WARFARE IN THE AMERICAN HOMELAND

WARFARE IN THE AMERICAN HOMELAND

POLICING AND PRISON IN A PENAL DEMOCRACY

Edited by
Joy James

Duke University Press

Durham and London

2007

© 2007 Duke University Press
All rights reserved
Printed in the United States of America on acid-free paper ∞
Designed by Heather Hensley
Typeset in Minion Pro by Tseng Information Systems, Inc.
Library of Congress Cataloging-in-Publication Data appear
on the last printed page of this book.

Acknowledgments for previously printed material and cred-
its for illustrations appear at the end of this book.

TO: OGGUN AND OSHUN

Neither slavery nor involuntary servitude, except as a punishment for crime whereof the party shall have been duly convicted, shall exist within the United States, or any place subject to their jurisdiction.

—THIRTEENTH AMENDMENT, SECTION 1,
U.S. CONSTITUTION

As a slave, the social phenomenon that engages my whole consciousness is, of course, revolution.

—GEORGE JACKSON

Contents

II. Policing and Prison Technologies

Preface: The American Archipelago

The contemporary world's work has become policing, halting, forming policy regarding, and trying to administer the movement of people. Nationhood—the very definition of citizenship—is constantly being demarcated and redemarcated in response to exiles, refugees, *Gastarbeiter*, immigrants, migrations, the displaced, the fleeing, and the besieged. The anxiety of belonging is entombed within the central metaphors in the discourse on globalism, transnationalism, nationalism, the break-up of federations, the rescheduling of alliances, and the fictions of sovereignty. Yet these figurations of nationhood and identity are frequently as raced themselves as the originating racial house that defined them. When they are not raced they are . . . imaginary landscape, never inscape; Utopia, never home.
—TONI MORRISON, "HOME"

There is a question of "voice" or "voices" here, perhaps this contestation over literary legitimacy is an issue of familiarity and validation, of comfort and recognition. Most readers will not recognize themselves or kin in these voices; over time, those numbers will likely diminish. The voices most necessary for this intellectual and political project—consider this anthology a manifesto, or something more lofty, or more debased—are not those best amplified in or by academe or government or corporate life, but those that occupy landscapes where practically no one wishes to walk, those only the most denigrated call "home." These voices register here as desperately needed for clarification. Of what? Our demise as a quasi-democratic state predicated on slavery and subjugation. Why this desperation? This is not an easy death.

Containment, police powers, state violence, global and imperial wars, and radiating rings of terror and counterterror foster the disappearance of bodies and rights. They render the concepts of "home" or "homeland" as coherent spaces of safety worth occupying an irony. When warfare is present and pervasive, and political, intellectual, emotional, and spiritual survival seem fairly precarious, to read those possessing neither authoritative voice nor roosts among academic, government, or corporate elites (even if their words appear in elite academic presses) constitutes an investment in "voice" as a political project.

The very project of elevating dismissed voices redefines the political functions of voice, writing and speaking. The political powers of narratives shared by prisoners and professors create a potential for either a mangled discourse of political performance and storytelling or a convergence of radical desire and will that crosses boundaries in a search for "home"—a democratic enclave, communities of resistance, a maroon camp. The request to explain the role of voices here (as made by one reader [and the press]) suggests a search for justification for the stories of "the displaced, the fleeing, and the besieged," and the revolutionary "slave," as having significance that warrants our attention—or, at least, equal attention or distracted or agitated attentiveness given to press, pentagon, or public-relations briefings.

The United States of America's democratic homeland diminishes (at least more noticeably for its more privileged occupants) as its police and prison archipelago grows. The voices that critically witness democratic delusions, demise, and change with perhaps the least romantic desires (or illusions) about the American homeland are found in narratives offered through the "Voices of Katrina" project organized by former Black Panther Party members in response to governmental devastation and abandonment in New Orleans. Or they are found in the voices in the "Black Genocide" project, which revisits the Civil Rights Congress's 1951 appeal to the United Nations in a book-length manuscript documenting crimes against black peoples in the United States. To charge and resist racial "genocide" or penal "slavery" (in this anthology, the voices that will define these terms emanate from bodies situated in conditions of caged existence) require narratives that depart from conventions. Such narratives offer new forms of instruction if one plans to be a "survivor"—or even a resistor. For instance, the "shoot-to-kill" edicts issued by the president and the governor of Louisiana for black Hurricane Katrina survivors overly determined as "looters" dictate that desperate, responsible, but not law-abiding mothers acquire bulletproof vests prior to taking bottled water, baby formula, and Pampers. Yet what instruction is to be taken from marginal voices if one plans to be a "liberator" in resistance to warfare and to survive uncaged as such? Perhaps instruction from political prisoners valued by conservatives would be useful.

During the heyday of the "Cold War" (one that feels decidedly won, unlike the current heated struggles against ever multiplying terrors), the United States waged domestic and foreign counterrevolutionary, or contra, wars against movements in the United States, Latin America, Africa, and Asia, largely against those racially fashioned as "minorities," as formerly colonized or enslaved peoples seeking greater democratic and economic freedoms. In the early 1970s, U.S. intelligentsia lauded a former political prisoner of the Soviet Union. Aleksandr Solzhenitsyn's *The Gulag Archipelago, 1918–1956* was published at the onset of the current U.S. prison explosion and circulated in the United States and western Europe as a valued testimonial against the former Soviet Union (or "evil empire," as it would be named by President Ronald Reagan in the 1980s). Its literary power and political insights are a testament to the author, who writes of the gulag, or prison and police network "scattered" geographically in an archipelago but psychologically "fused into a continent—an almost invisible, almost imperceptible country inhabited by the *zek*[1] people":

> And this Archipelago crisscrossed and patterned that other country within which it was located, like a gigantic patchwork, cutting into its cities, hovering over its streets. Yet there were many who did not even guess at its presence and many, many others who had heard something vague. And only those who had been there knew the whole truth.

Those seeking a more "whole truth" remain critically attentive to the "American homeland"—a democracy to which some pledge to give or take lives—and its archipelago, which encompasses some 700 U.S. military bases, with their attendant prisons and sporadic (CIA) interrogation or torture chambers scattered throughout the world. We have also noted the increasing police and military powers used by this homeland against "foreigners" and domestic dissidents in the households populated by the disenfranchised—poor people, people of color, women, queers, and the incarcerated.[2]

The homeland, idealized if not fetishized as a democratic site, displays tendencies for totalizing control. The numbers of incarcerated people in "empires" in evolutionary treks toward centralized police powers and penal democracies bear mentioning: In 1950, the number of people imprisoned in Stalin's Soviet gulags was 1,423 per 100,000. In 2000, the number of people under some form of penal control in the United States—prison, probation, parole, or jail—was 2,298 per 100,000[3]—this in penal systems and penal societies that can function without adequate or meaningful civilian or judicial oversight. Thus, the "evil empire," the enemy vanquished in the Cold War, has been surpassed. U.S.

attention given to stories of harrowing imprisoned life, and incisive political commentary, may stem not from an overwhelming concern for human rights or the humanity of the captive: A conservative former Russian prisoner provides a useful foil to contrast the evil empire with the good empire. Heralding the voices of imprisoned activists may also permit academic radicals a foil to position themselves as distinct from their "progressive" counterparts.

Whatever the games, the realization that power is centralized with only one military superpower has led to a battlefield, a contestation of democracy and "homeland" in which some intellectuals, such as the executive director of Amnesty International in his 2005 criticisms of torture and human-rights abuses at Guantánamo Bay, have denounced the "archipelago" of this democracy and the problem of expanding penal and police systems fueled by U.S. domestic and foreign policies.[4] It is a charting of this landscape that *Warfare in the American Homeland* seeks.

Warfare in the American Homeland: Policing and Prison in a Penal Democracy examines the sensibilities and the structures that enable a police and penal democracy to thrive. It connects the American homeland with the American prison and police mechanisms to argue that, at home and abroad, the United States wages war not just against criminals but also against people it constructs as such, i.e., against criminalized peoples. This anthology sketches political and cultural structures through which conflict between law and order and rebellion frame or disrupt an American prototype for normative state violence. This collection does not seek or posit uniform definitions of "warfare" or "imprisonment." Its various contributors differ in their progressive political ideologies; all identify themselves as active theorists or organizers against state police powers. In the absence of definitive dogma, theorizing about democracy and captivity— when one considers the historical black and indigenous presence on American soil, this nation has never known democracy in the absence of some form of institutional captivity—warfare and policing become more dynamic and, hence, more relevant to deciphering and rewriting the dominant political template.

Influenced by both political crises and the political theory and writings of radical theorists, *Warfare in the American Homeland* seeks to register some relevant response to crisis and violent death, the "carceral" and the policing effects of language that traces or maps over the racist and sexist aspects of warfare and social and state control. This book began in 2004 at what was then the height of the U.S. war in, and occupation of, Iraq and the scandals of abuse, torture, and killings in U.S.-administered prisons in Afghanistan, Guantánamo Bay, and Iraq. Some contributors note the expanding (complementary and intersectional) domestic police and foreign military powers and state ambitions rationalized by the growing need for "defense"—defense for or from a state that now, within its own borders, holds more than two million people captive in its jails, prisons, detention cells, juvenile facilities, "mental asylums," and death rows.[5] The vast majority of the detained are minorities, the marginalized people of the "household": African Americans, Latinos, Native Americans and Asians, and poor Euro-Americans.

Essays in this volume revisit the works of theorists and literary or political icons and subaltern thinkers and activists who refashion and reinvigorate political language and meaning. The contributors occupy varied positions and locations in the "household" of an imperial democracy. The essays follow in two parts: "I. Insurgent Knowledge" and "II. Policing and Prison Technologies." Many narratives, as noted in the bibliography, critique police powers (including the militarization of domestic police and the export of U.S. prison abuses to bases abroad). Fewer works offer insights into the border crossings of the American homeland's police and penal wars. In dynamically divergent writing styles, the essays and chapters that follow use biographies, pamphlets, meditations, diary entries, and analytical critiques reviewing social and political life and repression since the early 1970s. The originality of this volume emerges from its conscientious (and courageous, given the penal conditions of some of the contributors) content and from the ways in which the critical narratives are told. The chronology and cartography begin with the U.S. destabilization of one domestic liberation movement and progress to include a review of U.S. warfare against dissidents, "suspect" racially fashioned groups, and foreign national groups and states.

Imagine: Militant liberationists who lived years behind bars (some to die there) reframing the understandings of penal punishment not only as a form of U.S. domestic warfare but also as a foundation in an imperial democratic culture that gives you Abu Ghraib with occupation. Most Americans resist such imagination; despite the history of their homeland, these implications are not easily held about U.S. democracy.

This collection was sparked by encounters with a translation of Michel Foucault and colleagues' essay on the killing of George Jackson. The contributions and limitations of Jackson's theorizing, and Foucault's, shaped this endeavor. Still, Jackson's posthumously published *Blood in My Eye*, without the academic acclaim of Foucault's writings, declares war on a warring state and on state violence in a voice that is most difficult to encounter:

> Prestige bars any serious attack on power. Do people attack a thing they consider with awe, with a sense of its legitimacy? . . .
>
> We can stop the debate; prestige must be destroyed. People must see the venerated institutions and the "omnipotent administrator" actually under physical attack. . . . If the threat to power is truly revolutionary and the first step into revolutionary consciousness taken with a forceful attack upon prestige, we must anticipate reaction, accept repression's terror, and meet it with a counter-terror of our own. The gravedigger needs a bodyguard to protect him at this work, else the grave may be his own.[6]

As do many in the homeland, most of the writers here disavow or avoid militarist assertions that challenge a warring and policing state. (This should be self-evident; nonetheless, note the disclaimer and the right to self-defense.)

Yet during foreign or domestic wars, nationally legal (even if in violation of international law and treaties), or clandestine and illegal, reports of horror offer transport to whatever comes after—escalation, pacification, and imprisonment or peace. As Frederick Douglass's adage on power observes, peace must be purchased. The price of the ticket may not be Jackson's currency. Critiques of violence; analyses of technologies of information, penal and policing systems, economics, legal and military apparatuses, social stigma, and denigration are not small change. But they are not necessarily insurgent warfare, either. To abandon the conventional lingua franca that has failed to adequately express the depths of violent contradictions emanating from a prestigious democracy means to seek new voices.

Departing from homeland and home, seeing an archipelago within and beyond national borders, this volume brings witness to warfare and the voice of Nuh (pronounced "Noah") Washington, who died in 2000 in a New York prison. Incarcerated for nearly thirty years for political rebellion as a Black Panther and black liberationist, Nuh maintained that *victory* is not the vanquishing of colonizing and violent enemies. Rather, victory is the realization that collective knowledge of domination and resistance—painfully gained and painstakingly shared—has been preserved and passed on: one price paid for the ticket toward "home."

Notes

1. *Zek*, derived from the Russian word for "prisoner" (*zaklyuchenny*), is prisoners' slang for the captive class. Solzhenitsyn, *The Gulag Archipelago, 1918–1956*, x. Brady Heiner provided research for this reflection on Solzhenitsyn.
2. In May 2005, Irene Khan, executive director of Amnesty International, referred to the U.S. prison at Guatánamo Bay, Cuba, as "the gulag of our times." See Amnesty International, "Amnesty International Report 2005: Speech by Irene Khan at Foreign Press Association," May 25, 2005, available online at http://web.amnesty.org/library/index/ENGPOL100142005 (accessed July 2, 2005).
3. Wagner, *The Prison Index*.
4. The complexities and simplicities of safeguarding a democracy through consensus building premised on fear are embedded in legal narratives such as the omnivorous order of protection against an "imminent" danger that justifies police power, also known as George W. Bush's October 2, 2001, "Executive Order Establishing the Office of Homeland Security," sec. 3: "to coordinate the executive branch's efforts to detect, prepare for, prevent, protect against, respond to, and recover from terrorist attacks within the United States." Yet there are other, older narratives that speak of other, more familiar threats. Consequently, the Thirteenth Amendment to the U.S. Constitution, and the convict prison-lease system that followed, premised the internal threat to be the "black" and native "insurgents" or dissidents seeking greater democratic powers and fewer police mechanisms.
5. The widely cited figure of 2 million people incarcerated in the United States does not take into account the almost quarter-million youths held captive in juvenile detention facilities and those held in "mental asylums" (although more individuals suffering from mental illness are incarcerated in jails and prisons than in "mental asylums" or hospitals). Hence, the captive population is now near 2.5 million. See "Senator Collins Chairs Hearing on Warehousing Mentally Ill Children in Juvenile Detention Centers; Releases New Report with Representative Waxman Focusing on Nationwide Problem," July 7, 2004, available online at www.senate/gov/~affairs/index.cfm?FuseAction=PressRelease.Detail&Affiliation=C&PressRelease_id=747&Month=7&Year=2004 (accessed September 19, 2004).
6. Jackson, *Blood in My Eye*, 43.

Acknowledgments

Dylan Rodríguez and Brady Heiner shared labor and visions for this volume; this book exists as a response to their initiatives. Elliot Colla, Emily Blumenfeld, Sam Seidel, Dominique Stevenson, Nozomi Ikuta, José E. Lopez, and Alejandro Luis Molina also supported this anthology. Brown University's Undergraduate Teaching and Research Assistantship program and Dylan Rodríguez provided assistance for researcher Madeleine Dwertman. From 2004 to 2006, each summer, Maddy with painstaking research assistance participated in various struggles to bring these narratives forth. My thanks to all who contributed to this project and to all who have been supportive of its political endeavor to decipher and disentangle the mesh of democracy and captivity.

The American Archipelago: U.S. Prison Proliferation, 1900–2004

1900

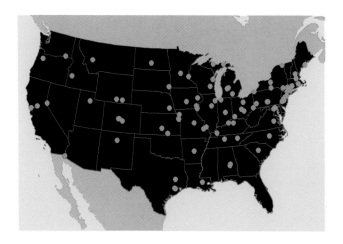

1940

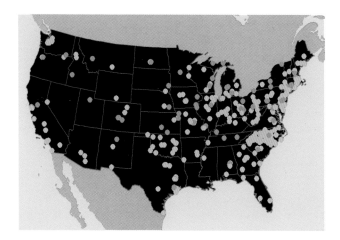

Figure 1 U.S. Prison Proliferation, 1900–2004, Designed by Rose Heyer. Data Source: U.S. Dept. of Justice, Bureau of Justice Statistics. *Census Of State And Federal Adult Correctional Facilities, 2000* [Computer file]. Conducted by U.S. Dept. of Commerce, Bureau of the Census. ICPSR ed. Ann Arbor, MI: Inter-university Consortium for Political and Social Research, 2004. State Corrections Departments, 2004. Cartography Source: U.S. Census Bureau, 2001. ESRI, 2000.

1980

2004

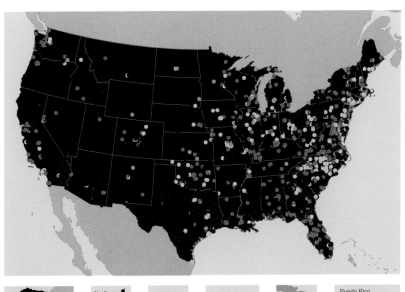

Year Prison Opened:　● 1778–1900　● 1901–1940　● 1941–1980　● 1981–2004

Violations

(for Emily)

Mississippi goddam. —NINA SIMONE, "MISSISSIPPI GODDAM," *NINA SIMONE IN CON-CERT*, 1964

A house is not a home. —LUTHER VANDROSS, "A HOUSE IS NOT A HOME," *NEVER TOO MUCH*, 1981

As an already- and always-raced writer, I knew from the very beginning that I could not, would not, reproduce the master's voice and its assumptions of the all-knowing law of the white father. Nor would I substitute his voice with that of his fawning mistress or his worthy opponent, for both of these positions (mistress or opponent) seemed to confine me to his terrain, in his arena, accepting the house rules in the dominance game. If I had to live in a racial house, it was important, at the least, to rebuild it so that it was not a windowless prison. —TONI MORRISON, "HOME"

There is something about violence and violations in the "household" that begs for silence.[1] And disavowal. Academe, one of the most influential gathering places of state and counter-state intellectuals, is one "household" in the American homeland and its expanding archipelago.[2] It is there that I sit while I write this essay. (Like predatory gentrification, academe has extended itself into my very kitchen.) The crafting and the shaping of this anthology, by academics, have occurred on a battlefield. In fact, the book was born in a state of war—specifically, the U.S. invasion and occupation of Iraq (sans Iraqi weapons of mass destruction or connections to al-Qaeda and September 11) and, what has really worried some, the effectiveness of Iraqi resistance movements a year after the world was informed that the war was over and the United States had won.[3]

Ostensibly, this work first raised its head in the expanding military theater of U.S. imperial aspirations and its domestic/foreign policy with their attendant human-rights abuses. Yet in truth, however you wish to define it, the smaller, closeted military theater (the "pit" as opposed to the amphitheater) permitted the ducking and dodging of difficult struggles precisely because academe is not the "streets." So what it and this academic engagement offer is not a political coalition (although old political ties and shared respect among some contributors indicate that coalitions exist and so manifest here—just not as an editorial process or text). Not a home, this literary intervention, a politics of sorts, challenges while it also reproduces containment.[4]

Trace the genealogy and map the penalscape and one finds that institutional intellectuals are rarely the "guerrilla intellectuals" that some academics emulate or necessarily the "native intellectuals" analyzed by Frantz Fanon. Nor, I believe, should they be: The "academic archipelago," with its increasing dependence on and enthrallment with corporatist and statist structures and funding, is not the most trustworthy of training camps for peace combatants seeking just distributions of power and wealth. Has the academic genealogist displaced the scientist who replaced the priest? Some see the roles of progressive academic intellectuals as synonymous with those of insurgent intellectuals, a conflation that produces considerable confusion about the function of political coalitions and the cooptation, commodification of "subjugated" forms of political power. This suggests to me that to project or to perform insurgency must be one of the technologies of warfare deployed, and perhaps delighted in, by a goodly, ungodly number of Americans. Ever present projections of apparitions of cultural characters such as John Wayne and Clint Eastwood—or, now, the white skins, black masks of the fugitive convict "Riddick" (Vin Diesel's "ambiguously raced" murderous con with a heart of gold) or *The Matrix*'s "Neo" or anime's hipster *Cowboy Bebop* bounty hunter "Spike Spiegel"—suggest how burdensome certain burdens can be for progressives in an ambitiously pugilistic, hero-addicted society.

When has the archipelago got you by the "*cojones*"?, to quote Secretary of State Madeleine Albright's castigation of the Cuban government's downing of the Miami-based, anti-Castro Brothers for the Rescue planes as they violated Cuban airspace. The answer: When your jailer dons drag to become you and usurps and reproduces your voice and politics without taking your place in the cell. Mimetic becomes apocalyptic in the penal landscape that is passing for a homeland—and logically so, for this is where death is manufactured.

Michel Foucault was right in (more than) one sense: There is no outside, particularly if the very voices of the physically subjugated become mimed by their surrogate guards who then perform as their liberators. Your own language and stories used against you? What violation, whether misdemeanor or felony. What violence, to be lectured on obedience with your own words, to have your own "bio-stories" reworked and recited back to you—now as spectacle turned captive audience—by anointed bard(s). Listen to the charge of "reverse racism or (hetero)sexism" or "class warfare" (in the absence of structural reversals of white supremacy, patriarchy, and capitalism) that supplants articulations of nonelite black, female, queer, or poor people's rage with the narratives of white victimization and racial or elite outrage, the verbal slippage of "by any means necessary" from the mouths of police and city or state officials in their assaults on and slaughters of black militants and their progeny (e.g., Philadelphia Mayor Wilson Goode's oration before the 1985 bombing of the MOVE Organization).[5] Or witness the bio-political power of the Pygmalion who projects Medea onto those who refuse to mammy. Finally, consider the academic "expert" and "re-articulation specialist" on the lives and narratives of those imprisoned in the household or its formal detention centers: Immigration Customs Enforce-ment—the former Immigration and Naturalization Service—holding cells, psychiatric wards, jails, police precincts, maximum security, death row, closets, or basements, hiding places from domestic batterers or the predation of aggres-sively "affectionate" adult kin. Consider all these "violations."

Yet the very calling out or detailing or analyzing of violations perhaps at times reproduces new forms of erasure, distortion, and violence. Thus, in the professionalism of prison discourse, the jailer (multitudinous rather than monolithic) may assume the position of the jailed in the rhetorical sense and mask his or her dual role as guard (or guardian of a certain order). There is a reality of non-duality, one that reveals that penal territory is so massive, so intri-cate, and so internalized that it circumscribes and burdens all. Hence, everyone is "incarcerated" in some sense, and captivity and violation are carceral shared experiences. Yet in maneuvers one can as a "theorist" or "performer" siphon off the political discourse of the imprisoned and hence engage in an elite form of criminality—identity theft. Such theft dispossesses the imprisoned of the labor and "wealth" they produce—the meanings and narratives of their confinement, the meanings and narratives of their resistance to repression, the meanings and narratives of their lives. (Curiously, with identity theft, those who have been robbed must prove that they themselves are not the thieves.)

Everything but the Burden is the title of the cultural critic Greg Tate's book on white and multicultural America's enthrallment with and appropriation of hip hop and black culture.[6] "Everything but the burden"—I grimace as I begin to trace and sketch my dialogue with elite voices, as an "elite" voice, chronicling the "gulag."

In spring 2004, I was introduced to an Italian translation of a section of Michel Foucault's and his coauthors' pamphlet *The Assassination of George Jackson*.[7] Having critiqued Foucault (Foucault will function as a convenient foil here) for his alleged past "erasures" of racist (and sexist) violence and terror in his text *Discipline and Punish*, I was curious but suspicious. The heated e-mail debates that ensued ended with my stating that Foucault's essay would be an important one that deserved a broader readership. I encouraged and promised to assist in its publication. That promise evolved into this anthology, the product of collective endeavors and battles. It is a product or construct, a discourse in which several of us, while attempting to tunnel our way out of a penal site—structural racism and sexism and the pathologizing of antiracist rebellion and slave resistance—found that we had merely dug ourselves into another prison corridor or cell.

It is fairly easy to begin as an ally "liberator" and slide into role playing as ally "appropriator." For instance, "white antiracists" or "people of color (POC)" are amorphous groupings that mask the ethnic chauvinism and anti-black racism that lie within. Such formations can provide a rainbow prism of hatreds and envy solidified by a refusal to "bow down" to blacks and their demands for recognition based on "exceptionalism." The quandary, though, for those who never sought genuflection is what is the value of recognition for the "uniqueness" of black bodies for whom white supremacist cultures and state policing practices in the United States have reserved an exceptional place: that of targets for excessive force and the penal site. What does it mean when "people of color" or antiracist whites wear the black body to exercise their grievances and outrage at white supremacy but maintain their distance (and disdain?) for the antithesis of whiteness.

Women, black women, even those intimately aware of trauma, can also violate and appropriate others, particularly if they are housed in the most repressive sites of the archipelago, its domestic (and foreign) prisons. For example, Asha Bandele's memoir, *The Prisoner's Wife*, offers an illustration of facile moves that glorify the mundane resistor by mapping over the narrative of the imperiled insurgent. Such moves extinguish the political risk and vulnerability that differentiate the "free" person, albeit one regulated to the household by racial-sexual stigma and practices, and the unfree person, locked in prison. Cloaking the middle-class author in the dress of the prison revolutionary George Jackson, the Readers' Club Guide for *The Prisoner's Wife* poses two queries that struck me as masking and violating gestures:

> *The Prisoner's Wife* features allusions to *Soledad Brother*, George Jackson's seminal portrait of the struggles, politics, and intricacies of prison life. How has Jackson's book—the work of a brave and embattled man—influenced our culture's perceptions of political imprisonment, racism, and the United States justice system?
>
> In what ways can we view *The Prisoner's Wife*—the work of an equally brave and similarly embattled black woman—as a useful, even indispensable, counterpoint (and complement) to the messages in Jackson's *Soledad Brother*?[8]

It is noted that the Readers' Club recognizes a black revolutionary. Yet, mimetic performance, even one that must cover Jackson's ideology as a militarist in order to appropriate and wear his iconic persona, is an equal-opportunity affair. Still, one must note that drag is not worn with equal risk—that is, those already designated part of the privatized realm for subordination, for example, black women such as Bandele, when performing insurrectionist, are likely to pay a heavier price for their theater than those designated part of the public realm of rulers and authoritative intellectuals and politicians such as white neoliberal or neoradical male intellectuals.

Some valued and mimed for their presentations of radicalism may never pay the price of the ticket (to use James Baldwin here) in the academic landscape, a surrogate for and derivative of the American penalscape. Useful registers—reliable in strategies to survive warfare—rather than globalizing genealogies offer precision. Remember the color codes of Homeland Security, red, orange, yellow flags as precautions against erasing or glossing over subjugated and insurgent knowledge.

Back to the foil. Consider Foucault's interview at New York's Attica prison.[9] Attica was the site of the state's killing of over thirty men, mostly African

American and Latino, who protested the slave-like conditions of subjugation. For Foucault in the Attica interview, crime is a "coup d'état from below." *Yellow*. The United States and its economic and political and social structures were and are founded on theft of (indigenous) land and (African) labor. Hence, the most significant criminals, and the least interested in battling the state, come from "above"—in property theft (white-collar crime), drug trafficking (money laundering is the most profitable; growers and street dealers garner only a fraction of the trade), and organized violence and murder rationalized as warfare— Vietnam, Kissinger's Cambodia. (Surely, state violence, Reagan's contras in Latin America and Southern Africa, the School of the America's training of death squads, the occupation of Iraq, and the theft of national and global resources and lives must register somewhere.) When the coup d'état from below meets the coup d'état from above, the reinforcement of the penalscape follows.[10]

What constitutes critical theory that can analyze this troubled symbiotic relationship?

Within the interview—which here serves as an illustration or contrast for my larger argument that the technologies of containment encompass "radical" academic discourse—coupled with the vanishing of state criminality in his narrative are Foucault's comments about Attica's architecture that refer to "Disneyland" (Baudrillard?) and the "cleanliness" of the prison halls (which he equates with nineteenth-century French parochial schools). *Orange*. Those who fear the physical terror of imprisonment may dissociate Attica from the "Magic Kingdom." Rather than foster a lack of imagination or theoretical verve, closer proximity to state captivity and violation shape even the gallows humor of the dead zones of the household and the penalscape. Those policed in virulent, violent fashions may have different cognitive skills that produce different, deeper meanings.

Foucault's comments about the physical structure of Attica disconcerted me but not some of the academic colleagues and students with whom I raised the issue. If they were disturbed, most did not acknowledge it to me. In fact, Foucault was usually vigorously defended against my ignorance of Foucault (although I imagine that the "discredited knowledge" that Toni Morrison notes as the affliction of all blacks must shape perceptions of ignorance and allow many to ignore the query, "Where are the people—my people?").[11] My animated or quiescent questions were met with silence. Perhaps *I* had committed some form of infraction?

Here's a violation that I—and any chorus member who marks the demise of (black/brown) renegades seeking freedom—will remember: In his interview, Foucault does not once mention the men who rebelled in Attica and who were *massacred* there (to use the terminology of Tom Wicker, the white, liberal *New York Times* writer). Not one man, not once, does he name. *Red*. To say nothing of the victims when one enters a mass graveyard is a breach of trust if one enters not as a national guardsman, or as Governor Nelson Rockefeller, or as an idle spectator or consumer, but as an ally.

Erasing a genealogy mapped by the "wretched of the earth" allows the non-wretched to print over their (our?) texts, to use insurgent narratives as recyclables. This is a practice of the police machinery and its technologies of warfare. Professed allies, "radical" theorists, are selective because they have that right and privilege. In one narrative, Foucault disappears all impoverished and imprisoned black/brown bodies, yet in another he presents, in painstaking delineation, the corpse of the revolutionary icon and prison rebel George Jackson; that killing in a California prison thirty years ago sparked the Attica rebellion and additional killings in a prison on the other side of the continent.

As did Jackson, the Attica captives and insurgents fashioned reformist and revolutionary moves and were murdered for those acts. Who witnesses this? Who supplants them? Who performs their guerrilla theater? Who loves what they represented and the families of their origins as they fashion new survival and liberation from war? Who understands that they were both violators and violated? And who comprehends that the most civil and surgical of violations, those that leave no mark on the physical body, would be erasure or dismemberment through mimetic performance that discredits the legacies of the "household"—their resistance.

Hence, the mesh of "revolutionary" desire and anxiety concerning the academic, elite cartographer and genealogist that I bring as editor to this work. A new "progressive radical" order can continue to elide the "household" that I am "forced" to occupy and, in complicity, reproduce. When the "household" of the disappeared—poor communities, prisoners, queers, red/black/brown peoples, women, children—reappears and dictates its own narrative, in its own voice, with its own unmitigated desires, surely that is, this is war.

Like many others, I am weary of warfare. Yet there are distinctions that I maintain between wars of survival and liberation and wars of conquest and annihilation. Like most, I fear violence and the realization that noncombatants largely are the victims of carnage or the designated targets. In contemporary warfare, since World War II in the foreign theater, the casualties have been in the majority women and children (giving perverse meaning to the chivalric chant, "Women and children first!"). In the domestic theater, women and children have always dominated the landscape of broken and scarred bodies and minds and disoriented souls. Still, exhaustion and terror cannot prevent movement; one must travel or become buried under the penal landscape. Those who don't resist violation don't survive. Some who enact survival and liberation possibilities do.

Transport requires mapping. *Warfare in the American Homeland: Policing and Prison in a Penal Democracy*, I hope, assists in locating race and gender "black holes" in authoritative texts; the undertheorizing of the "household"; and the resurgence of a (new) resistance to authoritative voices. It documents those who struggle and who stay present long enough to endure a battle or bear witness while attempting not to disappear the meaning of what they record. Some witness the raced-gendered-queered imprisoned body in order to investigate, interview, and be interrogated by those assigned to captivity—the poor, women, children, slaves, prisoners, laborers of the household, and those who resist.

Captives and rebels are not saints merely because they (or we) are exploited or abused. Some relegated to confinements seek rewards and approval for loyalties that "reproduce" the national(ist) "family" and its "coherence." According to the official, conventional narratives, it is safer to harbor and shelter within a penal democracy, despite its abusive excess. Some measure of safety is promised in exchange for obedience and conformity to and within the household. Is it not better to be a black woman in the Southern United States than a black woman in South Africa or Sudan?[12] In Sudan, Arab Muslim militia men (embraced by the terms of "people of color" and "Third World people"), in their ethnic cleansing and genocidal warfare, rape and mutilate African Muslim, Christian, and animist women, girls, and boys, cursing them with the Sudanese epithets of "black," branding survivors on their hands to ensure that private trauma enters public record. The archipelago is global, and so not always "American." There are multiple predations confronted and little adequate shelter—for some prey.[13]

Nevertheless, resistance, in all of its contradictions and imperfections, continues. In the United States, antiviolence activists in the "abolitionist" movement embrace violent men rather than jettison them to a "fatherly" state that punishes and destroys. Such activists grapple with what to do with the rapists, torturers, and the killers of children and women (and the lucrative market for sexual violence that dismembers). The antiviolence movement is multifaceted. In his essay "Killers" in a volume of writings by prisoners, Prince Imari A. Obadele describes and protests against "virtual rape"—male prisoners' "killing" of female guards with their eyes, masturbating in front of them as a form of warfare known as "taking the pussy." The women who do not report these violations are considered "good" women.[14] Obadele relates that he could care less about his female captors, yet he condemns the practice (for its implications for parolees): Predators require prey—don't they?—no matter what gender or on which side of the concertina wire.

In a collection that contests the homeland as predacious territory we explore both repression and resistance to violations that are ever present. *Warfare in the American Homeland* offers "critical thought" and political responsibility to the mapping of strategies based on peace and freedom as we imagine and fight for them. Having received much, not being so foolish as to attempt to rival the gift givers, we contribute our best in this moment of warring and loving—love and war so aptly expressed by Georgia Jackson to the captive after the burial of her seventeen-year-old Jonathan:

My dear only surviving son,

I went to Mount Vernon August 7th, 1971, to visit the grave site of my heart your keepers murdered in cold disregard for life.

His grave was supposed to be behind your grandfather's and grandmother's. But I couldn't find it. There was no marker. Just mowed grass. The story of our past. I sent the keeper a blank check for a headstone—and two extra sites—blood in my eye!!![15]

—JOY JAMES, 2004/2006

Notes

1. My understanding and critique of the "household" is situated in part in experience and in part in the political theory of Hannah Arendt. As a German Jew who survived Nazi genocidal campaigns during World War II, Arendt fought in the French Resistance and saw her mentors and friends Karl Jaspers and Martin Heidegger come to their own realizations about power, community, and violence. Jaspers was persecuted by the Nazis; Heidegger became one. Arendt's adopted country, the United States,

gave her the space and platform to advocate for the return of a mythic democracy, the Athenian polis. Such romantic revivalism both valorizes and solidifies American democracy as a bourgeois democracy, and self-avowed empire, while dismissing the implications of a master–slave dichotomy as fundamental to the democratic state and fails to issue a sustained critique of racialized and gendered exclusion and domination.

Arendt's theory of power as communication rather than domination is based on the division of space into the non- or pre-political, private realm and the political, public realm. Such a division engendered power as communication, according to Arendt, for the private realm of the household "freed" inhabitants of the public realm from labor and work, biological and material necessity. Seemingly undisturbed by the "issue," Arendt advocates an idealized political state, the Aristotelian polis, one which subverted and undermined power and politics by oppressing the household, built on enslavement and economic exploitation and forced relegation of captives to the "powerless" private realm. The subjugated provided the leisure that enabled the fabled Athenian elite (of propertied free men) to practice democracy. Subjugation constructed a restrictive public space dedicated to the ideal of power as communication, reason, and persuasion, a site advocating freedom but built on oppression. The practice of power as communication by an elite citizenry predicated on the enslavement and exploitation of the majority (women, children, men) is the historical reality of the United States: Frank Wilderson's "scandal"; Dylan Rodríguez's "forced passages." The historical legacy of genocide, slavery, and imperialism has created an archipelago in which democracy occupies a penal site. Arendt, like other progressive intellectuals, shares with the Black Panther Party, which was formed in 1966 against police brutality, a populist mandate: All power should reside with the people. She and her ideological contemporaries are merely much more restrictive about who constitutes "the people": see Arendt, *The Human Condition*.

Despite the ideological span between her liberalism and the "Marxism" of more contemporary authors, there are shared similarities. For instance, in *Empire*, Michael Hardt and Antonio Negri appear to construct an all-encompassing "multitude" as the new proletariat. Race seems irrelevant, as does gender, as categories that deserve serious analyses. A discussion of the predatory movements of this new proletariat does not occur. If radicals can make liberal gestures, then liberals can gesticulate as radicals. Amid these moving violations, who keeps score as such moves erase white supremacy and patriarchy and render empire and penal democracy a way of life for the subjugated and insurgent to suffer, endure, or expire? See Hardt and Negri, *Empire*. See also Amin, "Confronting the Empire" and *Empire of Chaos*.

2. In his translation of Aleksandr Solzhenitsyn's *The Gulag Archipelago, 1918–1956*, Thomas P. Whitney notes Solzhenitsyn's use of the archipelago as metaphor:

The *image* evoked by this title is that of one far-flung "country" with millions of "natives," consisting of an *archipelago* of islands, some as tiny as a detention cell in a railway station and others as vast as a large Western European country, contained within another country—U.S.S.R. This archipelago is made up of the enormous network of penal institutions and all the rest of the web of machinery for the police oppression and terror imposed throughout the author's period reference on all Soviet life. Gulag is the acronym for the Chief Administration of Corrective Labor Camps which supervised the larger part of this system.

See Solzhenitsyn, *The Gulag Archipelago, 1918–1956,* 616.

3. As of March 16, 2007, the Department of Defense recorded 3,197 U.S. military deaths of U.S. soldiers in Iraq in addition to 24,042 soldiers wounded in action: see U.S. Department of Defense, "OIF/OEF Casualty Update," available online at http://www .defenselink.mil/news/casualty.pdf (accessed March 18, 2007). According to CNN reports, an additional 258 deaths among coalition forces were reported at this time: see "Forces: U.S. and Coalition Casualties," CNN.com War Tracker, website, available online at http://www.cnn.com/SPECIALS/2003/iraq (accessed August 30, 2006). The Department of Defense has issued no authoritative estimates on the number of Iraqi civilian casualties. Iraq Body Count, a group of volunteer U.S. and British academics and researchers whose data have become a primary resource for the media, estimated between 59,236 and 65,160 Iraqi civilian deaths in March 2007 (see "Iraq Body Count," at http://www.iraaqbodycount.net, accessed March 18, 2007). In addition, a research team at Johns Hopkins University's Bloomberg School of Public Health in Baltimore published findings of a study in the medical journal *Lancet* strongly indicating that the U.S.-led invasion of Iraq in 2003 had resulted in more than 654,965 civilian casualties by fall 2006: See Roberts et al., "Mortality after the 2003 Invasion of Iraq: A Cross-sectional Cluster Sample Survey."

Reports on government deception, malfeasance, and "mismanagement" in the "war on terror"—including government use of terror and extensive killing of civilians in this expansive war—can be found in Amnesty International, "Beyond Abu Ghraib: Detention and Torture in Iraq," March 6, 2006, available online at http:// www.amnestyusa.org/countries/iraq/document.do?id=ENGMDE140012006 (accessed August 18, 2006); Amnesty International, "Iraq Killings of civilians in Basra and al-'Amara," May 11, 2004, available online at http://web.amnesty.org/library/ Index/ENGMDE140072004?open&of=ENG-IRQ (accessed June 1, 2004) (accessed June 1, 2004); "Report of the International Committee of the Red Cross on the Treatment by the Coalition Forces of Prisoners of War and Other Protected Persons by the Geneva Conventions in Iraq during Arrest, Internment, and Interrogation," February 2004, available online at http://www.globalsecurity.org/military/library/ report/2004/icrc_report_iraq_feb2004.htm (accessed June 6, 2004); and "Taguba

Report," Article 15–16 Investigation of the 800th Military Police Brigade, available online at http://www.cbsnews.com/htdocs/pdf/tagubareport.pdf (accessed June 6, 2004).

4. Bernice Johnson Reagon's wry commentary and cautioning observation about coalitions describes the false or unmet expectations that mark our intellectual and literary political endeavors and frustrations:

> Coalition work is not done in your home. Coalition work has to be done in the streets. And it is some of the most dangerous work you can do. And you shouldn't look for comfort. Some people will come to a coalition and they rate the success of the coalition on whether or not they feel good when they get there. They're not looking for a coalition, they're looking for a home! They're looking for a bottle with some milk in it and a nipple, which does not happen in a coalition. You don't get a lot of food in a coalition. You don't get fed a lot in a coalition. In a coalition you have to give, and it is different from your home (Reagon, "Coalition Politics," 359).

5. The MOVE Organization, its most prominent member being the death-row intellectual and former Black Panther Mumia Abu-Jamal, who joined after the 1985 tragedy, was decimated by an aerial bombing by police using Vietnam war surplus in Philadelphia. Eleven people died in the 1985 conflagration, including four children. For more information on MOVE, see *The Bombing of Osage Avenue*, dir. Louis Massiah (videocassette, 1986).

6. See Tate, *Everything but the Burden*.

7. See Groupe d'Information sur les Prisons (GIP), *Intolerable*, 3.

8. See Bandele, *The Prisoner's Wife*.

9. See Simon, "Michel Foucault on Attica." In September 1971, prisoners at New York's Attica rebelled against the prison administration's failure to address complaints about the poor living conditions. The uprising grew from solidarity among prisoners following the August killing of George Jackson by guards at California's San Quentin prison. More than 1,500 prisoners, across racial lines, seized the prison and held hostages for five days. Despite the warnings of observers and mediators selected by the prisoners, New York's Governor Nelson Rockefeller ordered that the prison be retaken by force. State troopers stormed the grounds; with high-powered rifles and shotguns, they fired some 4,500 rounds of ammunition at prisoners and the hostages. Forty-three people were killed, including Herbert Blyden, a signer of the Attica Liberation Manifesto, and 150 were injured, nearly all from the fire of the state troopers. Following the suppression of the rebellion, prisoners were tortured. Later in court, the sixty prisoners charged with inciting the rebellion were defended by a team of volunteer lawyers and supported by a national movement. By 1976, nearly all of the charges had been dismissed; in 2002, New York State awarded survivors an $8 million settlement. See Freedom Archives, "Thirty Years after the Attica Rebellion"

(sound recording, 2001), available online at http://www.freedomarchives.org; *Eyes on the Prize II: A Nation of Law? 1968–1971* (Blackside Productions, videocassette, 1987); and Wicker, *A Time to Die.*

10. Foucault states:

> But afterwards we met some psychologists who were clearly very nice people, very liberal, who saw things with a good deal of accuracy. For them, stealing the property of someone else, pulling off a holdup in a bank, committing prostitution, sleeping with a man if one is male, etc.—if those acts are psychological problems that they must help the individual to resolve, are they not also fundamentally accomplices to the system? Aren't they masking the fact that ultimately committing a misdemeanor, committing a crime questions the way society functions in a more fundamental way? So fundamental that we forget that it's social, that we have the impression that it's moral, that it involves peoples' rights. . . .
>
> And you see in what way one can present the problem. So that I subscribe completely to what you say, doesn't everything that concerns reintegration, everything that is a psychological or individual solution for the problem, mask the profoundly political character both of society's elimination of these people and those people's attack on society. All of that profound struggle is, I believe, political. Crime is "a coup d'état from below." (Simon, "Michel Foucault on Attica," 161)

For a discussion of Foucault's presentation of "racism," see Ann Laura Stoler, "Toward a Genealogy of Racisms."

11. See Morrison, "Rootedness," 342.

12. Rape and domestic violence against women and children in South Africa as an epidemic have been widely reported: see Amnesty International, "South Africa: Women, Violence, and Health," February 17, 2005, available online at http://www.amnestyusa.org/countries/south_africa/document.do?id=551AF81791C9B08580256F7300553101 (accessed August 28, 2006); Amnesty International, "Southern Africa: Women and Children Still Facing Discrimination and Violence," December 5, 2002, available online at http://web.amnesty.org/library/index/engafr030122002 (accessed July 20, 2004).

For reports of Arab (Muslim) militarists' murders of Muslim African men; rapes and mutilations of Muslim women, female and male children, and black Africans; and destruction of African mosques, see Human Rights Watch, "Darfur Destroyed"; Amnesty International, "Korma: Yet More Attacks on Civilians," July 31, 2006, available online at http://web.amnesty.org/library/Index/ENGAFR540262006?open&of=ENG-SDN (accessed August 28, 2006).

Documentation of the abuse of women in prison can be found in Amnesty International, "Abuse of Women in Custody: Sexual Misconduct and Shackling of Pregnant Women," March 2001, available online at http://www.amnestyusa.org/women/custody/abuseincustody.html (accessed July 10, 2004); idem, *"Not Part of My Sen-*

tence": *Violations of the Human Rights of Women in Custody*, 1999, available online at http://web.amnesty.org/library/Index/engAMR510011999 (accessed July 10, 2004). For a report of male rape in prison, see Human Rights Watch, *No Escape*.

13. In Greek mythology, Hercules sailed with Jason and the Argonauts in the quest for the Golden Fleece, a militarist campaign in pursuit of glory that led to slaughter and devastation. The second labor of Hercules, before his campaign with Jason, was to slay the Hydra; when one of its heads was cut off, two more grew in its place. The battle against an archipelago as Hydra recalls in my mind George Jackson's succinct disavowal in *Blood in My Eye* as he pursued war: "If one were forced for the sake of clarity to define [fascism] in a word simple enough for all to understand, that word would be 'reform.'"

14. See Prince Imari A. Obadele, "Killers," in James, *The New Abolitionists*.

15. One of the first printings of Jackson's *Blood in My Eye* (Bantam, 1972) attributes this statement to Lester Jackson; the reprint edition (Black Classic Press, 1990) offers no source, erasing Lester Jackson's name to leave a blank space on the page. I read these as mothers' words. Generally, it is women who birth and bury. So I give the bloodshot eyes to Georgia Jackson, not to the father Lester Jackson or to anonymity. The title of an interview with Georgia Jackson, "I Bought the Plot a Year Ago, I Knew They Would Kill Him" (*Sun Reporter* [San Francisco], August 28, 1971), supports this attribution.

PART I   Insurgent Knowledge

The essays in part I emphasize the policing and imprisonment of the black body (social construction) and the black rebel (political construction). Of the 2 million-plus incarcerated in the United States, 50 percent are people of African descent. Overwhelmingly, this majority is detained (or designated for executions) largely due to racial and economic bias in racial profiling and sentencing. Here, "insurgent knowledge" refers to the black or brown experiences of segregation, detention, surveillance and policing in a white-dominated state and society, and the radical experiences of resistance in overt and controversial manners recognized as political rebellion (and commonly condemned and criminalized as social deviance).

Addressing the "peculiar institution" of hyper- and excessive policing of the black social body, and the social death that ensues, Frank Wilderson's "The Prison Slave as Hegemony's (Silent) Scandal" references Frantz Fanon and Antonio Gramsci to explore the relationship between black positionality and civil society. Wilderson argues that this is an antithetical relationship, one that negates the black subject through material and symbolic violence perpetrated by the state. For Wilderson, not only civil society but also radical and social movements mirror the undemocratic, racist tendencies of the state. He extends his analysis to the prison abolition movement and its claims to be in service to the (black) "prison slave." According to Wilderson, both slavery and the modern prison-industrial matrix target the black body and are constructed on relations of direct force and terror, not of exploitation and capital. Thus, social movements that struggle for anticapitalist hegemony, he argues, render black positionality inconsequential and marked for social death.

Building on Wilderson's narrative, Dylan Rodríguez's "Forced Passages" analyzes how the prison regime has organized human immobilization and liquidation, extending its technologies beyond rituals of state executions and into the realm of a "fatal 'biopoliticality.'" Rodríguez maintains that the prison is fundamentally uninterested in "rehabilitation" and that, as a technology of violence, it has become centrally focused on containing, controlling, and punishing the bodies of white civil society's "incorrigibles." Rodríguez asserts that the prison proper manifests as a center for the reproduction of social formation, regimenting a necessary site of antisociality and civic/social death. "Forced Passages" looks to the coercive transatlantic transfer of enslaved Africans in the Middle Passage for a genealogy to elaborate the social logic of this carceral formation of mass incarceration.

In "Sorrow: The Good Soldier and the Good Woman," Joy James reflects on the death of gender and the rebirth of terror in the bodies of revolutionary soldiers shamed and refashioned in warfare against a repressive state. Her narrative, with its disruptive and disconcerting split page of parallel text, focuses and disrupts the reader's attention. James's explorations into the place of visibility and invisibility of black women radicals and revolutionaries who "soldier" create a reference for discussions of gendered violence and social death, discussions that both complement and contradict other gendered narratives in this section.

From the black liberation movement, a number of incisive texts on U.S. warfare and imprisonment have emerged. The contributions of the former Black Panther Party (BPP) leader and political prisoner Dhoruba Bin Wahad are presented in "War Within," an interview published in the early 1990s. Here, Bin Wahad describes the deadly Counterinsurgency Program (COINTELPRO) initiated by J. Edgar Hoover, former director of the FBI. Bin Wahad's narrative illustrates that the assassination of George Jackson, imprisoned intellectual and field marshal for the BPP, was not an isolated event. Rather, state violence against the Panthers, which led to the formation of the Black Liberation Army, and other black/brown/red revolutionary organizations, constituted unofficial government practice or policy. Through violence, manipulation of the media, and disinformation campaigns, the FBI waged warfare, destabilizing public support for the radical movements and removing leadership through exile, imprisonment, or death.

Bin Wahad's narrative of antiblack racism in domestic campaigns against liberation movements is updated and expanded in "Domestic Warfare: A Dialogue with Marshall Eddie Conway." A Black Panther political prisoner incarcerated for over three decades, Conway discusses the origins and legacies of COINTELPRO, encompassing a broader perspective. Referencing state violence from the FBI and police violence against poor blacks and other targeted populations vis-à-vis the alleged domestic "wars" on drugs and crime, Conway asserts that the absence of sustained radical resistance to state violence today is rooted in the trauma experienced by past revolutionaries and a growing, widespread fear of confronting the state.

In his April 1970 "Letter to Fay Stender," originally published in *Soledad Brother*, the "revolutionary icon," prison rebel, and martyr George Jackson chronicles the torture and abuse inflicted on African American prisoners by racist officials, guards, and inmates in California's Soledad Prison. The aim of the abuse is the mental and physical deterioration and, ultimately, annihilation of "deviant" bodies—particularly black bodies in resistance to the prison structure. Jackson's letter is a response to his attorney, Stender, who toured and investigated Soledad prison after Jackson, Fleeta Drumgo, and John Cluchette were indicted for killing the white prison guard Opie Mills. Jackson argues that the focus of any investigation must be the fascist aspects of the system itself—not the prisoners it produces. In an excerpt from his less well-known and more controversial book *Blood in My Eye*—completed a week before he was killed by guards on August 21, 1971, at San Quentin—Jackson asserts that revolution must aim for nothing less than the total destruction (not the seizure or reform) of the state and the entire system of existing property relations.

Jackson's narrative is juxtaposed with an excerpt from the pamphlet *The Assassination of George Jackson*, by Michel Foucault, Catherine von Bülow, and Daniel Defert, all members of the GIP (Prison Information Group). "The Masked Assassination" was first published in French in 1971, and is excerpted and translated here with a prefatory note by Sirène Harb. "The Masked Assassination" offers a sense of the far-reaching impact of George Jackson's death. Exploring the contradictions of mainstream U.S. media reports on the homicide of Jackson, Foucault and his co-authors argue that Jackson's death occurred at the moment that black and brown prisoners began to display a common front of resistance—and that his death was a premeditated murder on the part of prison guards. Referring to the assassination as an "act of war," the GIP collective prophetically (to date) asserts that his killers will never be prosecuted by U.S. courts. The GIP describes Jackson's pivotal role in organizing inside prisons as a form of effective "warfare"; consequently, his elimination was deemed "necessary" by state power.

State violence more commonly registers as a public act, most visually and viscerally in internment camps and prisons. The United States' practice of indefinitely detaining "enemy combatants"—both U.S. citizens and non-citizens—

without charge has focused some public attention on the historical internment of nearly 120,000 Japanese Americans during World War II. The internment of civilian populations, recognized as a violation of international law, includes not only the historical internments of American Indians, those of Japanese descent, and the recent interning of those of Arab descent in the "war on terror," but also the ongoing mass incarcerations of the African American and Latino populations in the name of the "wars" on crime and drugs.

Effective reactionary warfare manifests as wars on terror morphs into wars against liberation or independence movements (and vice versa). Oscar López Rivera's "A Century of Colonialism: One Hundred Years of Puerto Rican Resistance" examines the history of U.S. colonialism in Puerto Rico from 1898 and the twentieth-century Puerto Rican Independence Movement. Formerly active in the movement, Lòpez Rivera, one of the few incarcerated who identifies as a "prisoner of war" and one of the longest held politically incarcerated in the United States, discusses the movement's emergence, repression, and resurgence on the island and within Puerto Rican immigrant communities located primarily in poor, industrial centers of New York and Chicago. As with other organizations that challenged the U.S. government and elites, independentists' use of organized and armed resistance to protest and counter colonialism rendered the movement a primary target of state violence and the FBI's COINTELPRO.

This essay was the most difficult to obtain and edit for this volume. Rivera's work was handwritten and mailed out in installments to prevent confiscation of his writing by guards. Sent first to Quakers in the Midwest who had worked with Rivera for years, it was then edited and typed and sent to me at Brown University, where my research assistant, Madeleine Dwertman, and I continued the editing process. Given that Rivera has been incarcerated for some three decades; had, and has, limited access to library and resource materials; and faces the censorship powers of prison authorities and the editorial interventions of non-independentists, human-rights advocates, and academics, to assert that he wrote "freely" for this anthology would be to misspeak. The essay that appears in this volume is excerpted from a longer essay he sent on a century of U.S. colonialism and conquest in Puerto Rico and Puerto Rican resistance.

The Prison Slave as Hegemony's (Silent) Scandal

Frank B. Wilderson III

The Black experience in this country has been a phenomenon without analog.
—EUGENE GENOVESE, "EUGENE RIVERS'S CHALLENGE: A RESPONSE," *BOSTON REVIEW*,
OCTOBER/NOVEMBER 1993

There is something organic to black positionality that makes it essential to the destruction of civil society. There is nothing willful or speculative in this statement, for one could just as well state the claim the other way around: There is something organic to civil society that makes *it* essential to the destruction of the black body. Blackness is a positionality of "absolute dereliction" (Frantz Fanon), abandonment, in the face of civil society and therefore cannot establish itself, or be established, through hegemonic interventions. Blackness cannot become one of civil society's many junior partners: black citizenship and black civic obligation are oxymorons.[1]

In light of this, coalitions and social movements—even radical social movements such as the prison abolition movement, bound up in the solicitation of hegemony so as to fortify and extend the interlocutory life of civil society—ultimately accommodate only the satiable demands and finite antagonisms of civil society's junior partners (i.e., immigrants, white women, and the working class), but foreclose on the insatiable demands and endless antagonisms of the prison slave and the prison slave-in-waiting. In short, whereas such coalitions and social movements cannot be called the outright handmaidens of white supremacy, their rhetorical structures and political desire are underwritten by a supplemental antiblackness.

Assata Shakur's comments in her autobiography vacillate between being interesting and insightful and painfully programmatic and "responsible." The expository method of conveyance accounts for this air of responsibility. However, toward the end of the book, she accounts for coalition work by way of extended narrative as opposed to exposition. We accompany her on one of Zayd

Shakur's many Panther projects with outside groups, work "dealing with white support groups who were involved in raising bail for the Panther 21 members in jail."[2] With no more than three words, her recollection becomes matter of fact and unfiltered. She writes, "I hated it."

> At the time, i felt that anything below 110th street was another country. All my activities were centered in Harlem and i almost never left it. Doing defense committee work was definitely not up my alley. . . . i hated standing around while all these white people asked me to explain myself, my existence. i became a master of the one-liner.[3]

Assata's hatred of this work is bound up in her anticipation, fully realized, of all the zonal violations to come when a white woman asks her whether Zayd is her "panther . . . you know, is he your black cat?" and then runs her fingers through her hair to cop a kinky feel. Her narrative anticipates these violations-to-come at the level of the street, as well as at the level of the body.

Here is the moment in her life as a prison slave-in-waiting, which is to say, a moment as an ordinary black person, when she finds herself among "friends"—abolitionists, at least partners in purpose, and yet she feels it necessary to adopt the same muscular constriction, the same coiled anticipation, the same combative "one-liners" that she will need to adopt just one year later to steel herself against the encroachment of prison guards. The verisimilitude between Assata's well-known police encounters and her experiences in civil society's most nurturing nook, the radical coalition, raises disturbing questions about political desire, black positionality, and hegemony as a modality of struggle.

In *The Wretched of the Earth*, Fanon makes two moves with respect to civil society. First, he locates its genuine manifestation in Europe—the motherland. Then, with respect to the colony, he locates it only in the zone of the settler. This second move is vital for our understanding of black positionality in America and for understanding the, at best, limitations of radical social movements in America. For if we are to follow Fanon's analysis and the gestures toward this understanding in some of the work of imprisoned intellectuals, then we have to come to grips with the fact that, for black people, civil society *itself*—rather than its abuses or shortcomings—is a state of emergency.

For Fanon, civil society is predicated on the Manichaeism of divided zones, which are opposed to each other "but not in service of a higher unity."[4] This is the basis of his later assertion that the two zones produce two different "species," between which "no conciliation is possible."[5] The phrase "not in service of a higher unity" dismisses any kind of dialectical optimism for a future synthesis.

In "The Avant-Garde of White Supremacy," Steve Martinot and Jared Sexton assert the primacy of Fanon's Manichean zones (without the promise of higher unity), even in the face of American integration facticity. Fanon's specific colonial context does not share Martinot's and Sexton's historical or national context. Common to both texts, however, is the settler–native dynamic, the differential zoning, and the gratuity (as opposed to the contingency) of violence that accrues to the blackened position:

> The dichotomy between white ethics [the discourse of civil society] and its irrelevance to the violence of police profiling is not dialectical; the two are incommensurable whenever one attempts to *speak* about the paradigm of policing, one is forced back into a discussion of particular events—high-profile homicides and their related courtroom battles, for instance.[6]

It makes no difference that in the United States the "casbah" and the "European" zone are laid one on top of the other. What is being asserted here is an isomorphic schematic relation—the schematic interchangeability—between Fanon's settler society and Martinot's and Sexton's policing paradigm. For Fanon, it is the policeman and soldier (not the discursive, or hegemonic, agents) of colonialism that make one town white and the other black. For Martinot and Sexton, this Manichean delirium manifests itself by way of the U.S. paradigm of policing that (re)produces, repetitively, the inside–outside, the civil society–black world, by virtue of the difference between those bodies that do not magnetize bullets and those that do. "Police impunity serves to distinguish between the racial itself and the elsewhere that mandates it . . . the distinction between those whose human being is put permanently in question and those for whom it goes without saying."[7] In such a paradigm, white people are, ipso facto, deputized in the face of black people, whether they know it (consciously) or not. Whiteness, then—and, by extension, civil society cannot be solely "represented" as some monumentalized coherence of phallic signifiers but must first be understood as a social formation of contemporaries who do not magnetize bullets. This is the essence of their construction through an *a*signifying absence; their signifying presence is manifested by the fact that they are, if only by default, deputized against those who do magnetize bullets. In short, white people are not simply "protected" by the police. They are—in their very corporeality—the police.

This ipso facto deputization of white people in the face of black people accounts for Fanon's materiality and Martinot's and Sexton's Manichean delirium in America. What remains to be addressed, however, is the way in which the political contestation between civil society's junior partners (i.e., workers, white women, and immigrants), on the one hand, and white-supremacist institutionality, on the other hand, is produced by, and reproductive of, a supplemental antiblackness. Put another way: How is the production and accumulation of junior partners' social capital dependent on an antiblack rhetorical structure and a decomposed black body?

Any serious musing on the question of antagonistic identity formation—a formation, the mass mobilization of which can precipitate a crisis in the institutions and assumptive logic that undergird the United States of America—must come to grips with the contradictions between the political demands of radical social movements, such as the large prison abolition movement, which seeks to abolish the prison-industrial complex, and the ideological structure that underwrites its political desire. I contend that the positionality of black subjectivity is at the heart of those contradictions and that this unspoken desire is bound up with the political limitations of several naturalized and uncritically accepted categories that have their genesis mainly in the works of Antonio Gramsci— namely, work or labor, the wage, exploitation, hegemony, and civil society. I wish to theorize the symptoms of rage and resignation I hear in the words of George Jackson when he boils reform down to a single word, "fascism," or in Assata's brief declaration, "i hated it," as well as in the Manichean delirium of Fanon, Martinot, and Sexton. Today, the failure of radical social movements to embrace symptoms of all three gestures is tantamount to the reproduction of an antiblack politics that nonetheless represents itself as being in the service of the emancipation of the black prison slave.

By examining the strategy and structure of the black subject's absence in, and incommensurability with, the key categories of Gramscian theory, we come face to face with three unsettling consequences:

1. The black American subject imposes a radical incoherence on the assumptive logic of Gramscian discourse and on today's coalition politics. In other words, she or he implies a scandal.

2. The black subject reveals the inability of social movements grounded in Gramscian discourse to think of white supremacy (rather than capitalism) as the base and thereby calls into question their claim to elaborate a comprehensive and decisive antagonism. Stated another way, Gramscian discourse and coalition politics are indeed able to imagine the subject that transforms itself into a mass of antagonistic identity formations—formations that can precipitate a crisis in wage slavery, exploitation, and hegemony—but they are asleep at the wheel when asked to provide enabling antagonisms toward unwaged slavery, despotism, and terror.

3. We begin to see how Marxism suffers from a kind of conceptual anxiety. There is a desire for socialism on the other side of crisis, a society that does away not with the category of worker but with the imposition that workers suffer under the approach of variable capital. In other words, the mark of its conceptual anxiety is in its desire to democratize work and thus help to keep in place and ensure the coherence of Reformation and Enlightenment foundational values of productivity and progress. This scenario crowds out other postrevolutionary possibilities—that is, idleness.

The scandal with which the black subject position "threatens" Gramscian and coalition discourse is manifest in the black subject's incommensurability with, or disarticulation of, Gramscian categories: work, progress, production, exploitation, hegemony, and historical self-awareness. Through what strategies does the black subject destabilize—emerge as the unthought, and thus the scandal of—historical materialism? How does the black subject function within the "American desiring machine" differently from the quintessential Gramscian subaltern, the worker?

Capital was kick-started by the rape of the African continent, a phenomenon that is central to neither Gramsci nor Marx. According to Lindon Barrett, something about the black body in and of itself made it the repository of the violence that was the slave trade. It would have been far easier and far more profitable to take the white underclass from along the riverbanks of England and western Europe than to travel all the way to Africa for slaves.

The theoretical importance of emphasizing this in the early twenty-first century is twofold. First, capital was kick-started by approaching a particular body (a black body) with direct relations of force, not by approaching a white body with variable capital. Thus, one could say that slavery is closer to capital's primal desire than is exploitation. It is a relation of terror as opposed to a relation of hegemony. Second, today, late capital is imposing a renaissance of this original desire, the direct relation of force, the despotism of the unwaged relation. This renaissance of slavery—that is, the reconfiguration of the prison-industrial complex—has once again as its structuring metaphor and primary target the black body.

The value of reintroducing the unthought category of the slave by way of noting the absence of the black subject lies in the black subject's potential for extending the demand placed on state/capital formations because its reintroduction into the discourse expands the intensity of the antagonism. In other words, the positionality of the slave makes a demand that is in excess of the demand made by the positionality of the worker. The worker demands that productivity be fair and democratic (Gramsci's new hegemony; Lenin's dictatorship of the proletariat—in a word, socialism). In contrast, the slave demands that production stop, without recourse to its ultimate democratization. Work is not an organic principle for the slave. The absence of black subjectivity from the crux of radical discourse is symptomatic of the text's inability to cope with the possibility that the generative subject of capitalism, the black body of the fifteenth and sixteenth centuries, and the generative subject that resolves late capital's over-accumulation crisis, the black (incarcerated) body of the twentieth century and twenty-first century, does not reify the basic categories that structure conflict within civil society: the categories of work and exploitation.

Thus, the black subject position in America represents an antagonism or demand that cannot be satisfied through a transfer of ownership or organization of existing rubrics. In contrast, the Gramscian subject, the worker, represents a demand that can indeed be satisfied by way of a successful war of position, which brings about the end of exploitation. The worker calls into question the legitimacy of productive practices, while the slave calls into question the legitimacy of productivity itself. Thus, the insatiability of the slave demand on existing structures means that it cannot find its articulation within the modality of hegemony (influence, leadership, consent). The black body cannot give its consent because "generalized trust," the precondition for the solicitation of consent, "equals racialized whiteness."[8] Furthermore, as Orlando Patterson points out, slavery is natal alienation by way of social death, which is to say that a slave has no symbolic currency or material labor power to exchange.[9] A slave does not enter into a transaction of value (however asymmetrical), but is subsumed by direct relations of force. As such, a slave is an articulation of a despotic irrationality, whereas the worker is an articulation of a symbolic rationality.

A metaphor comes into being through a violence that kills the thing so that the concept may live. Gramscian discourse and coalition politics come to grips with America's structuring rationality—what it calls capitalism, or political economy—but not with its structuring irrationality, the anti-production of late capital, and the hyperdiscursive violence that first kills the black subject so that the concept may be born. In other words, from the incoherence of black death, America generates the coherence of white life. This is important when thinking about the Gramscian paradigm and its spiritual progenitors in the world of organizing in the United States today, with its overvaluation of hegemony and civil society. Struggles over hegemony are seldom, if ever, asignifying. At some point, they require coherence and categories for the record, meaning that they contain the seeds of antiblackness.

What does it mean to be positioned not as a positive term in the struggle for anticapitalist hegemony—that is, as a worker—but to be positioned in excess of hegemony; to be a catalyst that disarticulates the rubric of hegemony; to be a scandal to its assumptive, foundational logic; to threaten civil society's discursive integrity? In *White Writing*, J. M. Coetzee examines the literature of Europeans who encountered the South African Khoisan in the Cape between the sixteenth century and the eighteenth century.[10] The Europeans faced an "anthropological scandal": a being without (recognizable) customs, religion, medicine, dietary patterns, culinary habits, sexual mores, means of agriculture, and, most significant, character (because, according to the literature, they did not work). Other Africans, such as the Xhosa, who were agriculturalists, provided European discourse with enough categories for the record so that, through various strategies of articulation, they could be known by textual projects that accompanied the colonial project. But the Khoisan did not produce the necessary categories for the record, the play of signifiers that would allow for a sustainable semiotics.

According to Coetzee, the coherence of European discourse depends on two structuring axes. A "Historical Axis" consists of codes distributed along the axis of temporality and events, while the "Anthropological Axis" is an axis of cultural codes. It mattered very little which codes on either axis a particular indigenous community was perceived to possess, with "possession" the operative word, for these codes act as a kind of mutually agreed-on currency. What matters is that the community has some play of difference along both axes, sufficient in number to construct taxonomies that can be investigated, identified, and named by the discourse. Without this, the discourse cannot go on. It is reinvigorated when an unknown entity presents itself, but its anxiety reaches crisis proportions when the entity remains unknown. Something unspeakable occurs. Not to possess a particular code along the Anthropological Axis or the Historical Axis is akin to lacking a gene for brown hair or green eyes on an X or Y chromosome. Lacking a Historical Axis or an Anthropological Axis is akin to the absence of the chromosome itself. The first predicament raises the notion: What kind of human? The second predicament brings into crisis the notion of the human itself.

Without the textual categories of dress, diet, medicine, crafts, physical appearance, and, most important, work, the Khoisan stood in refusal of the invitation to become Anthropological Man. She or he was the void in discourse that could be designated only as idleness. Thus, the Khoisan's status within discourse was not that of an opponent or an interlocutor but, rather, that of an unspeakable scandal. His or her position within the discourse was one of disarticulation, for he or she did little or nothing to fortify and extend the interlocutory life of the discourse. Just as the Khoisan presented the discourse of the Cape with an anthropological scandal, so the black subject in the Western Hemisphere, the slave, presents Marxism and American textual practice with a historical scandal.

How is our incoherence in the face of the Historical Axis germane to our experience of being "a phenomenon without analog"? A sample list of codes mapped out by an American subject's Historical Axis might include *rights or entitlements*; here, even Native Americans provide categories for the record when one thinks of how the Iroquois constitution, for example, becomes the U.S. Constitution. *Sovereignty* is also included, whether a state is one the subject left behind or, as in the case of American Indians, one taken by force and by dint of broken treaties. White supremacy has made good use of the Indian subject's positionality, one that fortifies and extends the interlocutory life of America as a coherent (albeit imperial) idea because treaties are forms of articulation: Discussions brokered between two groups are presumed to possess the same category of historical currency, sovereignty. The code of sovereignty can have a past and future history, if you will excuse the oxymoron, when one considers that 150 Native American tribes have applied to the Bureau of Indian Affairs for sovereign recognition so that they might qualify for funds harvested from land stolen from them.[11] *Immigration* is another code that maps the subject onto the American Historical Axis, with narratives of arrival based on collective volition and premeditated desire. Chicano subject positions can fortify and extend the interlocutory life of America as an idea because racial conflict can be articulated across the various contestations over the legitimacy of arrival, immigration. Both whites and Latinos generate data for this category.

Slavery is the great leveler of the black subject's positionality. The black American subject does not generate historical categories of entitlement, sovereignty, and immigration for the record. We are "off the map" with respect to the cartography that charts civil society's semiotics; we have a past but not a heritage. To the data-generating demands of the Historical Axis, we present a virtual blank, much like that which the Khoisan presented to the Anthropological Axis. This places us in a structurally impossible position, one that is outside the articulations of hegemony. However, it also places hegemony in a structurally impossible position because—and this is key—our presence works back on the grammar of hegemony and threatens it with incoherence. If every subject—even the most massacred among them, Indians—is required to have analogs within the nation's structuring narrative, and the experience of one subject on whom the nation's order of wealth was built is without analog, then that subject's presence destabilizes all other analogs.

Fanon writes, "Decolonization, which sets out to change the order of the world, is, obviously, a program of complete disorder."[12] If we take him at his word, then we must accept that no other body functions in the Imaginary, the Symbolic, or the Real so completely as a repository of complete disorder as the black body. Blackness is the site of absolute dereliction at the level of the Real, for in its magnetizing of bullets the black body functions as the map of gratuitous violence through which civil society is possible—namely, those bodies for which violence is, or can be, contingent. Blackness is the site of absolute dereliction at the level of the Symbolic, for blackness in America generates no categories for the chromosome of history and no data for the categories of immigration or sovereignty. It is an experience without analog—a past without a heritage. Blackness is the site of absolute dereliction at the level of the Imaginary, for "whoever says 'rape' says Black" (Fanon), whoever says "prison" says black (Sexton), and whoever says "AIDS" says black—the "Negro is a phobogenic object."[13]

Indeed, it means all those things: a phobogenic object, a past without a heritage, the map of gratuitous violence, and a program of complete disorder. Whereas this realization is, and should be, cause for alarm, it should not be cause for lament or, worse, disavowal—not at least, for a true revolutionary or for a truly revolutionary movement such as prison abolition. If a social movement is to be neither social-democratic nor Marxist in terms of structure of political desire, then it should grasp the invitation to assume the positionality of subjects of social death. If we are to be honest with ourselves, we must admit that the "Negro" has been inviting whites, as well as civil society's junior partners, to the dance of social death for hundreds of years, but few have wanted to learn the steps. They have been, and remain today—even in the most antiracist movements, such as the prison abolition movement—invested elsewhere. This is not to say that all oppositional political desire today is pro-white, but it is usually antiblack, meaning that it will not dance with death.

Black liberation, as a prospect, makes radicalism more dangerous to the United States. This is not because it raises the specter of an alternative polity (such as socialism or community control of existing resources), but because its condition of possibility and gesture of resistance function as a negative dialectic: a politics of refusal and a refusal to affirm, a "program of complete disorder." One must embrace its disorder, its incoherence, and allow oneself to be elaborated by it if, indeed, one's politics are to be underwritten by a desire to take down this country. If this is not the desire that underwrites one's politics, then through what strategy of legitimation is the word "prison" being linked to the word "abolition"? What are this movement's lines of political accountability?

There is nothing foreign, frightening, or even unpracticed about the embrace of disorder and incoherence. The desire to be embraced, and elaborated, by disorder and incoherence is not anathema in and of itself. No one, for example, has ever been known to say, "Gee-whiz, if only my orgasms would end a little sooner, or maybe not come at all." Yet few so-called radicals desire to be embraced, and elaborated, by the disorder and incoherence of blackness—and the state of political movements in the United States today is marked by this very Negrophobogenisis: "Gee-whiz, if only black rage could be more coherent, or maybe not come at all." Perhaps there is something more terrifying about the joy of black than there is in the joy of sex (unless one is talking sex with a Negro). Perhaps coalitions today prefer to remain in-orgasmic in the face of civil society—with hegemony as a handy prophylactic, just in case. If through this stasis or paralysis they try to do the work of prison abolition, the work will fail, for it is always work *from* a position of coherence (i.e., the worker) on *behalf* of a position of incoherence of the black subject, or prison slave. In this way, social formations on the left remain blind to the contradictions of coalitions between workers and slaves. They remain coalitions operating within the logic of civil society and function less as revolutionary promises than as crowding out scenarios of black antagonisms, simply feeding our frustration.

Whereas the positionality of the worker (whether a factory worker demanding a monetary wage, an immigrant, or a white woman demanding a social wage) gestures toward the reconfiguration of civil society, the positionality of the black subject (whether a prison slave or a prison slave-in-waiting) gestures toward the disconfiguration of civil society. From the coherence of civil society, the black subject beckons with the incoherence of civil war, a war that reclaims blackness not as a positive value but as a politically enabling site, to quote Fanon, of "absolute dereliction." It is a "scandal" that rends civil society asunder. Civil war, then, becomes the unthought, but never forgotten, understudy of hegemony. It is a black specter waiting in the wings, an endless antagonism that cannot be satisfied (via reform or reparation) but that must, nonetheless, be pursued to the death.

Notes

Originally published in *Social Justice: A Journal of Crime, Conflict, and World Order* 30, no. 2 (2002): 18–27.

1. *Editor's note*: Frank Wilderson's original essay refers to the following as influential in his analysis: Fanon, *Black Skin, White Masks*; Gramsci, *Selections from the Prison Notebooks*; James, *Resisting State Violence*; and West, "Black Strivings in a Twilight Civilization."
2. Shakur, *Assata*, 224.
3. Ibid.
4. Fanon, *The Wretched of the Earth*, 38–39.
5. Ibid.
6. Steve Martinot and Jared Sexton, "The Avant-Garde of White Supremacy," April 27,

2002, available online at http://www.ocf.berkeley.edu/~marto/paradigm (accessed May 28, 2002), 6; emphasis added.

7. Ibid., 8.

8. Lindon Barrett, "The 'I' of the Beholder: The Modern Subject and the African Diaspora," unpublished paper presented at the Blackness in Global Contexts conference, University of California, Davis, March 28–30, 2002.

9. Patterson, *Slavery and Social Death*.

10. Coetzee, *White Writing*.

11. White supremacy transmogrifies codes internal to Native American culture for its own purposes. However, unlike immigrants and white women, the Native American has no purchase as a junior partner in civil society. Space does not permit me to discuss this fully here. Ward Churchill and others do explain how—unlike civil society's junior partners—genocide of the Indian, like the enslavement of blacks, is a precondition for the idea of America. It is a condition of possibility on which the idea of immigration can be narrativized. No web of analogy can be spun between, on the one hand, the phenomenon of genocide and slavery and, on the other hand, the phenomenon of access to institutionality and immigration. Thus, although white supremacy appropriates Native American codes of sovereignty, it cannot solve the contradiction that, unlike civil society's junior partners, those codes are not imbricated with immigration and access.

12. Fanon, *The Wretched of the Earth*, 37.

13. Ibid.

2

Forced Passages   Dylan Rodríguez

This essay considers the prison as a center for the reproduction of the American "Homeland" as a global locality, regimenting antisociality and mass-based civic and social death. I make two central arguments. First, I contend that the epoch of white-supremacist chattel slavery and its constitutive transatlantic articulation—the Middle Passage—elaborates the social and political logic of the current carceral formation that has been named and theorized as a qualitative "prison-industrial complex." There is a material and historical kinship between the prison as a contemporary regime of violence and the structures of racialized mass incarceration and disintegration prototyped in the chattel punishment and bodily disarticulation of enslaved Africans. Second, I argue that a foregrounding of the lineage of radical intellectuals imprisoned in the United States articulates a *theoretical vernacular of death*, one that disrupts hegemonic and "progressive" counterhegemonic public policy, academic and activist discourses, and their alleged critiques of prisons, policing, and the prison-industrial complex.

The Prison Regime as Middle Passage

In deploying the term "prison regime," I am differentiating both the *scale* and *object(s)* of analysis from the more typical macro-scale categories of "the prison," "the prison system," and, most recently, "the prison-industrial complex." The conceptual scope of this term similarly exceeds the analytical scope of prison policy and "the prison (or prisoner's) experience," categories that most often take textual form through discrete case studies, institutional reform initiatives, prison/prisoner ethnographies, and individualized biographical and autobiographical narratives. Rather, my working conception of the prison regime invokes a "meso" (middle, or mediating) dimension of processes, structures, and vernaculars that compose the state's modalities of self-articulation and "rule"— that is, its arrangement of official juridical as well as spatial *dominion* at the localized site of the prison.

I consider the terms of dominion to include both the conventional definition of a discrete territory controlled by a ruling order/state, as well as its ety-mological meaning derived from the Latin root term *dominium*, a conception of power that posits "absolute dominion in tangible things." The specificity of imprisonment as a regime of power is its *racial chattel logic*, or structure of non-humanization: To the extent that the (black) prisoner or "inmate" is conceived as the fungible property of the state (according to the Thirteenth Amendment to the U.S. Constitution, the "convict" is ready-made for actual "involuntary ser-vitude," or enslavement), the captive is both the state's abstracted legal property/ obligation and intimate bodily possession. Orlando Patterson's explication of the roots of slavery offers a useful framework through which to comprehend the root structure of this carceral-punitive regime:

> The Romans invented the legal fiction of dominium or absolute ownership, a fiction that highlights their practical genius. . . . By emphasizing the cate-gories of persona (owner) and res (thing) and by rigidly distinguishing be-tween corporeal and incorporeal things, the Romans created a new legal paradigm. . . . An object could only be a tangible thing. More important . . . property was no longer a relation between persons *but a relation between persons and things.* And this fiction fitted perfectly its purpose, to define one of the most rapidly expanding sources of wealth, namely slaves.[1]

Foregrounding the notion of *dominium* as the exercise of "inner power over a thing," Patterson's discussion provides a dynamic backdrop against which to sustain a theorization of "prison" and "imprisonment" as *processes, rituals, con-frontations, struggles, productions.* The prison regime constitutes an essential figure in the articulation of the state's *intelligibility* to its presumed audiences (including and beyond the formal polity) as well as to itself. Thus, to conceive a radical genealogy of the prison regime is to suggest that imprisonment, or captivity, encompasses a range of state and state-sanctioned practices, from the stridently ritualized to the arbitrary and informal, that manifest an otherwise abstracted sense and structure of "authority." Patterson continues,

> Those who exercise power, if they are able to transform it into a "right," a norm, a usual part of the order of things, must first control (or at least be in a position to manipulate) appropriate symbolic instruments. They may do so by exploiting already existing symbols, or they may create new ones relevant to their needs.[2]

The prison regime, in the process of attempting control over the symbolic, works through the *mediating material of the prisoner* as an embodied subject (to be distinguished from notions of the prisoner as "object" or objectified body). A persistent, guiding tension for the prison regime is therefore that between the power of *dominium* (absolute ownership, a power that is oblivious to consensus from "other areas of culture") and the regime's gestures toward "authority" as a production of respectability, common sense, and consent around the apparatus of its rule.[3]

This working conceptualization of the prison regime resonates with Michel Foucault's theorization of the displacement of the unitary sovereign power in modern and postmodern social formations. Foucault is famously concerned with the production of regimes of power through situated apparatuses and institutions (e.g., the asylum, the clinic, the prison, the military). In his lecture of January 14, 1976, Foucault contended:

> Our object is not to analyze rule-governed and legitimate forms of power which have a single center, or to look at what their general mechanisms or its overall effects might be. *Our object is, on the contrary, to understand power by looking at its extremities, at its outer limits at the points where it becomes capillary*; in other words, to understand power in its most regional forms and institutions, and especially at the points where this power transgresses the rules of right that organize and delineate it, oversteps those rules and is invested in institutions, is embodied in techniques and acquires the material means to intervene, sometimes in violent ways.[4]

The prison's operative "capillary" sites, where it exceeds official directive and juridical norm, are nowhere better excavated, documented, theorized, and centered than in the body of praxis generated by imprisoned radical intellectuals. Here, the theoretically conservative notion of "the Prison" as a formal state institution, defined by centralized protocols and rules, is displaced by a conception of the "prison regime" as a technology of power that works *through* the bodies of designated agents (guards, doctors, wardens, prison educators) and performs and materializes *on* the bodies of an immobilized subject population.

Foucault's "capillary power" may be recontextualized here as a literal designation for the materiality of the prison regime's method of violence as it manifests on the imprisoned subject's *bodily* capillaries, that is her or his viscerality—blood, skin, nervous system, organs. It is also a metaphoric designation for the manner in which power circulates, materializing through the form and move-ment of its outermost points. Capillaries, in the medical definition, are "the tiny blood vessels that connect the arterioles (the smallest divisions of the arteries) and the venules (the smallest divisions of the veins)." These blood vessels form crucial sites of passage for the transfer of the body's life-sustaining nutrients as well as for the spread of disease, infection, and impurities. "Although min-ute, the capillaries are a site where much action takes place in the circulatory system."[5]

The prison, as a capillary site for the production and movement of power, exerts a dominion that reaches significantly beyond its localized setting. This is to argue that the emergence of a reformed and reconceived prison regime as "a site where much action takes place in the circulatory system" of power and domination, has become central to constituting the political logic as well as the material reproduction of the United States' social formation. The prison regime, in other words, generates a technology of power that extends beyond and out-side the institutional formality of the Prison. Similarly, a radical genealogy of this regime must think significantly beyond and behind the current historical moment to comprehend fully the logic of its formation and sustenance.

Scholars such as Angela Y. Davis, Alex Lichtenstein, David Oshinsky, and others have closely examined the material continuities between U.S. racial-chattel plantation slavery and the emergence of the modern American pe-nal system. These studies bring crucial attention to the centrality of white-supremacist juridical, policing, and paramilitary regimes in the production of a carceral apparatus during the late nineteenth century that essentially repli-cated—and, arguably, exacerbated—the constitutive logic of the supposedly de-funct slave plantation. Lichtenstein, for example, argues convincingly that the transition from chattel slave to black prison labor in the post–Civil War South exemplified the "continual correspondence between the forces of moderniza-tion and the perpetuation of bound labor." He writes,

> In the postbellum South, at each stage of the region's development, convict labor was concentrated in some of the most significant and rapidly grow-ing sectors of the economy. Initially Southern prisoners worked on the rail-roads. . . . This decisive shift from private to public exploitation of forced black labor marked the triumph of the modern state's version of the social and economic benefits to be reaped from bound labor, in the name of devel-

oping a more . . ."progressive" economy. Thus, from Reconstruction through the Progressive Era the various uses of convict labor coincided with changes in the political economy of southern capitalism.[6]

By way of contrast Davis, in an extended examination of Frederick Douglass's historical understanding of the post-emancipation criminalization of black communities, offers a theorization of how "the prison system established its authority as a major institution of discipline and control for black communities during the last two decades of the nineteenth century," yielding a lineage of "carceral regulation" that arrived at "crisis proportions" a century later. Most important is Davis's foregrounding of the seamless linkage between the formal abolition of extant forms of racial chattel slavery in 1865 and the somewhat unheralded (albeit simultaneous) recodification and moral legitimization of a revised institution of enslavement, which would occur through the auspices of criminal conviction and imprisonment:

> When the Thirteenth Amendment was passed in 1865, thus legally abolishing the slave economy, it also contained a provision that was universally celebrated as a declaration of the unconstitutionality of peonage. "Neither slavery nor involuntary servitude, *except as a punishment for crime*, whereof the party shall have been duly convicted, shall exist within the United States, or anyplace subject to their jurisdiction." That exception would render penal servitude constitutional—from 1865 to the present day.[7]

Tracing the contemporary prison regime's points of origin to the juridical and material developments of the post–Civil War South—in particular, to its twinned and mutually constituting crises of economic modernization and managing/controlling a suddenly nominally "free" black population—is essential for a radical genealogy of the U.S. prison. To the extent that "the post–Civil War southern system of convict lease . . . transferred symbolically significant numbers of black people from the prison of slavery to the slavery of prison,"[8] the formation of the U.S. prison must be seen as inseparable from the relation of white freedom and black unfreedom, white ownership and black fungibility, that produced the nation's foundational property relation as well an essential component (with Native American displacement and genocide) of its racial ordering. In fact, the prison can be understood through this genealogy as one of the primary *productive* components of the U.S. nation-state's internal coherence (vis-à-vis the production of white supremacist hegemony through black bodily immobilization and punishment) and modernist expansiveness (as the prison replaced the "irrational" horrors of chattel slavery with the juridical "rationality" of the prison).

I am interested in stretching both the historical reach and conceptual boundaries of this genealogical tracing, however. While there are always and necessarily forms of *passage into* the temporalities and geographies of death, such as those of the slave plantation and post-emancipation prison, the contemporary case of the prison regime constitutes a site and condition of death *that is itself a form of passage.* This is to say that the prison is less a "destination" point for "the duly convicted" than it is a point of *massive human departure*—from civil society, the free world, and the mesh of affective social bonds and relations that produce varieties of "human" family and community. Hence, labor exploitation, the construction of unfree labor (what some have called a "new slavery"), and the mass confinement of a reserve labor pool are not the constitutive logics of the new prison regime, although these are certainly factors that shape the prison's institutional structure. Whereas forced labor (formal prison slavery) was at one time conceived as the primary institutional tool for rehabilitating imprisoned white men,[9] the proliferation of mass incarceration in the current era has reinscribed a logic of extermination.

Sharon Patricia Holland's meditations on the entanglement—in fact, the veritable inseparability—of death and black subjectivity indicts the very formation of a white Americana and its accompanying social imaginary vis-à-vis the never-ending presence (and imminence) of racial chattel slavery:

> It is possible to make at least two broad contentions here: a) that the (white) culture's dependence on the nonhuman status of its black subjects was never measured by the ability of whites to produce a "social heritage"; instead, it rested on the status of the black as a nonentity; and b) that the transmutation from enslaved to freed subject never quite occurred at the level of the imagination.[10]

Extrapolating Holland's central theses, I would add that, indeed, what *has* occurred is an inscription of the black nonhuman "nonentity" through the category of the imprisoned—hence illegal/extralegal/convict—subject. This is to argue that while the white social imagination has been unable to assimilate the notion of a "freed (black) subject" in its midst beyond cynical or piecemeal gestures of "inclusion" (which is to say that ultimately it really cannot assimilate blackness at all), the actual "transmutation" has been from the white social imagination of the slave to that of the (black) prisoner, or what Frank Wilderson theorized in the previous chapter as the new black "prison slave."[11]

The status of the enslaved–imprisoned black subject forms the template through which white Americana constructs a communion of historical interest, mobilizations of political force, and, more specifically, the production and proliferation of a regime of mass-based human immobilization. Thus, my theoretical centering of black unfreedom here is not intended to minimize or understate the empirical presence of "non-black" Third World, indigenous, or even white bodies in these current sites of state captivity but, rather, to argue that the technology of the prison regime—and the varieties of violence it wages against those it holds captive—is premised on a particular white-supremacist module or prototype that is in fact rooted in the history of slavery and the social and racial crisis that it has forwarded into the present.

The contemporary regime of the prison encompasses the weaponry of an institutionalized dehumanization. It also, and necessarily, generates a material rendition of the *non- and sub-human* that structurally antagonizes and de-centers the immediate capacity of the imprisoned subject to simply *self-identify*. Publishing in 1990 under the anonymous byline "A Federal Prisoner," one imprisoned writer offered a schematic view of this complex process, which is guided by the logic of a totalizing disempowerment and social disaffection:

> The first thing a convict feels when he receives an inconceivably long sentence is shock. The shock usually wears off after about two years, when all his appeals have been denied. He then enters a period of self-hatred because of what he's done to himself and his family.
>
> If he survives that emotion—and some don't—he begins to swim the rapids of rage, frustration and alienation. When he passes through the rapids, he finds himself in the calm waters of impotence, futility and resignation. It's not a life one can look forward to living. The future is totally devoid of hope.[12]

The structured violence of self-alienation, which drastically compounds the effect of formal social alienation, is at the heart of the regime's punitive-carceral logic. Yet it is precisely because the reproduction of the regime relies on its own incapacity to decisively "dehumanize" its captives en masse (hence, the persistence of institutional measures that pivot on the presumption and projection of the "inmate's" embodiment of disobedience, resistance, and insurrection) that it generates a philosophy of the captive body that *precedes* the logic of enslavement. Thus, the regime's logic of power reaches into the arsenal of a historical apparatus that was an essential element of the global formation of racial chattel slavery while simultaneously structuring its own particular technology of violence and bodily domination. What, then, is the materiality of the archetypal imprisoned body (and subject) through which the contemporary prison regime has proliferated its diverse and hierarchically organized apparatuses of racialized and gendered violence, most especially its technologies of immobilization and bodily disintegration?

I am arguing that a radical genealogy of the prison regime must engage in historical conversation with the massive human departure of the transatlantic Middle Passage, an apparatus and regime of capture and forced movement that outlined its own epochal conception of the non- and subhuman, the prototyping of normative black punishment in a white new world, and the blueprinting of the abject (*and durably captive*) black presence under the rule of Euro-American modernity. The Middle Passage foreshadows the prison as it routes and enacts chattel slavery, constituting both a passage into the temporality and geography of enslavement (crystallized by Patterson's conception of slavery as "natal alienation" and "social death"[13]) and a condition of existence unto itself—in particular, a spatially specified pedagogical production of black slave ontology.

I am especially concerned with the capacity of historically situated white-supremacist regimes to prototype novel technologies of violence and domination on black bodies—articulating in this instance through what Eric Williams considers the overarching "economic" logic of a transcontinental trafficking in enslaved Africans[14]—which in turn may yield technologies of power that become available to, and constitutive of, larger social and carceral formations, even centuries later. Thus, while the contemporary prison regime captures and immobilizes the descendants of slaves and non-slaves alike, I consider its technology of violence to be inseparable from a genealogy of transatlantic black/African captivity and punishment.

While the human volume of the Middle Passage has been a subject of empirical and methodological debate since the publication of Philip Curtin's *The*

Atlantic Slave Trade: A Census (1969), a loose consensus among historians has been attained since the 1999 release of the Cambridge University Press Trans-Atlantic Slave Trade database. David Eltis, drawing from a rigorous review of previous literature and elaborating from the Cambridge University data set, suggests a figure of about 11 million "exports of slaves from Africa" between the years 1519 and 1867.[15] Eltis, Curtin, Herbert S. Klein, Paul Lovejoy, David Richardson, Joseph Inikori, Stanley Engerman, and others have further estimated that between 12 percent and 20 percent of the enslaved perished during the transatlantic transfer, with a total of between 10 million and 15 million of the enslaved eventually reaching the Americas. It is important to note, for the genealogical relation I am examining here, that the vast majority of the seaborne deaths were the result of conditions endemic to the abhorrent living conditions of the slave vessels (the effects of contractible disease and malnutrition, for example, were exacerbated by the conditions of mass incarceration). Many others committed suicide and infanticide in an attempt to defeat the logic of their gendered biological expropriation and bodily commodification, while unknown numbers were killed in the process of attempting to overthrow their captors. The scale of biological death during the Middle Passage was astronomical and clearly genocidal.

Further, this process underwrote the innovation of a distinctive maritime architecture—literally, a seaborne and ship-bound geography devoted to the accumulation, storage, and biological preservation of an enslaved human "cargo." This technology of incarceration, famously portrayed by late-eighteenth-century British abolitionists in their lithograph "Stowage of the British Slave Ship Brookes" (see figure below), rendered a profoundly graphic conception of the racialized sub- and nonhuman as the spatial and existential underside of an expansive European New World millennium. Yet this mass-scale, transcontinental kidnapping must be examined in the context of the coerced transition that it induced by fiat.[16]

The Middle Passage constituted a liminal spatial and temporal site, a moment of commodity transfer between European business partners, as well as a profound site of transformation for the human beings mass incarcerated in the cargo holds of ships. It encompassed a moment of transition between discrete conditions of subjection and domination (from the upheavals of colonial conquest to the settlement localities of enslavement) as well as formed a condition

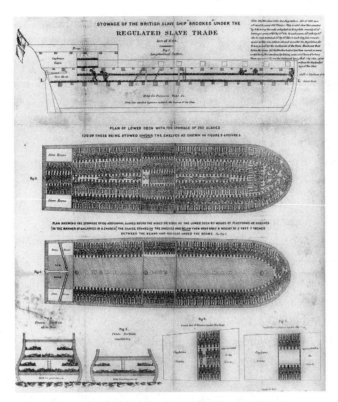

Figure 2 "Stowage of the British Slave Ship Brookes," circa 1790. Broadside, Rare Book Room, Library of Congress, Portfolio 282–43.

of existence unto itself. Confined to vessels floating in the Atlantic, enslaved Africans were, for their captors, precious live chattel investments in a limbo state between colonial conquest, enslavement (simultaneously commodity and labor value), and physical extermination. The Middle Passage was, at its spatial core, a site of profound subjective and communal disruption for captive Africans: Manifesting an epochal rupture from familiar networks of kinship, livelihood, and social reproduction, the voyage was the threshold of geographic, subjective, and bodily displacement for the transatlantic imprisoned. This African "New World" diaspora, fundamentally constituted and mobilized through conquest, genocide, and enslavement, was and is defined by a structure of immanent alienation from the material and psychic contexts that made operational indigenous African sociocultural forms and made their unique renditions of human community intelligible and consistent.

The manner in which the Middle Passage allegorized and materialized this unique destruction of human community, particularly its displacement and interruption of indigenous African tribal and communal subjectivities, illuminates how the construction of this seaborne mass incarceration entailed a production of power and domination that pivoted on significantly more than the logistical or economic pragmatics of a live commodity transport. While the human cargo certainly held a lucrative potential profit for slavers incumbent on their ability to bring their stock physically to market, there was far more at stake in the three-centuries-long institutionalization of this itinerant transatlantic "prison."

The Middle Passage was essentially a pedagogical and punitive practice that deployed strategies of unprecedented violence to "teach" captive Africans and coerce them into the methods of an incipient global ordering. Evidentiary fragments of this complex practice are reflected in the gathered historical data, which reveal that rates of survival for the enslaved during the era of the Middle Passage generally equaled or surpassed the survival rates of the European slave-ship crews. While the precise overall mortality rate of enslaved Africans during the transatlantic voyage remains a contested figure, Stephen Behrendt contends that, since "the primary aim of merchants was to minimize slave deaths in the middle passage to ensure a profitable voyage," the mortality rates for European crews were consistently higher than those of their captives, at times doubling or tripling their relative death counts. For the merchant slave traders, "minimizing crew mortality was a secondary consideration" to that of preserving their human chattel.[17] Curtin's focus on the mid- to late eighteenth century similarly reveals that "the death rate per voyage among the crew was uniformly higher than the death rate among slaves in transit at the same period." He argues in regard to this discrepancy in mortality rates that "the data are so consistent and regular . . . that this can be taken as a normal circumstance of the eighteenth-century slave trade."[18] Perhaps what is exceedingly horrific about the carceral technology of the Middle Passage is that it led to the death of breathtaking raw numbers of enslaved people while relatively successfully preserving slave life for the sake of auction and fungible bodily circulation.[19]

Thus, the planned survival of enslaved Africans was symbiotic to—rather than a logical contradiction of—their mass incarceration in vessel cargo holds. This structure of planned bodily preservation and mass bodily immobilization reflects the peculiar technology of domination and violence that conceived and persistently refigured the Middle Passage as a primary, long-term labor for the emergent transatlantic European and Euro-American civilization. Establishing an epochal precursor to the carceral technologies of the landlocked U.S. prison, the Middle Passage simultaneously (1) re-mapped enslaved black bodies; (2) prototyped a conception of the imprisoned/slave as the categorical embodiment of the sub- or nonhuman; and (3) reconfigured multiple scales of geography, constituting new conceptions of the continental (Europe/Africa/"New World") and (transatlantic) oceanic, while inventing new localities in the slave ship and plantation. Thus, the apparent commitment to preserving slave life on board the ships was more than an economic decision. Rather, keeping enslaved captives alive was integral to the production of the Middle Passage as a productive and socially constitutive modality of mass-based imprisonment that collapsed ontological violence into a regime of profound bodily punishment.

Elaborating the slave ship as precisely such a capillary site of power, Vincent Harding's incisive analysis of the Middle Passage further elaborates the symbiosis between the incipient white-supremacist racial formation of the transatlantic conquest and settlement and the ontological relation that characterized the capture, enslavement, and transfer of Africans:

> The ships were even more than prisons. Ultimately they provided black people with an introduction to the Euro-American state, for they were mini-states with their own polity, their own laws and government; the common sailors were the ships' own indigenous oppressed class. . . . At the core of the mini-states, prisons, and kennels it was always possible to discover the social, economic, and political scourges arising out of Europe: racism, capitalism, and the deep human fears they engender. The tie of the ships to European capitalism was evident in the decision to call them "slavers," and in their relationship to the slave "factories," and to the industrial factories at home which made the goods that they brought to trade for humans. To maximize profits, the ships had to herd as many Africans aboard as possible, and to exploit their own white crews.[20]

Harding brings attention to the technologies of human containment that were invented and refined at the site of the slave vessel. This portable and moving confinement, he tells us, was invested with an intensive and sophisticated—and profoundly brutal—technology of incarceration. Olaudah Equiano, predating

Harding's analogy of the ship as white nation-state, reconstructs his first impression of the slave vessel in his 1789 memoir *The Interesting Narrative of the Life of Olaudah Equiano*: "I could not help expressing my fears and apprehensions to some of my countrymen: I asked them if these people had no country but lived in this hollow place (the ship)."[21]

It was within the logic of this power relation—one that significantly exceeds the contained binary relation of torture as a structure of personalized violence and extracted "suffering"—that bodies were re-spatialized and space was re-embodied:

> The width allowed for each individual was no more than sixteen inches, and the passage between each of these rows of human packages was so small that it was impossible for a person walking by, however carefully, to avoid treading on them. Thus crammed together, like herrings in a barrel, they contracted putrid and fatal disorders, so that those who came to inspect them in a morning often had to pick dead slaves out of their rows, and to unchain their dead carcasses from the bodies of their wretched fellow-sufferers to whom they had been fastened.[22]

Such horrified European and Euro-American abolitionist descriptions of slave-ship geography, and the white humanist outcry they superficially convey, might be usefully reread in the context of Harding's interpretive framing. The death space of the slave ship, and the genocidal epoch of the Middle Passage, confined and produced bodies that were ambivalently situated between the categories of labor value, social death, and biological death. Less ambivalent, however, was the constitution of enslaved Africans as an emergent ontological category lurking just outside—and irreversibly, productively against—the historical telos of the European Enlightenment and modernity's mankind.

This ontological subjection, forged over a three-century span through the carceral technology of the Middle Passage, foreshadowed the enduring labor of generating the racialized unfree as the condition of possibility for the civil society of the white and free. As such, the humanist sensibility expressed by elements of the nineteenth-century European and Euro-American slavery and slave-trade–abolitionist movements begs the question of who, figuratively and literally, was entitled access to the domain of the "human."

Maria Diedrich, Henry Louis Gates Jr., and Carl Pederson, editors of the 1999 collection *Black Imagination and the Middle Passage*, offer a conceptualization of the transatlantic slave trade that can assist in complicating our temporal and spatial conception of the contemporary regime of imprisonment: "The Middle Passage . . . emerges not as a clean break between past and present but as a *spatial continuum* between Africa and the Americas, the ship's deck and the hold, the Great House and the slave quarters, the town and the outlying regions."[23] A genealogy of the contemporary prison regime awakens both the historical memory and sociopolitical logic of the Middle Passage. The prison has come to form a hauntingly similar spatial and temporal continuum between social and biological notions of life and death, banal liberal civic freedom and totalizing unfreedom, community and alienation, agency and liquidation, the "human" and the sub- and nonhuman. In a reconstruction of the Middle Passage's constitutive logic, the reinvented prison regime is openly articulating and self-valorizing a commitment to efficient and effective bodily immobilization within the mass-based ontological subjection of human beings.

Torture's Excess: "It Was Like Dying"

The contemporary prison, working within the genealogical lineage of the Middle Passage, constantly prototypes technologies premised on a re-spatialization of bodies and coercive re-embodiment of spaces. Robert Perkinson's description of the internal geography of the Florence, Colorado "control-unit" prison, among the first federal super-maximum prisons to be introduced in the early 1990s, invokes and refracts the historical image and imaginary of the slave ship's cargo hold:

> Each cell contains a three-foot-wide cement bed slab, a concrete stool and desk, a steel sink and toilet, and a three-by-three shower stall. A fluorescent light panel glares from the wall, illuminating other amenities like an electric cigarette lighter, an inmate duress switch (since the cells are essentially soundproof), an air grate, and, in some cells, a small television. Double doors shrink the cells by another three feet, trapping unreachable space between bars and the outer door. Only two window slits allow external light into the cage, one on the steel door staring into the empty hallway and another body-length sliver facing an empty courtyard. The shower, along with food slots in the door, allow for total isolation.
>
> Thus, the Florence ADX's very layout determines that it can be nothing but a chamber of sensory deprivation, designed to press inmates to the brink

of insanity by its very architecture. Modern electronics allow constant surveillance and supervision while prisoners themselves remain physically invisible, locked away from any direct human view or contact in compartments of solid steel.[24]

Extrapolating the immobilizing logic of the Florence ADX (Administrative Maximum Prison), the September 2001 issue of *Peacekeeper*, the official publication of the California Correctional Peace Officers Association (CCPOA), offers a propaganda piece valorizing the super-max prison's evolution into more sophisticated carceral techniques:

> Imagine the ultimate Big Brother of the prison system—tracking inmates twenty-four hours a day, 365 days a year. Well, guess what? It exists. Big Brother has arrived at Calipatria State Prison. . . .
>
> Every inmate wears a wrist-worn transmitter called PASS unit, which stands for Personal Activated Security Sensor. When an inmate arrives at the facility, he or she is enrolled into the system database by the system operator. The information typically entered consists of the inmates name, inmate identification number, housing/bed assignment and meal type. . . .
>
> The transmitter is installed on the inmate's non-dominant wrist. It is secured with screws that are tightened with a special torque screwdriver. The clips can only be removed by breaking them. . . .
>
> Officer A. Felty . . . believes the system is a great deterrent. "The inmates realize they are being constantly monitored and supervised, even when the officer's eyes are not on them. . . . Basically, he knows that escape is not an option, the removal of the bracelet is not an option because he is being constantly monitored—whether the officer is watching him or not."[25]

The totalizing spatial logic of Calipatria's "Big Brother" conveys a peculiar convergence between high technologies of panoptic discipline and the banal normalization of ritualized and immanent physical violence. Disciplinary biopolitical state power rearticulates through the state's self-justifying monopoly on legitimate forms of coercive bodily disintegration: This is to argue that, far from simply inscribing a more invasive and comprehensive form of discipline over its captive civically dead subjects, Big Brother represents a multiplication of the potential sites and scenarios of subjection and physical punishment. This high technology re-maps prisoners' bodies onto a virtual terrain, abstracting their bodily movements and gestures into a computerized grid of obedience and disobedience, submission and violation. Such innovations effect a re-spatialization of the prison itself, marking the extension and veritable omnipresence of the state's capacity to practice a violent domination over its "inmates."

While such advanced technologies of imprisonment are an epochal leap from the carceral practices of the Middle Passage, as a production of power and dominion they are constituted by an analogous—and, in some places, materially similar—social logic and historical trajectory. Located within an extended current genealogy of the slave vessel, there is a resurfaced familiarity in the prison's discursive emphasis and material production of effective mass capture, immobilization, and bodily disintegration. It is worth invoking Hortense Spillers's meditation on the captivity of the Middle Passage as a manner of illustrating a central genealogical linkage between apparently discrete and epochally distant carceral forms: "On any given day, we might imagine, the captive personality did not know where s/he was, we could say that they were culturally 'unmade,' thrown in the midst of a figurative darkness that exposed their destinies to an unknown course."[26] Echoing and recontextualizing Spillers, Jarvis Jay Masters's account of his initial entombment in San Quentin's death-row prison resonates a spatial and bodily encounter with the prison's more common modes of isolation and circumscription. His narrative echoes those of imprisoned African survivors of the transatlantic transfer (such as Cugoano, Equiano, and others) while supplementing the CCPOA's rosy tribute to the onset of the high-technology prison.[27]

> I will never forget when the steel cell door slammed behind me. I stood in the darkness trying to fix my eyes and readjust the thoughts that were telling me that this was not home—that this tiny space would not, could not be where I would spend more than a decade of my life. . . .
>
> I spread my arms and found that the palms of my hands touched the walls with ease. I pushed against them with all my might, until I realized how silly it was to think that these thick concrete walls would somehow budge. . . . The bed was bolted into the wall like a shelf. It was only two and a half feet wide by six feet long, and only several feet above the gray concrete floor.[28]

Old and new technologies of incarceration have collaborated in the emergence of the contemporary prison. Masters's description of the San Quentin cell reveals the constitutive logic that unifies "low" and "high" carceral technologies in the production of the prison regime while invoking the captivity of the Middle Passage as living and lived memory. To absorb the geographical breadth and technological depth of the prison regime's elaboration is to come face to face with the unprecedented levels of autonomy granted to—and extracted by—the prison to shape the social (and carceral) worlds. It is also to find an insurgent critique of imprisonment that moves from the sometimes eloquent, though consistently displaced, theoretical languages articulated by captive radicals and revolutionaries.

Interviewed in 1970 about his first experience under state captivity, the venerated imprisoned liberationist George Jackson recounted:

> The very first time, *it was like dying*. . . . Just to exist at all in the cage calls for some heavy psychic readjustments. . . . I never adjusted. I haven't adjusted even yet, with half my life already spent in prison. . . . *Capture, imprisonment, is the closest to being dead that one is likely to experience in his life.*[29]

Speaking from the experimental "High Security Unit" in Lexington, Kentucky, some twenty years later, the political prisoner Susan Rosenberg echoed Jackson's language in a manner that reveals an essential—though rarely elaborated—facet of the prison regime. Testifying in the award-winning 1989 documentary *Through the Wire*, Rosenberg said:

> [The High Security Unit is] a prison within a prison. . . . *The High Security Unit is living death.* . . . I believe that this is an experiment being conducted by the Justice Department to try and destroy political prisoners and to justify the most vile abuse of us as women and as human beings, and [to] justify it because we are political.[30]

Since the time of Rosenberg's testimony, the technology of the Lexington High Security Unit has circulated and metamorphosed, virus-like, through state and federal prisons across the country. On any given day, tens of thousands are held captive in these "super-max" prisons, while more than 2 million are incarcerated under the rule of Jackson's "cage"—that is, the venerable jail/prison/detention center. These various carceral forms have astronomically increased the numbers of both social and political prisoners held captive in conditions of low-intensity physical and psychological torture, as well as those subjected to high-intensity punishment and state-sanctioned mental or emotional disordering.[31] In the meantime, the expansion of youth prisons, mental-health facilities, and Homeland Security and immigrant detention centers in the past decades has been accompanied by a proliferation of conditions easily likened to both traditional and revised definitions of solitary and mass-based torture. Jamal al-Harath, in the aftermath of his release from the U.S. prison camp in Guantá-namo Bay, Cuba, in March 2004, concisely surmised the logic of his detention on flimsy suspicion of connection to Afghanistan's Taliban and the al-Qaeda network: "The whole point of Guantánamo was to get to you psychologically. . . . The beatings were not as nearly as bad as the psychological torture. Bruises heal after a week, but the other stuff stays with you."[32] Echoing Jackson's meditation on captivity as an approximation of death, and surfacing the indelible marks that "existing in a cage" permanently inscribes on body, soul, and psyche, al-Harath illuminates a form of subjection that exceeds the formal temporal and spatial boundaries of imprisonment. The Guantánamo detention, he says, will always stay with him, even as he reassumes the formal status of the free person in his homeland of Britain.

The notorious routines characterizing the rise of California's Security Housing Unit (SHU) prisons further extrapolates the particular white-supremacist logic that persists within the spectacle of the tortured imprisoned body. The video-taped 1994 murder of the black prisoner Preston Tate at the Corcoran State Prison SHU by correctional officers—one of whom prefaced the fatal shoot-ing by announcing, "It's going to be duck-hunting season"—obtained national attention in the mid- to late 1990s, accompanied by widespread reporting of the Corcoran guards' amused coercion of SHU prisoners into gladiator-style prison-yard fights (shooting many of them under the auspices of "trying to pro-tect another inmate or guard").[33] Perkinson, however, brings attention to the site of SHU's unseen, where regulated regimes of bodily violence are partnered with the "application of sophisticated technology to control prisoners' routines, movements, and even thoughts more than ever before." His investigation of the SHU/super-max prison's normative practices of psychological torture and bodily punishment illustrates a structuring—and, perhaps, paradigmatic—nar-rative for the regime's legitimated and lawful disintegration of particular racial-ized captive bodies:

On April 22, 1992, for example, Vaughn Dortch was stripped naked and pulled out of his cell by a Pelican Bay SORT [Special Operations Response Team] squad. According to court records, prison guards then carried Dortch shackled and gagged to the infirmary where six guards pressed him into a steel tub of scalding hot water for several minutes. Dortch, who is African American, told "60 Minutes" that the guards promised to give him a "Klan bath" and scrubbed him with a bristle brush until his skin started to peel away. "Looks like we're going to have a white boy before this is through," one of the assailants joked.[34]

Similar incidents are reconstructed in mind-numbing fashion throughout the memoirs, testimonials, and correspondence of people imprisoned in SHU and super-max facilities under U.S. sanction.[35] The sheer mass and repetition of such accounts render implausible the claims, frequently voiced by official and lay defendants of these punitive regimens, that such scenarios amount to a collection of isolated and exceptional episodes. In fact, it is clear that the Pelican Bay "Klan Bath" represents an allegory of both the disavowed regularity and racialized logic of the direct bodily disarticulation that forms the primary material expression of the prison regime's immediate dominion, at the spatial site of the captive's body.

Even the terms of "torture" may be insufficient nomenclature for this technology of immobilization, however. Conventional definitions consider the inflicting of bodily violence to be the means to some end, whether it is extracting information, coercing confessions, terrorizing populations, or otherwise. The United Nations Convention against Torture and Other Cruel, Inhuman or Degrading Treatment or Punishment, by way of prominent example, states:

> The term "torture" means any act by which severe pain or suffering, whether physical or mental, is intentionally inflicted on a person *for such purposes as obtaining from him or a third person information or a confession, punishing him for an act he or a third person has committed or is suspected of having committed, or intimidating or coercing him or a third person,* or for any reason based on discrimination of any kind, when such pain or suffering is inflicted by or at the instigation of or with the consent or acquiescence of a public official or other person acting in an official capacity.[36]

There is, however, no structuring *exterior* or *ulterior* motive to the state's technology of violence and domination in the super-max prison or within the broader production of the prison regime. The structurally manifest political desire of the prison regime's technology of immobilizing (and deadly) violence is, in the case of Jackson's inaugural imprisonment, Rosenberg's High Security Unit, Tate's fatal SHU yard, and Dortch's Klan Bath, intrinsic to the biopolitical technology of the "torture" itself—that is, the isolation, social liquidation, and immobilization of human beings on scales of flexible magnitude.

The organizing logic of the prison-industrial complex writ large is echoed and embodied in the *vernacular of death* spoken by radical captives such as Jackson and Rosenberg. Both, among countless of their (currently and formerly) imprisoned cohorts, invoke a conception of the prison within a continuum of dying, or "being dead," that crucially expands the historical scope of the prison regime's genealogical linkages to other forms of human domination and massively structured bodily violence.

The prison has become, akin to the Middle Passage, more than simply a means to an end. It is, in objective and in fact, an end in itself. The logic of imprisonment in the age of the prison-industrial complex involves a particular kind of social extermination that fundamentally alters the network of relationships (affective, economic, and otherwise) in civil society. The prison, in the lineage of the slave vessel, has become essential to the production of a new social formation: The technologies of social reproduction, juridically formalized civil death, and mass-based social death converge and collapse as the durable *geographic* (spatial) production of this regime. In turn, this spatialized intersection of oppressive technologies "places" and signifies the bloodwork of white ("multicultural") life and subjectivity, as it is insistently and fatally *lived* against black and Third World death and ontological subjection.

Notes

1. Patterson, *Slavery and Social Death*, 31; emphasis added.
2. Ibid., 37.
3. Ibid., 29.
4. Michel Foucault, "14 January 1976," in *"Society Must Be Defended,"* 27–28; emphasis added.
5. MedTerms Online Medical Dictionary, s.v., "Capillary," available online at http://www.medterms.com.
6. Lichtenstein, *Twice the Work of Free Labor*, 188–89.
7. Davis, "From the Prison of Slavery to the Slavery of Prison," 75–76; emphasis added.
8. Ibid., 75.
9. See Garland, "The Rationalization of Punishment"; Rotman, "The Failure of Reform."

10. Holland, *Raising the Dead*, 15.

11. Wilderson, "The Prison Slave as Hegemony's (Silent) Scandal."

12. A Federal Prisoner (anonymous), "A Mount Everest of Time," *San Francisco Chronicle*, "Sunday Punch" sec., October 7, 1990, 2.

13. Patterson, *Slavery and Social Death*.

14. Williams, *Capitalism and Slavery*.

15. Eltis, "The Volume and Structure of the Transatlantic Slave Trade." Outlining the historical debate over this figure, David Eltis, David Richardson, and Stephen Behrendt write that the empirical research that followed publication of Curtin's classic text "focused on the two centuries after 1660 when the transatlantic traffic in Africans peaked, [and] has used archival shipping data unavailable to Curtin. Usually interpreted as more reliable than Curtin's, the new findings have nevertheless tended to corroborate rather than challenge Curtin's original estimates of the totals involved." See Eltis et al., "Patterns in the Transatlantic Slave Trade, 1662–1867," 21. By way of reflection on this debate among historians of the human volume of the transatlantic slave trade, Joseph Inikori and Stanley Engerman wrote in 1992, "Inikori has suggested a global figure of 15.4 million. This figure has been contested by some scholars, and while the process of revision continues, it seems probably that the ultimate figure is unlikely to be less than 12 million or more than 20 million captives exported from Africa in the transatlantic slave trade." See Inikori and Engerman, *The Atlantic Slave Trade*, 6. Paul Lovejoy, another decade earlier in 1982, arrived at a figure remarkably close to both Curtin's and Eltis's, suggesting 11,698,000 "exported" enslaved Africans between 1450 and 1900, with approximately 9,778,500 surviving the transatlantic transport. See Lovejoy, "The Volume of the Atlantic Slave Trade," 477–78.

16. In addition to the books and articles already mentioned, it is worth noting the following texts for the purposes of providing a broad historical overview of the scholarship addressing the trade in enslaved Africans and the Middle Passage: Bennett, *Before the Mayflower*; Blassingame, *The Slave Community*; Carey, *The Slave Trade*; Curtin, *The Atlantic Slave Trade*; Diedrich et al., *Black Imagination and the Middle Passage*; Eltis and Walvin, *The Abolition of the Atlantic Slave Trade*; Harding, *There Is a River*; Kay, *The Shameful Trade*; Klein, *The Middle Passage*; Lott, *Subjugation and Bondage*; Manning, *Slave Trades, 1500–1800*; Northrup, *The Atlantic Slave Trade*; Patterson, *Slavery and Social Death*; Postma, *The Atlantic Slave Trade*.

17. See Behrendt, "Crew Mortality in the Transatlantic Slave Trade in the Eighteenth Century," 66; also quoted in Postma, *The Atlantic Slave Trade*, 47.

18. Curtin, *The Atlantic Slave Trade*, 282–83.

19. Postma, whose text culls from the recently available Oxford University CD-ROM database *The Trans-Atlantic Slave Trade* (2000) writes: "Because slaves were valuable investment property, ship captains kept careful records in logbooks and mortality lists of the dates and causes of death. . . . These records survive for about one-fifth

of the documented slave voyages and are now accessible through the Cambridge University Press Database. They show that on average twelve percent of the enslaved did not survive the ocean crossing, though there was considerable variation from one transport to another. Before 1700, death rates tended to be higher, averaging more than twenty-two percent. They decreased to about ten percent by the end of the eighteenth century, but rose again to nearly twelve percent during the years of illegal trading in the mid-nineteenth century." Postma, *The Atlantic Slave Trade*, 43–44.

20. Harding, *There Is a River*, 10–11.
21. Equiano, *Equiano's Travels*, 27.
22. Copley, *A History of Slavery and Its Abolition*, 124.
23. Maria Diedrich, Henry Louis Gates Jr., and Carl Pederson, "The Middle Passage Between History and Fiction," in Diedrich et al., *Black Imagination and the Middle Passage*, 8; emphasis added.
24. Perkinson, "Shackled Justice."
25. Nichol Gomez, "Big Brother Is Watching," *Peacekeeper*, September 2001, 39.
26. Hortense Spillers, "Mama's Baby, Papa's Maybe," in Spillers, *Black, White, and in Color*, 215.
27. In addition to Cugoano and Equiano, examples of narratives that articulate an autobiographical or generational memory of the Middle Passage can be found in such collections as Gates and Andrews, *Pioneers of the Black Atlantic*. The narratives of Mary Prince (1831), Old Elizabeth (1863), Mattie J. Jackson (1866), Lucy A. Delaney (1891), Kate Drumgoold (1898), and Annie L. Burton (1909) are similarly compiled in Gates, *Six Women's Slave Narratives*. The narratives of James Albert Ukawsaw Gronniosaw (1772), William Wells Brown (1847), Henry Bibb (1849), Sojourner Truth (1850), William and Ellen Craft (1860), Harriet Ann Jacobs (1861), and Jacob D. Green (1864) are anthologized in *Slave Narratives*. The autobiography and other narratives of Frederick Douglass are gathered in Gates, *Frederick Douglass*.
28. Masters, *Finding Freedom*, 4–5.
29. Yee, *The Melancholy History of Soledad Prison*, 121; emphasis added.
30. Nina Rosenblum, dir., *Through the Wire* (videocassette, New York: New Video Group, 1991); emphasis added.
31. According to a 1994 headline article in the *Progressive*, the opening of California's Security Housing Unit in 1989 at Pelican Bay State Prison led to thirty-six other states' following suit in the subsequent two years. "California Governor George Deukmejian said, in 1989, that Pelican Bay would serve as 'a model for the rest of the nation.' Unfortunately, he was right. At least thirty-six states have already built 'super-maxi' prisons like it, according to a 1991 report by Human Rights Watch": Paige Bierma, "Torture behind Bars: Right Here in the United States of America," *Progressive*, vol. 58, no. 7, July 1994, 21.

32. "Brit Tells Tale of Torture at Guantánamo," *Windsor Star*, March 13, 2004, C4.

33. While there is a significant body of reporting on the Corcoran incidents and the subsequent criminal trials of several guards, the following articles offer a clear overview of the fundamental issues. The comprehensive 2002 California Prison Focus (CPF) report "Corcoran State Prison 2001–2002: Inside California's Brutal Maximum Security Prison," is available online at the CPF website, http://www.prisons.org. The following news articles are listed in reverse chronological order: Jerry Bier and Mike Lewis, "Eight Correctional Officers Indicted: Corcoran State Prison Officials Accused of Orchestrating Inmate Fights as Entertainment," *Fresno Bee*, February 27, 1998, home ed., A1; Tom Kertscher, "Controversy at Corcoran Prison Is 10 Years Old: First Inmate Shootings Occurred Nine Months after Facility Opened," *Fresno Bee*, February 27, 1998, home ed., A16; Pamela J. Podger, "Corcoran Whistle-Blower Deals with Consequences Two Years Later: Richard Caruso Is Suing the State Department of Corrections," *Fresno Bee*, November 3, 1996, home ed., A16; Associated Press, "FBI Probes Fatal Shootings of Prison Inmates by Guards: Seven Convicts Killed at Corcoran Facility since 1988," *Fresno Bee*, October 28, 1994, A16.

34. Perkinson, "Shackled Justice."

35. While I have refrained from extensively quoting such texts here for the sake of space, as well as to protect the anonymity of those who have a possibility of obtaining parole release, a significant collection of personal and legal correspondence, as well as untranscribed audio-recorded interviews, has been amassed by CPF in its interviews with people imprisoned in SHU facilities. CPF can be reached at 2940 16th Street B-5, San Francisco, Calif. 94103; phone: (415) 252–9211; email: info@prisons.org. Similar material is being gathered by the organization Justice Now of Oakland, California, which focuses on the conditions of women's prisons. Justice Now can be contacted at 322 Webster Street, Suite 210, Oakland, Calif. 94612; phone: (510) 839–7654; email: cshaylor@earthlink.net.

36. United Nations Office of the High Commissioner for Human Rights, "Convention against Torture and Other Cruel, Inhuman or Degrading Treatment or Punishment," adopted December 10, 1984; emphasis added.

Sorrow: The Good Soldier and the Good Woman   Joy James

> The enemy culture, the established government, exists first of all because of its ability to govern, to maintain enough order, to ensure that a cycle of sorts exists between the various levels and elements of the society. "Law and Order" is their objective. Ours is "Perfect Disorder." Our aim is to stop the life cycle of the enemy culture and replace it with our own revolutionary culture. This can be done only by creating perfect disorder within the cycle of the enemy culture's life process and leaving a power vacuum to be filled by our building revolutionary culture.
> —GEORGE JACKSON, *BLOOD IN MY EYE*

> It is with much sadness that i say my last goodbye to Safiya Bukhari. She was my sister, my comrade and my friend. We met nearly thirty-five years ago, when we were both members of the Black Panther Party in Harlem. Even then, i was impressed by her sincerity, her commitment and her burning energy. She was a descendent of slaves and she inherited the legacy of neo-slavery. She believed that struggle was the only way that African people in America could rid ourselves of oppression. As a Black woman struggling in America she experienced the most vicious forms of racism, sexism, cruelty and indifference. As a political activist she was targeted, persecuted, hounded and harassed. Because of her political activities she became a political prisoner and spent many years in prison. But she continued to believe in freedom, and she continued to fight for it. In spite of her personal suffering, in spite of chronic, life-threatening illnesses, she continued to struggle. She gave the best that she had to give to our people. She devoted her life, her love and her best energies to fighting for the liberation of oppressed people. She struggled selflessly, she could be trusted, she was consistent, and she could always be counted to do what needed to be done. She was a soldier, a warrior-woman who did everything she could to free her people and to free political prisoners. . . . I have faith that the Ancestors will welcome her, cherish her, and treat her with more love and more kindness that she ever received here on this earth. —ASSATA SHAKUR, HAVANA, CUBA, AUGUST 29, 2003

Service Women

Family is a middle passage—one repeatedly returned to and reconstructed, or reinvented and reenacted. So, too, is war—a middle passage where hell is the birth canal.

State soldiers fight in family units on battlefields. The enslaved refashion family with their fictive kin. The imprisoned force its reappearance with manufactured gender roles. Revolutionary cadres forge family in underground armies. Youthful gangs reinvent it in the street. The corporate state polices and ritualizes it with legalistic trappings.

With notable mortality rates, the women—part Greek chorus and part cyborg—bear the brunt of this middle passage, this birthing. They create and are held captive by this primary social and political unit, one that reproduces and trains soldiers and so prepares society for life and killing.

In the Greek chorus, women are maternal (within state machinery and its military and police mechanisms, they are cyborg: part mechanistic enforcers for a democracy driven by constitutional amendments that humanize corporations and dehumanize people as penal slaves). In *Slavery and Social Death*, Orlando Patterson narrates the role of the Greek chorus as a gathering of slave women who defined freedom in juxtaposition to enslavement in the service of an elite and parasitical democracy, one built on the wealth and injustices that empire can imagine and fashion. Fed on slavery and imperialism, the Athenian polis shaped the private realm of captives to serve the public realm of senators and war makers. (Whereas Ancient Athens provides the mythic norm for America's penal democracy, the U.S. Constitution's Fourteenth Amendment creates its cyborg face, humanizing or granting civil rights to property—not predominately white-owned humans but predominately white-owned corporations—and its Thirteenth Amendment, which reduces captives to commodities by legalizing slavery for those duly convicted of a crime.)

In every armed conflict investigated by Amnesty International since 1999, the torture of women was reported, most often in the form of sexual violence.
—AMNESTY INTERNATIONAL, "RAPE AS A TOOL OF WAR" (2003)

MONTREAL—When the Belgian Defense Ministry earlier this year blamed North America for the world's worst ever genocide over its killing of millions of indigenous peoples, outrage at the claim spotlighted a topic that rarely enters the public realm. . . . The assertion was made as part of a display on Belgian peacekeeping worldwide, to mark the 10th anniversary of the genocide in Rwanda. . . . It claimed that 15 million native peoples have been murdered on this continent since Christopher Columbus landed in the Americas in 1492, and suggested that the extermination continues today.
—MARTY LOGAN, "INDIGENOUS PEOPLES DAY: GENOCIDE IT IS," *IPS NEWS* (AUGUST 9, 2004)

In June 1991, former National Guard Staff Sgt. Sharon Mixon was gang-raped by six soldiers. She was told by a military policeman, "That's what you get for being a woman in a war zone." Mixon decided not to report the assault to her commander.
—*ALL THINGS CONSIDERED*, NATIONAL PUBLIC RADIO (MAY 11, 2004)

The Bush administration has decided to pursue a 16-year-old effort to deport two Palestinian activists [Khader Hamide and Michel Shehadeh . . . allegedly affiliated with the Popular Front for the Liberation of Palestine] who as students distributed magazines and raised funds for a group the government now considers a terrorist organization, despite several court rulings that the deportations are unconstitutional because the

In the chorus of the oppressed, as distinct from that of the conqueror, the maternal woman—as good woman—manifests in opposition to colonizing warfare. She serves as the one who protects life in the roles of either the pacifist or the militarist freedom fighter, or as mother or daughter, the survivor who functions as the primary caretaker of the children, the aged, and male warriors. (Recall Black Panther Party women who marched chanting, "Set our warriors free! Free Huey!")

The chorus is political. Chroniclers memorize and narrate histories of repression and resistance; they create alternative archives, having recognized that the state will neither memorialize its insurgents and captives nor acknowledge its repressive wars. So maternal women (and their male counterparts) record familial pain and subversion in penal and war narratives, hold vigils, plan memorial services, and eulogize dead comrades while keeping stories—that rationalize killing and give meaning to dying—alive. All good girls can hope to become good women one day. Yet, the most hunted and embattled women, good soldiers, struggle with fairly limited recognition and approval. Their traumatic tales most often surface in memoirs or testimonials.

So, for example, having broken out of prison to live (and die?) in exile, the former Black Liberation Army (BLA) leader Assata Shakur—her $1million bounty assigned by Attorney General Alberto Gonzales brings new meanings to her memoir—notes of her comrade Safiya Bukhari: "She was a soldier, a warrior-woman who did everything she could to free her people and to free political prisoners." Safiya Bukhari survived the maiming medical practices of prison doctors (although her uterus did not), only to succumb to the standard black woman's diseases of hypertension, diabetes, obesity, and heart failure.

When I call for consolation, a white woman soldier imprisoned for years for anti-state warfare tells me that Safiya died months after white political prisoners were freed and BPP/BLA members were denied new hearings or parole; that Safiya collapsed hours after she buried her own mother—the grandmother who raised Safiya's young daughter the day her own daughter became a BLA fighter and fugitive, going underground only to surface for a eight-year prison term. I am told, in short, that Safiya likely died from grief.

Suffering, in the desert of state surgical strikes in military occupations, or the concrete muck of family violence in the households of police and military peacekeepers—or less patriotic batterers—is a maternal skill. Women, in diverse and distinct formations, fight for the state or the liberated territory and for family in varied configurations. As loyal or long-suffering, and so faithful, such fighters are simultaneously good women and good soldiers.

Suffering always bends and often breaks when it does not kill. The political context, though, determines the socially recognized value of the sufferer. Few have held observance for the sorrow of the Puerto Rican *independentista* Lolita Lebrón when her nine-year-old son drowned soon after she was captured as a prisoner of war (POW), as a fallen revolutionary soldier, following her 1954 attack on Congress. Lebrón's religious mysticism (as noted in her granddaughter's memoir, *The Ladies' Gallery*) flaws an iconic movement martyr, one further enshrined in suffering when she leaves prison for a few days, twenty-three years later, to attend the internment—

In Pennsylvania and some other states, inmates are routinely stripped in front of other inmates before being moved to a new prison or a new unit within their prison. In Arizona, male inmates at the Maricopa County Jail in Phoenix are made to wear women's pink underwear as a form of humiliation.

At Virginia's Wallens Ridge maximum security prison, new inmates have reported being forced to wear black hoods, in theory to keep them from spitting on guards, and said they were often beaten and cursed at by guards and made to crawl.

Corrections experts say that some of the worst abuses have occurred in Texas, whose prisons were under a federal consent decree during much of the time President Bush was governor because of crowding and violence by guards against inmates.

Judge William Wayne Justice of Federal District Court imposed the decree after finding that guards were allowing inmate gang leaders to buy and sell other inmates as slaves for sex. The experts also point out that the man who directed the reopening of the Abu Ghraib prison in Iraq last year and trained the guards there resigned under pressure as director of the Utah Department of Corrections in 1997 after an inmate died while shackled to a restraining chair for 16 hours. The inmate, who suffered from schizophrenia, was kept naked the whole time.

The Utah official, Lane McCotter, later became an executive of a private prison company, one of whose jails was under investigation by the Justice Department when he was sent to Iraq as part of a team of prison officials, judges, prosecutors and police chiefs picked by Attorney

General John Ashcroft to rebuild the country's criminal justice system.

—FOX BUTTERFIELD, "MISTREATMENT OF PRISONERS IS CALLED ROUTINE IN U.S.," *NEW YORK TIMES* (MAY 8, 2004)

The *New York Times* reports that there have been new releases of prisoners formerly held at Abu Ghraib. The photo shows a young man, age 17, being embraced by his mother and sisters. His body completely slumps into their protective arms. He is two years younger than my daughter. I am heartsick wondering if he will ever recover from his horror.

Muslim men are described as sexually humiliated at Abu Ghraib. And white women of the working class are used to "pussy whip" Muslim men. . . . Three of the torturers—Megan Ambuhl, Lynndie England and Sabrina Harman—so key to the pictorial narrative—are white women. The Brig[adier] General in charge of the prisons in Iraq, Janis Karpinski, is also a white woman. So is Maj[or] General Barbara Fast, the top U.S. Intelligence Officer who reviewed the status of detainees. . . .

Why in the Balkan wars was the raping of women a central narrative demonizing Serb nationalism while the rape and sexual humiliation of Muslim male prisoners [is] largely silenced? And, why, today is the central narrative Muslim men's humiliation [rape] while the violation of their women counterparts has been largely muted?

—ZILLAH EISENSTEIN, "SEXUAL HUMILIATION, GENDER CONFUSION AND THE HORRORS AT ABU GHRAIB," *PORTSIDE* (JUNE 2004, WEEK 3), HTTP://LISTS.PORTSIDE. ORG/CGI-BIN/LISTSERV/WA?A2=IND0406 C&L=PORTSIDE&T=0&P=190

We completed a documentary, *Every Mother's Son*, about police brutality during [Rudolph] Giuliani's term

and to be visited by thousands in a cemetery—following her daughter's suicide. Those who cannot read Lebrón's emotional silence may attempt to read *Assata: An Autobiography* but not see Shakur in her skirmishes against prison abortionists and terror in her raging, desperate determination to have a live birth. Rarely does public discourse acknowledge pregnant Black Panthers battered bloody by traumatized vets and refugees from counterrevolutionary wars, rebel soldiers who father without admittance to Veterans Administration hospitals.

Some have witnessed the grief fissures of Lila Lipscombe, in Michael Moore's film *Fahrenheit 9/11*. Coping with the death of her soldier son who had denounced the Iraqi invasion in a letter home months before he was killed, she daily unfurls an American flag on the exterior walls of her suburban home.

Embraced by U.S. nationalists and moviegoers, Lipscombe as a patriot is permitted public space, although a contested one, and visibly given respect for her sorrow in mainstream culture that rages against the state's betrayals—but not against the state, which appears more familiar than alien, and usually never appears as enemy culture to be disrupted with perfect disorder.

In contrast, another cadre of good women will have their stories preserved by political organizations and movements because their victimization comes at the hands of the penal democracy and its prison and police apparatuses, while they actively served the community or subaltern nation. This suggests that for most of the political public, it is not the privatized pain of women that gets recorded, retold, and raged against, but the torture and abuse of a people, *its* family, *its* females. The good woman, like the good soldier, only appears in service; at all other times, she is generally invisible or disappeared.

Service to the larger unit—which, of course, includes the self—appears in the political telling of public trauma. Such illustrations depict the heinous nature of captivity and racial and class warfare. Mamie Till Mobley's memoir, *Death of Innocence: The Story of the Hate Crime That Changed America*, recounts the murder of her fourteen-year-old child, Emmett, and becomes an act of resistance and soldiery in liberation warfare. Why else would a middle-class black woman have an open casket in 1955 for her only child—murdered, maimed, and decomposing? Why would a middle-class black woman instruct the undertaker not to "improve" on her son's appearances (instructions that were violated when dangling eyes and tongue were removed and orifices were stitched closed)?

The good soldier undertakes the public's demand to witness wounding and terror and to remember war victims but to keep stoic silence, as well. Such a witness in 1955 took nearly five decades for public commentators to hear, and for them to correct political memory and genealogy by locating a funeral held months before Rosa Parks's civil disobedience aboard a Montgomery bus as the birth of a movement (one that Martin Luther King Jr.'s Southern Christian Leadership Conference referred to as "the second reconstruction" and the Student Nonviolent Coordinating Committee, bearing the brunt of racial terror, labeled the "second civil war"). It was the visual narrative that Miss Parks had witnessed months earlier that led to her refusal to give up a seat on public accommodations as an act of soldiery.

(1994–2001) as mayor of New York City, told through the eyes of three mothers who lost sons to police violence and who have become spokespeople for police reform. . . . Iris Baez's son Anthony was killed during a pick-up football game on the streets of the Bronx in 1994, when a police officer put him in an illegal chokehold after the football hit the officer's car. Kadiatou Diallo's son Amadou was unarmed when he was shot 41 times in the doorway of his apartment building by four police officers [in 1999]. Doris Busch Boskey's son Gary (Gidone) Busch was pepper-sprayed, surrounded, and then shot to death by police while holding a small inscribed hammer, even though witnesses at the scene said it was clear he posed no threat.
—KELLY ANDERSON AND TAMI GOLD, "IN THEIR OWN WORDS," NEW YORK FOUNDATION FOR THE ARTS (JULY 4, 2004)

In 2005, 38.6 million people worldwide were living with HIV/AIDS, 24.5 million in Sub-Saharan Africa. Women make up 51 percent of those suffering from HIV; and Black Women account for 72 percent of all new HIV cases among women.

Over 25 million people have died since the first cases of AIDS were identified in 1981.
—UNAIDS, *2006 REPORT ON THE GLOBAL AIDS EPIDEMIC* (MAY 2006); LYNETTE CLEMETSON, "LINKS BETWEEN PRISON AND AIDS AFFECTING BLACKS INSIDE AND OUT," *NEW YORK TIMES* (AUGUST 6, 2004)

According to the U.S. State Department, between 600,000 and 800,000 people are trafficked across international borders annually; between 18,000 and 20,000 of those victims are trafficked into the United States. If trafficking within countries is included in the total world figures, official U.S. esti-

mates are that 2 to 4 million people are trafficked annually. However, there are even higher estimates, ranging from 4 to 27 million for the total number of forced or bonded laborers.
—FRANCIS T. MIKO, "TRAFFICKING IN PERSONS: THE U.S. AND INTERNATIONAL RESPONSE," CRS REPORT FOR CONGRESS (JULY 7, 2006)

Between 1993 and 2005, more than 400 women and girls were murdered in Ciudad Juárez and Chihuahua, Mexico; 20 percent of the cases involved sexual violence.
—AMNESTY INTERNATIONAL, "KILLINGS AND ABDUCTIONS OF WOMEN IN CIUDAD JUAREZ AND THE CITY OF CHIHUAHUA— THE STRUGGLE FOR JUSTICE GOES ON" (FEBRUARY 20, 2006)

Although the rate of offenses for females remains much lower than that for men . . . according to the FBI's [2003] Uniform Crime Report, females represented 23.3 per cent of all arrests in 2003. Additionally, 20.4 percent of all female arrestees were juveniles under age eighteen. Since 1995, the total number of female State and Federal prison inmates has grown 5 percent a year, compared to the 3.3 percent average annual growth for male prisoners.
— NATIONAL CRIMINAL JUSTICE REFERENCE SERVICES, "WOMEN AND GIRLS IN THE CRIMINAL JUSTICE SYSTEM," AT HTTP://WWW.NCJRS.GOV/ (APRIL 6, 2006)

In Rwanda between 250,000 and 500,000 women, or about 20 percent of women, were raped during the 1994 genocide. Ten years after the 1994 genocide, nearly all of these women have remained without legal redress or reparation.
—INTERNATIONAL RED CROSS, REPORT (2002), IN AMNESTY INTERNATIONAL, "MAKING VIOLENCE AGAINST WOMEN COUNT" (MARCH 5, 2004)

In mind when she resisted segregation and en route to jail was the picture of Emmett Till, an image provided by the mother as good woman and good soldier; one who defied government orders to keep the casket closed and refused to shield the public from the visual residues of law and order—lynching for a whistle at a white woman. So, the good women present trauma to their own children, witnesses to a mutilated child's corpse and the failure to soldier.

Tens of thousands came to the Chicago funeral for the burial, months before Miss Parks sat down. Hundreds of thousands saw the images of the mutilated body in black publications such as *Jet* (reflecting an insurgent twist on repressive cyber-communities created earlier by old postcards of lynchings captured in "Without Sanctuary" to contemporary digital [porn] abuse circulated at and beyond Abu Ghraib). For those viewed as good women, good soldiers, their narratives and stories, their sorrow, have space in the political, public world for retelling and remembering as long as they remain good servants.

It is service to the other, the non-self—for or against—the "enemy culture"—as family domesticity and captivity suggest multiple "enemy" formations—that makes the female a woman and a soldier, precisely laudable as a good woman and a good soldier. Good women protect and reproduce family (fictive, militarist, political). Good soldiers defend the nation-state or counter-state, the empire, or the liberated maroon societies.

What is the worth of a woman? Her service to nation formation or revolutionary formations, all of which is the refashioning of family. Who values a woman stripped of service? In a war time—perpetual time for an aggrandizing nation—a woman who does not soldier for empire or revolution against imperial ambitions is an anomaly as a political woman. (The value of women functioning as commodities determined by market forces is not addressed here.) If such a woman claimed public space and war status, her soldiering would be treasonous, would it not? For it serves neither state nor counter-state formations.

The good woman and the good soldier serve movements or entities larger than that of "woman." That is, they mingle and merge as socially significant when subordinate. The burka-beauty of the female guard of Louis Farrakhan or Muammar Qaddafi pose in photo ops, a visual testimony of aggregates of service women willing to die or kill for male insurgency (an inverse of Nikki Giovanni's poem exhortations to black men). Present photo ops of presidents greeting and speaking before troops display the black and female and black female serving bodies. It is that unity, that solidarity that assures of the formidable powers of law and order and ensures the long lifecycle of enemy cultures.

Bringing comfort to state or counter-state soldiers during times of war are women. Good soldiers birth and bury. Good women reassure and soothe. Females, exhausted by journeys and their attendant deaths and rebirths, who reinvent in hell the role of the midwife, simultaneously resist and replenish war. What would the traditional soldier, the male soldier, do without the good woman? Who would buttress battlefield horror by projecting real and symbolic antithesis—something to go home to, an ideal worth living and killing for?

In turn, what would white women in their forays against the object-subjects of their fear and envy

One transsexual/transgender person is murdered in the U.S. each month.
—NATIONAL COALITION OF ANTI-VIOLENCE PROGRAMS, REPORT (2004)

There are an estimated 27 million slaves worldwide.
—MSNBC, "MODERN DAY SLAVES" (FEBRUARY 27, 2004)

The Pentagon still lies about Agent Orange. . . . How did Iraq get weapons specific agents [and] . . . who was shipping it over there? . . . Clearly it was illegal. . . . I do not think the Pentagon wants to get into any of that so the cover-up goes on.
—FRANCIS A. BOYLE, "FACULTY LECTURE ON BIO/WARFARE/TERRORISM/ WEAPONS," UNIVERSITY OF ILLINOIS, CHICAGO (APRIL 18, 2002)

The Amazon rainforest in Brazil is home to over 60,000 plant species, 3,300 animal species, and 20 million people, including an estimated 180,000 indigenous people. In January 2001 the Brazilian government announced its plans for "Avança Brasil" (Advance Brazil), a U.S.$40 billion plan to cover much of the Amazon rainforest with 10,000 [kilometers] of highways, hydroelectric dams, power lines, mines, gas and oil fields, canals, ports, logging concessions and other industrial developments. Scientists predict that these planned developments will lead to the damage or loss of between 33 [and] 42 percent of Brazil's remaining Amazon forest.
—GREEN PEACE, "AMAZON REPORT" (2003)

Marital rape is recognized as a crime in only 51 countries. Only 16 nations have legislation specifically referring to sexual assault, while only 3 have legislation that specifically addresses violence against women as a category of criminal activity in itself.

—AMNESTY INTERNATIONAL, "MAKING VIOLENCE AGAINST WOMEN COUNT" (MAY 3, 2004)

Much of the evidence of abuse at the prison [in Abu Ghraib] came from medical documents, . . . [and] records and statements showed doctors and medics reporting to the area of the prison where the abuse occurred several times to stitch wounds, tend to collapsed prisoners, or see patients with bruised or reddened genitals.

—ROBERT JAY LIFTON, "DOCTORS AND TORTURE," *NEW ENGLAND JOURNAL OF MEDICINE* 351, NO. 5 (JULY 2004)

In 2000, a study of prisons in four Midwestern states found that approximately one in five male inmates reported a pressured or forced sex incident while incarcerated. About one in ten male inmates reported that that they had been raped. Rates for female inmates, who are most likely to be abused by male staff members, vary from seven percent in some facilities to twenty-seven percent in others.

The Department of Justice's Bureau of Justice Statistics report found that the number of formal complaints of sexual violence filed in adult prisons and jails increased nearly 16 percent, from 5,386 in 2004, to 6,241 in 2005. More than one-half of these complaints concerned staff sexual misconduct or harassment.

—STOP PRISONER RAPE, "THE BASICS ON RAPE BEHIND BARS," HTTP://WWW.SPR.ORG/EN/FACTSHEETS/BASICS.ASP (2004); STOP PRISONER RAPE, "GOVERNMENT PRISONER RAPE STUDY SHOWS INCREASE IN SEXUAL VIOLENCE REPORTS, RAISES CONCERNS ABOUT CORRECTIONAL AUTHORITIES' FOLLOW UP," WEBSITE (JULY 30, 2006)

(white men) and women or people "of color" in their battles of envy and fear with elite white women be or do without the antithesis of the "good woman"— the black woman, the site of "perfect disorder" in an enemy culture when she refuses to serve or pacify non-blacks nurtured by antiblack racism.

What can an "enemy culture" (Jackson's phrase tidily focuses war talk) not conceive and practice in familial, interpersonal, social, and international relations? Black female humanity. Nor can it envision the "perfect disorder" of association without coercion; the "perfect order" of democracy freed from police, law, parasitical relations to prison or slave bodies (and legalistic war documents such as the Thirteenth Amendment, which codifies slavery). In social-political formations, where police-as-law dies, freedom-as-political liberation lives.

Who soldiers for the death of law and the police? For the lives of those designated expendable or socially dead? Obviously few. Soldiers, like women, are captives, but captivity has specificity and rank, just like the military. A soldier's and woman's rank and status are determined not necessarily by acts but by their proximity to presence (whiteness and property) and distance from absence (blackness and captivity).

Good women reproduce family law, and so the police—hence, we reproduce law and order; the police disproportionately discipline and punish black and poor bodies, queer and female forms. Therefore, to seek to "elucidate" the meaning of "the prison within the prison state," as George Jackson urged, requires considering what would have to disappear (or be restricted to performance rituals cloistered on stage or screen): predator–prey formations.

The woman no longer beaten by man; the woman no longer servant to man; the black no longer servant or marked as prey and then castigated as predator; the black woman freed from the non-blacks and the non-women; and the child able to fend off adult predation—all this disrupts law-and-order schemes. All of this may be more perfect disorder than most can handle.

The "perfect disorder" that Jackson calls for seems to require a lot of dying: not just physical, but intellectual and political deaths in which the definition of "good," the signifier of the perfect functionary (and the perfect woman), is retired. Yet Jackson does not create the death or advocate for it. It is ever present. For the murderous gender misanthropes, the only "good" woman is a dead one—physically or psychically. For religious misogynists seeking the maternal martyr, the "good" woman is a dead soldier of god; ultimately, the dead good woman is the sacrificial lamb who first gives life to, then gives up life for, a fetus—the final service from a reproductive body that stills its own life instinct. To abort a penal democracy and family captivity in all its forms would indeed be an obscenity, a transgression against man and god-state.

"Good" is elusive and mercurial as a prefix to soldier, because soldiery is not an ontological state; it is a function. Hence, the "good" soldier (like the "good" woman) need only be proficient and obedient in her duties to merit acceptance or praise. Efficiency is not ethics. Perhaps a moral order that is not legalistic can be reclaimed. Perhaps the woman must die to "goodness" in order to tend as midwife to the "perfect disorder" of revolutionary culture. Such a death, when it leads to rebirth into a refusal to soldier (except for

In the United States, a woman is raped every 6 minutes; a woman is battered every 15 seconds.
—AMNESTY INTERNATIONAL, "BROKEN BODIES, SHATTERED MINDS: TORTURE AND ILL TREATMENT OF WOMEN" (2001)

Over 1.2 million children worldwide, including thousands in West Africa, are recruited from their homes each year by individuals seeking to exploit their labor. One child recalls: I made an appointment with the man to meet at Balanka, at night. . . . There were many other kids there—more than 300 of us in one truck, packed like dead bodies.
—HUMAN RIGHTS WATCH, "TRAFFIC IN CHILDREN" REPORT (AUGUST 2003)

From 1998 to 2001, the U.S.A., the U.K., and France earned more income from arms sales to developing countries than they gave in aid.
—ANUP SHAH, "THE ARMS TRADE IS BIG BUSINESS," HTTP://WWW.GLOBALISSUES .ORG/GEOPOLITICS/ARMSTRADE/ BIGBUSINESS.ASP (SEPTEMBER 7, 2004)

[People] taking the gloves off in interrogation is a thinly veiled reference to torture, but calling torture "stress and duress" or "abuse" is the homage paid to the still current imperative of denial. The presumptions that torture is both necessary and effective, and the implications of breaking the torture taboo by legalizing torture are shaping debates in the U.S.
—LISA HAJAAR, "TORTURE AND THE FUTURE," MIDDLE EAST REPORT (MAY 2004)

Reported incidents of anti-LGBT violence . . . rose from 1,720 in 2003 to 1,792 in 2004. Included in the rise in incidents for the year, was an 11 percent increase in anti-LGBT murders, which rose from 18 in 2003 to 20 in 2004. During 2004, the total number of victims rose

4 percent, from 2,042 in 2003 to
2,131 in 2004.
—NATIONAL COALITION OF ANTI-
VIOLENCE PROGRAMS, "ANNUAL REPORT
ON ANTI-LGBT HATE VIOLENCE
RELEASED" (APRIL 26, 2005)

The proportion of people living
in extreme poverty on less than
$1 a day dropped by almost half
between 1981 and 2001, from
40 percent to 21 percent of the
global population. In 1980, one out
of every ten poor people lived in
Sub-Saharan Africa. In 2000, the
figure rose to one out of every three.
Future projections predict that one
out of every two poor people will live
in Sub-Saharan Africa.
—WORLD BANK, "DRAMATIC DECLINE
IN WORLD POVERTY, BUT PROGRESS
UNEVEN" (APRIL 23, 2004)

From 2002 to the present, Human
Rights Watch estimates that at
least one thousand Afghans and
other nationals, many of which
are civilians, have been arrested
and detained by U.S.-led forces in
Afghanistan. Not a single person
detained in Afghanistan . . . [was]
afforded prisoner-of-war status
or other legal status under the
1949 Geneva Conventions. . . . The
Detainee Abuse and Accountability
Project has documented more than
330 cases in which U.S. military
and civilian personnel are credibly
alleged to have abused, tortured,
or killed detainees [in Afghanistan,
Iraq, and Guantánamo Bay]. . . .
Only a fraction of the more than
600 U.S. personnel implicated in
these cases—40 people—have
been sentenced to prison time.
—HUMAN RIGHTS WATCH, " 'ENDURING
FREEDOM': ABUSES BY U.S. FORCES IN
AFGHANISTAN" (MARCH 2004), AND "U.S.:
MORE THAN 500 IMPLICATED IN DETAINEE
ABUSE" (APRIL 6, 2006)

The U.S. Department of Defense
now spends half of its entire bud-

herself), betrays (state and counter-state) family formations. Given the varied and dangerous enemy cultures in warfare in the domestic realm, good women
like, and as, good soldiers reasonably fear the consequences of treason: penal isolation as social death
and the socially dead.

The Domestic Underground

In the United States, B.C.E. and A.C.E, have been
supplanted by pre- and post-September 11 for those
who reinvent a timeline that births new reality and
people. Watching PBS's *Lerhrer News Hour,* I was
pleased to note that the program's cultural corre-
spondent Elizabeth Farnsworth would be interview-
ing the African American feminist, and University
of California, Berkeley, professor, June Jordan to discuss her new memoir *Soldier: A Poet's Childhood.*

In one of her last interviews, June, who had had
recurring battles with breast cancer, thanked her
father, the frustrated Jamaican "race man" fractured
by U.S. racism, for the ritual late-night bed beatings
he had administered during her youth. He, she asserted, had made her into a soldier. Elizabeth said
nothing. I turned my head from the screen.

Only when I read *Soldier,* a few years later, did I
realize that the seven-year-old had interrupted the
bed beatings from the man who wanted everything
for his son-daughter and had arranged summer
camp and prep school in anticipation, an interruption that came late at night when she pulled a knife
from under her pillow and asked her father: "What
do you want?" Ill-prepared for such black women
soldiers in the pre-September 11 era, I shall try to
meet them now, noting that good soldiers are not
just good mothers and wives in the family matrix—
they are also good daughters.

Some years before June's book was published, I fumed while vacuuming the town house of my father (a retired lieutenant colonel and former ATF man) in a gated community in suburban Indiana. I rolled the upright Hoover over bullet shells and casings, noting the lack of suction to extract them from the carpet of his master bedroom. I struggled with plush pile for twenty minutes. Then I stopped. I realized from my own ROTC instruction and firing of weapons that vacuuming up live ammunition was potentially explosive. On my hands and knees I retrieved scores of bullets, around and under the king-size bed, and placed them in a container next to the seven(?) handguns and the shotgun that I had collected around the house. Checking to see that no bullets remained, I went to scrub the tub. Incapable of loading a gun and pulling a trigger—although amply trained as a career military officer and a Vietnam veteran (sent as an officer, allegedly in part to stop black troops from fragging—throwing hand grenades at their white officer corps to discourage [black] suicide missions)—my father had succumbed to a heart attack. ("Who really knows in these cases?" responds the coroner when I ask him for "cause of death.") Father decomposed and waited. I was summoned to Indiana by police and lawyers—themselves summoned by the adjoining town house residents who had summoned police to break down his front door weeks after his death. I collected the body; I cleaned up after him and readied his house for sale and his corpse, in closed casket, for an eighteen-gun salute military burial. (As my godmother insisted: What mattered was to respect his wishes, not my politics.)

What are the stories that women will not tell about soldiers returning from wars of occupation or from state prisons? About cleaning and caring

get on private military contractors; the top fifty contractors receive more than half of all the money.
—*MORNING EDITION*, NATIONAL PUBLIC RADIO (SEPTEMBER 30, 2004)

Physical pain amounting to torture must be equivalent in intensity to the pain accompanying serious physical injury, such as organ failure . . . or even death. . . . For purely mental pain or suffering to amount to torture . . . it must result in significant psychological harm . . . lasting for months or even years. . . . We conclude that the statute as a whole makes clear that it prohibits only extreme acts. . . . [For a defendant to be convicted of torture], even if the defendant knows that severe pain will result from his actions, if causing such harm is not his objective, he lacks the requisite specific intent even though the defendant did not act in good faith.
—U.S. DEPARTMENT OF JUSTICE, "MEMORANDUM FOR ALBERTO R. GONZALES, COUNSEL TO THE PRESIDENT" (AUGUST 1, 2002)

[In September 2004,] over 50,000 civilians . . . [had] died in the Darfur region of Sudan and over 1 million are internally displaced, while more than 170,000 have crossed the border into Chad. In over half of the towns burned, women reported rape as a tactic of warfare. The widespread rape of young boys has also been reported. . . . Despite the signing of the Darfur Peace Agreement in May 2006, grave violations of international humanitarian and human rights law continue unabated in Darfur.
—AMNESTY INTERNATIONAL, "DISTRESS, DENIAL AND DISAPPOINTMENT IN DARFUR: FINDINGS OF AMNESTY INTERNATIONAL VISIT TO DARFUR" (SEPTEMBER 21, 2004), AND "MORE KILLINGS AS 'PEACEKEEPING GAP' THREATENS IN DARFUR" (AUGUST 12, 2006)

As of September 30, 2004, there were an estimated 517,000 children in foster care. Children in foster care are three to six times more likely than children not in care to have emotional, behavioral and developmental problems. Children are eleven times more likely to be abused in State care than they are in their own homes, and die as a result of abuse in foster care 5.25 times more often than children in the general population.
—NATIONAL CLEARINGHOUSE ON CHILD ABUSE AND NEGLECT INFORMATION, "FOSTER CARE NATIONAL STATISTICS" (2003, 2005)

The four armed services, coordinated by the Joint Staff Urban Working Group, launched crash programs to master street-fighting under realistic third-world conditions. "The future of warfare," the journal of the Army War College declared, "lies in the streets, sewers, high-rise buildings, and sprawl of houses that form the broken cities of the world." . . . Artificial cityscapes . . . were built to simulate combat conditions in densely populated neighborhoods of [third-world] cities. . . . Today, many of the Marines [Army units] are . . . graduates of these Urban Warrior exercises.
—MIKE DAVIS, "THE PENTAGON AS GLOBAL SLUMLORD," HTTP://WWW .TOMDISPATCH.COM/INDEX.MHTML?PID =1386 (MAY 2004)

One in six U.S. prisoners is mentally ill. . . . There are three times as many men and women with mental illness in U.S. prisons as in mental health hospitals.
—HUMAN RIGHTS WATCH, "MENTALLY ILL MISTREATED IN U.S. PRISONS," OCTO- BER 2003

In over 178 countries, more than half a million children under 18 (some under 10 years old) have

for the emotionally and physically wounded, the suicidal, the violent and sadistic, the addicted, the manically depressed, the rape survivors and rapists, the misogynists whose stature as war casualties and tragic war heroes mitigates their excesses or at least their public condemnations?

Everyone who suffers and survives verbal, emotional, physical, and sexual misogyny and domestic battery soldiers. Domestic violence and state violence are so routinely practiced and deployed on the American landscape that they are normalized. They are rendered fully or partially invisible, given that female soldiery is underground.

The first battleground is the home. The first targets are usually the bodies of women and children. It is difficult to get accurate body counts of casualties of U.S. warfare. But if one factors in domestic violence with military violence, the numbers of casualties, including intergenerational trauma casualties, would have to be considerable, although not often considered by politicians and political analysts. The vast majority of those injured in domestic violence are women and their children. The vast majority of those injured in military and mercenary forays are women and their children.

The women beaten not by the state but by its victims, men who are casualties of state violence, returning vets from foreign wars or returning vets from domestic wars, have stories that are crowded out in the public realm, stories that are shushed. A "movement" woman battered by a "movement" man (or an imperial peacekeeper raped by another militarist) reports familial violence to whom? The incest survivor's dilemma: from which parental authority to seek sanctuary and shelter from the (possible) pending punishment for outing a familial predator? To whom does one report the rapes and beatings of female Air Force Academy cadets in Colorado Springs? Women soldiers on tour in Iraq? Female cops on patrol in New York or Los Angeles? Women warriors in antiwar/imperialist/racist organizations? Ultimately, it is all a "family" matter.

Good women and good soldiers care for the wounded. Bury the dead. Orchestrate pomp and ritual at military or political funerals. Create memorials despite domestic abuses. You can place any dead child from your womb on display, drape and fold any flag over a coffin, in variations of a color scheme— red, white and blue (for the United States and the territorial prey: Puerto Rico, Cuba, the Dominican Republic) or black, red, and green. Few good women get to tell, as Lisa Rios did while speaking about her suicidal husband, the rap star Christopher Rios—a Puerto Rican, or Boricuan, icon whose skillful lyrics prove a painfully engaging study in hard-core brutality—of their gratitude for a death that enabled them to survive spousal battery by a male survivor of childhood domestic violence (battery captured on home movies and replayed, with Lisa's authorization, in the posthumously released documentary *Big Pun: Still Not a Player*). What good women say of their state or counter-state soldiers—their kin, "Better him than me"?

Perhaps to soldier for nothing or no one but the female body means the unthinkable: to embrace a selfishness not found in the selflessness and sacrifice of nation building (whether that of empire or liberated zone). A self-embrace, female body of own female body, outside of "womanhood" and "soldiering," could bring a coherence to stories that make no

been recruited into government armed forces, paramilitaries, and civil militia. . . . An estimated 30 percent are girls. . . . Approximately one-fourth of these child-soldiers are Burmese. In Colombia, more than 11,000 child combatants, one-quarter to one-half female, fight for guerrilla and paramilitary groups. 11,000 children were involved in the last years of fighting in Angola. In, Liberia there are an estimated 21,000 child soldiers. [The] U.N. High Commissioner for Human Rights, Bertrand Ramcharan, stated in 2003 that: "One out of every 10 Liberian children may have been recruited into the war effort. Liberian children have suffered all kinds of atrocities, sexual violence, disruption of schooling and forced displacement."
—AMNESTY INTERNATIONAL, "CHILD SOLDIERS: A GLOBAL ISSUE" (2004), "CHILDHOOD DENIED: CHILD SOLDIERS IN AFRICA" (JULY 2004), AND "CASUALTIES OF WAR: WOMEN'S BODIES, WOMEN'S LIVES" (OCTOBER 13, 2004)

Each year, more than 15,000 women are sold into sexual slavery in China. Two hundred women in Bangladesh are burned with acid by husbands or suitors. More than 7,000 women in India are murdered by their families and in-laws in disputes over dowries. In South Africa, a woman is shot dead by a current or former partner every 18 hours.
—AMNESTY INTERNATIONAL, "VIOLENCE AGAINST WOMEN" (2004)

Between May and November 1967, the U.S. Tiger Force platoon, created to spy on enemy forces in Vietnam, killed over 327 civilians. "They dropped grenades into underground bunkers where women and children were hiding—creating mass graves . . . frequently tortured and shot prisoners, severing ears and scalps for souvenirs. . . . [A] four-and-a-

half year Army investigation sub-
stantiated numerous war crimes
but no one was prosecuted. . . .
Mr. Rumsfeld, whose office declined
to comment . . . served his first
stint as secretary of defense under
President Gerald Ford beginning in
November 1975—the same month
the Tiger Force investigation was
closed.
—"TIGER FORCE SPECIAL REPORT,"
TOLEDO BLADE (OCTOBER 3, 2003)

Over the last 250 years, 97 percent
of America's original forests have
been logged.
—"WARCRY," "BURNING TO BREATH
FREE: ECO-ACTIVIST GETS 23-YEAR
SENTENCE FOR TORCHING SUV'S!,"
EARTH LIBERATION FRONT PRISONERS
SUPPORT NETWORK, HTTP://WWW
.SPIRITOFFREEDOM.ORG.UK/PROFILES/
FREE/BURNING.HTML (2004)

[George W.] Bush's environmental
record is appalling. . . . He murdered several thousand civilians
to install an oil pipeline in Afghanistan for his industry spon-
sors, supports ethnic cleansing in
Palestine in pursuit of hegemony
in the Middle East, is gearing up to
massacre countless more Iraqis for
oil, sabotaged the Kyoto Protocol,
subsidizes suvs, and yet, no one
has called him an "eco-terrorist,"
and no court has dared hold him
accountable.
—JEFF LUERS, EARTH LIBERATION
FRONT PRISONERS, HTTP://WWW
.SPIRITOFFREEDOM.ORG.UK/PROFILES/
FREE/BURNING.HTML (2004)

One in four LGBT people are battered
by a partner. . . . In 2004 alone,
there was a 35 percent increase in
serious injuries and a 71 percent
increase in deaths or murders that
occurred as a result of the violence.
—KRISTEN LOMBARDI, "ON ANOTHER
DOMESTIC VIOLENCE FRONT," *BOSTON
PHOENIX* (AUGUST 8, 2003); ANDY HUMM,
"LGBT DOMESTIC VIOLENCE RISES," *GAY
CITY NEWS* (JULY 21–27, 2005)

sense, and a silence to silencing that masks trauma. Fill in silences that disappear embattled women. Only the traumatized have an incoherence—one too daunting for me to edit—and absence of self that allow them to describe and mask the horror of a black partner who attempts suicide while fleeing imprisonment and the state's torturous COINTELPRO (torture used overwhelmingly against black and indigenous rebels) with the words—written by a "wife" and potential contributor to this volume—for the hunted, despairing: He "accidentally shot himself in the head."

Battered women have their tongues cut out, or they self-inflict the procedure or perform it on girls and younger women (students and daughters) when their batterer(s) requires protection—that is, when he is not really, truly from the enemy culture, or when women actually belong to "law and order." A chorus of soldier or slave women en route to hospitalize, divorce, or inter rebel brothers, fathers, husbands, sons censor. To whom could a woman soldier tell a complete story? Especially when the male kin has been feminized by male violations administered by the state: cattle prods placed on the genitals of captured militants, police beatings, death and rape (threats) in penal captivity, shootings in foreign wars, eleven-year-old suicide bombers and watching them explode. And then some, many, dream of being released to go home to some woman's bed—a woman who now has in her keep another feminized tortured body and psyche, besides her own, to administer to.

Who works in the underground? Domestic workers and revolutionaries. There, good women and good soldiers all—they vacuum. What is sucked away in the cleaning for academic speeches, political archives, and public spectacles or consumption may be a private suffering and sorrow that defies order. Will war stories that refuse to be told in the absence of the female body restore the missing and dismembered? Or shall, in the presence of the "burning energy" of women in hospital wards and burial sites, war stories with their ever present eulogies be told in the most condensed script, such as that offered by Assata in honor of kin: "The Ancestors will welcome her, cherish her, and treat her with more love and more kindness than she ever received here on this earth."

Women now make up more than 75 percent of registered migrant workers from Indonesia, 70 percent from the Philippines, and 69 percent from Sri Lanka.
—HUMAN RIGHTS WATCH, "ASIA'S MIGRANT WORKERS NEED BETTER PROTECTION" (SEPTEMBER 1, 2004)

In Bosnia and Herzegovina 20,000–50,000 women were raped during five months of conflict in 1992. In some villages in Kosovo, 30–50 percent of women of child bearing age were raped by Serbian forces.
—AMNESTY INTERNATIONAL U.K., "AMNESTY INTERNATIONAL LAUNCHES GLOBAL CAMPAIGN TO STOP VIOLENCE AGAINST WOMEN" (MARCH 5, 2004)

[The] U.N. High Commissioner for Refugees estimates that women and children comprise 70–80 percent of the world's refugee and internally displaced population.
—AMNESTY INTERNATIONAL, "STOP VIOLENCE AGAINST WOMEN" (2004)

DHORUBA BIN WAHAD

Dhoruba Bin Wahad (Richard Moore) was born in the South Bronx in 1944. A member of a Bronx gang, the Disciple Sportsmen, during his teens, Bin Wahad entered prison at eighteen and served a five-year sentence. On his release in 1968, he joined the newly formed New York chapter of the Black Panther Party (BPP). Bin Wahad worked on tenants' rights, police brutality, and drug-rehabilitation programs in Harlem, the South Bronx, and Brooklyn. To curtail drug abuse, he worked in coalition efforts with the Young Lords Party and Young Patriots Party to develop the Lincoln Detox Center, a hospital-based rehabilitation center that used acupuncture rather than methadone maintenance for drug addiction.

The New York Police Department (NYPD), in complicity with FBI COIN-TELPRO operatives, indicted Bin Wahad and twenty other leaders of the New York BPP, the "New York 21," on April 2, 1969, on more than one hundred conspiracy charges that included plots to assassinate New York City police officers and dynamite city department stores, a botanical garden, a police station, and a railroad right-of-way. The charges were without foundation and were later dismissed. However, in the aftermath of the arrests and warrants, the New York 21 were incarcerated, and the New York BPP leadership was decimated. Bin Wahad and Michael Cetewayo Tabor were released on bail and fled the country during the trial because of a plot initiated by the FBI to incite the national BPP leadership, under Huey Newton, to kill them. After two years in prison and an eight-month trial, the New York 21, including Bin Wahad and Tabor in absentia, were acquitted. Jury deliberations lasted less than an hour, and the verdict was returned on May 13, 1971. Bin Wahad returned to the United States but remained underground.

In June 1971, the NYPD apprehended Bin Wahad outside a Bronx "after-hours" bar frequented by drug dealers and their associates, which he was attempting to rob. He was charged with the attempted murder of two police officers, Thomas Curry and Nicholas Binetti, who had been attacked in Manhattan two months earlier. The case set the precedent for what became known as the Joint Terrorism Task Force, an investigative effort among NYPD, New York State Police, and the FBI. After three trials in the case of *People v. Dhoruba Bin Wahad*, Bin Wahad was convicted in July 1973 and sentenced to twenty-five years to life. Two years later, the Church Committee Senate hearings brought COINTELPRO under (semi-)public scrutiny, and Bin Wahad's lawyers filed a civil-rights action to obtain all documents pertaining to him and the BPP in New York. Five years later, they received more than 300,000 highly excised, barely readable documents that disclosed forged letters, phone calls, and anonymous articles aimed at defaming the BPP. Documents also contained over two hundred previously undisclosed pages of three FBI reports on Bin Wahad's case, including a record of an anonymous call to the police in which the prosecution's key witness, Pauline Joseph, exonerated Bin Wahad. The defense received the final set of "Newkill" (an acronym referring to killings in New York that the agency wanted to connect to the BPP) documents in 1987, twelve years after the initial civil-rights action to procure the evidence. Citing the inconsistency and possible perjury of Pauline Joseph in the 1973 trial and conviction, Dhoruba Bin Wahad and his lawyers filed for a retrial. A New York Supreme Court granted a retrial on March 22, 1990, and released Bin Wahad from prison. The District Attorney's Office dismissed his case on January 19, 1995, formally ending the twenty-six year struggle that began with the New York 21 case in 1969.

Following two lawsuits in 1995 and 2000, Dhoruba Bin Wahad received settlements for personal damages from the FBI and the City of New York, respectively. With these funds, Bin Wahad founded the Campaign to Free Black and New Afrikan Political Prisoners (formerly the Campaign to Free Black Political Prisoners and Prisoners-of-War) and established the Institute for the Development of Pan-African Policy in Accra, Ghana.

War Within: A Prison Interview   Dhoruba Bin Wahad

Dhoruba Bin Wahad: My name is Dhoruba Al Mujahid Bin Wahad, formerly Dhoruba Moore. I'm a political prisoner. I've been incarcerated in New York State for nearly nineteen years, which I guess makes me one of the longest-held political prisoners in the world, a notoriety I do not seek, but there it is. My imprisonment was a result of my activities in the black community as a member and leader of the Black Panther Party. Right now there are over a hundred political prisoners and prisoners of war incarcerated in the United States and serving exceptionally long sentences, and most of them are black militants and former members of the Black Panther Party. My case has received a considerable amount of notoriety in that I was one of the original defendants in the New York Panther 21 conspiracy case, which involved an indictment against the leadership of the New York chapter of the Black Panther Party in April 1969.

Q: And you were part of that original indictment?

Bin Wahad: Yes. At that particular time, the Black Panther Party was under full-force attack from the U.S. government, which subsequently destroyed the Black Panther Party. I used to travel around the country speaking about that case and other political cases, so I always had to go through a lot of changes with the FBI at the airports, State Troopers pulling us over on the highway, the whole nine yards. It became really crazy. I felt I was in a war. I would walk down a street, and if kids threw firecrackers, man, I would duck. The only reason we wouldn't shoot back was that we had a policy to see who it was first. It stayed that way until I was arrested. You could see by some of the photos how I looked. I looked like one of those POWs in the early stages of the battle outside Laos—you know, Vietnam. I was completely shell-shocked. I had a combat mentality. It was a question of survival. It was them or me. I was targeted as a "Black extremist" and put into the U.S. government's "Agitator Index" and "Black Extremists" files. These files were meant to identify and target certain leaders and spokespersons of the black struggle for human rights so that they could be neutralized and otherwise taken out of circulation.

Q: The sentence you're serving now—was that on charges unrelated to the 21 trial?

Bin Wahad: It's unrelated to the 21 case, but it's a continuation of the political repression that was aimed at myself and at the Black Panther Party at that time. You see, when I was acquitted in absentia in the 21 case, I was a fugitive, forced underground by the FBI's Counterintelligence Program [COINTELPRO].[1] COINTELPRO had devised a plot to incite the national leadership of the Black Panther Party to assassinate me and some of my comrades.

Q: How did you become aware of that?

Bin Wahad: During my civil suit against the government, around 1980, I eventually got them to release a bunch of documents under the heading "Travel of BPP National Leadership." And one of these documents indicated that there was, in fact, a counterintelligence program aimed at creating a split between the New York Black Panther Party and the BPP national headquarters. The FBI wanted to sow suspicion in the minds of national leadership—specifically, Huey P. Newton, David Hilliard, and the Central Committee in Oakland, California, that the New York Black Panther Party members were out to kill them.[2] They would go about this very systematically. They would send letters to Huey P. Newton purporting to come from New York Panthers who were disgruntled because they didn't adhere to the instructions of the Central Committee. They would also capitalize on individual differences, on the sexism and on the regionalism within the Black Panther Party. You should remember that the BPP was a national organization, and when you travel across the country you see that each city has a different rhythm and style. The FBI would try to use these differences to divide the Black Panther Party. One operation specifically mentioned that I was opposed to representatives of the Central Committee who were stationed in New York to administer the everyday affairs of the Black Panther Party after the Panther 21 arrests. The Panther 21 were the leadership of the New York chapter of the Black Panther Party, and for a number of years they were in prison, so the office of the Black Panther Party sent cadres and other field workers to New York to help run the party. So when I was released on bail, the FBI started a program to sow dissension between myself and the individuals who were left in prison and between myself and the individuals who were put in leadership positions from the West Coast. And this resulted in my being demoted in rank; this resulted in friction between myself and the leadership, which was already under stress, and culminated in threats on my life during the time of the Panther 21 trial. It was a result of these threats on my life that I had to flee underground during a crucial point in my trial, and the government tried to portray my disappearance as an admission of guilt. Of course, it was all designed to prejudice the jury, because the evidence in the case was very weak. I imagine the state thought that if the Panthers who were on bail fled right before the deliberation, that would sort of sway the jury into believing that they were guilty. But that had nothing to do with it. We had to jump bail because the Counterintelligence Program had devised a plot to kill us. Of course, we became very paranoid. I felt that I was always under pressure. Since the BPP leadership had chosen me to be released on one hundred thousand dollars' bail, I felt the Black Panther Party had a one-hundred-thousand-dollar investment in me. I couldn't sleep in the same place two nights in a row. I always had to have people on security with me.

Q: What happened then?

Bin Wahad: While I was a fugitive, two New York City police officers were shot and wounded as they were guarding the home of Manhattan District Attorney Frank Hogan. The following day, two New York City police officers were shot and killed in Harlem. Now, both of these shootings were claimed by the Black Liberation Army [BLA]—

Q: Which was a clandestine group?

Bin Wahad: Yes. According to the U.S. Senate Church Committee on terrorism in the United States, the Black Liberation Army grew out of the Black Panther Party. The way it's portrayed in official documents is that the Black Liberation Army represented the hardcore militants within the Black Panther Party who were dissatisfied with legitimate struggle, with legitimate protests. Of course, that's not true. The racist repression of the Black Panther Party is what motivated the Black Liberation Army. The destruction of the Black Panther Party, the splitting of the Black Panther Party into hostile factions, is what led to that particular development of the black underground in the United States. These activists, who could no longer function safely above ground, had to flee for their survival. So I was a fugitive. I was underground when these two officers were shot on May 19, 1971, and the BLA claimed responsibility for these shootings. At that time, the black community was enraged by the continual murder of black youth by the police and the ongoing, racist police brutality that was being inflicted on the black community. The black underground retaliated in this way. I wasn't involved in any of these shootings, but because of my notoriety around the Panther 21 case, because of my vocal opposition to the criminal-justice system in New York, I became a prime target for a frame-up around the shooting of these two officers. I maintained then, and I maintain now, that I was innocent of that shooting.

Subsequently, as a result of my filing a suit in Federal District Court in Manhattan, I obtained approximately 300,000 pages of FBI documents on the Black Panther Party, on myself, and on the Counterintelligence Program, and these documents clearly indicate that (1) I was a target of the Counterintelligence Program of the U.S. government and the New York law-enforcement agencies; and, (2) I was innocent of the charges for the murder of these two officers. When we first got these documents, they were heavily excised. I filed this suit against the U.S. government in 1975, and it took over five years for me to prove that the government was lying about its COINTELPRO role in my case. . . .

At first, the U.S. government and the police denied involvement in any such counterintelligence activities. They did this for several months. They tried to overturn the civil complaint on purely technical grounds. We survived that. For almost five years, they stonewalled it. It so happened that at that particular time, a suit was being litigated in Chicago in the case of Fred Hampton.[3] . . .

Years later, a suit was filed against the Chicago Police Department by the family of Fred Hampton, and it was during the litigation of that suit that certain documents came to light. Some of these documents had my name on them, and they were not among the documents that were turned over to me during my suit. So when this was brought to the attention of the federal judge, she got a little upset and ordered the U.S. government to turn over everything with my name on it. . . . Then we started producing certain documents from the FBI that indicated that the source for the FBI was the intelligence unit of the New York City Police Department.

Q: Have you received any of those NYPD documents?

Bin Wahad: We received about three hundred irrelevant documents—surveillance of demonstrations. They said they lost the whole file. . . . They miraculously found this whole room stacked from floor to ceiling with documents. Their next legal maneuver was to claim that the newly found documents were privileged material, so we had to fight a motion in court for privilege. It's these types of dilatory tactics that in any other case would not have been tolerated by the court.

Q: Why were they tolerated in your case?

Bin Wahad: Because it clearly showed that the law-enforcement agencies of the U.S. government and the State of New York had broken the law in order to put me away. And because of the political nature of the case, because of the police officers that were shot, the lives of those police officers that were involved, the credibility and the political interests of the Policemen's Benevolent Association and other agencies, it required that the courts bend over backward in order to give them the opportunity to destroy the evidence, doctor evidence, or conceal it, and that's what the court did. And it still does that today. To this very day, the suit is pending. It's been pending since 1975. It's one of the longest pending suits in the Seventh District Court.

Q: Could you describe what COINTELPRO was and give some indications of its breadth?

Bin Wahad: In the Church Committee report, there's a glossary [with] the different acronyms and accepted terminology that are used in the intelligence community.[4] "Counterintelligence" usually and universally means to counteract the intelligence operations of a foreign power. However, COINTELPRO, as implemented by the FBI, was aimed at countering the rise in political power of a domestic national minority—specifically, primarily, black people. . . . The implementation of the Counterintelligence Program transcended mere investigation. It was in effect a domestic war program, a program aimed at countering the rise of black militancy, black independent political thought, and at repressing the freedoms of black people in the United States. The Counterintelligence Program can be seen as a program of war waged by a government against a people, against its own citizens. It was a program of domestic warfare.

It could be compared, in some respects, to the counterintelligence activities that were carried out in Southeast Asia around the time of the Vietnam War. I have specifically in mind . . . the secret war in Laos that was carried out by the CIA. Of course, the analogy has its limitations. The military in Laos, for instance, were able to carry out larger operations. There was a counterinsurgency program secretly financed by the U.S. government through the CIA that destroyed whole villages in regions of Laos. We could say that this was not the case in the United States, but it was just a matter of scale here, and proportion. . . . During the early '60s, at the height of the Civil Rights Movement and the human-rights movement, the police in the United States became increasingly militarized. They began to train out of military bases in the United States. The Law Enforcement Assistance Act (LEAA) supplied local police with military technology—everything from assault rifles to army personnel carriers.[5] So the Counterintelligence Program went hand in hand with the militarization of the police in the black community, with the militarization of the police in America. . . . The so-called intelligence community developed and honed its skills at domestic repression under the guise of local law enforcement and the Counterintelligence Program.

Q: What do you think were the ideological and political justifications that they were hoping to present to the public?

Bin Wahad: One of the things that motivated the militarization of the police in the United States was racism. They really believed that black people and national minorities, people of color, American Indians, Puerto Ricans, and Chicanos represented a serious threat to the internal security of the United States. And I think that that was based on the historical fact that these national minorities had been subjugated by a racist system for centuries and that, if they were to exercise the full panoply of political, economic, and social rights, the American system as such, in its Eurocentric character, could no longer carry out its mission. The mission of the American nation-state is to perpetuate European hegemony over the Third World and over people of color. Political education and the development of political awareness was one of the main goals of the Black Panther Party. In fact, the BPP never posed a serious military threat to the U.S. government. It was the popularity of our Ten-Point Program, our belief in the guaranteed right of everyone to food, clothing, decent housing, free health care, education, etcetera, that terrified the government and motivated them to launch an all-out attack against us.

Q: But one of the immediate ways of doing that was to criminalize, as you say, independent-thinking people of color, to present them as criminals.

Bin Wahad: Well, yes, that has always been a unique characteristic of political repression in the United States, going back to slavery. When we look at the history of the development of slave laws, in the antebellum South, we see that there was a whole legal system put into place to keep the African enslaved. Anyone that rebelled against this legal system was in effect a criminal. They were subject to be prosecuted by the courts. The slave codes were, in effect, penal codes in many parts of the country. And it's not a coincidence that today the United States denies that it has any political prisoners, based on the fact that everybody in prison is convicted of a crime. I mean, we didn't just pop out of the ground this morning. Everything has a history. And it's no coincidence that the prosecutorial agencies of the state make no distinction between political repression and law enforcement.

Q: What have been the long-range effects of COINTELPRO on the black community?

Bin Wahad: The most devastating effect of the Counterintelligence Program in the black community in America has been the vacuum of leadership that it created. Now, this vacuum was filled in the 1970s by individuals who survived the repression of the 1960s because they were not involved in front-line struggles. And the ones who had been involved in these struggles were thoroughly intimidated by the awesome devastation [caused by] the Counterintelligence Program. I think the deaths of Malcolm X and Martin Luther King [Jr.] and the destruction of certain militant organizations created a vacuum in the black community, and this vacuum was filled in many cases by political charlatans, opportunists, and individuals who were less than uncompromising in their stand against race repression and racist domination.

Q: So you're suggesting that King and Malcolm X were probably targets of COINTELPRO?

Bin Wahad: Well, I have no doubt that they were. I think that the events surrounding the deaths of both Malcolm X and Dr. Martin Luther King indicate that the U.S. government had a hand in manipulating forces to murder them. If we go back historically into the demise of all potent revolutionary black leaders, we'll see that almost in every instance other black people were used to murder them or to compromise their struggle.

Q: What about COINTELPRO's effects internationally?

Bin Wahad: The purpose of the Counterintelligence Program on the international level was the isolation of blacks from the international community. And it was this purpose that I believe was at the root of the deaths of both Malcolm X and Dr. Martin Luther King, because both of these black leaders had begun to speak about international issues and attract an international audience. The majority of the so-called black leaders who do enjoy a degree of international credibility are those who usually collaborate with U.S. foreign-policy interests. So the Counterintelligence Program, in my view, had an international component, and its operations on the international level were carried out by the CIA.

The CIA had a program similar in form and objective to COINTELPRO called "Operation Chaos." It dealt with domestic surveillance and international surveillance of domestic activists, and to this very day no one knows the depths of that program.

But I think the objective of the Counterintelligence Program on the international level was the isolation of the blacks from the events of the Third World and that this isolation was a very important aspect of U.S. foreign policy. It has been consistent U.S. government policy, regardless of whether the administration has been Republican or Democrat. In its attempt to portray itself as a bastion of freedom, of free speech, of human rights, the United States has consistently had to overcome the racist origins of its own foreign policy and its own interests. American foreign policy and interests are Eurocentric. Yet the majority of the nations of the world are people of color. So the COINTELPRO operations that were aimed at muting the voice of blacks in the international arena were a very important component in maintaining U.S. supremacy over the Third World. We need to examine that, and we need to examine how it is that we have come into the position where sports figures and entertainers can travel abroad and act as spokespersons for black people, act as our representatives abroad. This is a sad state of affairs, and black people need to put this dynamic in check. . . .

Q: The FBI sought to present the Black Panthers and other militants as criminals, but actually one of the results of the repression was that it did force people to use arms in an offensive instead of a defensive manner. Do you see that as one of the effects of COINTELPRO?

Bin Wahad: When we talk about methods of resistance, we need to understand a basic principle. And that basic principle is that repression breeds resistance. And the more vicious and physical the repression, the more intense and physical the resistance. A lot of people do not understand that the Black Liberation Army, as an idea and as a concept, was a response to the brutal repression of the Black Panther Party and the legalization of that repression. Even though the FBI and other government agencies wiretapped the phones and homes of activists within the Black Panther Party and other organizations, these wiretaps, by and large, were illegal. They were not supported by existing law. They were wiretaps that were authorized by Attorney General John Mitchell solely under his authority. So here you have an agency that purportedly is committed to defending the law and defending the U.S. Constitution breaking the law and bending the law in order to repress elements in society that it views with disfavor. That has been typical of law-enforcement agencies. The state, the national-security state—which America is—has one overriding interest, and that is to protect and defend itself against its own citizens. Anything that the police did, anything that the investigative agencies of the government did in order to defend the national-security–state interests, was considered legal, was considered "justifiable." . . .

Q: Why do you think you in particular, and the Black Panther Party generally, became such an obsession for the U.S. government?

Bin Wahad: I think it was psychosexual. . . . I say that only partly tongue-in-cheek. One of the things that scares white America is the thought of assertive black manhood. They cannot deal with the threat that it represents to white male supremacy. And some of that is psychosexual. The idea of black men standing up in America in a paramilitary array, so to speak, with guns—it scares the hell out of white folks. It was the idea that had to be destroyed. The individuals may not have represented a significant physical threat to the U.S. government; it was the idea that black men had the right to defend themselves against white aggression. That's psychosexual. Women tend not to be perceived as as great a threat, and often for this reason when they become revolutionaries they break the sexist mold. Historically, black women were always at the forefront of the struggle. Certainly, Harriet Tubman, Sojourner Truth, and Assata Shakur, among others, inspired fear in the white man's heart. During slavery, men and women were forced to work side by side in the field. They were whipped and tortured with equal vehemence. The psychosexual component of our oppression was evident in the extent to which violence against us took on a sexual flavor. White males have always been allowed unhindered access to black women. In fact, rape was an essential feature of the chattel-slave system, used to dominate, humiliate, and control black women. Lynchings invariably involved the dismemberment of sexual organs (breasts, penises, testicles). These acts were condoned because black men and women were typically viewed as animals or chattel, subhumans. So when you stand up in the twentieth century with a gun in your hand, and you're not presenting a middle class amenable to the "reason" of white standards and white values, then you become a threat. But the power of that threat didn't just come from nowhere. . . . I'm not saying that the only underlying motivation for our oppression is psychosexual; that would be overly simplistic. But this is what lurks behind the notion of black people armed for their own defense—fear of black potency. The idea of black self-defense couldn't be tolerated.

Q: Some psychosexual elements are evident even today?

Bin Wahad: Yes, and they have to do with black assertiveness. America gets very belligerent with its prerogatives if its rights are trampled on by other people, especially Third World people or people of color. And the first thing they want to do is send in the Marines. They get real macho. They talk about the right to self-defense, the right to be armed, you know, the armed citizenry. But there is definitely a dual standard here. White male supremacy is a given. Black subordination is also supposedly a given, and the Black Panther Party changed that. It's no coincidence that law-enforcement agencies, staffed mainly by white macho males, just went berserk at the mere thought of black people, mostly black men, shooting back at them. I mean, they went crazy. The fear of black men and black males is so pervasive in this society that a mob in Bensonhurst or a mob in Howard Beach could murder [black] men just based on the fact that they're in the neighborhood, or that they look at you in a certain way, or that they wear their hat a certain way, or that they carry themselves a certain way, with aggressiveness.[6] I found this same fear throughout my time in prison, that it's very difficult to deal with prison officials unless they feel that you are being subservient. And me, being the type of individual that I am, I don't feel or act like I'm subservient. I recognize that I'm in prison, but that's as far as it goes. I mean, it's not my prison. If it was my prison, I wouldn't be here, right? There's a basic assumption that as a black you are expected to communicate in your demeanor and in the tone of your voice that you believe you are inferior and they are superior. And when you refuse to do that, you have a problem. And if you have no power, you become the victim of the problem. My point was that the Black Panther Party had to be destroyed because of the idea that it represented, black assertiveness and black self-defense, that this should be achieved by any means necessary—in fact, by the same means, if necessary, that white people would employ to defend themselves. And the system couldn't tolerate that. . . .

Q: What are white people about, and how does that affect the nation-state?

Bin Wahad: When I use the term "white people," I'm talking about a certain cultural–historical continuum, as opposed to individuals. Because, as you know, individuals are capable of transcending certain sociological and ideological limitations. But at the same time, we're all soldiers of history, I guess, we're all in the same stream of history. So when I say white people, I'm talking about a social, economic, and historical confluence of forces that determines the social being and consciousness of large segments of people and informs their relationships with each other. That's basically what I mean when I say that. The European historical experience is the experience of self-alienation. And the reinforcement of that experience through the political and economic establishment of the modern nation-state has led to the present situation that we're in. If we check out any aspect of Europe's involvement in the world, we'll see that alienation and greed have been the primary motive forces in everything they do. That alienation has manifested itself in their encounters with aboriginal cultures. Just my limited reading of Europe's colonization and appropriation of the North American continent shows me that they had a certain mindset that came from the European historical experience. The fundamental contradiction of that mindset is the human alienation from self and nature, a seeing, a perceiving of oneself as being over and above nature. It's a unique feature of European culture. I mean, no other people have that, not to that degree. Eastern cultures are more holistic, more unified in their approach to life and in their approach to the struggles of life. But it's that contradiction, inherent and inculcated in the European historical experience, that has transformed the nature of the world. . . .

Q: When you were in the Black Panther Party, what sort of work were you doing?

Bin Wahad: I used to organize chapters and branches of the Black Panther Party throughout the State of New York and along the Eastern seaboard, down to Maryland. . . .

The type of work we did at that time revolved around trying to better the conditions of black people in the inner city, in housing, in school, in welfare, in hospital care. We opened free hospital clinics so that people could be tested for sickle-cell; we secured volunteer doctors from different hospitals around the city; we opened free breakfast programs to feed children during the school months. That's the type of activity that we engaged in. And, of course, we also organized self-defense patrols in the black community. We advocated that black people arm themselves against racist attack. That seems to be the part of our agenda that got the most attention.

Q: I wanted to read you a selection from the Panther 21 statement delivered to Judge Murtow: "Does not your constitution guarantee man's freedom, his human dignity against state encroachment, or does the innate fear of the rebellious slave in the heart of the slave master continue to this day to negate all those guarantees in the cases of Black people?"

Bin Wahad: We had divided up the writing up of that statement, and I wrote that part. The key phrase in there is the innate fear in the slave master for the slave, for his rebelliousness. The so-called rebellious slave was the one that was always singled out for a special type of treatment, as an example and a signal to the rest of the slaves that—this is what will happen to you if you rebel against our power and against our system. And often the rebellious slave, the strong black slave, would be subject to heinous physical torture. . . .

Why do we always have to talk about reconciliation, healing wounds of a racial division when black people die, but when white people die they talk about revenge, they talk about justice, about putting someone away for life?

There's no reconciliation there. Why? Because the value of a black life and the value of a white life are different. It's completely obvious, and no one questions that. And the politicians, the white politicians that stand up and say that's not true, and if I became mayor I would punish these men to the fullest extent of the law, etcetera, they're hypocrites. You only hear them when one of us gets killed. Because they fear the attitude of black people should change from trying to fit into the American dream of white folks to destroying it. That's the fear. So it's only the reconciliation when we die. It's justice when they die. . . . My point is to say that one is a crime, and the other one is a crime because of race, it is based in a racist historical continuum. . . .

Q: Could you outline the nature of the repression that the United States visited on the Black Panther Party?

Bin Wahad: . . . One of the objectives of the initial memo regarding the Counterintelligence Program vis-à-vis the black movement was to prevent the rise of a messianic leader who could unite black people. You have to understand that the individuals who run and control the system have the entire apparatus of academia at their disposal. Some of the best minds of the world can be found in the institutions of higher learning in the United States. And these individuals are paid and contracted by the U.S. government to analyze how we think, how we feel, to analyze every facet of our existence, to conduct experiments on us emotionally, psychologically, and physically. This has been done. So the Counterintelligence Program when it was implemented against black people was a war strategy that fed on the weaknesses of blacks.

There was nothing haphazard or incidental about COINTELPRO. In the documents, former FBI Director J. Edgar Hoover talks about the standards of moral conduct that hold sway in the African American community. And being racist, he says that these standards are essentially low-life standards, they're different from white standards, so you really can't embarrass these Negroes by calling them names and showing that they're corrupt in certain ways, because they're not like us, you see? . . .

And a lot of these tactics were brought home to the United States and employed in the black community. A lot of police officers got their initial training in counterinsurgency and counterintelligence in Vietnam. Some police officers went on sabbaticals to serve in the Phoenix Program during the Vietnam War.[7] Concepts like block watches and community patrols and community outreach programs were all further developments of the ideas and concepts that were outlined to destroy the Vietcong—the village watcher, the spy who could inform the police as to who was an NLF [National Liberation Front] cadre and who wasn't.[8] These techniques, the techniques of disinformation, of counterinsurgency—they were brought home. The war was brought home to the United States. When we used to say that the war was being fought in our community at home, the peace movement, which was predominantly white, predominantly liberal, ignored us. They didn't want to confront and deal with their racism. It was all right to talk about "Stop the war in Vietnam," because that threatened their future. They could be the ones to be drafted. But they didn't want to deal with the war in Watts, with the war in Buttermilk Bottom in Atlanta, with the war on Hastings Street in Detroit. They didn't want to deal with that because that was too close to home. . . . [9]

Q: Do you think the white American left stood by as the Black Panther Party was destroyed?

Bin Wahad: Yes, I think so. The Black Panther Party absorbed the rage and the repression that would have normally been visited on the white left. I mean, every time I read one of these "'60s Revisited" interviews or books where they will go to a 1960s radical and they will ask, "What was it like?" and the white radical might be sitting up in a yuppie bar and, you know, he's a corporate executive, and he says, "Well, it was wild, man. . . ."

Meanwhile, you have blacks who are in the grave, who are in prison, who are in exile, and they don't have that privilege of reflecting. Essentially, white America said to their children: "All right, you sowed your wild oats, you did your thing, now come into the system." White privilege was always there for them to come back to; it was never there for black people. The system was taking no prisoners, no hostages, when it came to repressing us. But when it came to repressing their own children, the really "crazy" ones, the ones who meant what they said and were really out there, they dealt with them, like Marilyn Buck or the Ohio Seven.[10] But then again, the class basis of the Ohio Seven is completely different; they come from working-class families, they're poor.

Q: Could you tell us more about the sorts of strategies the FBI used against the Black Panther Party?

Bin Wahad: There were a number of strategies. It depended on what they wanted to achieve. Their primary goal was, of course, to achieve the total discreditation of the Black Panther Party. If they could have discredited the Black Panther Party in the eyes of black people without putting everybody in jail, I'm reasonably certain that they would have done it. There is one document, a memo from the San Francisco FBI field office to bureau headquarters, that says that the underlying purpose of the Counterintelligence Program is to bring home to black youth that if they adhere to, or succumb to, the revolutionary philosophies or ideologies, they will be dead revolutionaries. The document says—I'm still paraphrasing—that black youth need something to believe in, and we have to prove and show to them that it's better to be accepted by the system than to tear it down. They wanted to prevent the passing on of ideas that the Panthers represented to black youth. And they were successful at that. In my mind, this was the most painful document to read because of the condition that black youth are in today. They have no understanding of history, of their past. They have become, to a large extent, very nihilistic. They have succumbed to the base materialism and materialistic attitudes of American society. I mean, look at the gangs in [Los Angeles], and the gangs in Chicago, and in New York City. Black youth are cut off from any sense of purpose or direction, from any sense of social responsibility and political struggle. That was the reason the Black Panther Party had to be destroyed.

One of the first objectives was to "prevent the rise of a Mau-Mau rebellion in the United States." COINTELPRO utilized all types of tactics. One tactic was identifying effective leaders within the Black Panther Party and then creating rumors around these particular individuals so that the leadership would feel threatened and therefore neutralize them. Another tactic was to develop contradictions within the party over money. In one memo, J. Edgar Hoover says that the three things a "Negro" wants most are money, a white woman, and a Cadillac. (Laughs.) That's the way he said it, you know. (Laughs again.) . . .

Q: The final question, [concerning] counterinsurgency in Vietnam and counterintelligence here at home, in the United States: Do you see a relationship between those two and the subsequent development of counterterrorism?

Bin Wahad: Sure. Once the Counterintelligence Program had been successful in destroying the ability of the Black Panther Party to work overtly in the black community, and splitting its leadership, forcing certain individuals underground, then it changed its gears into a counterinsurgency or anti-urban-guerrilla program. In fact, the document names changed. It changed from COINTELPRO, or Black Nationalist Hate Groups, to Urban Guerrilla Black Nationalist Hate Groups. So the strategies changed. In fact, in 1971 the FBI convened a series of seminars in which it brought together police chiefs from all different parts of the country, and of various intelligence units, and gave them seminars on the threats of urban terrorism and the threat of the black underground, the BLA, the FALN [Armed Forces of National Liberation],[11] the Weather Underground, and various other organizations that were considered terrorists in the United States. As a result of this, certain programs came into being. One program was called Prison Activist Program. In this program, correction officers from all over the country were brought together at the Marine Base in Quantico [Virginia] for workshops, and they were shown how they could play a crucial role in monitoring the activities of political prisoners, their visitors, and individuals in the street. Each facility had an officer that was identified as the individual who would be the liaison with the FBI. So that, like in my case, if the officers shook down my cell and found some "subversive literature," they would take the literature from my cell, and that literature would wind up in the hands of the FBI. Mine was the first case in which the New York City police, New York State Police, and the FBI joined forces to conduct an investigation into the shooting of police officers. This was formalized later into what we now know as the Joint Terrorism Task Force. My case was the pilot project for that, as one of the memoranda of a police inspector indicated.

And the tactics that were used to disrupt the overt organizations became purely military tactics. That's when you see the development of SWAT [Special Weapons and Tactics] teams in the United States. They first came as a result of the clashes between the Black Panther Party and the police throughout the country, when the police would raid Black Panther offices. The Black Panther offices tended to be fortified and heavily armed because we actually believed in self-defense. Therefore, when they would attack the office, they would have APCS—armored personnel carriers—and helicopters. So they started to develop their special weapons and armed tactics. SWAT team tactics. And these SWAT team tactics were basically . . . Basic Unit Tactics utilizing advanced weaponry training that you find in the military, adapted to the urban situation. A lot of the experienced personnel in these situations were Vietnam vets. In New York, it's the same thing with the Emergency Service Unit. So, yes, there is a direct correlation between the anti-insurgency that the United States fought abroad and the repression of the black movement in the United States. By way of another example, we can see that the development of special forces, of quick emergency response teams, have coincided with the development of these units on the local police—and national level. Every police department that's worth its salary has a SWAT team, a special weapons and tactics squad. Every one. I mean, it goes with the territory now. These tactics are designed to deal with the rising tide of militancy or contain that discontent.

Another example is this so-called war on drugs. Drugs were always used in the Third World as a mechanism of economic and political control. The classic example is China and the Opium Wars, the introduction of opium into China in order to facilitate European exploitation and dominance. So the military is being touted, and recruited, to fight the war on drugs, at least at the borders. The whole idea of a war on drugs is a domestic war policy. It's a code word for "keep the black and Latino and surplus labor and youth in their place." And what's their place? Prison. Build more prisons. You can't employ them, you can't educate them, because the economy can't provide jobs for them. I mean, this is clear. So how do you deal with this? You declare a war on drugs, and you build armies, based on waging this war on drugs. In Los Angeles, where we have these nihilistic gangs, youth gangs, going around, shooting each other with MAC-10S and AK-47S, the people are screamin' and hollerin,' "We need more cops!" And more cops you'll get. You'll see them on the Geraldo Rivera show kicking in doors, and how do they look? They look just like a SWAT team going into a village in

Vietnam. That's what they look like! The only thing, they didn't land in a helicopter. They come in a van, they jump out, and they're armed to the teeth. Sure. I mean, we should understand *glasnost*.[12] The nature of *glasnost* is that the Europeans who control the Soviet empire and those who control the European empire realize that they have a common historical root. Now they have a common destiny: to maintain their control over the Third World. The contradiction is no longer East–West; it's North–South. So that being the case, there has to be some type of ideological basis for unity. It's no longer cool to say the communists are the enemy. Now they're coming over, they're hanging out. Before you know it, you'll have joint maneuvers between the Soviet Navy and the U.S. Navy. Who are they maneuvering for, if they aren't fighting each other anymore? We're talking about nuclear disarmament, so we're talking about building a conventional arsenal. Who are the major suppliers to the arsenals of the Third World? The same parties that are talking about *glasnost*. So "anti-terrorism" substitutes itself for "anticommunism." Anti-terrorism substitutes itself for blatant racism. It's no longer chic to say that you should hang black folks by a tree and lynch them, so what you do is you declare them terrorists and you shoot 'em in the head. That's the significance, in a nutshell, of how terrorism is replacing certain catchwords in the United States.

Notes

Originally published in Jim Fletcher, Tanaquil Jones, and Sylvère Lotringer, eds., *Still Black, Still Strong: Survivors of the U.S. War against Black Revolutionaries* (New York: Semiotext(e), 1993), 9–56. The interview was conducted by Chris Bratton and Annie Goldson in fall 1989 at Eastern Prison in Napanoch, New York, approximately seven months before Dhoruba Bin Wahad was released on his own recognizance after his conviction was vacated. The interview also appears in Bratton and Goldson's documentary film *Framing the Panthers* (NEA McArthur Foundation, 1991).

1. *Editor's note*: During the era of the Black Panther Party, the primary purpose of the FBI's COINTELPRO, as J. Edgar Hoover wrote in a 1966 memorandum, was "to expose, disrupt, misdirect, discredit, or otherwise neutralize the activities of black nationalist organizations and groupings, their leadership, spokesmen, membership, and supporters." Through violence, manipulation of the media, and disinformation campaigns, the FBI aimed to both destabilize the public-support base of the movement and remove its leaders from public discourse through exile, imprisonment, or death. COINTELPRO was "dismantled" in the late 1970s, but the Joint Terrorism Task Force was created to continue its repressive program. See Dhoruba Bin Wahad,

"COINTELPRO and the Destruction of Black Leaders and Organizations (Abridged)," in James, *Imprisoned Intellectuals*, 97–106; Churchill and Vander Wall, *Agents of Repression*; and idem, *The COINTELPRO Papers*.

2. *Editor's note*: David Hilliard, an early member of the Black Panther Party, served as chief of staff of the organization.

3. Fred Hampton, leader of the Chicago chapter of the Black Panther Party, was assassinated (along with Mark Clark) in a pre-dawn raid on December 4, 1969, by Chicago police, who were assisted by the FBI. Hampton was a prime target of FBI COINTELPRO operations because of his success in building alliances among Chicago street gangs (such as the Blackhawk Rangers, Young Lords, and Young Patriots). His murder is among the most visceral examples of state counterrevolutionary violence inside the United States. See *Eyes on the Prize II: A Nation of Law? 1968–1971* (Blackside Productions, videocassette, 1990); Howard Alk dir., *The Murder of Fred Hampton* (Film Group, videocassette, 1971). See also "Domestic Warfare: A Dialogue with Marshall Eddie Conway," in this volume.

4. *Editor's note*: The U.S. Senate's Church Committee (named after Senator Frank Church, Democrat of Idaho) was assembled in 1973. The committee's proceedings, which were published in 1976, concluded by stating: "The Government has often undertaken the secret surveillance of citizens on the basis of their political beliefs, even when those beliefs posed no threat of violence or illegal acts on behalf of a hostile foreign power. . . . Groups and individuals have been harassed and disrupted because of their political views and their lifestyles." In 1986, a federal court determined that COINTELPRO was responsible for at least 204 burglaries by FBI agents, the theft of 12,600 documents, the use of 1,300 informants, 20,000 illegal wiretap days, and 12,000 bugs. See "Results of the 1973 Church Committee Hearings," available online at http://pw1.netcom.com/~ncoic/cia_info.htm (accessed June 22, 2004).

5. *Editor's note*: Passed during the administration of Lyndon B. Johnson, the LEAA created the Office of Law Enforcement Assistance and provided funds for professionalizing state and local law-enforcement agencies.

6. *Editor's note*: In 1989, a mob of white youths shot and killed a sixteen-year-old black youth, Yusuf Hawkins, who had gone to Bensonhurst, New York, to look at a used car. Similarly, in 1986 a gang of white youths beat three black youths and murdered one, Michael Griffith, when their car broke down in the predominantly white neighborhood of Howard Beach, New York. See DeSantis, *For the Color of His Skin*; Hynes and Drury, *Incident at Howard Beach*.

7. *Editor's note*: In 1965, the CIA launched a computer-driven program designed to "neutralize," through assassination, kidnapping, and systematic torture, the civilian infrastructure that supported the insurgency in South Vietnam. Renamed the "Phoenix Program" by 1968, program operations resulted in the deaths of at least 20,000 supporters or suspected supporters of the Vietcong.

8. *Editor's note*: In 1960, widespread opposition to Ngo Dinh Diem, president of South Vietnam, 1955–63, led to the official sanctioning of the formation of the NLF. Although communists dominated the NLF leadership, noncommunists who opposed the South Vietnamese government also joined. The NLF trained and equipped a guerrilla force (formally organized as the People's Liberation Armed Forces in 1961 but commonly known as the Vietcong) to overthrow the Diem government and reunify Vietnam.

9. *Editor's note*: Buttermilk Bottom in Atlanta, Hastings Street in Detroit, and Watts in Los Angeles were predominantly black, inner-city areas damaged by riots between 1965 and 1967.

10. *Editor's note*: Marilyn Buck is a political prisoner serving a virtual life sentence in Dublin, California, for her work with the Black Liberation Army. See Marilyn Buck, "The Effects of Repression on Women in Prison," in this volume. The "Ohio Seven," white, antiracist activists in the United Freedom Front and Sam Melville/Jonathan Jackson Unit, claimed responsibility for a series of bombings of government and military buildings and corporate offices, including those of the South African Airlines in New York City. They were convicted in 1986 by a federal court in Brooklyn of bombings against U.S. military facilities and contractors and other businesses profiting from South African apartheid. See "Raymond Luc Levasseur," in James, *Imprisoned Intellectuals*, 227–30.

11. *Editor's note*: The Fuerzas Armadas de Liberación Nacional (Armed Forces of National Liberation, or FALN) was an underground organization that resisted U.S. colonization of Puerto Rico. Between 1974 and 1980, the FALN took numerous actions against U.S. military, government, and economic sites in Puerto Rico. By 1980, the U.S. government had captured members of FALN who were later convicted of charges that ranged from bomb making and conspiracy to armed robbery and given sentences of thirty-five to ninety years. Many FALN activists served fourteen to nineteen years in prison. See Oscar Lòpez Rivera, "A Century of Colonialism: 100 Years of Puerto Rican Resistance," in this volume; Susler, "Unreconstructed Revolutionaries," 145.

12. *Editor's note*: *Glasnost* (openness), the Soviet policy initiated by Mikhail Gorbachev in the late 1980s, was designed to promote a policy of openness in public discussions, government receptivity to the media and foreign leaders, and détente between the East and the West.

References

Bin Wahad, Dhoruba. "Cointelpro and the Destruction of Black Leaders and Organizations." *Bulletin in Defense of Marxism* (May 1993): 22–26.

———. "Dhoruba Bin Wahad: Veteran Black Panther and Nineteen-Year Political Prisoner" (interview with Bill Weinberg). *Shadow* 36 (March 2002). Available online at http://shadow.mediafilter.org/mff/s36/s36.dbw.html (accessed October 24, 2004).

———. "Speaking Truth to Power: Political Prisoners in the United States." Pp. 269–78 in *Criminal Injustice: Confronting the Prison Crisis*, ed. Elihu Rosenblatt. Boston: South End Press, 1996.

Boyd, Herb. "Ex-Panther's Lawsuit Settled." *Black World Today*, December 9, 2000.

Fraser, Gerald C. "FBI Files Reveal Moves against Black Panthers." *New York Times*, October 19, 1980, A1.

People of the State of New York v. Dhoruba Bin Wahad, Formerly Richard Moore. Lexis 1232. NY Sup. Ct., February 8, 1990.

Richard Moore v. New York State Board of Parole. Lexis 11746. NY Sup. Ct., November 14, 1990.

Valadez, John, dir. *Passin' It On*. Videocassette. New York: First Run/Icarus Films, 1992.

MARSHALL EDDIE CONWAY

While serving in the U.S. Army, Marshall Eddie Conway was transformed by studying Malcolm X. Deeply disaffected with the armed forces, he left with an honorable discharge in 1967. After returning to his hometown of Baltimore, Maryland, he became active in the Congress of Racial Equality and helped integrate the Sparrows Point Fire Department, which he remembers as being largely composed of Klan sympathizers. Conway recalls "being one of the first blacks in the Fire Department. I had a real experience with organized racism. It . . . pushed me to a more militant stand in order to just maintain employment. That made me realize that it was time to do something more serious."[1]

In April 1969, Conway joined the Baltimore chapter of the Black Panther Party (BPP). There, he helped to expose and expel a key FBI COINTELPRO infiltrator, Warren Hart. Under FBI directives, Hart "founded" the Baltimore BPP and subsequently used his leadership position to gain access to the Panther Central Committee, reporting his findings to the National Security Agency (NSA). Conway's disruption of Hart's domestic espionage led to his being targeted by COINTELPRO.

On the evening of April 24, 1970, two police officers were shot in West Baltimore by three men walking by their police car. One, Officer Donald Sager, died. Nearby, Officer Michael Nolan was involved in a foot chase and gunfire exchange with one of the men, who eventually escaped. The police apprehended Jack Johnson Jr. and James Powell—both were later identified as members of the Black Panther Party—near the scene of the shooting, hiding under the porch of a house. Ammunition and a .38 caliber handgun were allegedly found on the ground near them. The next morning, another gun was supposedly found at the arrest site, hidden under a sandbox. A ballistic expert later testified that the bullet removed from the skull of Officer Sager during an autopsy was a .38 caliber. Powell and Johnson were subsequently charged with first-degree murder.

Two days later, police arrested Eddie Conway at Baltimore's main post office, where he worked, charging him with murder and attempted murder. No physical evidence connected Conway with the shootings. The warrant for his arrest was premised on information provided by an informant for the FBI, apparently working as a COINTELPRO operative. In 1990, the prosecuting attorney, Peter Ward, recalled at the trial: "The greatest difficulty in the State's case was that we didn't have any direct evidence and we didn't have a direct eyewitness. There were a lot of incriminating circumstances that we had to tie together to form a total picture."[2]

The state developed its prosecution of Conway through several tactics. Johnson, who was deeply implicated in the shooting through direct physical evidence, was given immunity from prosecution in return for implicating Conway in the crime. When Johnson took the witness stand, he invoked his Fifth Amendment rights. Officer Nolan, at the trial, was shown two sets of photos and asked to point out which of the photos matched the man he saw running into an alley at night and with whom he had exchanged gunfire. Conway's picture was the only mug shot placed in both sets. Charles Reynolds, a prisoner placed in Conway's cell for four days, claimed that Conway had "confessed" to him. Reynolds asked for a favorable recommendation to the Michigan Parole Board in exchange for his testimony; he was later revealed to have been a paid government informant and provided the only additional testimony linking Conway to the shootings.

Absent competent legal defense, Marshall Eddie Conway, who chose not to participate in the trial, was convicted and sentenced to life imprisonment plus thirty years. Some twenty-one Panthers, former BPP members, and close community activists were either arrested or were fugitives at the time of Conway's arrest.

While imprisoned, Conway earned two associate's degrees and a bachelor's degree and is currently completing his master of arts degree. He has founded and led numerous prison educational programs and led legislative initiatives to improve basic living conditions for Maryland prisoners. He currently works with legislators and activists to reopen public hearings on the government's illegal Counterintelligence Program, seeking amnesty for political prisoners incarcerated under COINTELPRO.

5

Domestic Warfare: A Dialogue

Marshall Eddie Conway

Marshall Eddie Conway: [It] is important to be able to understand the climate that existed in the late 1960s and early 1970s in the world that impacted . . . what was going on in America. There was the war in Vietnam, which was a major proponent of international politics, and . . . antiwar demonstrations and activities all around the world in relationship to Vietnam. But there were also wars of liberation in Angola, Mozambique, Guinea Bissau. There was war of liberation in Cambodia, Laos . . . in Uruguay, in Peru, in South America, and on pretty much every continent. In the Philippines, there was an active struggle to throw off the Marcos regime. So around the world, the ruling class or the multinational corporation owners were being threatened by local forces of opposition that were trying to change the relationship of property in their particular areas. They were trying to gain control over their territories and trying to gain control over the means of production in one way or another and make that work in their interest.

In America, as that was happening, there sprung up several movements—the Black Panther Party being one of the most widely recognized; the American Indian Movement being another one; and the anti-imperialist struggle that included the SDS [Students for a Democratic Society], the Weather Underground, the hippie movement or the counter-culture movement. These movements, the activists in these movements, the concepts and the ideas of these movements [were effective] in terms of changing property relationships, in changing how people work together across the board, from community to community, recognizing that there was a common struggle in the white community, the black community, the Native American community, the Asian community, the Latino community. This . . . [posed] a threat to the owners of production, and . . . caused a reaction. . . .

As the Black Panther Party started dealing with food programs, with survival programs, in terms of supplying clothing and stuff, dealing with programs that was allowing them to gain some independent control of resources coming through their community, the government decided to disrupt the Black Panther Party and other groups like that. . . . They infiltrated agent provocateurs and informers in the groups in such a way that they created a climate of suspicion within the groups. That was like the first level of warfare that was launched against the groups.

Dylan Rodríguez: Can you clarify what an "agent provocateur" is?

Conway: Well . . . a normal informer can work for any police agency or anybody and can come in and basically spy on people, report back what is going on, give information, steal records, take pictures, etc. But an agent provocateur is different. An agent provocateur actually goes into an organization and creates illegal activities, creates conspiracies around illegal activities. . . . The Baltimore chapter of the Black Panther Party and the Maryland state chapter . . . [and] all the rest of the chapters in Maryland fell under Baltimore: The Maryland state chapter of the Black Panther Party was set up by an agent provocateur who worked for the National Security Agency.[3] He had spent twenty years in the military; he got out of the military, and they hired him to set up the Black Panther Party in Baltimore and allowed him to become part of the National Steering Committee of the Black Panther Party in Oakland [California] from his position as being head in Maryland.

Now what he did was that he initiated certain activities as the captain among the Panthers—he sent Panthers out to do things that were illegal, and because he was in charge, because most of them were new recruits and a lot of them were being trained directly by him, they didn't know that these were not the things that needed to be done. The consequence of it is that some of them end up getting arrested; at least one of them end up getting killed in a robbery attempt; some of them just disappeared with like no real record of what ever happened to them. . . . Agent provocateurs caused groups to run afoul of the law-enforcement agencies at the behest of the law-enforcement agencies. In one particular case that's reported in materials, a Baltimore agent provocateur had a confrontation with police outside of our headquarters . . . seven or eight other Panthers kind of came to his assistance, got involved, and in a confrontation, end up being arrested. A month later it was discovered that this particular person had been working all along for the police department and had created that kind of scenario.

There have been cases where agent provocateurs have shot at police, ran into the front door of the Panther headquarters, being members of that particular Panther group, ran through the building, ran out the back door, and the police had surrounded that building and attacked the people inside who was completely unaware of what was going on and end up being involved in a shootout, end up getting themselves murder charges, etcetera, end up spending two or three years in jail. The agent provocateur kept on going, and it was only years later that it was discovered what happened. So this is the kind of thing that agent provocateurs do. But they do far more. "Tommy the Traveler" was like infamous. He was shooting in people's windows, he planted bombs, so Gene Roberts, in New York, which was Bobby . . . [Correctional facility: "You have one minute left to talk."]

[Conversation resumes] **Angela:** I have a question about the agent provocateur. . . . Was there ever an instance where you caught one before any illegal activity took place, and if so, what steps did you use to get him out of the organization?

Conway: Well, in fact, the agent provocateur I was talking about that set up the Baltimore chapter . . . Warren Hart was his name . . . was the defense captain. We discovered him during the process of investigation. Since they had the office bugged and everything else, they informed him, and he fled the country. In fact, he showed up two years later in Canada, and he had infiltrated the All-Afrikan Peoples' Revolutionary Party, which was the organization that Stokely Carmichael [Kwame Toure] had established.[4] And he was discovered up there, and he fled to the Caribbean, and after that I don't know what happened to him, but in most cases when agent provocateurs were discovered, they were put in the front of the [*Black Panther*] newspaper. They were basically exposed around the country, all the chapters were warned about them, their pictures were posted, a rundown on who they were and what they had been doing and who they were operating on behalf of—whatever information was available. That happened in most cases. In some cases, there was actual violence on the ground: In the case of Ericka Huggins, Bobby Seale in New Haven [the Connecticut trial], in particular, an agent provocateur had been exposed by another agent provocateur.[5] In fact, that also happened in Baltimore.

What tends to happen in some of these cases was that there were agents from various agencies. There might be a local police agent or informer; there might be a State Police agent or informer; there might be a special prosecution informer or agent; there might be a military-intelligence FBI agent; there might be a National Security agent; and in most cases, these agents did not know who told on who. It was unique in California in the sense of Luis Packwood and Melvin "Cotton" [Smith] and several other agents out in California. They worked together and kind of knew each other. But in most local chapters, agents [ran] operations under deep cover, and they were operations to point fingers at other people and keep attention off of themselves, so suspicion rose in various chapters about information leaking or a bug being found planted or some other kind of thing. Everyone would be pointing the finger at other individuals, and in some cases these other individuals might have in fact been agents also and unknown to the agents or the people who have been calling them out, and there actually violence occurred. Some people were disappeared; some people were actually assassinated; and in a couple of places, some people were tortured. But for the most part, the official authorized policy was exposure through the newspaper. . . .

When Malcolm X was assassinated, there's a famous picture of him lying on the stage, and a guy is bending over him on the stage giving him mouth-to-mouth resuscitation. This guy was named Gene Roberts. He went on to join the Black Panther Party and the New York 21, which is one of the famous political trials of the Black Panther Party, initiated by an agent provocateur, in which they claim the Panthers were going to bomb the [New York] Botanical Garden, the Macy's department store, the Brooklyn Bridge, Long Island. . . . With this elaborate conspiracy in which twenty-one Panthers ultimately got locked up, there were plans, etcetera. They did two years in jail, and during the trial it was discovered that Gene Roberts, who had been Malcolm X's bodyguard—the same guy that had been on the stage giving him mouth-to-mouth resuscitation—was actually an official police officer working for the New York City Police Department as a deep-cover agent. [In the Panther 21 case], he had provided the plan, encouraged conspiracy, led the discussion, even brought to the meeting fake dynamite to instigate this particular plot. The result of it was that all of the Panthers were released after two years, but it took the main leadership of the New York chapter out of circulation for two years because of this activity.

This is how agent provocateurs operate. They come in; they create these kind of climates, right? In addition to agent provocateurs, it was a high-profile attempt to let everyone in the neighborhood know that the Panther Party was under surveillance in your neighborhood. An actual observation post set up in the neighborhood with cameras in the windows across the street, monitoring the car traffic, monitoring the door traffic, agents changing shifts going in and out—I mean it was, like, obvious that these officers [had put the BPP] under surveillance. And the idea was not directed at the Panthers themselves but directed at the community in the sense of, "You don't want to go in there." It was intimidation for the community at large. It was like, "You'll be observed, there will be files on you, you'll get yourself in trouble." This was another level of harassment that the government was doing to intimidate the community about interacting around the legitimate stuff. Whether they were coming in about a problem they were having with the electricity company or rent problems, or whether they were coming in because they needed food or they needed clothing, or whether they wanted to support the breakfast program or get some medical aid, it didn't matter to the government or government agency. Their job was to intimidate people in such a way as to cause them not to come in. When Panther vehicles traveled around the city, they were constantly stopped, harassed, ticketed, or just in a high-profile way, you know, being made aware that "We know who you are, we know where you are, we know what you're doing." Those things were . . . psychological. I think [J. Edgar] Hoover said at some point, "We don't have to have a spy in every office, but we just need to make you think that we have a spy in every office," and then in most cases people will turn on themselves and turn on each other. The high-profile harassment and observation of the activists in rallies, speaking engagements, in the work area [continued].

The IRS, the FBI, and a number of other agencies were contacting the employers of Panthers or Panther supporters. They were contacting the supporters of the breakfast program. People who would donate in a consistent manner, they would get a letter saying, "You're supporting un-American activities"; "We're going to tell your costumers"; "There will be a boycott of your establishment"; etcetera. So these letters were going out, kind of in secret, saying "Fire this guy. He's a Panther"; "Fire this woman. She's associated with the Panther Party"; "This teacher on her off-duty time actually teaches black children to hate white people." . . .

They did a lot of this, but the most infamous one was they actually created a comic book that they had distributed around the breakfast program, using the agent provocateurs. I believe it was, like, two defense captains . . . took the comic book, which they had produced and printed, and inserted it into the breakfast program, and [our opponents] held it up and said, "Look what they are teaching."[6] [The FBI] smeared the breakfast program to supporters and distributors all across the country using that method, and then these people went to Washington [D.C.] and actually testified in front of the Senate hearing dressed up in the Panther uniform, the leather jacket, the sham, the dark shades, you know, and they looked like poster children for the Black Panther Party. And the whole time, they had been agent provocateurs. And they used that testimony to say that this was the greatest internal threat. This is the [congressional] testimony that led up to Hoover saying [of the Black Panther Party] in 1968: "This is the greatest internal threat to the security of America." . . .

When this kind of behavior did not [deter black, white, Latino, Native American] people from working together and people in the community from supporting those programs, the government intensified its warfare in a sense that people started being assassinated. . . . In several cases, people just disappeared. But in other cases, people were just shot in the street as a result of the government manipulation of other groups, rival groups, hostilities that had existed or were instigated by either agent provocateurs. . . .

In my case, I was actually a victim of an assassination attempt. In the early 1970s while I was incarcerated, I formed a Black Panther Party chapter in the Maryland Penitentiary, and out of a population of 1,200 people, there was maybe 100 Panthers in the population at the time actually engaged in political education, organizing survival programs, that kind of stuff. One day, a guy actually approached . . . nervous and kind of red, and he said, "Look, you know, I've been knowing you and you've been doing good work here . . . and I didn't think you had any ill feelings toward me and if it was anybody else but you we wouldn't be talking." So I noticed the guy, his hands [here] in his jacket, he's got a knife, he's got like a bottle of some sort of fluid in his hand. . . . So I'm, like, you know, this is a problem. I am talking to him, and he's saying, "Well, they told me . . . that you were going to have me knocked off." So I'm, like, well, "Who is this? When did this happen? What's going on? And that's not something that's gonna happen."

So we talked, and what had happened was he had been in the psychological ward. Somebody had hit him in the head a day or two before. The lieutenant that worked in the day shift . . . told him to stay out of the ward the next day because I had ordered the Panthers to kill him. And then they let him out, and they never said anything to me, and I never knew anything about this. So he was armed, and he was ready to actually attack me in fear of his own life. Because he knew the kind of work I was doing. He actually took a minute to talk to me, and because I was completely caught off guard, unprepared, it was the last thing on my mind. Once I discovered that, I took him to the lieutenant and confronted the lieutenant and tried to find out why did they tell this guy this? And if that was true, why didn't you tell me? Why didn't you lock me up? You know? How could you come in on a night shift, when you are off, and tell him that and let him out and then not pull me in for investigation or something? So we end up going and talking to the warden, and it was kind of clear from there on in if something happened to me, in there, you know, this group [of the lieutenant's] . . . would be held responsible inside the jail and outside the jail. . . . But that was out of the blue, you know. I mean, that was completely out of the blue, and had this guy not talked to me, I could have very well been seriously hurt or killed. . . .

This is the kind stuff that they were doing, and people didn't know what was going on and didn't understand. To some degree, it's like, Why would a lieutenant do that? To some degree, it didn't even make any sense, but at that time I was organizing the prisoners into a labor union, and I'm thinking, well, this is a good thing, and it'll improve the lives of the prisoners. It'll give us minimum wages. It'll make us industrious. It'll help us get out, etcetera. You know, it's a good thing. But obviously it represented a threat to the people that were running the prisons. . . . That was the kind of power the guards had. This is the early 1970s, and the guards still have some degree of that power, but it's less now because it's easier for them to be exposed. But during that time it was harder for them to be exposed because they kept prisoners isolated in such a way and they controlled the media in such a way that whatever happened in there, their version was the only version that reached the media, and in most cases it was distorted.

There were actual assassination attempts. There were actual assassinations . . . mysterious bombings and other kind of activities that enforced the paranoia . . . to the point where a Panther, for their own safety, would involve themselves in underground activities, or they would separate themselves completely from the Panther Party and the struggle itself, because it was clear that there were unprovoked attacks. There were gang activities directed toward the Panthers. There were other organizational activities directed toward the Panthers by manipulating elements in both of the groups [East Coast and West Coast Panthers] to actually create a conflict. This level of warfare went on to the point where people start going underground. And they start fighting back and resisting on some level. . . . The Panthers created the Black Liberation Army [BLA]; a number of other groups participated in the Republic of New Afrika;[7] the American Indian Movement; the Weather Underground. . . . Other groups started resisting what was clear then—a pattern of government attacks and assassinations and just falsified imprisonment. . . .

Sormeh: As a political prisoner . . . what does it mean in your opinion to be political? What beliefs or ideologies qualifies one as "political"?

Conway: It's where you're at in location, on the one hand. It's where you're at historically in today's world. There's political prisoners all over the world in various countries. No country recognizes political prisoners, per se, in their country. But all countries recognize political prisoners in other countries. For instance, in China you have a number of dissidents, a number of religious disciples, you have a number of "pro-democracy" activists, and they are recognized in America as political prisoners in China. But, of course, they are not classified that way in China. The same thing could be true in Vietnam or Cuba. There are people in opposition to the political systems there, and they're classified by the Cubans or the Vietnamese as "dissidents." They are classified by the capitalists or Western democracy as "political prisoners." The same is true here in America by the virtue of the fact that the system is a capitalist system. In most cases, people that have an ideology—anticapitalism, socialism, communism, anarchists—and [are] in opposition to the capitalists are classified, in my mind, as political prisoners. . . .

Rodríguez: What does that mean for people who don't have a systematic ideology?

Conway: Well, there is a broader kind of debate going on in America. . . . On the one level, because of the way in which the American system was set up and the plight of black or people of color and poor and oppressed people, some people actually say that all 2.1 million prisoners in America are in fact political prisoners because of the economics and the economic relationship. Only poor people go to jail, and if you're rich or you have connections in most cases you don't go to jail, except in . . . [Correctional facility: You have one minute left to talk.] Okay, I'm gonna have to call back. . . .

[Conversation resumes] **Sormeh:** Earlier you said that to be [a political prisoner is to be] against capitalism, because capitalism is the current state of America. Because it's also white supremacist. Do you think being against white supremacy would qualify one as being political?

Conway: Yes, in fact what happens is in political prisoners, it's a wide range—it's like Plowshares people, for instance, that are opposed to nuclear weapons and nuclear war.[8] They don't necessarily . . . have a political ideology, maybe liberation theology . . . [but are] in opposition to certain political policies and trends, and their behavior reflects that by the activities they take, and as a result they go to jail. That makes them political prisoners. . . . [I]n fact, in this prison here, there was a young guy, Terrance Johnson.[9] He was fifteen years old when . . . he was mistakenly locked up by being identified as his older brother. They took him into the police station, and they took him in the back, and two 250-pound police officers commenced to beating him in the cell. He wrestled the gun away from one of them and shot both of them, killed one, wounded the other, and . . . they gave him, like, twenty-five years or something like that because they realized two things: (1) He was the wrong person; (2) He's, like, a little, skinny fifteen-year-old; and (3) The police were actually beating him up and in the heat of all that he panicked and shot 'em. There was a campaign for his release, and in fact he became a political prisoner in the sense there was an egregious wrong being done. It was clear that if this had been any other child innocently locked up, other than a young black child, then he would have been released and rewarded. So, yeah, white supremacy is one of the things if you're in opposition to that, then your activities are political.

If you're an environmentalist, if you're concerned for the well-being of the planet, if you're concerned about the well-being of the globalization trend, those things cause people to protest the policies of the multinational corporations, and so that makes them, if they get locked up as a result of that . . . whether collectively or singularly, political prisoners. But that's also true in Russia. . . . The people that opposed the Russian system, for whatever reason they opposed it, are in fact political prisoners in that environment, and they are antisocialist or anticommunist. So, it's where you're at and it's what you do and it's also what happens to you.

Rodríguez: Talk a little bit more about what a political prisoner would be in the current context, where we don't have a viable set of liberation movements that people would be attached to. What does it mean to be a political prisoner without organization and without widespread, activist ideologies taking hold among different kinds of people who are in liberation struggles? What's a political prisoner without a liberation struggle?

Conway: The answer in my opinion would be that an activist [is] a person that stands up to injustices, a person [who] for whatever reason takes the position that this or that is wrong, whether they do it based on ideology . . . [or what] is morally right, whether it's in the interest of the community or themselves. . . . Just being beaten by police with flashlights, for instance, and it results in them being prosecuted, it results in them being harassed or locked up, jailed, and so on, they in fact become political prisoners. Now, I think that there's a universal classification for political prisoners, and that's movement-related, activity-related, ideologically related, in a sense that . . . these people were engaged in political activity. But I also have learned over the thirty-some years of being in jail that a lot of people become political prisoners, become conscious and become aware and act and behave based on that awareness after they have been incarcerated for criminal activity or other kinds of activities. That's on one level.

On another level, I'm also aware, like I pointed out about the Terrance Johnson case, there are people who are forced into the position of political prisoners because of some act of the government or some opposition they have presented to the government. In the case of Plowshares activists, even though they were pouring blood on missiles, it was a political act that got them locked up and has them now facing years or so in prison, so this is a different level. So you can operate based on your principles and you can operate in opposition to what appears to be corruption, a morally wrong or legally wrong activity, and you can do it as an individual or you can do it as a collective and . . . if you have operated, you are a political prisoner. . . .

There has always been this activity from the federal government since after the Civil War to suppress movements. It started off with the early labor movements in the 1880s—that is, it started off against the Grangers, the Populist movement in the Midwest, and so on.[10] It eventually rolled into the World War I antiwar movement, the Workers of the World, industrial unions.[11] There was always the attempt to dismantle, disrupt, or deport [activists]. Movements were attacked illegally by breaking and entering, attacked by vigilantes, etcetera. This stuff went through World War II, the McCarthy era [in the 1950s], and by the time of the Panthers, the liberation movement and so on, there was experience that was gained by the CIA, which was initially the OSS [Office of Strategic Services], during World War II.[12] . . . Behind the active line, they undermined the Germans, the French forces, they undermined activities in Italy, France, etcetera. They used these activities, and there's a good book out called *Killing Hope*.[13] They used these activities in the late '40s, early '50s to undermine European governments [in France, Germany, Italy, Greece] that were being formed after World War II that had a socialist or communist bent. . . . In Iraq and Iran, movements that were progressive in nature . . . were actually putting people in power who were anti-American, anti-multinational corporations. [The CIA] used various counterintelligence programs to destroy those movements, and in most cases they put in movements that were pro-capitalism and favorable to [the United States]. As a result of the success they had around the world, they brought those programs home [as] counterintelligence programs against the domestic opposition that was developing.

They were using the drugs initially to finance the secret clandestine wars in Laos and in central and south Vietnam. In Cambodia, they were actually taking drugs out of the country and into the United States in very different ways, and they were selling those drugs and financing illegal armies that were controlling [parts] of Laos, central Vietnam, and Cambodia. These drugs ended up in the poor communities, and they used these drugs to help undermine the liberation movements that were occurring in the poor communities in America. In the late 1960s and the early 1970s, an explosion of drugs, an explosion of films, songs, portrayals of the superfly, hip . . . drug imagery and drug culture was spread, and that happened in conjunction with a number of soldiers returning from Vietnam having been introduced to drugs in Vietnam and strung out and eventually brought those same habits home. Well, the federal government used the agencies. They took the stuff that they were doing against the Black Panthers [and] they turned it to some degree into DEA [Drug Enforcement Agency] activity, and they used surveillance, informers, agent provocateurs, the IRS, and other agencies to wage a war against the larger community.

The relationship to that and unemployment is key. We talk now about runaway jobs and runaway factories, but that stuff started in the 1970s. At some point, the industrial bases, the manufacturing base of America was shipped overseas to low labor markets where they had two-dollar-a-day workers. They moved their plants out, but as a result of moving those plants out, there was massive unemployment in the urban areas. Then the only viable means of economic gain was to sell drugs, distribute drugs, or get caught up in the drug economy and the drug culture. The main-line manufacturing jobs were gone, so that's a relationship there. [The government] used those drugs to come into the communities, to find out who was doing what in the communities to actually turn those drug dealers, drug users, drug informers against the liberation movement and the liberation-movement people. At the same time they were doing that, there was a third type of activity going on, and it was basically known as "model cities." It was in relationship and in conjunction to affirmative action. They used those model-cities programs to take away the "middle-class" professional, intellectual elements in the community that would buy into this program or that program and in terms of small businesses running this center or running that shop. They used that to take away—it's really like a pacification program—to take away elements that might have been instrumental in building a solid liberation movement for black independence or black self-determination. So the relationship between the jobs being gone, the drugs coming in, COINTELPRO actually becoming codified and official, because that's what happened with the DEA and so on, these things became legal. The RICO [Racketeer Influenced and Corrupt Organizations] Act and all of these things were actually authorized by law at some point.[14] . . .

The RICO Act focused on conspiracy. If one part of an organization does something, the entire group and its associates are participants in the specific act. They used RICO then. Now the PATRIOT Act has actually codified those things that were illegal activities, like the illegal entry of the so-called black-bag operations that the FBI would do—they would break in, photograph stuff, they would steal stuff. . . . In fact, it's against the Bill of Rights, illegal search and seizure [Article IV]. [The PATRIOT Act] actually authorizes that activity for sixty to ninety days without even informing anybody that that kind of activity has occurred. From COINTELPRO, from those days, they build on that stuff, legal coverage for that stuff. They actually turn those kind of activities into laws, and now those are impacting on everybody, from the point of reading your health records to checking your business stuff. . . . They have the right to go in the library and request the materials that you're reading; the right to go into your computer database and look at what websites you visit with the program; they have the right to monitor your telephone if you are associated with somebody that's under investigation, even if you're not under investigation and you're not accused of anything. It's a roving surveillance now. . . . Say five years ago you donated money to a Palestinian charity that's now been classified on the "terrorist" list. You can be subject now to investigation for something that was not illegal five years ago that you did. The government has, without the American population fully appreciating it, actually established, in my mind, a level of fascism that's so sophisticated that it's almost invisible, but it exists. . . .

Jollee: In your thesis, you provided a number of factors for the downfall of the Black Panther Party. One of them is the overemphasis on recruiting of the underclass. So when you were talking about drugs in lower-class neighborhoods and the importance of the middle-class element and the "model-city" thing, why do you think that the emphasis of the underclass was a negative factor? Was it because they were more vulnerable to agent provocateurs? Why do you think the middle class is such an important element for the movement?

Conway: Well, I think initially that overemphasis on using that particular class of people became a problem [based on] behavior that was already in place that hadn't been corrected in terms of putting an ideology in place, putting a discipline in place. There was a certain degree on the street level of resistance to repression that takes on a physical form in poor communities. You'll see it every week. Well, I don't know if you will now, but it used to be that Friday, Saturday, Sunday nights there would be fights. There would be a certain level of violent resistance. There would be a certain kind of interaction with the police. The police would be in the black community, in the poor communities. They would be busting people in the heads. There would be bottles thrown, bricks thrown, and there would be resistance. There would be toe-to-toe, knock-down, drag-outs, beat-down kind of situations that were occurring. This was a normal kind of response, and these behaviors came into the Black Panther Party. In moments of conflict, tempers flared; the behavior exhibited itself. It was easy for agent provocateurs to manipulate that kind of behavior. It was easy for agent provocateurs to jump out and create something, and everybody else would say, "OK, we've got to support you." . . . I guess my emphasis is on the need—and I think we were doing it to a great degree, because the Panthers were a wide-range mix, even though they say at the highest point it was only 5,000 [members], for a wide mixture of people from professional, middle class, youth, men, women, to what I call the lumpen proletariat." [Correctional facility: "You have one minute left to talk."] Even intellectuals, but let me call back. . . .

[Conversation resumes.] **Conway:** The other side of that was the middle class, professionals, people that I thought, and I think, [were] distracted away from the movement. [They] were providing skills that other people were learning, all of these things were learnable skills, but . . . at some point you actually have [to have] a basis of producing a newspaper; you have to have the wherewithal to run logistically a food-distribution [program]; you have to have a certain level of skill, even though we were training people, sort of like barefoot doctors, to do first aid and sickle-cell–anemia [testing] and medical care. But you have to start with a basis. You have to start with some skill level. You have to start with people that have been trained somewhere in order to move forward. I think those people were siphoned off and taken away from the movement.

Jollee: So when you talk about . . . resistance to oppression by the lower class and the Friday night police brutality against the lower-class people, doesn't that complicate the definition of political "prisoners"?

Conway: Well, the definition of political prisoner is complicated anyway, because, depending on who you talk to and when you talk to them, there's opinions of all 2 million people that are presently incarcerated in the prison system as being political prisoners. There's all the way down to a narrow group of 150 to 200 people. There are some people that don't even recognize the Islamic Jihad as political prisoners. There's probably close to 1,000 of those people in various jails around the world in fact under control of America at Guantánamo Bay and so on. So it depends. . . . [T]hat definition is probably going to be debated forever for what actually constitutes a political prisoner, and to a great degree I see political prisoners on three different levels, as I think I expressed earlier. . . . There are obviously domestic and other kind of activities that don't qualify, given the nature of the economic system itself and the impact of oppression on people and how they tend to take that oppression out on each other in a domestic setting. I think Frantz Fanon's [work on the] "native intellectuals" [states that], for fear of challenging the oppressor itself, . . . the [colonized] internalize violence [and conflict on each other].[15] . . .

Conway: In my experience, I've only been in a couple of major jails . . . for the most part the [prison] populations don't recognize opposition to the American political system. I'm talking 90 percent of the population don't recognize that there is a . . . "problem" with the relationship to the legal economic system, and in most cases they feel they have made some sort of major mistake in their life, in their life choices. Those mistakes resulted in them coming to jail or constantly coming to jail. They kind of accept that [and] figure out what they can do to re-insert themselves into the economic system so that they can become entrepreneurs. In the sense of Christopher Columbus, they want to exploit somebody and get wealthy. . . . I think the prison population [has] more support for the mechanisms of the capitalist system and the concepts of the capitalist system than for change or an understanding that there is a need to change. . . . For the most part, there is in the minds of prisoners [that this is] a good system. . . .

Sormeh: Do you think it becomes problematic when what Fanon calls the "native intellectual" organizes or disciplines what you call the "lumpen proletariat"? . . .

Conway: I don't. It depends on where that organizing goes, and what that organizing is based on. . . . If the ideology [that] the intellectual organizes with is an ideology that supports the well-being and the benefit of the masses, the lumpen proletariat, the poor and oppressed class, there's gonna be an integration between those elements, from the lower class, the middle class, the intellectual. But if the ideology is the ideology that's being promoted by the middle class or the intellectuals. . . . I mean, if you come, if you join the masses and in the interest of the masses, like Ché Guevara, and in their interests you use that intellectual ability . . . to work to cover those goals, then there's an integration there that will shake that movement forward. . . .

Rodríguez: I think that's precisely what happened at the site of the university with so-called people of color, and especially with Africana, black studies, and ethnic studies departments, which were conceived as a way not just to organize with the so-called lumpen proletariat but also to open up, actually to program or deprogram for poor people of color. What you see now is actually a kind of replication of the model-cities–program approach.

Conway: Yeah, initially those black student unions and whatnot sprung from the Black Panther movement, in a lot of cases, and certainly sprung from the Black Liberation Movement, and they were designed to bring a consciousness and education to the broader community, to influence those universities, university policies, and to expand . . . participation in those institutions for the benefit of the black community. I think now probably what you have is people that benefit culturally and intellectually, but that doesn't come back to the community. It's lost that connection between what the community needed and what's actually going on. That wasn't the initial concept when it was developed, and it's similar to the model-cities program in a lot of cases then.

Rodríguez: I have a question [that] leads into the discussion of the efforts to reopen an investigation or tribunal of the legacies of COINTELPRO and the absence of any sustained discussion among so-called U.S. leftists, especially white leftists, about the existence of ongoing domestic warfare against black and Third World people. There's just no conversation of it. I want to get your thoughts on why.

Conway: Initially, I would think that there was the impact of COINTELPRO, and even the neo-COINTELPRO programs, because COINTELPRO was technically supposed to end in the early 1970s. It was discovered that there would still be operations in the late 1970s—the Sanctuary Movement that was bringing in people from El Salvador and Guatemala and other South American places where they had military dictatorships and people were being murdered.[16] [People] were discovered to be under the federal government FBI investigation, scrutiny, infiltration into the 1980s. The American Friends Service Committee was discovered even into the 1990s to be under scrutiny and investigation by police agencies and government agencies. I think the movements, the white left, as well as the movements in the black liberation [movement] and other movements . . . were actually traumatized. When I talk to people in the past thirty years, there's serious trauma that resulted from COINTELPRO. . . . I think the movement itself not only was traumatized, but I think the remnants of it, the people that were left, in some degree panicked. I think that they are just starting to recover to some small degree with a new generation of people. I think the activists of my generation, in their fifties and their sixties, [were] not only traumatized, not only panicked, but in some cases, in most cases, they burned out.

I think that through the 1980s and the early 1990s, there was such a degree of demonization, if I can use that term, predatoriness, or criminalization. *Boyz in the Hood, Menace 2 Society*, the predatory young black male, and now female, has created an image, and even in the movement, and in most other communities, that basically has led to people being terrified of the black community and elements of the black community. . . . That terror has led to a tentative justification of—or, at least, apathy toward—the attacks that are constantly being launched. . . . I mentioned earlier the flashlight beatings. That stuff goes on in our community all the time. Everywhere across the country, there's a low-intensity warfare going on. Folks are being shot. But the mass media has created that imagery and the feeling of insecurity among the American population, [and] it's accepted those images as the prevailing image. In other words, it's hell down there, and whatever's going on down there is going on down there, and we don't want to get involved. There's drugs, criminal activity. They deserve it. It's dangerous. It's because of the low-intensity warfare that exists between the haves and the have-nots [that] it's easy to fall into the pattern, into the belief, that these people are detrimental and need to be controlled, and whatever's being done to control them is acceptable, and there's no point in speaking out about it because we are at risk in our community if they are not controlled. . . . Young people are fighting to overcome these stereotypes now. . . . It's small pockets of protests here and there, but for the most part you don't have any kind of staying activity around the military occupation of the community, because a lot of the people in the community feel threatened, feel at risk, feel insecure because of the economics and the conflict between the haves and the have-nots. . . .

[When] you start supporting things that are in your neighborhood, you actually have to get down there, you actually have to put your body on the line, so to speak. It becomes uncomfortable . . . and I think to a great degree, that's part of it. . . . You can't discount the fact of white supremacy, and don't for any reason think that white supremacy means that's just what white people think, because there's actually a number of people of color in here with me that are white supremacists or influenced greatly by that whole concept. They are pro-American, pro-war—they're brought into that whole concept. It's easier to do things that you can do and [be] safe [when] you don't have to confront the ruling class, you don't have to confront the forces of oppression that's down on the street. You don't have to confront the opposition.

Maybe I'm taking a leap here, [but] that's kind of how fascism is. It's always easier on the fascists [for progressives] to protest things that are distant, but it's unacceptable and dangerous to involve yourself in domestic activities. There's a penalty, there's a sanction about domestic involvement, and there's just a tentative OK if you're talking about [Abu Ghraib], South America, or policies in China. . . . It gives the appearance of freedom of speech, freedom of opposition, but if that opposition or that speech takes on concrete conditions and contradictions that are internal and domestic, then there's a violent [Correctional facility: "You have one minute left to talk."] swift reaction against those elements that's bringing that to attention. . . .

[Conversation resumes.] On the one hand, you have consciousness, whether it's anarchist, whether it's socialist or communist or environmentalist, or whatever you have this interest to make changes and so on. But on the other hand, you have privilege. You have not just privilege, but you have a perspective of the world. Your paradigm is influenced by different factors. In other words, you don't know, you don't see, you don't feel, you don't experience the violence that occurs and the repression and the opposition that occurs in the black community, with the police forces keeping the black community under tight rein. In your community, you don't experience that. You don't understand that "Officer Friendly" in your community turns into a storm trooper in poor communities. You don't understand when people say they experience racism . . . they can't get a job, they can't get loans, they can't get things. You don't experience it because there is a certain amount of . . . comforts and material accumulation that has resulted from white supremacy and of colonizing the world that has insulated you in a sense that you're comfortable. . . .

Even if you don't have privileges, you can recognize [that] opportunities exist throughout the community. If you're talking socialist, whatever leftist politics, you still see reform, electoral reform, and other kinds of reform as a method by which you can achieve your ends. Things can be changed. We can move forward with this. There is no need for a radical confrontation with the system. Things can't be that bad. There's a tendency to blame the victim: "Well, they just don't have the skills. Well, they just don't behave in the right way, they don't take the opportunity." So there's a different paradigm at work based on material [conditions], based on historical accumulation of wealth, based on institutional protections, based on a psychology that basically says, "Look, we made great advances in the last 200 years, and look at the rest of the world." . . . Unconsciously, there's a paradigm that develops based on all of those things that people can't really appreciate. They can't walk a mile in our shoes. They can't see where we're at, because they really don't understand where we're at. I mean, they can read it, they can hear about it, they can even come through and see an incident here or there that they basically say is an exception, or they can get an impression of something but they don't understand, that this is our life. So they don't respond in the same way, and they don't see the same thing we see. In fact, they tend to think that we might be exaggerating the things that we are saying, or we might be overly sensitive—in short, get over it. . . .

Sormeh: In the context of white supremacy, because white people have the right to live or the right to bodily safety, whereas people of color, especially black people, don't, at what point or junction do you see political alliance with white people possible, if it is at all?

Conway: Well, of course, political alliances with all people [are possible]. You know, white supremacy, even though it's pervasive and universal in many ways, is still an ideology. Racism is another ideology. Nationalism is a different kind of ideology. I think all ideologies at some point somewhere have to be called into question in such a way that we look at them and see how they work to create unity. And when I say nationalism, I'm saying the kind of nationalism that divides the human race. I think we need to be looking at the things that unify the human race, and when we're talk about unifying the human race, we have to cease talking about white folks, as well as Native Americans, Latinos, blacks. So there is that possibility of alliances, and there's always been alliances, to some degree, and every alliance is going to bring its own baggage and it's going to bring its own limitations, and those alliances need to be developed in such a way that there's a common goal and a common struggle.

Notes

Editor's note: The phone dialogue took place between Marshall Eddie Conway and Dylan Rodríguez and his ethnic studies class at the University of California, Riverside, in July 2004. Dominique Stevenson assisted in facilitating the dialogue; Raquel España transcribed the interview. The research and draft for the introduction were provided by Dylan Rodríguez.

1. Marshall Eddie Conway Support Committee, "Baltimore Black Panther Fights for Justice," press release, July 17, 1998. See also Conway, "Imprisoned Black Panther Party Members"; and "Marshall Eddie Conway," in Committee to End the Marion Lockdown, *Can't Jail the Spirit: Political Prisoners in the United States*, 102.

2. *Baltimore City Paper*, February 15, 1990.

3. *Editor's note*: On October 24, 1952, President Harry Truman, in a secret memorandum, established the NSA as a separately organized agency within the Department of Defense. The NSA, which relocated to Fort Meade, Maryland, in 1956, became the largest intelligence agency in the U.S. government. Its responsibilities included communications intelligence, coordination of specialized activities to protect U.S. information systems, and direction of foreign intelligence information. NSA officials or operatives also used technology to target and disrupt domestic dissidents, such as the Black Panther Party. See Harry Truman, "Truman Memorandum," October 24, 1952, available online at http://jya.com/nsa102452.htm (accessed August 18, 2004);

Bamford, *Body of Secrets*; "National Security Agency," available online at http://www
.nsa.gov (accessed August 18, 2004).

4. *Editor's note*: After a 1966 imperialist coup in Ghana, Kwame Nkrumah, the first
Ghanian president (1964–66), called for the formation of the All-Afrikan People's
Revolutionary Party (A-APRP). Nkrumah founded the A-APRP in 1972 with the aid
of Stokeley Carmichael (Kwame Toure), former chairman of the Student Nonviolent
Coordinating Committee and prime minister of the Oakland chapter of the Black
Panther Party, to coordinate African revolutionary parties. See Nkrumah, *Handbook
of Revolutionary Warfare*; Carson, *In Struggle*; "Dedication to the A-APRP," available online at http://www.members.aol.com/aaprp/index.html (accessed August 18,
2004).

5. *Editor's note*: In 1971, Ericka Huggins and Bobby Seale, along with other members
of the Black Panther Party (who came to be known as the "New Haven 9"), stood
trial in New Haven for the May 1969 murder of Alex Rackley, a member of the New
York chapter of the BPP who was suspected of being a police informant. Seale and
Huggins were acquitted by a hung jury. George Sams, Warren Kimbro, and Lonnie
McLucas were convicted on various charges for Rackley's murder. It is alleged that
George Sams, who identified Rackley as an informant and called for his execution,
was himself an FBI agent provocateur. See Edward Jay Epstein, "The Black Panthers
and the Police: A Pattern of Genocide?" *The New Yorker* (February 13, 1971); Freed,
Agony in New Haven.

6. *Editor's note*: In the late 1960s, as part of their efforts to destroy the Black Panther
Party's free breakfast program, the FBI distributed a twenty-four-page coloring book
featuring pictures of black youth shooting pigs dressed as policemen. Claiming that
the book was created by the Panthers, the FBI sent it to Safeway Stores, Mayfair Markets, and the Jack-in-the-Box Corporation to discourage contributions to the free
breakfast program. See U.S. Senate, "The FBI's Covert Action Program to Destroy
the Black Panther Party," final report of the Select Committee to Study Government
Operations with Respect to Intelligence Activities, April 23, 1976, available online
at http://www.raven1.net/cointelpro/churchfinalreportIIIc.htm (accessed August 18,
2004).

7. *Editor's note*: The Republic of New Afrika (RNA), organized by Imari A. Obadele I
in 1968, called for the creation of an independent black nation spanning the states
of Alabama, Georgia, Louisiana, Mississippi, and South Carolina. Members of the
RNA, which was founded on principles of black self-determination, cooperative economics, and community self-sufficiency, referred to themselves as "New Afrikans."
They named a provisional RNA government, with Obadele as president, and their
demands include that the U.S. government pay $400 billion in reparations for the
injustices of slavery and racism. Now based in Washington, D.C., the RNA continues

to advocate the establishment of an African American nation in the U.S. South. See Sundiata Acoli, "An Updated History of the New Afrikan Prison Struggle," in James, *Imprisoned Intellectuals*, 138–64; Obadele, *Revolution and Nation-Building*; and idem, "A People's Revolt for Power and an Up-Turn in the Black Condition."

8. *Editor's note*: The Plowshares Movement began in 1980 when the brothers Daniel and Philip Berrigan, along with six others, entered a General Electric weapons-manufacturing plant in King of Prussia, Pennsylvania, and hammered and poured their blood on nuclear warheads. The name of the movement came from the book of Isaiah's injunctions to "beat swords into plowshares." Since 1980, there have been over fifty Plowshares actions. See Berrigan, *The Trial of the Catonsville Nine*; Berrigan and Wilcox, *Fighting the Lamb's War*; Laffin, *Swords into Plowshares*; and Carol Gilbert, "Ponderings from the Eternal Now," in this volume.

9. *Editor's note*: In 1978, Terrance Johnson, a fifteen-year-old resident of Prince George's County, Maryland, was falsely arrested on suspicion of breaking into a vending machine. Johnson, who maintains that the arresting officers, James Brian Swart and Albert Claggett IV, abused him in an interrogation room to coerce a confession, grabbed Swart's pistol and killed both officers. Johnson was found innocent of one of the killings by reason of temporary insanity but was given a twenty-five-year sentence for manslaughter for the other. Johnson served sixteen years before being released in 1994, the longest prison term anyone has ever served for manslaughter in the State of Maryland. See *The Diamondback: An Independent Student Newspaper*, University of Maryland, College Park, 1996, available online at http://www.inform. umd.edu/News/Diamondback/1996-editions/04-April-editions/960416-Tuesday/ ED-Cop_killer,_Esq (accessed September 14, 2004).

10. *Editor's note*: In 1867, Oliver H. Kelley, an employee of the U.S. Department of Agriculture, organized farmers into the Patrons of Husbandry to facilitate the development of new farming methods. Known as the Grangers, this group of farmers influenced the passage of regulatory legislation to counter price fixing by railroads and grain-storage facilities. The Grangers' cooperative endeavors made them targets of anticommunist sentiment and repression. Out of the Granger movement grew the Populist movement of the 1890s. The Populist Party, which focused on economic reform and a redistribution of wealth, endorsed labor unions and advocated for workers' rights. See Zinn, *A People's History of the United States*.

11. *Editor's note*: In 1905, representatives of forty-three groups who opposed the conservative policies of the American Federation of Labor formed a more radical organization, the Industrial Workers of the World (IWW). The IWW, unlike other labor organizations, welcomed immigrants, advocated reform of the economic system, and spoke out against U.S. involvement in World War I. Ibid.

12. *Editor's note*: In July 1942, during World War II, President Franklin D. Roosevelt cre-

ated the OSS to replace the former American intelligence system, Office of the Co-ordinator of Information (OCI). The purpose of the OSS was to collect and analyze information about enemy nations and to sabotage their morale and war potential. The OSS was disbanded in 1945, and many of its functions were assumed by the CIA and directed against domestic "enemies" of the state. See Office of Strategic Services Operation Groups, home page, available online at http://www.ossog.org (accessed August 16, 2004).

13. *Editor's note*: See Blum, *Killing Hope*.

14. *Editor's note*: In 1970, Congress passed the RICO Act, Title 18, U.S. Code, secs. 1961–68. At the time, Congress's goal was to eliminate the negative impact of "organized crime" on the nation's economy. The RICO Act, however, which allows courts to try individuals soley based on their membership in or association with an organization, has been used repeatedly to justify the mass arrest and incarceration of radical activists. To read the text of the RICO Act, see "Racketeer Influenced and Corruption Organizations," available online at http://usinfo.state.gov/usa/infousa/laws/majorlaw/rico/rico.htm (accessed August 16, 2004).

15. *Editor's note*: See Fanon, *The Wretched of the Earth*.

16. *Editor's note*: During the Reagan administration in the 1980s, the U.S. government supported or funded Latin American death squads in Central American and South American countries engaged in civil war. U.S. support contributed to refugees and an estimated 70,000 political killings in El Salvador; 20,000 deaths from the contra war in Nicaragua; 200 political "disappearances" in Honduras; and 100,000 deaths largely of indigenous peoples in Guatemala. The Sanctuary Movement, which emerged in response to these human-rights violations and the inhumane treatment of war refugees, was organized primarily by churches and other religious groups to aid refugees and oppose U.S. foreign policy. When the Sanctuary Movement became a target of FBI activity, its members reported more than three hundred incidents of harassment from 1984 through 1988, including the theft or damage of papers, files, and computer documents. See Coutin, *The Culture of Protest*; Tomsho, *The American Sanctuary Movement*.

GEORGE JACKSON

George Lester Jackson was born on September 23, 1941, on the West Side of Chicago, the second of Georgia and Lester Jackson's five children. The family settled in the Troop Street Projects, where truancy and conflicts with the police became routine for George Jackson. In 1956, seeking to protect his son, Lester Jackson transferred his post office job to Los Angeles. Yet soon after settling in Los Angeles, George began to have serious confrontations with the law. After an attempted burglary and possession of a stolen motorcycle (which he claimed to have purchased), he was sent to Paso Robles School for Boys, an institution of the California Youth Authority. In Paso Robles, during his seven-month sentence, he read the works of Rafael Sabatini and Jack London.[1]

In 1958, a few months after his parole, Jackson and several friends were arrested for robberies to which he pled guilty. He escaped from Bakersfield Jail and was recaptured to serve the rest of his sentence. After his release, on September 18, 1960, he allegedly drove the getaway car after his friend robbed a gas station of seventy-one dollars. He agreed to confess in return for a light sentence; the judge gave him one year to life, a sentence designed to allow judicial flexibility but that ultimately proved to be a life sentence for George Jackson. Initially sent to Soledad prison, he was transferred at least four times during his incarceration. During his first years, he and his close friend James Carr gained power and respect within prison as the leaders of a gang called the Wolf Pack. Each year, Jackson was denied parole because of infractions.

W. L. Nolen, a major figure in the black liberation movement, was the first to introduce Jackson to radical philosophy. As Jackson's disciplinary record grew, he was forced to spend up to twenty-three hours a day in solitary confinement. There he read Karl Marx, V. I. Lenin, Leon Trotsky, Friedrich Engels, Mao Tse-tung (Zedong), and other political theorists. In 1968, Jackson, Nolen, David Johnson, Carr, and other revolutionary convicts began leading "ethnic-awareness classes"—study groups on radical philosophy. These meetings led to the formation of the Black Guerrilla Family, a revolutionary organization (described by authorities as a "gang") that proclaimed black prisoners' rights to self-defense.

In January 1969, Jackson and Nolen were transferred to Soledad Prison, notorious among racist prisons. In the O Wing, which housed Soledad's most dangerous captives, racial tension led to the closing of the exercise yard. Nolen and five other black inmates were preparing civil suits against the O Wing guards for their complicity in creating a dangerous and racially divisive atmosphere.

On January 13, 1970, guards reopened the O Wing exercise yard and released a racially mixed group of prisoners, fully aware of the potential for violence.[2] The fight that began was ended by the marksman Opie Mills, who fired four shots, killing the African American inmates Nolen, Jackson's mentor, Cleveland Edwards, and Alvin Miller and wounding a white prisoner.[3] Three days later, a Monterey County grand jury ruled the deaths "justifiable homicide." Following the publicizing of the ruling, a guard, John V. Mills, was thrown to his death from the third tier of Y Wing, George Jackson's cellblock.

One month later, with no physical evidence, Jackson, Fleeta Drumgo, and John Cluchette were indicted for killing Mills. Huey P. Newton requested that his attorney, Fay Stender, meet with Jackson. After doing so, Stender subsequently formed the Soledad Brothers Defense Committee, which eventually was headed by Angela Y. Davis. Stender also arranged for the publication of *Soledad Brother: The Prison Letters of George Jackson.*[4]

On August 7, 1970, Jackson's seventeen-year-old brother, Jonathan, entered the Marin County Courthouse—with weapons registered in the name of Angela Davis—during the trial of the prisoner James McClain, who was charged with the attempted stabbing of a Soledad guard. Jonathan Jackson armed McClain and, with the prisoner witnesses Ruchell Magee and William Christmas, took the assistant district attorney, Judge Harold Haley, and three jurors into a van parked outside. Following state procedure on escapes, law-enforcement officers fired on the parked van holding Jackson, the prisoners, and their hostages, killing Judge Haley, Christmas and McClain, and Jonathan Jackson, and wounding Magee and several hostages.

During an escape attempt on August 21, 1971, guards shot George Jackson in the back. The exact events still remain unclear. *Blood in My Eye* was completed a week before Jackson's death.

Soledad Brother and
Blood in My Eye (Excerpts)

George Jackson

"Letter to Fay Stender"

Dear Fay,

On the occasion of your and Senator Dymally's tour and investigation into the affairs here at Soledad, I detected in the questions posed by your team a desire to isolate some rationale that would explain why racism exists at the prison with "particular prominence."[5] Of course the subject was really too large to be dealt with in one tour and in the short time they allowed you, but it was a brave scene. My small but mighty mouthpiece, and the black establishment senator and his team, invading the state's maximum security row in the worst of its concentration camps. I think you are the first woman to be allowed to inspect these facilities. Thanks from all. The question was too large, however. It's tied into the question of why all these California prisons vary in character and flavor in general. It's tied into the larger question of why racism exists in this whole society with "particular prominence," tied into history. Out of it comes another question. Why do California joints produce more Bunchy Carters and Eldridge Cleavers than those over the rest of the country?[6]

I understand your attempt to isolate the set of localized circumstances that give to this particular prison's problems of race is based on a desire to aid us right now, in the present crisis. There are some changes that could be made right now that would alleviate some of the pressures inside this and other prisons. But to get at the causes, you know, one would be forced to deal with questions at the very center of Amerikan political and economic life, at the core of the Amerikan historical experience. This prison didn't come to exist where it does just by happenstance. Those who inhabit it and feed off its existence are historical products. The great majority of Soledad pigs are southern migrants who do not want to work in the fields and farms of the area, who couldn't sell cars or insurance, and who couldn't tolerate the discipline of the army. And of course prisons attract sadists. After one concedes that racism is stamped unalterably into the present nature of Amerikan sociopolitical and economic life in general (the definition of fascism is: a police state wherein the political ascendancy is tied into and protects the interests of the upper class—characterized by militarism, racism, and imperialism), and concedes further that criminals and crime arise from material, economic, sociopolitical causes, we can then burn all of the criminology and penology libraries and direct our attention where it will do some good.

The logical place to begin any investigation into the problems of California prisons is with our "pigs are beautiful" Governor [Ronald] Reagan, radical reformer turned reactionary. For a real understanding of the failure of prison policies, it is senseless to continue to study the criminal. All of those who can afford to be honest know that the real victim, that poor, uneducated, disorganized man who finds himself a convicted criminal, is simply the end result of a long chain of corruption and mismanagement that starts with people like Reagan and his political appointees in Sacramento. After one investigates Reagan's character (what makes a turncoat) the next logical step in the inquiry would be a look into the biggest political prize of the state—the directorship of the Department of Correction.

All other lines of inquiry would be like walking backward. You'll never see where you're going. You must begin with directors, assistant directors, adult authority boards, roving boards, supervisors, wardens, captains, and guards. You have to examine these people from director down to guard before you can logically examine their product. Add to this some concrete and steel, barbed wire, rifles, pistols, clubs, the tear gas that killed Brother [Fred] Billingslea in San Quentin in February 1970 while he was locked in his cell and the pick handles of Folsom, San Quentin, and Soledad.[7]

To determine how men will behave once they enter the prison it is of first importance to know that prison. Men are brutalized by their environment—not the reverse.

I gave you a good example of this when I saw you last. Where I am presently being held, they never allow us to leave our cell without first handcuffing us and belting or chaining the cuffs to our waists. This is preceded always by a very thorough skin search. A force of a dozen or more pigs can be expected to invade the row at any time searching and destroying personal effects. The attitude of the staff toward the convicts is both defensive and hostile. Until the convict gives in completely it will continue to be so. By giving in, I mean prostrating oneself at their feet. Only then does their attitude alter itself to one of paternalistic condescension. Most convicts don't dig this kind of relationship (though there are some who do love it) with a group of individuals demonstrably inferior to the rest of the society in regard to education, culture, and sensitivity. Our cells are so far from the regular dining area that our food is always cold before we get it. Some days there is only one meal that can be called cooked. We never get anything but cold-cut sandwiches for lunch. There is no variety to the menu. The same things week after week. One is confined to his cell twenty-three and a half hours a day. Overt racism exists unchecked. It is not a case of the pigs trying to stop the many racist attacks; they actively encourage them.

They are fighting upstairs right now. It's 11:10 A.M., June 11. No black is supposed to be on the tier upstairs with anyone but other blacks but—mistakes take place—and one or two blacks end up on the tier with nine or ten white convicts frustrated by the living conditions or openly working with the pigs. The whole ceiling is trembling. In hand-to-hand combat we always win; we lose sometimes if the pigs give them knives or zip guns. Lunch will be delayed today, the tear gas or whatever it is drifts down to sting my nose and eyes. Someone is hurt bad. I hear the meat wagon from the hospital being brought up. Pigs probably gave them some weapons. But I must be fair. Sometimes (not more often than necessary) they'll set up one of the Mexican or white convicts. He'll be one who has not been sufficiently racist in his attitudes. After the brothers (enraged by previous attacks) kick on this white convict whom the officials have set up, he'll fall right into line with the rest.

I was saying that the great majority of the people who live in this area of the state and seek their employment from this institution have overt racism as a *traditional* aspect of their characters. The only stops that regulate how far they will carry this thing come from the fear of losing employment here as a result of the outside pressures to control the violence. That is O Wing, Max (Maximum Security) Row Soledad—in part anyway.

Take an individual who has been in the general prison population for a time. Picture him as an average convict with the average twelve-year-old mentality, the nation's norm. He wants out, he wants a woman and a beer. Let's say this average convict is white and has just been caught attempting to escape. They may put him on Max Row. This is the worst thing that will ever happen to him.

In the general population facility there are no chains and cuffs. TVs, radios, record players, civilian sweaters, keys to his own cell for daytime use, serve to keep his mind off his real problems. There is also a recreation yard with all sorts of balls and instruments to strike or thrust at. There is a gym. There are movies and a library well stocked with light fiction. And of course there is work, where for two or three cents an hour convicts here at Soledad make paper products, furniture, and clothing. Some people actually like this work since it does provide some money for the small things and helps them to get through their day—*without thinking* about their real problems.

Take an innocent con out of this general population setting (because a pig "thought" he may have seen him attempting a lock). Bring him to any part of o Wing (the worst part of the adjustment center of which Max Row is a part). He will be cuffed, chained, belted, pressured by the police who think that every convict should be an informer. He will be pressured by the white cons to join their racist brand of politics (they *all* go under the nickname "Hitler's Helpers"). If he is presidposed [*sic*] to help black he will be pushed away—by black. Three weeks is enough. The strongest hold out no more than a couple of weeks. There has been *one* white man only to go through this O Wing experience without losing his balance, without allowing himself to succumb to the madness of ribald, protrusive racism.

It destroys the logical processes of the mind, a man's thoughts become completely disorganized. The noise, madness streaming from every throat, frustrated sounds from the bars, metallic sounds from the walls, the steel trays, the iron beds bolted to the wall, the hollow sounds from a cast-iron sink or toilet.

The smells, the human waste thrown at us, unwashed bodies, the rotten food. When a white con leaves here he's ruined for life. No black leaves Max Row walking. Either he leaves on the meat wagon or he leaves crawling licking at the pig's feet.

Ironic, because one cannot get a parole to the outside prison directly from o Wing, Max Row. It's positively not done. The parole board won't even consider the Max Row case. So a man licks at the feet of the pig not for a release to the outside world but for the privilege of going upstairs to o Wing adjustment center. There the licking process must continue if a parole is the object. You can count on one hand the number of people who have been paroled to the streets from o Wing proper in all the years that the prison has existed. No one goes from o Wing, Max Row straight to the general prison population. To go from here to the outside world is unthinkable. A man *must* go from Max Row to the regular adjustment center facility upstairs. Then from there to the general prison population. Only then can he entertain thoughts of eventual release to the outside world.

One can understand the depression felt by an inmate on Max Row. He's fallen as far as he can into the social trap, relief is so distant that is very easy for him to lose his holds. In two weeks that little average man who may have ended up on Max Row for *suspicion* of *attempted* escape is so brutalized, so completely without holds, that he will never heal again. It's worse than Vietnam.

He's dodging lead. He may be forced to fight a duel to the death with knives. If he doesn't sound and act more zealous than everyone else he will be challenged for not being loyal to his race and its politics, fascism. Some of these cons support the pigs' racism without shame, the others support it inadvertently by their own racism. The former are white, the latter black. But in here as on the street black racism is a forced *reaction*. A survival adaptation.

The picture that I have painted of Soledad's general population facility may have made it sound not too bad at all. That mistaken impression would result from the absence in my description of one more very important feature of the main line—terrorism. A frightening, petrifying diffusion of violence and intimidation is emitted from the offices of the warden and captain. How else could a small group of armed men be expected to hold and rule another much larger group except through *fear*?

We have a gym (inducement to throw away our energies with a ball instead of revolution). But if you walk into this gym with a cigarette burning, you're probably in trouble. There is a pig waiting to trap you. There's a sign "No Smoking." If you miss the sign, trouble. If you drop the cigarette to comply, trouble. The floor is regarded as something of a fire hazard (I'm not certain what the pretext is). There are no receptacles. The pig will pounce. You'll be told in no uncertain terms to scrape the cigarette from the floor with your hands. It builds from there. You have a gym but only certain things may be done and in specified ways. Since the rules change with the pigs' mood, it is really safer for a man to stay in his cell.

You have work with emoluments that range from nothing to three cents an hour! But once you accept the pay job in the prison's industrial sector you cannot get out without going through the bad conduct process. When workers are needed, it isn't a case of accepting a job in this area. You take the job or you're automatically refusing to work, even if you clearly stated that you would cooperate in other employment. The same atmosphere prevails on the recreation yard where any type of minor mistake could result not in merely a bad conduct report and placement in the adjustment center, but death. A fistfight, a temporary, trivial loss of temper will bring a fusillade of bullets down on the darker of the two men fighting.

You can't begin to measure the bad feeling caused by the existence of one TV set shared by 140 men. Think! One TV, 140 men. If there is more than one channel, what's going to occur? In Soledad's TV rooms there has been murder, mayhem, and destruction of many TV sets.

The blacks occupy one side of the room and the whites and Mexicans the other. (Isn't it significant in some way that our numbers in prison are sufficient to justify the claiming of half of all these facilities?)

We have a side, they have a side. What does your imagination envisage out of a hypothetical situation where Nina Simone sings, Angela Davis speaks, and Jim Brown "splits" on one channel, while Merle Haggard yodels and begs for an ass kicking on another.[8] The fight will follow immediately after some brother, who is less democratic than he is starved for beauty (we did vote but they're sixty to our forty), turns the station to see Angela Davis. What lines do you think the fighting will be along? Won't it be Angela and me against Merle Haggard?

But this situation is tolerable at least up to a point. It was worse. When I entered the joint on this offense, they had half and we had half, but out [sic] half was in the back.

In a case like the one just mentioned, the white convicts will start passing the word among themselves that all whites should be in the TV room to vote in the "Cadillac cowboy." The two groups polarize out of a situation created by whom? It's just like the outside. Nothing at all complicated about it. When people walk on each other, when disharmony is the norm, when organisms start falling apart it is the fault of these whose responsibility it is to govern. They're doing something wrong. They shouldn't have been trusted with the responsibility. And long-range political activity isn't going to help that man who will die tomorrow or tonight. The apologists recognize that these places are controlled by absolute terror, but they justify the pig's excesses with the argument that we exist outside the practice of any civilized codes of conduct. Since we are convicts rather than men, a bullet through the heart, summary execution for fist-fighting or stepping across a line is not extreme or unsound at all. An official is allowed full range in violent means because a convict can be handled no other way.

Fay, have you ever considered what type of man is capable of handling absolute power. I mean how many would not abuse it? Is there any way of isolating or classifying generally who can be trusted with a gun and *absolute* discretion as to who he will kill? I've already mentioned that most of them are KKK [Ku Klux Klan] types. The rest, all the rest, in general, are so stupid that they shouldn't be allowed to run their own bath. A *responsible* state government would have found a means of weeding out most of the savage types that are drawn to gunslinger jobs long ago. How did all these pigs get through?! Men who can barely read, write, or reason. How did they get through!!? You may as well give a baboon a gun and set him loose on us!! It's the same in here as on the streets out there. *Who* has loosed this thing on an already suffering people? The Reagans, [Richard] Nixons, the men who have, who own. Investigate them!! There are no qualifications asked, no experience necessary. Any fool who falls in here and can sign his name might shoot me tomorrow from a position thirty feet above my head with an automatic military rifle!! He could be dead drunk. It could really be an accident (a million to one it won't be, however), but he'll be protected still. He won't even miss a day's wages.

The textbooks on criminology like to advance the idea that prisoners are mentally defective. There is only the merest suggestion that the system itself is at fault. Penologists regard prisons as asylums. Most policy is formulated in a bureau that operates under the heading Department of Corrections. But what can we say about these asylums since none of the inmates are ever cured. Since in every instance they are sent out of the prison more damaged physically and mentally than when they entered. Because that is the reality. Do you continue to investigate the inmate? Where does administrative responsibility begin? Perhaps the administration of the prison cannot be held accountable for every individual act of their charges, but when things fly apart along racial lines, when the breakdown can be traced so clearly to circumstances even beyond the control of the guards and administration, investigation of anything outside the tenets of the fascist system itself is futile.

Nothing has improved, nothing has changed in the weeks since your team was here. We're on the same course, the blacks fast losing the last of their restraints. Growing numbers of blacks are openly passed over when paroles are considered. They have become aware that their only hope lies in resistence [*sic*]. They have learned that resistence is actually possible. The holds are beginning to slip away. Very few men imprisoned for economic crimes or even crimes of passion against the oppressor feel that they are really guilty. Most of today's black convicts have come to understand that they are the most abused victims of an unrighteous order. Up until now, the prospect of parole has kept us from confronting our captors with any real determination. But now with the living conditions of these places deteriorating, and with the sure knowledge that we are slated for destruction, we have been transformed into an implacable army of liberation. The shift to the revolutionary antiestablishment position that Huey P. Newton, Eldridge Cleaver, and Bobby Seale projected as a solution to the problems of Amerika's black colonies has taken firm hold of these brothers' minds.[9] They are now showing great interest in the thoughts of Mao Tse-tung, [Kwame] Nkrumah, [V. I.] Lenin, [Karl] Marx, and the achievements of men like Ché Guevara, [Vo Nguyen] Giap, and Uncle Ho [Chi Minh].[10]

Some people are going to get killed out of this situation that is growing. That is not a warning (or wishful thinking). I see it as an "unavoidable consequence" of placing and leaving control of our lives in the hands of men like Reagan.

These prisons have always borne a certain resemblance to Dachau and Buchenwald, places for the bad niggers, Mexicans, and poor whites.[11] But the last ten years have brought an increase in the percentage of blacks for crimes that can *clearly* be traced to political-economic causes. There are still some blacks here who consider themselves criminals—but not many. Believe me, my friend, with the time and incentive that these brothers have to read, study, and think, you will find no class or category more aware, more embittered, desperate, or dedicated to the ultimate remedy—revolution. The most dedicated, the best of our kind—you'll find them in the Folsoms, San Quentins, and Soledads. They live like there was no tomorrow. And for most of them there isn't. Somewhere along the line they sensed this. Life on the installment plan, three years of prison, three months on parole; then back to start all over again, sometimes in the same cell. Parole officers have sent brothers back to the joint for selling newspapers (the Black Panther paper). Their official reason is "Failure to Maintain Gainful Employment," etc.

We're something like 40 to 42 percent of the prison population. Perhaps more, since I'm relying on material published by the media. The leadership of the black prison population now definitely identifies with Huey, Bobby, Angela, Eldridge, and antifascism. The savage repression of blacks which can be estimated by reading the obituary columns of the nation's dailies, Fred Hampton, etc., has not failed to register on the black inmates.[12] The holds are fast being broken. Men who read Lenin, [Frantz] Fanon, and Che don't riot, "they mass," "they rage," they dig graves.

When John Cluchette was first accused of this murder he was proud, conscious, aware of his own worth but uncommitted to any specific remedial action.[13] Review the process that they are sending this beautiful brother through now. It comes at the end of a long train of similar incidents in his prison life. Add to this all of the things he has witnessed happening to others of our group here. Comrade Fleeta [Drumgo] spent eleven months here in O Wing for possessing photography taken from a newsweekly. It is such things that explain why California prisons produce more than their share of Bunchy Carters and Eldridge Cleavers.

Fay, there are only two types of blacks ever released from these places, the Carters and the broken men. The broken men are so damaged that they will never again be suitable members of any sort of social unit. Everything that was still good when they entered the joint, anything inside of them that may have escaped the ruinous effects of black colonial existence, anything that may have been redeemable when they first entered the joint—is gone when they leave.

This camp brings out the very best in brothers or destroys them entirely. But none are unaffected. None who leave here are normal. If I leave here alive, I'll leave nothing behind. They'll never count me among the broken men, but I can't say that I am normal either. I've been hungry too long. I've gotten angry too often. I've been lied to and insulted too many times. They've pushed me over the line from which there can be no retreat. I *know* that they will not be satisfied until they've pushed me out of this existence altogether. I've been the victim of so many racist attacks that I could never relax again. My reflexes will never be normal again. I'm like a dog that has gone through the K-9 process.

This is not the first attempt the institution (camp) has made to murder me. It is the most determined attempt, but not the first.

I look into myself at the close of every one of these pretrial days for any changes that may have taken place. I can still smile now, after ten years of blocking knife thrusts and pick handles; of anticipating and faceless sadistic pigs, re-acting for ten years, seven of them in Solitary. I can still smile sometimes, but by the time this thing is over I may not be a nice person. And I just lit my seventy-seventh cigarette of this twenty-one-hour day. I'm going to lay down for two or three hours, perhaps I'll sleep. . . .

Seize the Time.

From *Blood in My Eye*

As a slave, the social phenomenon that engages my whole consciousness is, of course, revolution.

The slave—and revolution.

Born to a premature death, a menial, subsistence-wage worker, odd-job man, the cleaner, the caught, the man under hatches, without bail—that's me, the colonial victim. Anyone who can pass the civil service examination today can kill me tomorrow. Anyone who passed the civil service examination yesterday can kill me today with complete immunity. I've lived with repression every mo-ment of my life, a repression so formidable that any movement on my part can only bring relief, the respite of a small victory or the release of death. In every sense of the term, in every sense that's real, I'm a slave to, and of, property.

Revolution within a modern industrial capitalist society can only mean the overthrow of all existing property relations and the destruction of all insti-tutions that directly or indirectly support existing property relations. It must include the total suppression of all classes and individuals who endorse the present state of property relations or who stand to gain from it. Anything less than this is reform.

Government and the infrastructure of the enemy capitalist state must be destroyed to get at the heart of the problem: property relations. Otherwise there is no revolution. Reshuffle the governmental personnel and forms, without changing property relations and economic institutions, and you have produced simply another reform stage in the old bourgeois revolution. The power to alter the present imbalances, to remedy the critical defects of an advanced industrial state ordered on an antiquated set of greed-confused motives, rests with control over production and distribution of wealth. If the one percent who presently control the wealth of the society maintain their control after any reordering of the state, the changes cannot be said to be revolutionary.

The prerequisite for a successful popular revolution is that the victors totally junk the old machinery of state. Lenin stressed in the *State and Revolution*: "One thing especially was proven by the commune, viz. that the working class cannot simply lay hold of the ready-made state machinery and wield it for its own purposes." And again: "the working class must break up, smash the ready-made state machinery, and not confine itself merely to laying hold of it." The reason is simple enough: A popular revolution means a revolution by and for the popular classes. Its ultimate aim is to bring all classes into one, that is, destroy the class state![14]

Revolutionary change means the seizure of all that is held by the one percent, and the transference of these holdings into the hands of the remaining ninety-nine percent. If the one percent are simply displaced by another one percent, revolutionary change has not taken place. A social revolution after the fact of the modern corporate capitalist state can only mean the breakup of that state and a completely new form of economics and culture. As slaves, we understand that ownership and the mechanics of distribution must be reversed. The problems of the Black Colony and the Brown Colony, those of the entire ninety-nine percent who are being manipulated, can never be redressed as long as the necessary resources for their solution are the personal property of an extraneous minority motivated solely by the need for its own survival. And that extraneous minority will never consider the proper solutions. We have this on record from a voice speaking from inside the Fourth Reich—a Lieutenant Governor of California orating in public on poverty: "One-third of the population will always be ill-housed, ill-clothed, and ill-fed. Many urban problems are really conditions that we cannot change or do not want to incur the disadvantages of changing." His "one-third" statement was a calculated understatement.

To the slave, revolution is an imperative, a love-inspired, conscious act of desperation. It's aggressive. It isn't "cool" or cautious. It's bold, audacious, violent, an expression of icy, disdainful hatred! It can hardly be any other way without raising a fundamental contradiction. If revolution, and especially revolution in Amerika, is anything less than an effective defense/attack weapon and a charger for the people to mount *now*, it is meaningless to the great majority of the slaves. If revolution is tied to dependence on the inscrutabilities of "long-range politics," it cannot be made relevant to the person who expects to die tomorrow. There can be no rigid time controls attached to "the process" that offers itself as relief, not if those for whom it is principally intended are under attack *now*. If the proponents of revolution cannot learn to distinguish and translate the theoretical into the practical, if they continue to debate just how to call up and harness the conscious motive forces of revolution, the revolutionary ideal will be the loser—it will be rejected.

The principal reservoir of revolutionary potential in Amerika lies in wait inside the Black Colony. Its sheer numerical strength, its desperate historical relation to the violence of the productive system, and the fact of its present status in the creation of wealth force the black stratum at the base of the whole class structure into the forefront of any revolutionary scheme. Thirty percent of all industrial workers are black. Close to forty percent of all industrial support roles are filled by blacks. Blacks are still doing the work of the greatest slave state in history. The terms of our servitude are all that have been altered.

The Black Colony can and will influence the fate of things to come in the U.S.A. The impact of black revolutionary rage actually could carry at least the opening stages of a socialist revolution under certain circumstances—not discounting some of the complexities created by the specter of racism. However, if we are ever going to be successful in tying black energy and rage to the international socialist revolution, we must understand that racial complexities do exist.

When the Minister of Defense and Servant of the People [Huey P. Newton] attacks the strategy of the Amerikan Communist Party and the liberal-left revisionists for their failure to devise a policy which takes into account the special circumstances of Yankee-style racism, he is not attacking communism and the collective ideal. He is questioning the Communist Party and other less committed sections of the left revolutionary movement about their awareness of the unique problems presented by a particularly vicious and immediately threatening racism.

My brother Jonathan, a communist revolutionary to the core, writing me in June of 1969, theorized as follows:

> We are quite obviously faced with a need to organize some small defenses to the more flagrant abuses of the system now. I mean this in a military sense. The period of disorganized activity, of riots and rallies, and purely political agitation/education has come to a close. The violence of the opposition has brought it to an end. We cannot raise consciousness another millimeter

without a new set of tactics. Long-range political ploys alone are not practical for us. To me, the concept seems to assume that someday in the distant
future we'll produce a 700-pound flea to fight the Paper Tiger. That's not too
likely to happen. While we await the precise moment when all of capitalism's
victims will indignantly rise to destroy the system, we are being devoured
in family lots at the whim of this thing. There will be no super-slave. Some
of us are going to have to take our courage in hand and build a hard revolutionary cadre for selective retaliatory violence. We have numbers on our
side if the whites who support revolutionary change can prevent this thing
from degenerating into race war. The picture of the U.S. as a Paper Tiger is
quite accurate, but there is a great deal of work to be done on its destruction
and I'm of the opinion that if there is a big job of growing to do, the sooner
begun the sooner done.

Both Huey and Jonathan are understandably calling for the programmed
revolution to take into account the fact of racial genocide. Jonathan is calling
from his grave, adding another voice to the many thunderous graveyard affir-
mations which, for us blacks, speeds the revolution to its ultimate issue.

In order to develop revolutionary consciousness, we must learn how revolutionary consciousness can be raised to the highest point by stimuli from the
vanguard elements. We recognize and appreciate the decades of hard, sometimes dangerous work done in the name of revolution by the older socialist
parties. Perhaps we wouldn't exist at all were it not for their efforts. It is our sin-
cere wish to operate in complete harmony with these older groups. But we must
create new impetus and greater intellectual and physical energy if the forces of
reaction are not to win another extended reprieve. A joint effort will make the
task of overwhelming our common enemy all the simpler. But if our present
differences cannot be reconciled by an honest and fearless search for the correct
way, then we will be forced to take the foundation of correct ideals and theory
into our own hands and build a positive and more practical superstructure ap-
plicable to the circumstances surrounding our lives. In his *Guerrilla Warfare*
Lenin wrote: "New forms of struggle, unknown to the participants of the given
period, inevitably arise as the given social situation changes, the coming crisis
will introduce new forms of struggle that we are now unable to foresee."[15]

In other words, the old guard must not fail to understand that circumstances
change in time and space that there can be nothing dogmatic about revolution-

ary theory. It is to be born out of each popular struggle. Each popular struggle must be analyzed historically to discover new ideas. In the words of John Gerassi: "Building from one to the other, eventually the revolutionary cadre would become equipped with a theory rooted in experience, broadened by historical knowledge, tested by combat, and fortified by reflection."[16]

After ten or fifteen generations of laboring on a subsistence level, after a hundred and forty years of political agitation and education, we grow impatient—not that we fail to understand the risks and complexities of antiestablishment warfare. We simply want to live.

Notes

"Letter to Fay Stender" was originally published in Jackson, *Soledad Brother*, 9–28; the excerpt from *Blood in My Eye* was originally published in *Blood in My Eye*, 7–13.

1. Jackson, *Soledad Brother*, 14. See also *Blood in My Eye* and "Toward the United Front"; Mann, *Comrade George*; Sabatini, *The Writings of Rafael Sabatini*; London, *The Call of the Wild*, "The Pen," and "Pinched"; Foner, *Jack London, American Rebel*.
2. Durden-Smith, *Who Killed George Jackson?* 177.
3. Ibid.
4. In 1979, eight years after George Jackson's death, Fay Stender was shot, allegedly by a member of the Black Guerilla Family for not supporting Jackson's militarist politics. She suffered severe injuries that led to her paralysis. Stender committed suicide in May 1980. See Liberatore, *The Road to Hell*.
5. *Editor's note*: At the time, Fay Stender was George Jackson's attorney.
6. *Editor's notes*: Alprentice "Bunchy" Carter, former leader of the Slaussons street gang, was radicalized by the writings of Malcolm X during his four-year incarceration in Soledad prison. In 1968, he chartered the Southern California chapter of the Black Panther Party (BPP) and assumed the position of deputy minister of defense. Carter, along with the Southern California BPP leader John Huggins, was shot and killed by members of Ron Karenga's US at Campbell Hall, University of California, Los Angeles, on January 17, 1969. These murders were facilitated by COINTELPRO, which carried out operations aimed to create dissension between the BPP and Ron Karenga's US.

    Eldridge Cleaver was convicted in 1957 of assault with intent to kill and spent time in San Quentin and Folsom prisons. While incarcerated, he immersed himself in revolutionary texts and, when paroled in 1966, became senior editor of *Ramparts* magazine. In 1967, he joined the BPP and became its minister of information. After a shootout with the police in 1968, Cleaver fled the country and became a primary leader of the international chapter of the BPP in Algiers.

7. *Editor's note*: See Aptheker, *Morning Breaks*, 12–13.

8. *Editor's note*: A famous African American jazz vocalist and pianist, Nina Simone wrote about racial and sexual injustices in many of her songs. An important figure in the civil-rights struggle, Simone is perhaps best known for "Mississippi Goddam," which she wrote in response to the 1963 bombing of a church in Alabama and the killing of four young black girls. Nina Simone died an expatriate in France in 2004.

   Angela Y. Davis, a black intellectual, feminist, and human-rights advocate, worked with the Black Panther Party but is better known as a communist and leader of the Soledad Brothers Defense Committee. In 1970, Davis was placed on the FBI's Ten Most Wanted list on false charges connected to the attempt by George Jackson's younger brother, Jonathan, to free prisoners by taking hostages at the Marin County courthouse. Jonathan used weapons registered in Davis's name. Davis went underground, given the repressive political climate. A massive FBI hunt culminated in one of the most famous political trials in recent U.S. history. During her sixteen months of incarceration, an international "Free Angela Davis" campaign was organized. Davis was acquitted of all charges in 1972. See Davis, *Angela Davis* and *The Angela Y. Davis Reader*.

   Jim Brown, a famous African American football running back, is a member of the National Football League Hall of Fame. Merle Haggard is a notable white country-and-western singer.

9. *Editor's note*: In October 1966, in Oakland, California, Huey P. Newton and Bobby Seale co-founded the Black Panther Party for Self-Defense (later renamed the Black Panther Party) and wrote a ten-point political platform, "What We Believe" and "What We Want." When Newton was found guilty of manslaughter in September 1968 after a police officer was killed in a shootout, Bobby Seale, along with Eldridge and Kathleen Cleaver, launched the "Free Huey" campaigns. Newton, Cleaver, and Seale, all of whom occupied key leadership positions in the BPP, were targeted by the FBI's COINTELPRO program. See Jones, *The Black Panther Party [Reconsidered]*.

10. *Editor's note*: Kwame Nkrumah, who became the first president of independent Ghana in 1957, played a key role in Ghana's independence struggle and was instrumental in organizing the 1945 Pan-African Congress.

   Vo Nguyen Giap, a Vietnamese general who studied guerrilla warfare in China with Mao Zedong, was instrumental in the founding of the Vietminh, became Army commander-in-chief of the Vietminh in 1946, and is credited with the 1954 defeat of the French at Dien Bien Phu. During the Vietnam War, Giap directed the military strategy of North Vietnam and served as deputy prime minister and minister of defense under Ho Chi Minh.

11. *Editor's note*: Both Dachau and Buchenwald, concentration camps under Nazi Germany, were part of Adolf Hitler's "final solution" for European Jews.

12. *Editor's note*: The Chicago Black Panther leaders Fred Hampton and Mark Clark were killed by Chicago police, assisted by the FBI, on December 4, 1969, in a pre-dawn raid. Families and survivors of that raid eventually received a settlement from the government.

13. *Editor's note*: John Cluchette and Fleeta Drumgo, along with George Jackson, were charged in 1970 with the death of the Soledad prison guard after Opie Mills, an expert marksman, killed three African American inmates during a fight in the O Wing exercise yard. They came to be known as the Soledad Brothers, and their case drew attention to racist prison conditions.

14. Gerassi, *The Coming of the New International*, 40.

15. V. I. Lenin, "Guerrilla Warfare," *Proletary*, no. 5, September 30, 1906.

16. Gerassi, *The Coming of the New International*, 42.

ABOUT THE TRANSLATION SIRÈNE HARB

Published in France on November 10, 1971, "The Masked Assassination" originally appeared as the second part of a pamphlet, *The Assassination of George
Jackson (L'Assassinat de George Jackson)*,[1] prepared by the Prison Information
Group (Groupe d'information sur les prisons [GIP]).[2] The GIP published two
pamphlets before this one: *Investigation in Twenty Prisons (Enquête dans 20
prisons)* and *Investigation in a Model Prison: Fleury-Mérogis (Enquête dans une
prison-modèle: Fleury-Mérogis)*.[3] Part I of *The Assassination of George Jackson*
includes two interviews in which George Jackson explores, among other things,
the importance of military and political cadres, consciousness-raising among
the prisoners, and the role of women in the Black Panther Party. The first interview, "The Struggle in the Prisons (*La Lutte dans les prisons*)," was published by
the Black Panther Intercommunal News Service on August 23, 1971. The second
interview, "The Politics of the Black Panther Party (*La Politique du Black Panther Party*)," was conducted on July 28, 1971, in San Quentin, by a journalist from
the *Berkeley Tribe*. The second part of the pamphlet includes three sections:
"The Masked Assassination (*L'Assassinat Camouflé*)," "After the Assassination
(*Après l'Assassinat*)," and "Jackson's Place in the Prison Movement (*La Place de
Jackson dans le movement des prisons*)."

The French theorist and activist Jean Genet, one of the most ardent supporters of the Black Panther Party, provided the preface to the pamphlet and texts
prepared by the GIP. It was at his suggestion that the GIP devoted a communiqué on media coverage of George Jackson's death in San Quentin.

The GIP prefaces its title page with the following statements:

The death of George Jackson is not a prison accident. It is a political assassination.

In the United States of America, assassination was, and still is, a form of
political action.

This pamphlet does not propose to fully explain the events of August 21,
1971, which took place in the prison of San Quentin: for the time being, at

least, these events are not fully understandable. Through this brochure, we wanted to answer two questions:

1. Who was this human being (*vivant*) whom they wanted to kill? What type of threat did he carry, despite the fact that he only carried his chains?
2. And why did they want to kill this death, to stifle it under lies? Why was it still perceived as a form of threat?

To answer the first question, we have chosen to present some of the most recent interviews in which George Jackson examines the revolutionary function of the movement in prisons.

To answer the second question, we have analyzed some pieces of information and some documents that were published directly after the death of Jackson.

The Masked Assassination

Michel Foucault
Catharine von Bülow
Daniel Defert

For a number of weeks, American newspapers have published articles about Jackson's death. Many divergences exist between all, or almost all, of these articles. Impossibilities and contradictions appear at every stage. One article claims that the events started at 15:10, another at 14:25. One article describes the revolver as a 9 mm; another as a .38 caliber. One article reports that Jackson wore a wig; another claims he did not. On Saturday, the whole event was described as a thirty-second blaze; on Monday, it became a long massacre of thirty minutes.

Most of this information comes directly from the administration of the penitentiary. A man whose account of his neighbor's death is half as incongruous as the story told by the director of San Quentin about Jackson's death would be immediately accused of the crime, but this will not happen to the director of San Quentin.

Jackson has already said it: What is happening in the prisons is war, a war having other fronts in the black ghettos, the army, and the courts. There was a time when an imprisoned militant was a soldier outside of combat. For the ruling power, prison represented, after murder, the most effective weapon against its adversaries. Today, the imprisoned revolutionary militants and the common-law prisoners, who became revolutionaries specifically during their detention, paved the way for the war front to extend inside prisons. This struggle is terribly uneven since all of the weapons (as can be noted from the recent events in Attica) are in the hands of one party. Despite this fact, such a struggle worries the American administration, since it has become clear that court sentences will not be able to stop it. Scandalous verdicts have transformed the prisoners into militants, and, in turn, the struggle in prisons has rendered court sentences derisory, whatever they might be. At this stage, the ruling power is left with one resort: assassination.

Jackson's assassination will never be prosecuted by the American justice system. No court will actually try to find out what happened: It was an act of war. And what the ruling power, the administration of the penitentiary, and the reactionary newspapers have published must be considered as "war communiqués."

This means that they fulfill some tactical exigencies, they serve a specific purpose, and they stimulate the struggle on the internal front.

It is therefore pointless to try to find out what is more or less accurate in the communiqués of the administration. Rather, it is sufficient to know the purpose that this or that statement would serve and what the administration sought to achieve and gain through its use.

A few hours after Jackson's death, Jim Park, associate warden of the prison, gave the first version of the events:

—Everything took place in thirty seconds. It was 3:10 in the afternoon—that is, "a little more than an hour after the end of visiting time"

—The incident took place in the maximum-security cellblock of the prison, where the "worst of the incorrigibles" are locked up. Seventeen to twenty inmates were involved in it; among them were Jackson, the other two Soledad Brothers ([Fleeta] Drumgo and [John] Clutchette), and [Ruchell] Magee (implicated, along with Angela Davis, in the events of August 7, 1970).[4]

—"What exactly was Jackson's role? Was he the leader?" Jim Park was asked. "He was the first to leave his prison cell, and he had a revolver in his hand. I leave it up to you to draw your own conclusions."

—This revolver was a .38 caliber. We don't know if he used it or not. Anyway, the five victims (three guards, two white inmates) were stabbed with knives, which were either smuggled in or fabricated inside the prison. Two other guards were injured in the same way.

—Less than one minute after the beginning of the riot, Jackson fled the maximum security cellblock, running. [Johnny] Spain, another inmate, was with him. Jackson was directly shot down, Spain was slightly wounded.

—The guards only fired one or two effective shots. The remaining ones (some thirty or so) were intended to warn the inmates and force them to leave their cells and lay down in the yard.

What are the purposes that this first version serves?

To depict an abrupt, violent, and absurd riot, without a specific reason or objective, and emphasize the prompt and impeccable response of the police.

But this was merely a hasty first operation, designed to answer the most urgent needs. Other operations were necessary, and they were enacted over the subsequent days. Undoubtedly, the American administration needed Jackson's death. He was the main exponent of the revolutionary movement in the prisons; thus, it was necessary to eliminate him. But this administration feared that his assassination would provoke an explosion and lead to the reinforcement of the revolutionaries. Consequently, there was a series of operations, which took the form of communiqués, news, and disclosures. Their goal was the manipulation of public opinion—at least, that of the people who were yet "undecided"—and to prepare a certain number of repressive measures. This counteroffensive tactic aimed to achieve five goals:

1. Compromise those black and white lawyers who provide legal and political assistance to the inmates.
2. Plant the seeds of suspicion about the complicity of the entire black community.
3. Present the guards, whose reputation had been devalued, in a more positive light.
4. Destroy the unified front of resistance formed by black and white prisoners.
5. Detract from the prestige of the black figures who led the struggle in the prisons, along with the common-law and political prisoners.

First Operation: "The Suspect Lawyer"

The outline of the events imposes its "logic": Jackson's death must be directly linked to a visit, a lawyer's visit—a lawyer who had ties with blacks and radicals and who, acting as an illegal courier, must have provided the instruments of the drama.

1. THE CHRONOLOGY OF EVENTS

According to the first version, the riot started at 3:10 P.M., an hour after the end of visiting time. This is also the chronology reported by *The Oregonian* of August 23.

But:

—The events "started immediately after the end of visiting time" (*New York Times*, August 23).

—The events took place at 3:10, "at the time when the visits were over" (*San Francisco Chronicle*, August 24).

—At 2:35 P.M., Jackson was led back to the maximum-security cellblock, and the events started at that specific moment (*San Francisco Chronicle*, August 24).

—At 2:27 P.M., Guard DeLeon signed the log confirming that Jackson had been led back to the maximum-security cellblock. Jackson pulled out his revolver a few seconds later (*New York Times*, September 3).

2. THE SMUGGLED REVOLVER

—Jim Park [the associate warden of San Quentin] claims, "Apparently a gun was smuggled in" (*San Francisco Examiner*, August 22).

—Louis S. Nelson, warden of San Quentin Prison, revealed that Jackson had received a visit on Saturday, August 21, at the beginning of the afternoon. Nelson did not want to reveal the identity or the profession of the visitor, but in a slip of the tongue, he spoke of the table that separated Jackson from the "attorney." Nelson "supposed" that [the] visitor introduced the revolver. "But how was it possible," Nelson was asked, "for the visitor carrying a gun to go through the metal detector?" He replied, "In life, anything is possible" (*New York Times*, August 23).

—The officials disclose the name of the lawyer: Stephen Bingham. He is young, white, and progressive; he participated in a number of sit-ins at Berkeley, collaborated with Martin Luther King Jr., and, in March 1970, defended three men accused of violence against an agent during a court session in the trial of the Soledad Brothers (*San Francisco Chronicle*, August 23, August 24).

—Bingham arrived at San Quentin at two in the afternoon, with a young woman who registered under the name Anderson. The young woman had a briefcase. Since she was denied access to the visiting area, she gave the briefcase to Bingham. When he entered the visiting area with the briefcase, the metal detector reacted. The briefcase was opened, and it contained an apparently functional tape recorder. Some working parts had been taken out of the machine to conceal a gun (*San Francisco Chronicle*, August 24).

—Bingham and the young woman entered the visiting area together and spoke with Jackson. It is noted that the young woman is in communication with a female lawyer from the East Bay (*San Francisco Chronicle*, August 24).

—The address given by the young woman is that of the Black Panthers in Oakland (*San Francisco Chronicle*, August 24).

—The address of the young woman is 2230 10th Street, Berkeley (*San Francisco Chronicle*, August 25).

—The revolver had been acquired by the Black Panthers in Reno (*San Francisco Chronicle*, August 23).

—Bingham and his companion had arrived at San Quentin at 10:15 in the morning. Since Bingham was not Jackson's official defense attorney, he had to get a visit permit, but Miss Anderson was denied one. Bingham met with Jackson in the visiting area at 13:25 (*New York Times*, September 3).

—During this meeting, Bingham gave Jackson not only the revolver but also two ammunition clips and a wig (*New York Times*, September 3).

—Bingham completely disappeared; Bales, the prosecutor, has officially charged him with five murders, on the basis of a California state law that does not discriminate between perpetrators of crimes and their accomplices (*New York Times*, September 3).

Second Operation: "The Black Conspiracy"

In what will follow, the objective is to demonstrate that, in this war waged in prisons, the whole black community must be considered suspect; women and children are combatants masked as civilians.

—Officials disclosed information about an escape plan that they had "discovered." A former prisoner [James E. Carr] who was Jackson's cellmate sent Jackson a letter through a lawyer. Jackson had written a response on the back of the letter. The former prisoner slipped the letter in his pocket. During the pressing, an employee found the letter and gave it to the officials, who, "to avoid raising his [Carr's] suspicion," made a copy of it and then put it back in the pocket (*San Francisco Chronicle*, August 24).

—In this letter, Jackson asked his sisters to "hide some pistols in the heels of their shoes"; he enclosed a "diagram to show them how to get past the metal detector." Furthermore, the women must have hidden tubes of explosives in their vaginas. Jackson also indicated how one could interrupt the prison's electrical current, and he requested that he be picked up in "a four-wheel drive vehicle."

On August 1, Jackson received a visit from two sisters with three children. Jim Park, associate warden of San Quentin, thinks that the purpose of the visit was to "test" and "measure the effectiveness of the detector." In fact, one of the children was discovered to have metal buckles on his shoes and his belt; the three of them carried concealed toy pistols.

Officials made no public disclosure of the escape plan and the suspicious visit of the family because, they claim, they did not want to "prejudice Jackson's position prior to his trial," which was due to take place soon in San Francisco (*San Francisco Chronicle*, August 24).

—In fact, next to Jackson's body in the San Quentin yard, they found not only a gun and two ammunition clips but also a bottle containing [an] explosive substance (*San Francisco Chronicle*, August 24).

Third Operation: "The Nonviolent Guards"

The inmates were in possession of all of the weapons, resorted to all sorts of tricks, and were the source of all of the violence. Confronting them were the guards—unarmed, impotent, and distracted. The blacks are the ones waging permanent war while the whites always attempt to maintain a lenient order. If the guards don't want to be the first and only victims, they will have to resort, as Jim Park said, "to old corrective methods." *They, too*, will one day have to be armed.

1. THE REVOLVER SMUGGLED DURING THE VISIT

—Usually, when taken to the visiting area, Jackson was handcuffed, and his arms were shackled to a chain around his waist. But "because of his cooperative behavior lately," it was decided to remove his chains for the duration of the visit (*New York Times*, September 3).

—In the visiting room, there is frequently a barrier separating inmates and visitors. That day, between Jackson and the lawyer, there was only a table (*New York Times*, August 23).

—According to prison regulations, a guard is to continuously surveil the small visiting room where Jackson met with Bingham. It is the visiting room usually reserved for those visiting prisoners condemned to death. On August 21, only one guard was assigned to surveil the main and the small visiting rooms. He wasn't able to keep his eyes permanently fixed on Jackson (*San Francisco Chronicle*, August 24).

2. THE ARSENAL IN THE HAIR

a) What Was Jackson's Hair Like?

—Towering Afro-style hair (*Oakland Tribune*, August 24).
—An African hairstyle of average length (*San Francisco Chronicle*, August 24).
—For some time, Jackson wore a watch cap on his head. It is under this watch cap, and not under his hair—or probably "a combination of both"—that Jackson concealed and transported the weapon (*San Francisco Chronicle*, August 24).
—The guards have spoken of a wig that was later found jammed in a cell toilet. They maintained that it could be related to the events of August 21, but they did not indicate how (*San Francisco Chronicle*, August 24).
—One of the guards had had the impression that Jackson was wearing a wig, but had never said anything. He did not disclose this piece of information until after the wig had been discovered (*San Francisco Chronicle*, August 25).

b) Of What Did the Arsenal Consist?

—A .38 caliber revolver (*San Francisco Examiner*, August 22).
—A 9 mm revolver of foreign origin (*New York Times*, August 23).
—A 9 mm Spanish-made Llama (*San Francisco Chronicle*, August 23).
—An Astra M600 (*San Francisco Chronicle*, August 24).
—A short 9 mm Llama [Llama Corto], five inches long; not a standard Llama, which is eight inches long (*San Francisco Examiner*, August 29).
—A revolver which is eight inches long, five inches tall, and 1.5 inches wide. In addition, under his wig, Jackson carried two full ammunition clips (*New York Times*, September 3).

—After his return to the maximum-security cellblock, Jackson pulled out his revolver and shot the man who was frisking him (*San Francisco Chronicle*, August 23).

—The guard who was frisking Jackson noticed in his hair something that resembled the point of a pencil. The guard asked him what it was and, instead of responding, Jackson pulled out the revolver. According to some sources, the revolver was not loaded, so Jackson loaded it and then overpowered the "surprised" guards, who stood helpless (*San Francisco Chronicle*, August 24).

—When the incident was taking place, there was, on the ground floor of the cellblock, a total of six guards, one of whom was noncommissioned. Three guards were in the corridor that leads to the cells (*New York Times*, August 23; *San Francisco Chronicle*, August 23).

—Jackson had just been returned to the maximum-security cellblock by Guard DeLeon. Rubiaco was in front of Jackson, frisking him. Behind Jackson, Officer McCray was supervising. Rubiaco noticed something in Jackson's hair and tried to grab it, but Jackson jumped aside, whipped off his wig, grabbed the revolver and the two ammunition clips, swept one of the clips into the revolver, and turned toward the guards, whom he neutralized (*New York Times*, September 3).

Fourth Operation: The Black Massacre

The American administration has constantly used racism to fight the revolutionary movement in the prisons. However, at present, the front of the war no longer lies between the black inmates and the white inmates but, rather, between all the revolutionary inmates on the one side and the administration (and all those who serve it, be they guards or inmates) on the other.

For the officials, it is crucial to break this new front at all costs and to reestablish as soon as possible in the prisons the virulent racism against black inmates. Therefore, they have to show that the events at San Quentin do not belong to a *new* stage in the political struggle but, rather, constitute a return to the *old* practice of savage massacre.

1. JACKSON'S PARTICIPATION

—Jackson fled from the cellblock thirty seconds after having brandished the revolver. (Five men had their throats slashed by "other inmates") (*San Francisco Examiner*, August 22).

—Jackson pulled out his revolver and forced the guards to open all of the cells on the ground floor. Immediately after, he exited the building and was killed. Everything took place within thirty seconds, but the guards were not able to regain control of the cellblock until after a quarter of an hour. They found five bodies. When he was asked why these people were killed, the Associate Warden replied: "It could have been in retaliation for the shooting of Jackson" (*New York Times*, August 23).

—Using an automatic lever, Jackson opened all of the cells on the ground floor. It was shortly after 14:35. "In the ensuing half hour," Jackson and a companion executed the massacre. It wasn't until 15:10 that Jackson exited the building and attempted to escape (*San Francisco Chronicle*, August 23).

—In Jackson's cell were found, piled on top of each other, four dead bodies and one wounded guard; the murderers had not noticed that he was alive.[5]

—To prevent them from recognizing their assassins, the victims had been blindfolded (*San Francisco Chronicle*, August 27).

2. THE SAVAGERY OF THE MASSACRE

—All the victims had their throats slashed within thirty seconds (*San Francisco Examiner*, August 22).

—The duration of the massacre was half an hour. Using half a razor blade, Jackson and the other inmates attempted to slit the throats of their hostages. However, since the blade was dull, they were forced to use it like a saw. A number of shots from a firearm forced them to retreat to the back of the building; they dragged their victims, continuing to slash their throats (*San Francisco Chronicle*, August 23).

—Since the razor blade was dull, a fingernail clipper was used to puncture the jugular artery of one of the guards.[6]

—Autopsies of the victims. Jere Graham: two stab wounds to the chest, another two to the abdomen, a bullet to the back of the head. Frank De-Leon: throat slashed on both sides, a bullet to the back of the head, a facial wound caused by a dull object, strangled with an electrical wire. Paul Krasenes: three razor blade slashes to the throat, another to the right side of the torso, strangled with an electrical wire. John Lynn: four wounds on the right side of the neck, two on the left side. Ronald Kane: severed artery on the right side of the throat (*San Francisco Chronicle*, August 24).

3. THE DEATH OF THE WHITE INMATES

—The revolting blacks killed, in addition to the three guards, two white inmates because "they [the revolting blacks] didn't like them" (*San Francisco Examiner*, August 22).

—There were four white inmates on the ground floor of the maximum-security cellblock. When Jackson forced the guards to open the doors of the cells, two of the inmates, realizing that the blacks were going to kill them, re-closed the cell door; this act saved their lives (*San Francisco Chronicle*, August 24).

—The blacks killed two white inmates because they were tier tenders,[7] and the blacks could never become tenders (*San Francisco Chronicle*, August 24).

—The two tier tenders had just finished working in the kitchen. They remained in their cells. The mutineers asked: "We're breaking out. . . . Are you with us?"—"We won't get in your way . . . but we don't want in."—"Then you're against us." And they were killed (*San Francisco Chronicle*, August 25).

—The two white tier tenders were killed while they were still working in the kitchen (*New York Times*, September 3).

Fifth Operation: "The Irresponsible Leader"

Jackson was perceived as the leader of the revolutionary movement in the prisons. For the administration, it was crucial to physically eliminate him. However, this administration also wanted to destroy the public image (so that Jackson would not survive) and the function (so that no one would take his place). Consequently, it needed to weave the "right" narrative to make the general public believe that Jackson had dragged the other inmates into an endeavor without an exit strategy, and that this endeavor aimed to achieve his exclusive, personal goals. Thus, this administration also had to represent him as someone who abandoned his companions in the middle of the struggle and attempted to escape alone.

—A collective escape attempt, of which Jackson seems to have been the leader (*San Francisco Examiner*, August 22).

—Jackson intended to escape before his trial with the other two Soledad Brothers, which was to take place shortly thereafter. By discovering the revolver in his hair, the guards frustrated his plot. It is exactly at this point that Jackson stirred up the riot (*San Francisco Chronicle*, August 24).

—For the trial, Jackson and his accomplices had prepared a plan of action somehow similar to that of August 1970. He wanted to use a revolver in court. When he saw that his plan was discovered, he dragged his companions down with him (*San Francisco Chronicle*, August 24).

—From the outset of the riot, Jackson was trying to escape (*New York Times*, August 23).

—When the alarm was sounded, Jackson attempted to escape. He fled the maximum-security cellblock and ran toward the seven-meter-high wall. He was killed by two bullets: one to the head, the other to the heel (*San Francisco Chronicle*, August 24).

After the Assassination

On August 23, the preliminary hearing for the events at Soledad took place. A bullet-proof sheet of glass separated the court from the public, including the journalists. The public was so outraged by the attitude of the judges that it pounded on the glass, yelling, "Pigs, pigs." Two days later, Cluchette's mother was expelled from the court after a crisis that the authorities described as hysterical; blacks and police clashed in the courtroom. On August 23, Cluchette handed over to lawyers a petition signed by twenty-six inmates of San Quentin who had witnessed the drama of Saturday. The petition was written on the back of a greeting card sent to one of them and bearing the inscription, "I live to love you." At different stages, the petition was rejected by the judges, who considered it irrelevant. Lawyers read it to the public and the press outside the courtroom. The petition addressed the assassination of Jackson:

We, the undersigned, each being held incommunicado, because of suffering from both wounds and internal injuries inflicted upon our persons by known and unknown agents of Warden Louis S. Nelson. Through their agents, Warden Nelson and Associate Warden James L. Park killed a man called George Jackson and plotted the assassination of the undersigned who refused to be involved in the conspiracy of the functionaries of the State.

The text continues, recounting instances of physical maltreatment and torture; it also asks that investigations be conducted and forms of protection offered to the inmates. The lawyers who were able to see some of the inmates in the maximum-security cellblock confirmed the horrible conditions; it was also noted that Ruchell Magee was in extremely bad condition.

The prisoners also succeeded in leaking another longer text to the outside:

We, the twenty-seven united black, brown, and white prison-slaves of the maximum security cellblock of San Quentin penitentiary, are the victims of an assassination conspiracy, exactly like the one which ended the life of our comrade G. L. Jackson, assassinated on August 21.

The scene had been staged to suggest an escape attempt, but what really happened was a conspiracy to assassinate the Soledad Brothers, and with them Ruchell Magee and the rest of the fighters for freedom. . . . Since August 21, we twenty-seven have been directly experiencing fascism in its roughest form. We have been subjected to every form of brutality; we have been kicked and beaten with clubs, tortured with lit cigarettes and pins; we have been abused, spat on, dragged on the ground, etc. All of this while we are enchained like animals, spread naked on the grass. . . . Every day they threaten our lives: we will be poisoned, asphyxiated; we will never leave the maximum security cellblock alive; we will never receive a trial; and our lawyers will not be able to help us because they too will be killed, etc. In this prison, there are black, brown, and white comrades who don't belong to any particular political organization. All that we are asking for is the support of the people in our daily struggle. Among us there are men who don't read Marx, Lenin, Engels, or Mao; there are some who don't know how to read even a sentence. What we are affirming now is this: we need everyone's help, whether s/he is an outlaw, a pimp, a prostitute, a priest or a doctor of philosophy. . . . We are not grieving, we are not crying over the death of our beloved comrade George

Jackson. He brought courage to our hearts and spirits, and he taught us how to pursue his ideals. He made the ultimate sacrifice, and his black blood is the nourishment that gives us the resolution to fight against the crushing forces of oppression. We will vindicate him, because we are the ones who knew him best and loved him the most.

It is clear that there was no escape attempt but, rather, an assassination, a premeditated crime against Jackson. For some time, the director of the California Department of Corrections, R. K. Procunier, had been spreading rumors that trouble might break out at San Quentin. The guards wanted to kill Jackson and other "dangerous" prisoners, to make people believe that there was a collective escape attempt. Jackson, who knew very well that the guards wanted his skin above all, succeeded in reaching the yard, where he was killed. By doing so, he rendered unsustainable the "pre-packaged" official version of the events and prevented the massacre of the other prisoners. This explains why the lawyers and the other inmates said that George Jackson had sacrificed his life. It is possible, then, that the guards and the two prisoners were killed in a brief battle following Jackson's assassination. Park, associate warden of the prison, stated that some of the murders probably happened "in retaliation for the shooting of Jackson."

Jackson had known for some time that he was constantly under the threat of death. On the one hand, it might come from an inmate conditioned by racism and lured by the promises or terrified by the threats of the guards. On the other hand, it might be directly engineered by the guards themselves. The graveness of this threat increased in tandem with the development of Jackson's political consciousness and prestige. The probability that the events of Soledad would be discussed in court while Jackson was still alive became increasingly scarce. There were numerous attempts to eliminate Jackson, and his letters from prison are a testament to this. On March 19, 1971, the former Soledad prisoner Allan Mancino wrote that one night in January 1970, Spoon, a guard, and Moody, a captain, had pulled him out of his cell and asked him to kill Jackson. (Moody then asked me directly if I was willing to kill George Jackson. He said that he didn't need another Eldridge Cleaver.)

In this atmosphere of death that permanently surrounded him, Jackson faced extremely hard challenges: "I may run, but all the time that I am, I'll be looking for a stick! A defensible position!"[8]

And in such a climate heavy with death, he advanced the political education of his parents:

With each attempt the pigs made on my life in San Quentin, I would send an SOS out to my family. They would always respond by listening and writing letters to the joint pigs and Sacramento rats, but they didn't entirely accept that I was telling them the truth about the pig mentality. I would get dubious stares when I told them about the lieutenants and the others who propositioned some of the most vicious white convicts in the state: "Kill Jackson, we'll do you some good." You understand, my father wanted to know why. And all I could tell him was that I related to Mao and couldn't kowtow. His mind couldn't deal with it. I would use every device, every historical and current example I could reach to explain to him that there were no good pigs. But the task was too big, I was fighting his mind first, and his fear of admitting the existence of an identifiable enemy element that was oppressing us because that would either commit him to attack that enemy or force him to admit his cowardice. . . .

I was leading up to the obvious fact that black women in this country are far more aggressive than black males. But this is qualified by the fact that their aggression has, until very recently, been within the system—that "get a diploma boy" stuff, or "earn you some money." Where it should have been the gun. Development of the ability for serious fighting and organized violence was surely not encouraged in the black female, but neither was it discouraged, as it was in the case of the black male."[9]

This political education resulted in a level of consciousness for Jackson's mother, which made her declare, after the assassination of her son, "Both of his legs looked like they'd been cut. He just looked so mangled, it's pitiful. . . . He said they were trying to kill him. They wanted to kill George, they wanted to kill George years ago."[10]

Jackson said:

It's no coincidence that Malcolm X and M. L. King died *when* they did. Malcolm X had just put it together (two and three [sic]). I seriously believe, they knew all along but were holding out and presenting the truth in such a way that it would affect the most people situationally—without getting them damaged by gunfire. You remember what was on his lips when he died. Vietnam and economics, political economy. The professional killers could have murdered him long before they did. They let Malcolm rage on muslim [*sic*] nationalism for a number of years because they knew it was an empty ideal, but the second he got his feet on the ground, they murdered him.[11]

The same thing can be said about Jackson: He was killed specifically when the time he had announced and worked for came, when a growing awareness among "the blacks, the browns, and the whites" allowed for the identification of the deceptive traps of organized racism. This process marked the beginning of the formation of a unified resistance front, specifically within the prisons. There is something inside us that often pushes us to believe that the interventions of the ruling power, when they aren't just, are at least diabolical and well-calculated. This is not true; everything eludes this power and its control, including its own actions and its conspiracies. The assassination of Jackson is one of these phenomena, a defensible position, as Jackson would say, that revolutionaries can transform into a cause.

Jackson's Place in the Prison Movement

In the black revolutionary movement, Jackson wanted to be perceived as a militant. However, the most crucial aspect of his reflections resides in the theorization of the relationship between military and political actions.

This is a fundamental issue that was at the origin of the split between [Huey] Newton and [Eldridge] Cleaver. Cleaver reproached Newton for what he called his "pacifism," his "legalitarianism," in short, his "revisionism." By contrast, Cleaver advocated the immediate passage to armed struggle, which he considered as the supreme form of political struggle.

Jackson, the militant, condemned the military activism of the Weathermen and their actions, organized without strategic preparation and the political support of the masses. He gave his support to Newton and his popular action programs, such as the free distribution of snack meals to black children in the ghettos. These programs will be increasingly threatened by fascist repression specifically because they enable the black community to organize itself. Such a causal relation informed Jackson's belief that these programs will soon become inconceivable without a military cadre.

For at least two years, Jackson was in charge of the preparation of this military protection, and specifically from within the prisons, where disarmed and heavily shackled men train for war. This is Jackson's grand initiative. Two profoundly connected facts made it possible: On the one hand, the entire black avant-garde lives under the threat of prison, and many of its leaders are held there for long periods of time; on the other hand, under the influence of this presence, other prisoners, in turn, become politicized. One of these prisoners, for example, when asked about his plans for after his release, answered, "To help my people." Hence, it is not only in the ghettos, in the factories, in the rebellions in the military, but also in the prisons that solid nuclei of resistance, elements of the armed cadre, are forming and being formed.

These pre-visions overturn many commonly accepted ideas in the history of the working-class movement about the population of the prisons.

From within the prisons, Jackson prepared the military protection necessary for political work; such a form of preparation was unstable, weakened by the threat of systematic murder practiced by the authorities. That's the reason why, outside the walls of the prisons, political organizations launch military operations to rescue and liberate some inmates, specifically those whose lives are threatened by imminent death. In this context, Angela Davis became a symbol of heroism for black people, when she was accused (despite belonging to a pacifist, legalitarian communist party[12]) of contributing to the bold action of support, undertaken from the outside on August 7, 1970, to rescue Soledad prisoners. From both sides of the walls, the army of the prisoners and the army of the people are preparing themselves for the same war of liberation.

In this movement, Jackson occupies a fundamental position. He is one of the first revolutionary leaders to acquire his political education entirely in prison. As he states, "I have all the theory . . . and I've put my books aside now."[13] He is also the first whose political action was carried out exclusively in prison. He is the first to carry out a class-based analysis of the prisoners and define their specific role in the revolutionary process:

> You would be very surprised to see how these particular lumpen in here accept class war and revolutionary scientific socialism, once they understand [that] our real historical contribution was not the African feudalism of U.S. and other government stooges, but the agricultural communal existence described by [W. E. B.] DuBois, [Earl] Ofari [Hutchinson], and others.[14]
>
> All these cats in here are lumpen, that's all I've ever been—it has not damaged my capacity to love. . . . Then all these brothers are similar. Violent, yes,

but ninety percent tenderness. It can be seen in the intense longing for community. Even out there, the unconscious one looks for parties and gatherings with a passion, that's a reaction, Pat, to the absence of community, no family or clan or national ties, so they search for parties, dances, etc., in their love for and longing for community, commune-ity.

That's what helps define us as a class.

I have spent eleven years—from the age of eighteen to twenty-nine—caged up like an animal for a crime that would have earned the average person six months or a suspended sentence.[15]

Ten years in prison for seventy dollars is a political experience—an experience of hostage, of a concentration camp, of class warfare, an experience of the colonized.

In prison, Jackson implemented his theory of communism through his daily practices. He shared money and books; he taught his brothers how to read and write; he helped to develop their political consciousness; and he organized them so that they could fight, by all necessary means, fascist methods of repression and dehumanization.

Daily violence and the permanent threat of death constitute the most rigorous tools for learning class hatred and the vigilance and astuteness of war. It's an experience of warfare. The people's liberation army will find its Ho Long and its "revolutionary outlaws" not in the mountains but in the prisons. The revolutionary role that Jackson attributed to the prisoners was that of the protection of political work—a military cadre, a sacrificial role. Through their support of [George] Jackson, Drumgo, Clutchette, and the three Soledad Brothers, Jonathan Jackson and Angela Davis played an instrumental role in bringing the movement in favor of the prisoners to a critical stage of its development.

Traditionally, this type of support is one of the forms of democratic struggle, effectuated through marches, demonstrations, and meetings. Kidnapping a judge in a full courtroom, Jonathan Jackson denounced the justice system as the indubitable instrument of fascist repression practiced by the United States. This same justice system, with its white judges and its white jurors, consigned hundreds of thousands of African Americans to the bloodthirsty guards of concentration camps. In this context, Jonathan Jackson demonstrated that the act of supporting prisoners constitutes a form of war.

Jackson's death is at the origin of the revolts that exploded in prisons, from

Attica to Ashkelon.[16] Prison struggle has now become a new front of the revolution.

Notes

Editor's note: Some also attribute authorship of this pamphlet to Gilles Deleuze, but research was unable to support this claim. "The Masked Assassination" was originally published in GIP, *Intolerable 3*. The translation is by Sirène Harb.

Translator's note: The version reprinted here differs from the original in that changes were made to correct the spelling of some proper names (for instance, Charline was replaced with Charlene and Rane with Kane); the use of "Chronicle" and "Examiner" in some references to the *San Francisco Examiner* and *San Francisco Chronicle* (*San Francisco Examiner* is the title of the Sunday edition of the *San Francisco Chronicle*); and some inaccuracies (for example, in one section, Jim Park was referred to as "warden" of San Quentin instead of "associate warden").

1. *The Assassination of George Jackson* (*Intolerable 3: L'Assassinat de George Jackson*) is the third in a collection of four GIP pamphlets. The first two were published by Champ Libre, and the other two were published by Gallimard. The back cover of the first pamphlet cites what the GIP finds intolerable: "courts, cops, hospitals, asylums, school, military service, the press, television, the State." See GIP, *Intolerable 4*.

   According to Artières et al., *Le Groupe d'information sur les prisons*, 105: "After the break with Champ Libre, the choice of Gallimard is probably due to the links [the publisher] had with Michel Foucault, Jean Genet, and Catherine von Bülöw."

2. Foucault announced the creation of the GIP in a statement presented on February 8, 1971, in Saint Bernard Chapel, in the Montparnasse train station. The statement was published in March 1971 in *Esprit*. It stresses the importance of denouncing the bleak conditions of life in prisons and the complex repercussions of the institutional gaze on individual lives. Because of the tone and spirit of the statement, Foucault was perceived as its main author and the GIP as "his new organization"; the statement listed Foucault's home address, 285 Rue Vaugirard, as the GIP mailbox. See Eribon, *Michel Foucault*, 225.; Miller, *The Passion of Michel Foucault*, 188.

3. GIP, *Intolerable 1*; idem, *Intolerable 2*.

4. *Editor's Note*: Ruchell Magee, who was serving a life sentence in San Quentin prison, was present at the August 7, 1970, trial of James McClain when Jonathan Jackson entered the Marin County Courthouse. Magee assisted Jonathan Jackson, along with the prisoners James McClain and William Christmas, in taking Judge Harold Haley, the district attorney, and members of the jury hostage. As the only prisoner who survived the guards' gunfire, Magee was indicted by a Marin County Grand Jury, along with Angela Davis, in a joint charge of first-degree murder (of Judge Harold Haley), kidnapping, and conspiracy. Magee and Davis filed to have their cases severed be-

cause Magee, acting as his own counsel, needed to seek judicial recognition that he had been falsely imprisoned in the state penitentiary for almost eight years. By establishing that his original conviction was illegal, Magee planned to demonstrate just cause for his participation in the August 7 events at the Marin County Courthouse. See Aptheker, *Morning Breaks*; Davis, *Angela Davis*.

5. *Translator's note*: The authors provided neither source nor citation for this statement in the original.

6. *Translator's note*: A newspaper account reports that the jugular vein was punctured.

7. *Translator's note*: Tier tenders are "inmates who serve food and pick up laundry in the adjustment center [maximum-security cellblock] and thus have some degree of freedom": "The Quentin Violence—First Inside Account," *San Francisco Chronicle*, August 24, 1971, 18.

8. Jackson, *Soledad Brother*, 249.

9. Ibid., 33–34, 229.

10. *Translator's note*: This quotation comes from an interview with Georgia Jackson, George Jackson's mother, titled, "I Bought the Plot a Year Ago, I Knew They Would Kill Him" (*Sun Reporter* [San Francisco], August 28, 1971, 24).

11. Jackson, *Soledad Brother*, 237.

12. *Translator's note*: Angela Davis is a member of the Communist Party of the United States of America; her ideological affiliation is with its leftist wing, formerly led by the black militant Charlene Mitchell.

13. *Translator's note*: The quote is from Pat Gallyot, "George Jackson, a Beautiful Black Warrior," *Sun Reporter* [San Francisco], August 28, 1971, 2.

14. *Editor's note*: Earl Ofari Hutchinson's publications include *The Myth of Black Capitalism* (New York: Monthly Review Press, 1970) and *Let Your Motto Be Resistance* (Boston: Beacon Press, 1972).

15. *Translator's note*: One part of this quote is from Gallyot, "George Jackson, a Beautiful Black Warrior," 2.

16. *Editor's note*: In September 1971, responding to George Jackson's killing by San Quentin prison guards, administrators, and dehumanizing and racist prison conditions, 1,500 African American, Puerto Rican, and white prisoners seized control of Attica, a maximum-security prison in New York. *Translator's note*: Eight days after the events in the maximum-security prison of Attica, Palestinian inmates began revolting in the Israeli prison of Ashkelon.

OSCAR LÓPEZ RIVERA

Oscar López Rivera was born in San Sebastian, Puerto Rico, in 1943 and moved to Chicago at fourteen to live with his sister. Drafted into the U.S. Army, he served in the Vietnam War (1965–66), where he was awarded the Bronze Star. In 1967, López Rivera returned to work in Chicago's Puerto Rican community, where he became active in struggles for improved community health care, education, and employment; an end to police brutality; and Puerto Rican independence. A community organizer for the Northwest Community Organization, he helped to found the Rafael Cancel Miranda High School (now known as the Dr. Pedro Albizu Campos High School), the Juan Antonio Corretjer Puerto Rican Cultural Center, FREE (a halfway house for convicted drug addicts), and ALAS (an educational program for Latino prisoners at Stateville Correctional Center in Illinois).

During his many years of involvement with the Puerto Rican struggle for independence, López Rivera has never claimed affiliation with any political organization or movement. His community and political activism, however, made him a target of U.S. government repression. López Rivera was captured on May 29, 1981; convicted of seditious conspiracy ("to overthrow the government of the United States in Puerto Rico by force"), armed robbery, and lesser charges; and sentenced to fifty-five years in prison. In 1988, López Rivera was given an additional fifteen years for "conspiracy to escape" and sent from Leavenworth to the maximum-security prison in Marion, Illinois, before his transfer to the ADX (Administrative Maximum Prison) in Florence, Colorado. He is currently incarcerated in the U.S. Penitentiary in Terre Haute, Indiana.

President Bill Clinton offered leniency to twelve Puerto Rican political prisoners/prisoners of war in 1999. Due to his political principles, López Rivera rejected Clinton's offer of a pardon to reduce his sentence to ten years. During his incarceration, Rivera has written many short stories and articles for *Libertad* and *Patria Libre*. In the unabridged essay, written from his prison cell, Rivera describes colonization and resistance in Puerto Rico. The excerpted version presented here recounts, when the United States invaded and occupied Puerto Rico in 1898, how it installed a military governor who was unfamiliar with the country, its culture, and its language, and began an "Americanization" process that would alter a national economy and create an outflow of émigrés seeking relief from colonization. Sovereign prior to the U.S. invasion, with self-determination decreed by Spain's Charter of Autonomy, Puerto Rico changed radically into a new formation, in which policing and punishment for dissidents would become routine aspects of "nation building."[1]

The Jones Act of 1917 offered a "hybrid citizenship" to Puerto Ricans, according to Rivera, imposing the responsibilities of citizenship without political or legal representation.[2] When Puerto Ricans became eligible for the draft following the passage of the Jones Act, the U.S. Selective Service called thousands for military duty. Those who refused the draft or challenged the act became targets for imprisonment.

FBI Director J. Edgar Hoover used COINTELPRO to destroy the Puerto Rican Independence Movement, as he would use it decades later to destabilize the Civil Rights Movement and destroy the black liberation movement.

A Century of Colonialism: One Hundred
Years of Puerto Rican Resistance   Oscar López Rivera

The u.s. invasion and its aftermath:
assimilation, repression, and resistance

When the u.s. government militarily invaded and occupied Puerto Rico in 1898, General Nelson Miles told the Puerto Rican people that it was his government's intention to bestow upon them the freedom, liberty, and democracy for which they yearned. But the government's actions and measures had nothing to do with freedom, liberty, or democracy. It named and installed a governor, plucked from the military, who knew nothing about Puerto Rico nor even spoke Spanish. It devastated the native economy by devaluing the Puerto Rican currency by sixty percent and imposing the u.s. dollar. It forced the peasants off the land— including emigration to far-away places like Hawai'i—in order to make room for agro-business and the military, and to bring down the native population. It attacked everything Puerto Rican, especially the culture and the national identity, imposing English as the language of public instruction and introducing the protestant church in order to accelerate the assimilation process. In less than three years, Puerto Rico had been transformed from an autonomous nation with its own government to a colony of the u.s.a.

Before the invasion, the Puerto Rican people had forced Spain to grant them a Charter of Autonomy. In *Violations of Human Rights in Puerto Rico by the U.S.*, Luis Nieves Falcón notes that:

> The Charter, a binding international covenant formally negotiated between representatives of the Puerto Rican people and the Spanish Crown, granted a series of important rights and powers to the insular government of Puerto Rico, including the authority to establish its own currency, to enter into commercial treaties, and to possess the authority to approve or reject treaties or agreements made by Spain which would affect the economic interest of Puerto Rico. Most significant, Article 44 provided that the charter could

not be amended except upon the request and approval of the Puerto Rican people.[4]

Colonialism was the perfect status for the u.s. imperialistic designs, and the government did whatever it took to keep it that way. As soon as Puerto Ricans began to criticize the occupation, the latter's immediate response was to repress, persecute, criminalize, and imprison those who dared to challenge it. These repressive and punitive measures have been part and parcel of the u.s. colonial rule from the moment of the invasion to the present.

The first Puerto Ricans to be attacked by the u.s. government were journalists who owned small newspapers and had published articles critical of the military occupation and the absence of freedom, and democracy. Evaristo Izcoa Díaz, owner of the newspaper *La Bomba*, was the first victim. He was sentenced to one year of hard labor in prison and his newspaper was confiscated. This experience devastated his health; he died soon after he was released from prison, at the age of thirty-six. Other journalists, such as Manuel Guzmán Rodríguez, Tomás Carrión Maduro, Julio Medina González, and Félix Medina González, faced similar punishment and abuse. Although they were a bit luckier than Izcoa Díaz, the u.s. government never stopped harassing and persecuting them. So much for the freedoms of speech and the press. Other Puerto Ricans who were persecuted, repressed, and even imprisoned soon after the invasion and occupation were those who opposed the imposition of the English language for public education and [the] u.s. government's other efforts to assimilate Puerto Ricans. Along with journalists, the anti-assimilationists became the first Puerto Rican political prisoners. Ever since then, the u.s. government has continued to send Puerto Ricans to prison for wanting freedom, independence, and democracy.

World War I, forced citizenship, and cannon fodder

Because the u.s. government intended to keep Puerto Rico as its colony and to use it for its own ends, it decided to use Puerto Ricans as cannon fodder as it prepared to enter World War I. In order to achieve this goal, it invented and imposed, through the adoption of the Jones Act of 1917, a hybrid form of u.s. citizenship against the expressed wishes of the Puerto Rican people.[5] This hybrid citizenship imposed on Puerto Ricans all the responsibilities of u.s. citizenship but without any political or legal representation. Its purpose was not to make

Puerto Ricans u.s. citizens, but to make them eligible for the draft. Only three months after the Jones Act was passed, the u.s. selective service called thousands of Puerto Ricans for military duty. Puerto Ricans who refused the draft or condemned the hybrid citizenship became the new targets of u.s. repression, persecution, criminalization, and imprisonment. According to José "Ché" Paralatici, at least seventy-five Puerto Ricans were imprisoned for refusing to serve in the u.s. armed forces during the lifetime of the military draft from World War I to after the Vietnam War.[6] Some served prison sentences as long as five years. During the same period, more Puerto Ricans per capita had served in the u.s. armed forces than u.s. citizens from any of the states of the union.

The Puerto Rican Nationalist Party: popular support and government repression

After the first three decades of colonial rule, the Puerto Rican masses were fed up with their colonial status and dire economic conditions. Along came the Puerto Rican Nationalist Party (PRNP), led by Don Pedro Albizu Campos—a charismatic Harvard-trained lawyer, leader, and organizer. In 1934, his success in leading 125,000 sugarcane workers on strike frightened the sugar barons and shook the political establishment. The u.s. government and north american business interests weren't willing to allow the Puerto Rican Nationalist Party (PRNP) to continue winning the hearts and minds of the Puerto Rican people, especially those of the workers. So, in response, a group of u.s. officials—Governor Blanton Winship, Col[onel] E. Francis Riggs (head of the Puerto Rican police), Cecil Snyder (u.s. attorney for Puerto Rico), Robert Cooper (federal judge), and from Washington, J. Edgar Hoover (head of the federal bureau of investigation)—hatched a plan to slam the brakes on the Nationalist Party and silence the demand for freedom, liberty, and democracy. Their plan was to criminalize the leadership of the Nationalist Party, and all the political activities dealing with the issue of Puerto Rico's independence.

Under Riggs, the police became an agency of provocateurs, torturers, and murderers. According to Ronald Fernández, it was under Riggs' authority that four members of the Nationalist Party were killed by the police in what became known as the Río Piedras Massacre.[7] The PRNP people could not let such a heinous crime go unpunished, and on February 23, 1936, Hiram Beauchamp and Elias Rosado executed Riggs. In return, the police killed both of them after arresting and taking them to police headquarters. Riggs's death emboldened u.s.

attorney Cecil Snyder to bring criminal charges against the top leadership of the PRNP. Don Pedro Albizu Campos, Juan Antonio Corretjer, et al., were charged with seditious conspiracy, a law used during the u.s. civil war. Since the jurors couldn't come up with a unanimous guilty verdict in the first trial, u.s. attorney Snyder decided to bring the Nationalists to trial again. But for the second trial, he handpicked the members of the jury to ensure a "guilty" verdict. In a letter in support of clemency for the Nationalist prisoners, one of the jurors, Mr. Elmer Ellsworth, wrote to president [Franklin] Roosevelt:

> In making this statement to you concerning the jury's deliberation I can't refrain from saying that my associates on the jury all seemed to be motivated by a *strong if not violent prejudice against the Nationalists and were prepared to convict them regardless of the evidence.*[8]

Ten of the jurors were north american residents in Puerto Rico, and the two Puerto Ricans were closely associated with north american business interests. This jury found Don Pedro Albizu Campos, Juan Antonio Corretjer, Luis E. Velázquez, Clemente Soto Vélez, Erasmo Velázquez, Julio H. Velázquez, Pablo Rosado Ortiz, and Juan Gallardo Santiago guilty of seditious conspiracy to overthrow the u.s. government in Puerto Rico by force.

Judge Cooper's role in the plan was to instruct the jurors so that they would have no alternative than to find the Nationalists guilty. This was confirmed by Mr. Ellsworth's letter, quoted above, where he described the judge's response to his question regarding whether Albizu Campos' published articles could be used as the sole basis for a "guilty" verdict. "The judge expressed himself on the question in such language that I was obliged to arise in the jury box and ask him whether he meant yes or no. Confronted with the necessity for a definite answer he finally replied in the affirmative." The other role Judge Cooper played was to give the Nationalists the maximum possible sentence, without regard for justice or the u.s. system of jurisprudence. By the time Cooper was finished, he had sent most of the Nationalist Party's leaders to prison with the harshest possible sentences.

J. Edgar Hoover's role went on even after the plan had come to an end. He initiated the Counter-Intelligence Program (COINTELPRO) in order to do away with the forces fighting for Puerto Rico's independence. Hoover never stopped investigating and persecuting Don Pedro Albizu Campos, and continued to keep files on him even after Don Pedro Albizu Campos had died. The plan and its nefarious consequences were described by Congressman Vito Marcantonio in a speech to the u.s. congress in 1939:

> In five years as governor of Puerto Rico, Mr. Blanton Winship destroyed the last vestiges of civil rights in Puerto Rico. Patriots were framed in the very executive mansion and railroaded to prison. Men, women, and children were massacred in the streets of the Island simply because they dared to express their opinion or attempted to meet in free assemblage. Citizens were terrorized.[9]

Of the numerous crimes committed against the Puerto Ricans, the bloodiest and most horrific is known as the "Massacre of Ponce." On Palm Sunday, March 21, 1937, the members of the PRNP had planned to hold a march. But at the last minute, their permit was revoked under direct orders from Governor Winship. The Nationalists decided to go on with the march. The police, knowing the Nationalists were going to proceed with the march, set up an ambush. According to the evidence gathered by the American Civil Liberties Union, the trap was set up from all sides, so that no one could get out of it. The police fired on a totally unarmed and defenseless crowd, leaving nineteen people dead and over 200 wounded.[10]

Between 1935 and 1940, at least forty-five members of the Puerto Rican Nationalist Party were sent to prison. Some served days, some served months, some served years. Some were sentenced to life in prison, and after serving some years were found innocent. The harshest sentence was the one given to Don Pedro Albizu Campos. Even after completing his sentence in the united states penitentiary of Atlanta, he was not allowed to return to Puerto Rico until 1947.

World War II, softer colonialism, and more cannon fodder

When the u.s. government was getting ready to enter World War II, it eased its choke-hold on the Puerto Rican liberation movement and began some reforms in order to gain more Puerto Ricans for cannon fodder and to obtain the support of the Latin American nations for the war. It even went as far as to offer the governorship of Puerto Rico to Don Pedro, as long as he would not raise the issue of Puerto Rican independence. Don Pedro refused it.

The most obvious change the u.s. government instituted was to allow the people to elect a governor for the first time, in 1948, after having governors from the u.s. imposed on them for fifty years. Another major change was the trans-formation of a monoagriculture economy to one based on light industry and tourism. What it didn't change was its colonial domination. The u.s. congress still retained absolute power over Puerto Rico. Neither did it stop repressing, persecuting, and criminalizing Puerto Ricans who wanted freedom, justice, and democracy for their homeland. The decade of the 40s ended with more than eighty Puerto Ricans having experienced prison because they refused to serve as cannon fodder for the u.s. armed forces.

The Jayuya Insurrection and massive repression

The decade of the 50s began ominously for the Puerto Rican forces struggling for Puerto Rican freedom, justice, and democracy. Puerto Rico felt the weight of the cold war and McCarthyism, which were defining the politics of u.s. imperialism. The new colonial administration, headed by governor Luis Muñoz Marin, was a farce. Following the orders of its master, it got ready to smash any opposition to the colonial regime by passing laws, setting up the courts, and preparing the police and the national guard. The main target was the Puerto Rican Nationalist Party, which had been re-organizing and rebuilding itself after the return of Don Pedro Albizu Campos. It also got ready to create a political structure, which in 1952 became known as "Estado Libre Asociado de Puerto Rico"—the Free Associated State of Puerto Rico—in order to get Puerto Rico off the United Nations list of non-governing countries (a.k.a. colonies).

For the Nationalist Party, the new colonial administration was even less acceptable than the previous one. The Nationalist Party, conscious of what was at stake, had no other choice than to call for insurrection. On October 30, 1950, in the town of Jayuya, Blanca Canales—a social worker—raised the Puerto Rican flag, and declared the "Republic of Puerto Rico." The insurrection had begun. The town of Jayuya had been taken over by members of the Puerto Rican Nationalist Party. Unfortunately, the other insurrectionary forces were unable to replicate the success enjoyed by the ones in Jayuya. They were overwhelmed by the police and national guard that were prepared and waiting for the insurrection to start. Many Nationalists were killed and wounded and over one thousand persons were hauled off to prison, including Don Pedro and mostly all the leaders of the PRNP.

Two days later, November 1, 1950, Griselio Torresola and Oscar Collazo went to Blair House, where president Truman was residing, to execute him. But they were unable to accomplish their mission. Griselio and a guard were killed in the shoot-out and Oscar was badly wounded. He was captured, tried, and sentenced to death; but in 1952, president Truman commuted his sentence to life in prison.

Soon after Don Pedro and the other members of the party were sent to prison, their torture began. Don Pedro let it be known to the world he was being subjected to radiation torture. His health quickly began to deteriorate. But the government's official response was that his charges were the rantings of a demented man. Today we know Puerto Rican prisoners were subjected to radiation experiments, which was nothing less than government-sponsored torture.[11]

In its quest to smash the Nationalist Party, the government employed the dirtiest of tactics. Whole families were sent to prison. Wives were given long sentences for preparing food for their husbands and children. No one identified as a supporter of Puerto Rican independence could get jobs in the public sector. And in the private sector, it often only took a visit to the employer by the fbi or the police and he or she would end up getting fired. People who owned their own businesses lost them. It really was an all-out attack. The government was not going to allow any opposition to take root and flourish.

In December 1953, the u.s. government forced the U.N. to remove Puerto Rico from the list of territories and colonies. Only twenty-two countries voted in favor of removing Puerto Rico from the list; eighteen voted against it; and nineteen abstained.[12] This underhanded move was a tremendous blow to the PRNP, because in 1945—when the United Nations was founded—the United Nations had succeeded in placing Puerto Rico on that list which meant the u.s. government had to submit a yearly report to the U.N. explaining its process by which it allowed the Puerto Ricans to exercise self-determination.

But the nationalists refused to be silenced and ostracized by that prison which is colonialism. On March 1, 1954, a commando unit, led by Lolita Lebrón, responded by attacking the us. congress. With Lebrón were Rafael Cancel Miranda, Andrés Figueroa Cordero and Irvin Flores Rodríguez. The four walked into the u.s. congress and opened fire; Lolita, draped with the Puerto Rican flag, told the world Puerto Rico was a u.s. colony and such a crime and tyranny would not be tolerated by those who love freedom, justice, democracy, and the homeland. For their heroic acts [in which no one was killed, but five congressmen were injured], they were sentenced to [fifty-year] prison terms.

Prison also became a torture chamber for many brave and courageous women and men of the Nationalist Party, who experienced the ordeal of losing their mental or physical health or who witnessed that ordeal suffered by others.[13]

By the end of the decade of the 50s, over 500 women and men had been sent to prison by a government that used the dirtiest tactics, including Kangaroo courts and laws that were later declared unconstitutional. For those Puerto Ricans who were to continue to struggle, more repression, persecution, and criminalization loomed large over the horizon.

The 1960s: Vietnam, ROTC, and COINTELPRO

Along with the dawning of the 60s came COINTELPRO—the fbi's counter intelligence program, that aimed to bring havoc to the Puerto Rican Independence Movement, as well as the Black Panther Party and the American Indian Movement.

On August 4, 1960, J. Edgar Hoover sent a COINTELPRO memorandum to the special agent in charge (sac) of the San Juan office, telling him that: "You should bear in mind that the Bureau desires to disrupt the activities of these organizations [seeking independence for Puerto Rico] and is not interested in mere harassment."[14] On June 12, 1961, Hoover sent another memorandum instructing the sac in San Juan to:

> Delve deeply into that part of their lives which does not show on the surface; for example, we must determine their capabilities of influencing others, capabilities of real leadership, why the intense desire for Puerto Rico's independence, what they expect to gain from independence, and the support they have from other leaders and rank and file members. We must have information concerning their weaknesses, morals, criminal records, spouses, children, family life, educational qualifications, and personal activities other than independence activities.[15]

Copies of this memorandum were sent to the fbi offices in Chicago and New York.

Although the Independence Movement was more fragmented and remained under state-sponsored attack at the start of the decade, it was also showing signs of renewal and the will to continue the struggle. It had divided into three factions, each with its own ideology and political program. The Puerto Rican Independence Party (PIP) continued its efforts to achieve an Independent Puerto Rico through the electoral process. The Nationalist Party, the hardest hit by the government's attacks and weakened because its main leaders were still in prison, continued with its insurrectionary program. The *Movimiento Pro Independencia* (MPI) had adopted Marxism/Leninism as its ideology and was advocating a proletarian revolution. It was the latter that was attracting the youth, especially from the University of Puerto Rico (UPR).

The Puerto Rican Independence Party suffered a major set back in the 1960 gubernatorial elections. The support it received at the ballot box was only a fifth of the votes it had received in 1952, when it had received over twenty-five percent of the vote, making it the second most popular party. By 1960, it had been reduced to such insignificance that governor Luis Muñoz Marín publicly declared the issue of Independence for Puerto Rico to be dead. Within this political environment, the fbi unleashed its criminal activities, implementing J. Edgar Hoover's instructions. Informers, provocateurs, police, and reactionary Cubans who had settled in Puerto Rico began the campaign of dirty tricks to create dissent, character assassination, and to foment antagonisms within and among the organizations.[16] They were also involved in a campaign of terror—sniping at leaders, firebombing the headquarters of the *Movimiento Pro Independencia* and destroying the presses of the independentist newspaper *Claridad*.[17] These attacks didn't deter the Independence Movement which condemned the u.s. war in Vietnam and supported the young men who refused the draft and opposed the ROTC program at the UPR and the u.s. military presence in Puerto Rico.

The UPR campus became polarized as political activity grew, and the war radicalized much of the student body. The government saw this radicalization as a major threat and intensified its campaign of repression. To protect themselves, groups within the Independence Movement began to create clandestine organizations. The first to appear on the scene was the *Comandos Armados de Liberación* (CAL). In February of 1968, CAL publicly declared its aims: the national liberation of Puerto Rico through armed actions; an end to monopolistic control of industry by u.s. firms; and the expulsion of u.s. firms from Puerto Rico. It declared u.s. imperialism to be its enemy and let it be known that it would take drastic measures to ensure no Puerto Rican who was opposed to serving in the u.s. armed forces would be sent to prison. CAL and other clandestine organizations carried out several armed propaganda actions, causing millions of dollars in damage. Their main targets were u.s. firms and the u.s. military.[18]

The government retaliated by using the informers and *agents-provocateurs* to bring criminal charges against the most radical organizations. The Puerto Rican Socialist League (LSP), led by Don Juan Antonio Corretjer, became a primary target. The LSP's leadership faced charges that carried lengthy sentences of hundreds of years. A few years later all the charges were dropped because the whole case had been fabricated by informers and *agents provocateurs*. But the damage to the LSP had been done.[19]

By the end of the 60s, over fifty Puerto Ricans had been detained, arrested, and/or convicted because of their involvement with the struggle for Puerto Rican independence and sovereignty or for opposing the war and refusing to serve in the u.s. armed forces. In the Puerto Rican diaspora other Puerto Ricans had met the same fate. But the struggle for freedom, justice, and democracy continued.

The 1970s: Vieques and Culebra, armed repression, and defense

The decade of the 70s started and ended in political turmoil. Some have called it one of the "bloodiest and most repressive in Puerto Rico's history." The government continued fabricating cases and keeping independentists tied up in the courts. The situation at the UPR only grew worse and more tense.

The UPR administration, instead of dealing with the issues the students were raising, transformed the campus into an armed police camp. On March 4, 1970, while the students held a demonstration against the ROTC program, the riot police responded with live ammunition fire. Antonia Legares Martínez, a student who was watching the event from the balcony of her dorm, was killed by a stray police bullet. Hundreds of students were injured, some were arrested, and student leaders who were identified as independentists were suspended. The following day, CAL executed two navy soldiers in retaliation for Antonia's death. In a communiqué, CAL gave notice to the government that none of the repressive measures used against Puerto Ricans would be tolerated. From that moment on the campus became a tinder-box waiting to explode. On March 11,

1971, while the students were commemorating Antonia's death, the riot police, members of the ROTC program, and right wing forces opened fire on the students. It became a pitched battle and at the end three policemen had been killed, including the commander of the riot police.

The right wing forces burned the offices of the PIP and businesses of independentists. At police headquarters, the students who had been arrested and their lawyers were assaulted. The UPR was shut down for a month and many of the students were suspended for life. Humberto Pagán was charged with the killing of the police commander. He was released on bail and flew to Canada in fear for his life. The u.s. government demanded his extradition; but the Canadian government refused. In 1973, he returned to Puerto Rico to face trial and was acquitted of all charges because there was no evidence linking him to the killing.

At the same time that the UPR students were protesting against the ROTC Program another group was protesting against the navy's use of Culebra as a target range and for other military exercises. For decades, the u.s. navy had been using the islands of Vieques and Culebra without any respect or regard for the health and safety of the residents or the environment. In January of 1971, the Independence Movement started a civil disobedience campaign and occupied the restricted areas of the navy's firing range in Culebra. They built a chapel and set up a camp. The courts ruled the activists had to leave the restricted area controlled by the u.s. navy or be evicted. A group of about twenty, including Rubén Berríos (the President of the PIP), were arrested. Most were imprisoned for up to three months. But the civil disobedience activities continued until 1975, when the navy finally left Culebra.

By the middle of the decade, the Independence Movement showed signs of strength and rejuvenation. It was mobilizing more people, waging a better organized struggle, functioning at both the public and clandestine levels, and getting bolder. Not only were these signs visible in Puerto Rico, but also in the diaspora. The fbi then declared the Puerto Rican Independence Movement a primary threat to the country's internal security. Right wing terrorists began to operate. And from within the ranks of the police a death squad emerged, consisting of policemen with close ties to the fbi.

On January 11, 1975, while the Puerto Rican Socialist Party was commemorating the birthday of the Puerto Rican independentist leader Eugenio Maria

De Hostos, a bomb placed by a right-wing terrorist group killed a twenty-eight-year-old independentist and an eleven-year-old boy, both of whom were attending the ceremony. Two weeks later, another clandestine organization, the Armed Forces of National Liberation (FALN), placed a bomb in Fraunces Tavern in response. The FALN communiqué warned the government that any dastardly act, such as the one of January 11 committed against the Puerto Rican people, would be met with a retaliatory response.[20]

One new weapon the fbi and the prosecution (u.s. Justice Department) used against the Independence Movement was the federal grand jury. The government began to use the federal grand jury to criminalize and imprison independentists: The first Puerto Rican sent to prison for refusing to testify before a grand jury was Lureida Torres Rodríguez, a young teacher who had moved to New York in 1974. She was charged with contempt of the grand jury and spent three months in prison. Between 1976 and 1979, eleven independentists or supporters of the Puerto Rican Independence Movement were imprisoned for contempt because they refused to be part of any witchhunt of the u.s. government. Like the fabrication of cases, the use of the grand jury became a potent weapon to put independentists in prison, tie them up in the court's maze, and force the Independence Movement to spend precious human and economic resources. After years of using these weapons, the individuals targeted and the Independence Movement were going to suffer exhaustion. And that exhaustion was a victory for the government.

The year 1978 was marked by several events: the return home of Andres Figueroa Cordero (one of Puerto Rico's National Heroes, who had been released from prison by President Jimmy Carter in December 1977 because he was dying of cancer); the takeover of the Chilean Embassy [consulate] in Puerto Rico by Pablo Marcano and Nydia Cuevas; the capture of William Guillermo Morales in New York after he was injured when a bomb he was making accidentally exploded.

There was also the appearance in Puerto Rico of at least two clandestine organizations claiming support for Puerto Rico's independence but in reality having been organized by the police. The central character in these organizations was Alejandro González Malavé, an undercover policeman who passed himself off as a revolutionary. On July 25, 1978, he led two young independentists to Cerro Maravilla, where the police waited in ambush. Arnaldo Dario Rosado, a twenty-two-year-old unemployed worker, was shot point blank while on his knees, begging the policeman not to kill him. Carlos Soto Arriví, a seventeen-year-old student and the son of one of Puerto Rico's distinguished writers, died in an ambulance a few minutes later. This became known as the Cerro Maravilla Massacre. Facts about this horrific and abominable event were revealed in 1983.[21]

Two events brought great jubilation to those who love Puerto Rico and struggle for its freedom and total independence. The first was the escape from prison by William Guillermo Morales, who was able to cut a hole in a window and jump to freedom, despite having lost his fingers in an explosives accident.[22] The other event was the return to Puerto Rico of the four National Heroes: Lolita Lebrón, Irvin Flores, Rafael Cancel Miranda and Oscar Collazo López. At the time of their release they were the longest held political prisoners in u.s. history.[23]

The decade closed with the death of Angel Rodríguez Cristóbal, a schoolteacher and farmer, who was completing a six-month sentence at the federal correctional institution (fci) in Tallahassee, Florida. Along with twenty other activists, Angel had entered the restricted area in Vieques to stop the navy from carrying out its military exercises. In court, he declared himself a prisoner of war, because he had been arrested while acting as a fighter for Puerto Rico's independence. Prison officials said that he had committed suicide. But those who knew him well could not accept the jailers' official story. Angel was not suicidal. He was a family man who enjoyed the love and respect of his family, his community, and the Independence Movement, a distinguished and respected leader of the Puerto Rican Socialist League, a Vietnam Veteran, and he only had two more weeks left to complete his sentence. The physical evidence showed a big gash on his forehead and bruises that were signs of physical struggle.

In retaliation, three clandestine organizations (the Organization of Revolutionary Boricua Volunteers [ovrb]; the Armed Revolutionary Force of the People [farb]; and the *Macheteros*), which operated in both Puerto Rico and the diaspora, attacked a navy bus on its way to Sabana Seca Naval Base and killed two soldiers. A communiqué explaining the action was issued by the clandestine organizations: Every killing of a Puerto Rican patriot committed by the government would be met with revolutionary retaliation. By the end of the decade, ninety-eight Independentists in Puerto Rico and in the diaspora had been imprisoned and over one dozen Independentists had been killed by the police death squad, by the regular police, and by the right wing terrorist group assisted by the fbi.[24]

The 1980s: Capture of a new generation of Puerto Rican political prisoners; revelations of gross colonial abuses

In the decade of the 1980s, the government continued using the federal grand jury to attack the Independence Movement, but the prosecution added the new charge of "criminal contempt" to use against non-collaborators. In the past, those who refused to testify before the grand jury were charged with civil contempt and could be imprisoned only for the duration of the grand jury—up to eighteen months. With the new charge, the prosecution could ask for a maximum sentence of fifteen years. Between March 1980 and November 1989, at least sixteen non-collaborators were imprisoned. Eight of them were charged with "criminal contempt" and sentenced to several years in prison. Seven were non-Puerto Ricans who were targeted because of their solidarity with Puerto Rico's struggle for self-determination. And six of them were convicted for refusing to testify.

A month after the government had started targeting Independentists for the grand jury onslaught, eleven Puerto Ricans—Elizam Escobar, Ricardo Jiménez, Adolfo Matos Antongiorgi, Dylcia Pagán, Edwin Cortés, Alicia Rodríguez, Ida Luz Rodríguez, Luis Rosa, Carlos Alberto Torres, Haydeé Torres, and Carmen Valentín—were captured in Evanston, Illinois. They declared themselves "prisoners of war," and demanded that the government recognize their rights under international law and turn them over immediately to the proper international jurisdiction.

The issue of jurisdiction over Puerto Rico was crucial and fundamental for the eleven because the u.s. government's jurisdiction was illegal on two grounds. First, the Treaty of Paris of 1898, used by the u.s. government to force Spain to cede Puerto Rico as war booty, was in violation of the Charter of Autonomy. Puerto Rico did not belong to Spain for the latter to cede, and it wasn't *nullius terra* for the u.s. to take over and control. At the time the Treaty was signed there were close to one million Puerto Rican citizens, and their rights should have been respected by the Spanish and u.s. governments. Second, Puerto Rico was and is a colony of the u.s., and colonialism was considered a crime against humanity. The eleven refused to recognize the jurisdiction of the u.s. government over Puerto Rico and over themselves in order to avoid abetting a crime against humanity.

The government responded to their demand by criminalizing them. It used the media to depict them as "terrorists." Their bail was set at millions of dollars. While in detention they were subjected to physical and psychological abuses by policemen, sheriffs, fbi agents, u.s. marshals, prosecutors, judges, and jailers. Ten of them were charged with seditious conspiracy in a courtroom in Chicago.[25] They were also given charges by the state of Illinois. The other prisoner, Haydeé Torres, was turned over to the jurisdiction of New York, and was sentenced to life in prison. Because she refused to collaborate or give the material evidence the government demanded, she was physically attacked.

Because they refused to participate in the trial or defend themselves, they knew they had been found guilty and condemned before the farce had begun. The courts were biased and prejudiced. This became obvious during the sentencing process when one of the judges told Carmen Valentín that the only reason he didn't sentence her to death was because the law didn't allow him to do so. He sentenced her to ninety years in prison. The disproportionately lengthy sentences received—as documented by attorney Jan Susler—were one of the reasons cited by President Bill Clinton when he gave clemency to most of the Puerto Rican political prisoners in 1999.[26]

The treatment the eleven received in the courts and during their detention set the pattern for the way other Puerto Rican freedom fighters would be treated in the future. Edwin Cortés, Alberto Rodríguez, José Luis Rodríguez, and Alejandrina Torres were captured in 1983, in Chicago. They were kept in segregation, locked in cells twenty-three hours per day without access to fresh air or sunlight, to the telephone, to regular family visits, or to proper medical treatment. Alejandrina was kept in the same male unit with Eddie and Alberto. Her cell had a window that made it impossible for her to have any privacy. When she had to use the toilet, male guards and prisoners could see her. Their bail was set at millions of dollars.

The prosecution and the fbi tried to make their trial another Kangaroo court. But Judge George Leighton, an African American, did not let them. José Luis Rodríguez, who used a legal defense, was allowed to make his case; the judge sentenced him to five years' probation. And he sentenced the other three, who assumed the same prisoner of war position as the eleven, to thirty-five years each.

Cruel and unusual punishment continued to be used against the political prisoners, especially against Alejandrina. In one of the gulags, she was sexually assaulted by the jailers. And when the Special Housing Unit (SHU) was opened in Lexington, Kentucky, she along with other female political prisoners were kept there to break their spirit and will [see Laura Whitehorn's essay " Resisting the Ordinary" in this volume]. The SHU conditions were so outrageous a court in Washington, DC ruled the prisoners were being subjected to "cruel and unusual punishment." The public demand and outcry for justice forced the bureau of prisons to close it down, and to transfer the women to other prisons.

Haydeé Torres and Ida Luz Rodríguez were also warehoused in a control unit—in Alderson, West Virginia. They were the only two prisoners in the unit, but could neither speak to nor see each other. They were totally dependent on the jailers. They were kept locked twenty-three hours per day in their cells, and had no human contact except with the jailers. They couldn't receive visits, even legal ones, together. It took a massive campaign to get them out of such deleterious conditions.

On August 30, 1985, about 200 fbi agents, wearing camouflage uniforms and bulletproof vests and armed with all types of weapons, carried out a quasi-military operation against the homes of several Independentists who were members of the *Macheteros*. Filiberto Ojeda, leader of the *Macheteros*, resisted the attack on his home. He fired a machine gun at the fbi, and an agent was wounded in the exchange. When enough neighbors had been alerted, Filiberto gave up his firearm and didn't resist arrest. At least fourteen people were arrested in Puerto Rico, and at least three others were arrested in the u.s. and Mexico.[27]

At the same time the fbi was carrying out the raids in Puerto Rico, agents were arresting Juan Segarra Palmer in Texas, Anne Gassin (who later became a government witness) in Boston, and in Mexico, the Mexican police were arresting Luz Berríos and her two small children. She and the children were threatened and tormented by the police for four days before they were turned over to the u.s. authorities.

The fourteen who had been arrested were taken to a courtroom in Hartford, Connecticut—where it was impossible for an impartial trial to be carried out. The scene in Hartford was very similar to the one in Chicago in 1980. The prisoners had been stigmatized by the media, and the public had been poisoned with hatred and fear. In *Prisoners of Colonialism: The Struggle for Justice in Puerto Rico*, Ronald Fernández explains:

> When they finally entered a Connecticut courtroom on September 3, 1985, authorities shaped public opinion in—for Hartford, Connecticut—totally unprecedented fashion. Main Street looked like Beirut or Bosnia. Dogs, machine guns, sharpshooters, flack jackets, and one fellow wearing as many bullets draped over his chest as Rambo in Vietnam.[28]

The fourteen faced charges related to the seven million dollar expropriation of a Wells Fargo armored car. In 1983, Victor Gerena, a security guard working for Wells Fargo, drugged and put to sleep two of his co-workers and took seven million dollars. After the expropriation, according to the government, he moved to Cuba and has lived there since.

In an unprecedented move, the court refused to set bail for some of the prisoners. As a result, Filiberto Ojeda Ríos and Juan Segarra Palmer became the longest-held detainees without bail in u.s. history; at least three others whose charges were later dropped were kept in detention for up to sixteen months.

The *Macheteros* opted for a legal defense but with much political content. Throughout the proceedings the issue of colonialism, the abuses the government had committed, and the crimes committed by the fbi were publicly aired. Three of the defendants had the charges dropped and the others were given sentences ranging from one to sixty-five years in prison. Filiberto Ojeda Ríos was tried in absentia and given a fifty-five-year sentence. Because Ojeda Ríos was facing charges in Puerto Rico for preventing the fbi from invading his home, that case took precedence. Judge Carmen Vargas Cerezo allowed him to defend himself and to do so in Spanish (a victory in and of itself because all proceedings in the u.s. federal court in Puerto Rico are conducted in English). He successfully presented his case, arguing that he had the right to defend his home from an illegal invasion. A Puerto Rican jury agreed and found him not guilty. After the trial, the court allowed him to remain in Puerto Rico under house arrest, wearing an electronic bracelet until the trial in Hartford. A year later he took off the bracelet and sent it to the media with a message about his decision to go underground again. Ever since then, the fbi has been trying to capture him. A reward of one million dollars has been offered for information leading to his arrest—but there have been no takers.

Between 1980 and 1989, about fifty-nine Independentists and supporters of the Puerto Rican Independence Movement were imprisoned. But conspirators and assassins like Governor Carlos Romero Barceló and the fbi agents responsible for the Cerro Maravilla Massacre were never brought to justice.

The 1990s and Beyond: Dirty tricks, partial victories, and continuing struggle

During the decade of the 90s, the government focused its attack on the Juan Antonio Corretjer Puerto Rican Cultural Center in Chicago. The Center had earned a solid reputation for its work with the Puerto Rican community and for its support of Puerto Rico's independence. It was where the campaign to free the Puerto Rican political prisoners was started and where much of the work was being done. The fbi had attempted to close it down in the mid 1980's, but the Puerto Rican community thwarted the attempt by giving the Center the support it needed.

After failing to shut down the Center, the fbi planted an informer and *agent-provocateur* there named Rafael Marrero. He had moved to Chicago from Puerto Rico, and established a relationship with the sister of political prisoners Alicia and Ida Luz Rodríguez to gain legitimacy. He started working at the Center and projected the image of a dedicated worker. Once established, he began to advocate for more radical politics and armed struggle. He also criticized the work being carried out at the Center and labeled it "reformist."

Dr. José Solís Jordán and his family moved to Chicago in 1992. He was a professor at DePaul University. Marrero began to befriend him, and soon their two families became close. On 10 December, 1992, an organization called the *Frente Revolucionario Boricua* took responsibility for bombing a u.s. army recruitment center in Chicago. Marrero mailed letters with newspaper clippings about the bombing to some of the Puerto Rican political prisoners, and started trying to recruit people for the new clandestine organization.

The work of the Center came under Marrero's attack. He started employing the same tactics the fbi had used in Puerto Rico during the decades of the 60s and 70s—character assassination of the leaders, fomenting dissent and sowing confusion. As part of his smear campaign, he also published a tabloid, *El Pito*, which mysteriously appeared at Puerto Rican businesses just before key community celebrations. Then, suddenly, he disappeared.

Soon after Marrero's disappearance, the Center's work came under a media attack—especially from the *Chicago Sun-Times* and the *Tribune*.[29] The Center had established a working relationship with the Roberto Clemente High School. According to the media, massive fraud was being committed. The money assigned for poverty programs, the media alleged, was being spent by the Center to fund the campaign to free the Puerto Rican political prisoners. The media used Rafael Marrero as the source for their allegations. The fbi and the u.s. attorney for Chicago called for an investigation. The CEO of the Chicago Public Schools seized the opportunity to attack the programs the Center and Clemente High School had instituted. And the Illinois State legislature began to hold hearings. Marrero testified about the alleged fraud. But after all the media red-baiting and fear-mongering, the attacks by the fbi and the u.s. attorney, and the hearings there wasn't a scintilla of evidence of any fraud. As an informer and agent-provocateur, Rafael Marrero had wreaked havoc on the hard community work the Center had carried out at Clemente High School for years. Many relationships were destroyed. The distrust and hatred that had been sown deeply affected the work of the campaign to free the Puerto Rican political prisoners.

In 1997, the fbi arrested Dr. José Solís Jordán in San Juan, Puerto Rico on charges of participating in the December 10, 1992 recruiting station bombing. During the arrest, the fbi asked him to incriminate others, particularly the executive director of the Center, my brother José López. Solís Jordán refused and was forced to go to Chicago to face trial. Rafael Marrero was the star witness. Under oath, Marrero testified that he had worked for the fbi, and that he made and placed the bomb. But it was Solís Jordán who was found guilty and sentenced to fifty-one months in prison. After completing his sentence, Dr. Solís returned to his wife and five children in Puerto Rico and to his job at the University of Puerto Rico.[30]

The destruction caused by the government in its quest to destroy the Puerto Rican Independence Movement cannot be quantified or redressed. But there are examples that reveal how blatant and rampant the abuses and destruction were. The case of Erich Rodríguez García, who was released from prison after serving a twelve-year sentence, is very illustrative. Judge Hiram Sánchez Martínez, in the resolution exonerating Erich, wrote:

Finally we want to consign that cases like this illustrate the fragility of the justice administration system when corrupt policeman and unscrupulous investigating attorneys unite to subvert the judicial process and using the legitimacy of judicial power take away from the citizen the precious right of his/her freedom.[31]

In a lawsuit that Erich Rodríguez García filed for wrongful conviction and for damages caused to him and his family, he alleged that the police, the colonial department of justice, fbi agents, and the u.s. attorney for Puerto Rico were aware that the evidence used against him had been planted and the case fabricated, yet they allowed him to be imprisoned for twelve years. When the government started the case against him, he was twenty-years-old, married, and with an infant daughter. He will never be able to make up for what he lost.

On September 10, 1999, eleven Puerto Rican political prisoners were released from prison. President Clinton, granting clemency, acknowledged the political nature of the case and the disproportionately lengthy sentences received. These eleven men and women were among the fifteen whose release had been sought by thousands of people who participated in an international human rights campaign; two others have been released since then. Carlos Alberto Torres and I remain in prison. The eleven were welcomed home as national heroes in Chicago and Puerto Rico.[32]

The fbi, with the support of the legislative branch of the government and other government bureaucrats, mobilized forces to condemn the decision. Ninety-five senators and 311 members of Congress voted to condemn Clinton's decision to release the independentists. The Committee on Government Reform, chaired by Congressman Dan Burton, (R-IN), called Clinton's decision reckless and claimed that it sent a dangerous message. In its report, the committee concluded: "that the offer of clemency to unrepentant terrorists who have done nothing to discourage violence or solve unresolved crimes diminishes our moral authority in the fight against international terrorism."[33]

If Congressman Burton and his committee were so concerned with the u.s. authority to fight international terrorism, then why didn't they condemn President George H. W. Bush, who in 1992 used his clemency power to pardon Dr. Orlando Bosch, the Cuban American responsible for the bombing of a Cuban plane that killed all seventy-three passengers on board? Since 1992, Bosch has been linked to other terrorist acts, including the plan to assassinate

Fidel Castro in Panama. His two associates, Guillermo Novo Sampol and Luis Posada Carriles were in a Panamanian prison for the plot. Guillermo Novo Sampol and Luis Posada Carriles were given clemency by President Miralla Moscoso—the outgoing president of Panama. When Novo Sampol arrived in Miami, he was given a hero's welcome. That's international terrorism blessed by the u.s. government.[34]

In April 1999, one of the largest and most successful civil disobedience campaigns in Puerto Rico's history began. On April 19, 1999, David Sanes Rodríguez, a guard working at the u.s. navy base, was killed by a bomb dropped by a u.s. navy plane that was conducting a military exercise. The navy tried to deal with this death in the same arrogant and insensitive way it had throughout the sixty years it had occupied Vieques. But the Puerto Rican people, galvanized by the injustice, called for the immediate closing of the base and the departure of the navy from Vieques. Camps were set up in the areas occupied by the navy, and people took turns occupying those camps for a full year. In May 2000, the u.s. federal court in Puerto Rico ordered the activists to leave the restricted area. The navy had been stopped from using it for over a year. When the activists refused to leave, the police, the military police, and u.s. marshals moved in, arrested the protesters and destroyed the camps. But the arrests and destruction of the camps didn't stop the civil disobedience campaign; on the contrary, it grew even stronger.[35]

The civil disobedience campaign went on, stopping the navy many times from carrying out its military exercises. Between 1999 and May 2003, hundreds of people were imprisoned. The total number of people arrested, according to José "Ché" Paralitici [director of the All Puerto Rico for Vieques Committee], were 1,640 in Puerto Rico and over 300 in the u.s. They were sentenced to a total of 9,586 days (twenty-six years, two months, and twenty-six days). George W. Bush finally agreed to close the base in May 2003.

May 1, 2003, thousands of people congregated in Vieques to celebrate the departure of the navy. The victory was real, although the struggle continues to have the land cleaned up and returned to the people.[36] At midnight when the celebration started, some of the participants made bonfires with the junk left behind by the navy. But for the government, the burning of the junk was a crime. Twelve persons, mostly Vieques residents, were charged for destroying the junk and a u.s. federal judge gave them sentences ranging from probation to five years in prison and fines.

For over sixty years, the navy caused irreparable damage to the environment, the flora and fauna, and the residents of Vieques. It forced half of the population to emigrate, destroyed the Island's economy, and killed or caused the death of many people. For all the crimes it committed, the navy was never condemned by the government. But, thousands of Puerto Ricans were criminalized and imprisoned for wanting Vieques to be free of any military presence and for its residence to live in peace, in a clean and safe environment, and to develop their economy.

Conclusion

For over a hundred years, Puerto Rico has been a place of u.s. colonialism and Puerto Rican resistance. Our nation has been invaded, our language and culture attacked, and we have been forced to be u.s. citizens in order to serve as cannon fodder. Our leaders and their supporters have been persecuted, smeared, imprisoned, tortured, and killed. Our territories have been bombed, poisoned, and violated. Yet, our people have resisted, and continue to resist. After a hundred years of colonialism, it's time for Puerto Rico to exercise its right of self-determination, to be a free, sovereign, and democratic nation, and to take its place in the community of nations.

Notes

The research and draft for the introduction to this chapter and research assistance for notes were provided by Madeleine Dwertman. As noted earlier, Rivera's essay was handwritten and mailed in installments to prevent confiscation by guards; it has passed through many hands and has been subjected to many editorial interventions, some of which Rivera has found distressing. For that reason, we have chosen to publish the essay without further intervention.

1. In *Violations of Human Rights in Puerto Rico by the U.S.*, Luis Nieves Falcón notes that the charter granted "the authority to establish its own currency, to enter into commercial treaties, and to possess the authority to approve or reject treaties or agreements made by Spain which would affect the economic interest of Puerto Rico. Most significantly, Article 44 provided that the charter could not be amended except upon the request and approval of the Puerto Rican people." Falcón, *Violations of Human Rights in Puerto Rico by the U.S.*, 237.

2. *Editor's note*: On March 2, 1917, President Woodrow Wilson signed the Jones-Shafroth Act, which gave Puerto Ricans U.S. citizenship and individual civil rights and separated the executive, judicial, and legislative branches of the Puerto Rican govern-

ment. The governor and the president of the United States, however, maintained the power to veto any law passed by the legislature, and the U.S. Congress possessed the power to stop any action taken by the legislature in Puerto Rico. The United States maintained control over governmental and economic matters and exercised authority over mail services, immigration, and defense. See Library of Congress, "Jones Act," available online at http://www.loc.gov/rr/hispanic/1898/jonesact.html (accessed September 29, 2004).

3. Fernández, *Prisoners of Colonialism*.

4. The charter "could not be amended except upon the request and approval of the Puerto Rican people." Of course, this key provision of the charter was violated by the 1898 Treaty of Paris, through which Puerto Rico fell under U.S. control as war booty after Spain's defeat in the Spanish American War. See Falcón, *Violations of Human Rights in Puerto Rico by the U.S.*, 237.

5. *Editor's note*: On September 23, 2005, the anniversary of *Grito de Lares*, the first Puerto Rican uprising against Spain, the FBI assassinated in his home in Hormigueros, Puerto Rico, Filiberto Ojeda Rios, founder of the Armed Revolutionary Independence Movement and key leader of the FALN and *Macheteros*. Ojeda Rios, sentenced in absentia by the United States in 1992 for his alleged participation in the 1973 Wells Fargo robbery, in Puerto Rico in 1990, went underground after being unanimously absolved by a Puerto Rican jury. According to eyewitness accounts, the FBI operation included three hundred FBI agents, two helicopters, more than thirty vehicles on land, and approximately twenty-four sharpshooters. While the FBI fired over one hundred shots at his home, Ojedo Rios fired only ten in self-defense. Autopsy reports indicated that Ojeda Rios was hit with a single bullet in his right clavicle and bled to death because the FBI prevented him from receiving medical attention for nearly twenty hours. Following widespread public outcry, allegations from Puerto Rican officials, and denouncement from the Puerto Rican Truth and Justice Commission, which stated Ojeda Rios's death was "without any doubt, a political assassination," FBI Director Robert S. Mueller ordered an independent Justice Department investigation into the incident that is currently still underway.

See: Democracy Now!, "FBI Assassinates Puerto Rican Nationalist Leader Filiberto Ojeda Rios," September 26, 2005, available online at http://www.democracynow .org/article.pl?sid=05/09/26/1434229 (accessed October 5, 2005); International Action Center (IAC), "IAC Statement on the Assassination of Filiberto Ojeda Rios," available online at http://www.iacenter.org/puertorico/puerto-filiberto092805.htm (accessed October 5, 2005); Tom Soto, "FBI Terror Attack in Puerto Rico," *Worker's World*, September 27, 2005, available online at http://www.workers.org/2005/world/ filberto-ojeda-1006/ (accessed October 3, 2005); Simon Watts, "FBI Probes Puerto Rico Shoot-out," BBC News, September 27, 2005, available online at http://news.bbc .co.uk/2/hi/americas/4287118.stm (accessed October 3, 2005).

6. Jose Ché Paralatici, *Sentencia Impuesta: 100 Años de Encarcelamientos per la Independencia de Puerto Rico* (San Juan: Ediciones Puerto, Inc., 2004).

7. Ronald Fernández, *Prisoners of Colonialism: The Struggle for Justice in Puerto Rico* (Monroe: ME: Common Courage Press, 1994).

8. Marcantonio, "Five Years of Tyranny"; emphasis added

9. *Editor's note*: Vito Marcantonio delivered a speech entitled "Five Years of Tyranny" before the U.S. Congress on August 14, 1939. The full text of this speech is reprinted in *Congressional Record—House*, 14 August 1939, available online at http://www .cheverote.com/reviews/marcantonio.html (accessed August 12, 2006).

10. *Editor's note*: See Alfredo López, *Doña Licha's Island—Modern Colonialism in Puerto Rico* (Boston: South End Press, 1987); Fernández, *Prisoners of Colonialism.*

11. *Editor's note*: For information on radiation experiments on Puerto Rican prisoners, see Fernández, *Prisoners of Colonialism.*

12. *Editor's note*: See Resolution 748 (VIII), 73(e) of the United Nations charter; United Nations, "General Assembly Resolutions, 8th Session," available online at http://www .un.org/documents/ga/res/8/areas8.htm.

13. Heriberto Marín, who spent close to nine years behind bars, writes about the ordeal of the Díaz family. Don Ricardo Díaz, a prominent leader of the PRNP in Arecibo; his wife, Leonides Díaz; his sons Ricardo and Angel; his brother-in-law; and his nephew, Hipólito, were all arrested, convicted, and sentenced to multiple life sentences. Hipólito Díaz was killed during the insurrection. After several years in prison, Angel Díaz's mental health began to deteriorate. When his son was no longer mentally sane, Don Ricardo became terribly ill, stopped eating and communicating, and stayed in bed, staring at the ceiling. Doña Leonides was declared innocent after being behind bars for over seven years. Months later, Don Ricardo and his sons were released from prison because of poor health; all three were soon dead. See Marín, *Eran Ellos.*

14. *Editor's note*: This memorandum is quoted in Paul Wolf, comp., "COINTELPRO: The Untold American Story," presented to the United Nations World Conference against Racism, 2001, available online at http://www.icdc.com/~paulwolf/cointelpro/coinw car3.htm (accessed October 1, 2004).

15. *Editor's note*: J. Edgar Hoover, "Memorandum," August 4, 1960. This memorandum is also quoted in Juan Gonzalez, "FBI Campaign in Puerto Rico Lasted More than Four Decades," *Puerto Rico Herald*, May 24, 2000.

16. *Editor's note*: Omega 7, a U.S.-based right-wing terrorist organization of Cuban exiles that opposed Fidel Castro's government, is believed to be responsible for the bombing of *El Diario* in 1978. See Anya K. Landau and Wayne S. Smith, "Keeping Things in Perspective: Cuba and the Question of International Terrorism," Center for International Policy, November 6, 2001, available online at http://ciponline.org/cuba/ cubaandterrorism/keepingthingsinperspective.htm (accessed October 3, 2004).

17. *Editor's note*: *Claridad* printing presses were bombed at least five times during the 1970s. The independence movement furnished police with detailed information about perpetrators, yet no trials were ever held on the island in connection with these bombings. See "COINTELPRO: The Untold Story of American Repression," *Third World Traveler*, available online at http://www.thirdworldtraveler.com/FBI/COINTELPRO_Untold_Story.html (accessed September 29, 2004).

18. *Editor's note*: See "Puerto Rico Libre!" *Arm the Spirit*, vol. 13, June–July 1992, available online at http://www.etext.org/Politics/Autonome.Forum/ATS.Magazines/ats13-july-1992.txt (accessed January 17, 2005).

19. Juan Antonio Corretjer, who spent time in a prison in Atlanta, Georgia, with Albizu Campos after the *Grito de Jayuya*, founded the LSP, a small clandestine independence group founded on principles of revolutionary Marxism. The LSP forged bonds with other organizations in Latin America and the Young Lords and *independentistas* in the United States.

    Editor's note: For information on U.S. use of the Federal Grand Jury to incarcerate members of radical Puerto Rican organizations, see Deutsch, "The Improper Use of the Federal Grand Jury."

20. *Editor's note*: In an April 1997 statement submitted to the U.S. House Resources Committee Hearings on proposed legislation concerning the status of Puerto Rico, Puerto Rican political prisoners explained their position on the use of violence in the struggle for Puerto Rican independence:

    > Invoking the right under international law to use all means available does not mean we used them with no respect for human life, even when colonialism is a disrespect for the human life of a nation, a crime perpetrated against all citizens, regardless. It has always been the practice and purpose of groups participating in the independence struggle to take all possible measures to ensure that innocent people are not harmed. Our actions, for the most part symbolic, have had the objective of focusing the attention of the U.S. government on the colonial conditions of Puerto Rico, and not of causing terror to the citizens of the U.S. or Puerto Rico. However, that is not to deny that in all liberation processes, there are always innocent victims on all sides. In the case of Puerto Rico, there are fewer caused by those who struggle for independence in comparison with other liberation movements, taking into consideration as well the disproportionate size of the contenders. In our case . . . we learn from past experiences with a sense of self-criticism, always in the context of our just cause, seeking to end colonialism, a crime against humanity. Activities caused by other contradictions as a result of the system that predominates in the United States cannot interfere with the efforts for our release or the struggle to end our colonial situation.

    The full text of this statement is available online at http://www.prisonactivist.org/quesalgan/RCS.html (accessed November 4, 2004).

21. The 1983 hearings held by the colonial legislature regarding the Cerro Maravilla Mas-

sacre clearly demonstrated why colonialism was declared a crime against humanity. The policemen who had assassinated Arnaldo Dario Rosado and Carlos Soto Arrivi testified that a young undercover agent named Alejandro González Malavé, who worked for the police as an informer since he was sixteen years old, had lured the two young men into a phony clandestine organization, the "Movimiento Revolucionario Armado," which had been organized by the police, supervised by the FBI, and originated by then-governor Carlos Romero Barceló, the superintendent of police, the head of police intelligence division, and agents of the FBI. For five years, the colonial justice department and the federal justice department had colluded to cover up the massacre.

The most telling testimony was given by the taxi driver [Julio Ortiz Molina], who was kidnapped and forced to drive the three to Cerro Maravilla. He was almost killed in the police shootout. But from the first statement he gave to the police [in which he disclosed witnessing the police beat the two men and heard gunfire after the surrender], until he testified in the hearings he never changed his story. The police and the attorney from the justice department tried to force him to change it to make it compatible with the official version, but he refused. Finally, the assassins told the truth and confirmed what the taxi driver had been saying all along—that the police had committed a massacre.

After the hearings, [five Puerto Rican] policemen were sentenced to [five to thirty years in] prison and the justice department's attorney was censured. But the real culprits and those in the federal justice department who covered up the crime were never prosecuted or brought to justice. The fact that a colonial governor, the superintendent of police, and employees of a federal agency had conspired and carried out such a heinous crime showed how criminal colonialism was and continues to be.

One positive result of the hearing was the elimination of the notorious police intelligence unit. It was the unit responsible for spying and keeping files on Independentists. In 1987, the police were ordered to turn over the files to the more than 100,000 Independentists who had been persecuted for years by this police unit.

Editor's note: Two investigations by the Puerto Rican Justice Department in 1978 and in 1981 absolved the police of all wrongdoing and concluded that Arriví and Rosado had opened fire and the police had shot in self-defense. The *New York Times* states that Governor Romero Barceló visited U.S. Attorney General Benjamin R. Civiletti in December 1979. Shortly after the visit, Romero Barceló, formerly a Republican, declared himself a Democrat and began to support Jimmy Carter's presidential campaign. Barceló claimed that he could deliver Puerto Rico's forty-one Democratic Party convention votes to Carter. On April 25, 1980, the Justice Department's civil-rights division closed its investigation for "lack of evidence." Rubén Berros, president of the Puerto Rican Independence Party, and Juan Mari Bras, secretary-general of the Puerto Rican Socialist Party, demanded a Senate investigation in Puerto Rico.

See "Senators Asked to Study Puerto Rico Killing Inquiry," *New York Times*, August 11, 1980.

The case was reopened in 1980 when Lieutenant Julio C. Andrades of the Puerto Rican police, who participated in the operation, accepted immunity and testified that the two suspects had surrendered and were killed while unarmed. During the Senate hearings, Miguel Cartagena Flores, a detective in the intelligence division, delivered six hours of testimony, corroborating this version of events. The hearings resulted in the conviction of ten former Puerto Rican police officers on counts of perjury and obstruction. The U.S. Justice Department, however, refused to release many important documents to Puerto Rican officials, leading some to believe that the FBI was involved in perpetrating and covering up the killings. The FBI's 1984 investigation of its own behavior, however, found no wrongdoing. See Reginald Stuart, "Ten Puerto Rican Police Indicted in Cover-Up of '78 Killings," *New York Times*, February 7, 1984; "New Inquiry in Puerto Rico Shootings," *New York Times*, August 23, 1984; "Ex-Justice Official Cites 'Coverup' By FBI in '78 Puerto Rico Shootings," *New York Times*, May 9, 1992; "Fourteen Years Later, Puerto Rico Rests Its Case," *Washington Post*, May 18, 1992.

Five Puerto Rican police were eventually convicted of murder and received sentences ranging from five to thirty years. The commander of the intelligence unit responsible for the same murders was released on parole after six years in prison. See Susler, "Unreconstructed Revolutionaries."

22. Around the same time Edwin Cortés, Alberto Rodríguez, José Luis Rodríguez, and Alejandrina Torres were captured in Chicago, Mexican Interpol was apprehending William Guillermo Morales in Puebla, Mexico. His capture had been ordered by the FBI. There was a shootout between the police and William's companion. Two policemen were shot (one of them died soon after), and the companion was killed. William was tortured. An international campaign was organized asking the Mexican government not to extradite him to the u.s., but the Mexican government acknowledged that his was a political case. He was allowed to go to Cuba, where he received political asylum, after he completed his five-year sentence.

23. *Editor's note*: Andres Figueroa Cordero was granted executive clemency in December 1977. The other four were granted executive clemency in 1979, after over twenty-five years in prison. See "An Interview with Elizam Escobar," in Torres and Velázquez, *The Puerto Rican Movement*, 235.

24. See Fernández, *Prisoners of Colonialism*.

25. *Editor's note*: The "sedition laws," created by the Alien and Sedition Acts of 1798, allowed the imposition of up to twenty-year prison terms when two or more people "conspire to overthrow, put down, or to destroy by force the government of the United States, or to levy war against them."

26. *Editor's note*: See Susler, "Puerto Rican Political Prisoners."

27. *Editor's note*: News reports indicate that 200 FBI agents raided over thirty-seven residences and offices in Puerto Rico on August 30, 1984, including those of writers thought to be supportive of the independence movement. The agents arrested eleven individuals with supposed links to the *Macheteros*, who were suspected of involvement in the 7 million dollar Wells Fargo robbery on September 12, 1983. In addition to those arrested in Puerto Rico and transferred to Hartford, Connecticut, for the trial, six individuals were seized in Boston, Dallas, and Mexico. The primary suspect, Victor M. Gerena, was given sanctuary by Cuba. See "Eleven to Be Extradited in $7 Million Theft," *New York Times*, September 2, 1985, 24; "Wells Fargo Robbery Suspects Appear in Hartford Court," *New York Times*, September 4, 1985, A25; Manuel Suarez, "FBI Discerns Big Gain on Puerto Rico Terrorists," *New York Times*, September 8, 1985, 39; Edwin McDowell, "Writers Assail FBI Seizures in Puerto Rico," *New York Times*, October 2, 1985, B9.

28. Fernández, *Prisoners of Colonialism*.

29. *Editor's note*: According to a 1998 *Chicago Sun-Times* article, Marerro testified that Jose E. López, the founder of the cultural center and head of the *Movimiento de Liberación Nacional Puertorriqueno* (MLN), which the FBI identified as the aboveground arm of the FALN, aimed to "take over the local school council [of Clemente High School], control the hiring of the school principal, and take over the Chapter 1 funds" and divide them "among the community organizations the MLN controls." López denounced the accusations as "nothing but lies" and indicated that the government has never proved any ties between the FALN and MLN. See Al Podgorski, "Clemente Funds Traced; Sent to Terrorists' Allies, Panel Told," *Chicago Sun-Times*, March 5, 1998, 3.

30. For more information on José Solís Jordan, see José Solís Jordan, "This Is Enough!" in James, *Imprisoned Intellectuals*, 271–91.

31. Paralitici, *Sentencia Impuesta*, 295–96; translated by Oscar López Rivera.

32. *Editor's note*: The eleven Puerto Rican *Independentistas* released on parole on October 10, 1999, were Edwin Cortés, Elizam Escobar, Ricardo Jiménez, Adolfo Matos, Dylcia Pagán, Alberto Rodríguez, Alicia Rodríguez, Ida Luz Rodríguez, Luis Rosa, Alejandrina Torres, and Carmen Valentín. On Tuesday, July 26, 2005, the United States Parole Commission released Edwin Cortés, Elizam Escobar, Ricardo Jiménez, Adolfo Matos, Dylcia Pagán, Alberto Rodríguez, and Alejandrina Torres from parole.

Juan Segarra Palmer, who accepted Clinton's clemency offer to serve an additional five years of a fifty-five-year sentence, was released on January 3, 2004. Antonio Camacho Negrón, who refused the clemency offer due to its restrictive conditions, was released on August 17, 2004 after serving fifteen years (maximum sentence).

Those currently incarcerated include: Oscar López Rivera; Carlos Alberto Torres (serving a seventy-eight-year sentence); and Haydee Beltràn (sentenced to life in prison).

See: Melendez. Laura Rivera. "Hundreds Greet Nationalist Freed After Nineteen Years in Prison." *Puerto Rico Herald*, 25 January 2004, available online at http://www .puertorico-herald.org/issues/2004/vo18no5/Media3-en.shtml (accessed July 10, 2005); "Puerto Rican Political Prisoners and Prisoners of War Released: ¡Que Viva Puerto Rico Libre!," available online at http://www.prisonactivist.org/quesalgan/ turningtide.html (accessed July 9, 2002).

33. *Editor's note*: This statement is quoted in "Puerto Rican Patriots Are Greeted with Heroes' Welcome," *Chicago Militant*, vol. 63, no. 22, September 27, 1999.

34. *Editor's note*: See "Cuban Charge d'Affaires to Panama to Return," *Havana Journal*, August 30, 2004, available online at http://havanajournal.com/politics_comments/ A2411_0_5_0_M/ (accessed January 24, 2005).

35. *Editor's note*: See Barreto, *Vieques, the Navy and Puerto Rican Politics*.

36. *Editor's note*: For discussion of environmental damage in Vieques and civil disobedience to protest it, see Robert F. Kennedy Jr., *Outside*, October 2001, 80–84, 114–16.

References

Hanley, Charles. "America's Political Prisoner: When the Revolution Comes Home." *Los Angeles Times*, June 14, 1998.

Jericho Movement. "Oscar López Rivera." Available online at http://www.thejericho movement.com (accessed June 30, 2004).

Prison Activist Resource Center. "Oscar López Rivera." Available online at http://www .prisonactivist.org (accessed June 30, 2004).

United States v. Oscar López et al. Lexis 1483. U.S. Dist., February 25, 1987.

United States v. Oscar López, et al. Lexis 7552. U.S. Dist., August 14, 1987.

PART II   Policing and Prison Technologies

The essays in part II explore the penal conditions and police surveillance directed in the "free" and penal worlds at blacks, whites, women, Muslims, Asian Americans, Puerto Ricans, and Native Americans. This part begins with the profiling of "suspects" in organized campaigns for racial control, as explored in Jared Sexton's "Racial Profiling and the Societies of Control." Sexton discusses the relationship between state-sanctioned racial profiling in the United States and the contemporaneous rearticulation of what we might term "martial common sense" after the Cold War. Sexton traces linkages between the consolidation of the prison-industrial complex as a racial project of mass incarceration and the emergence of an official discourse of "rising international terrorism" and "proliferating rogue states" supposed to present a "post-political" threat to the stability of global civil society. He explores the connections between domestic policing and militarism abroad, specifically with respect to the ideologies of racial difference (tacitly endorsed by progressives) fabricated in each domain. Sexton maintains that these parallel trends construct a new historical bloc that forges an uneasy alliance against the menace of an atavistic black population, even as the United States mobilizes citizen-soldiers against "new" enemies in theaters of foreign war or in the crosshairs of local counterterrorist campaigns.

Alongside racialization, religion has merged in U.S. policing and military campaigns as "acceptable" criteria for excessive force and repression. Hishaam Aidi's "Jihadis in the Hood: Race, Urban Islam, and the War on Terror" argues that, since the capture of John Walker Lindh, the Marin County "black nationalist"-turned-Taliban, and the arrest of the would-be terrorist José Padilla, a Brooklyn-born Puerto Rican ex-gang member who found Islam while in prison, terrorism experts and columnists have warned of the "Islamic threat" in the American underclass and alerted the public that the ghetto and the prison system could supply a "fifth column" to Osama bin Laden. Aidi argues that assessments of an "Islamic threat" in the American ghetto are sensational and ahistorical. Critiquing the campaigns to stem the "Islamic tide," Aidi reviews prison and hip-hop culture to explore why alienated black and Latino youths gravitate toward an Islam that functions as a "culture of resistance."

Prison repression fosters various cultures of resistance. The voices of women prisoners appear in Marilyn Buck's "The Effects of Repression on Women in Prison." Prisons, according to Buck, an antiracist white revolutionary incarcerated for her work with black liberation movements, function as small city-states, in which the denizens—prisoners—are subject not only to society's laws but also to the ever changing, arbitrary power of the overseers and keepers. Drawing on her own experiences in federal prison—Buck is serving a virtual life sentence in a California prison for her associations with the Black Liberation Army—and those of other female prisoners, predominantly "social" prisoners, Buck describes how the prison as a repressive mechanism produces social and psychological alienation and decay.

The state also punishes human-rights pacifists who express dissent through nonviolent illegal acts. Sister Carol Gilbert's "Ponderings from the Eternal Now" presents her sentencing statement and collection of letters written as diary entries between October 2003 and July 2004 while she was incarcerated at Alderson Penitentiary. Gilbert, a Plowshares activist and member of the Jonah House Community, has twice been found guilty of "depredation of U.S. Government property" and served time in prison for actions taken to oppose U.S. manufacturing of nuclear warheads. She discusses the United States' violation of international law and subsequent criminalization of individuals who act to uphold these laws. Her monthly letters from prison—with their spiritual commitment to nonviolence that illustrates the diversity of resistance narratives to U.S. warfare—offer a view of the daily prison regime and routine exploitation and dehumanization of inmates (and their participation in social demise).

Amid the horror of the revelations of torture of prisoners by American soldiers in Iraq, Afghanistan, and Cuba's Guantánamo Bay, some journalists highlighted the presence of torture in U.S. prisons. Yet, according to Laura Whitehorn's "Resisting the Ordinary," few examined standard, daily abusive operating procedures and routines at U.S. penal sites. Whitehorn argues that torture and institutional abuse are similarly geared toward the destruction of the human personality. Looking at humiliation as one aspect of torture, Whitehorn relies on examples from her personal experiences in federal prison and administrators' dehumanizing acts against other prisoners to describe how "ordinary" practices become acceptable even when they fall within the categories of torture and abuse. Whitehorn discusses the difficulties in countering abuse when it is defined as "standard operating procedure." Incorporating into her essay excerpts from personal correspondence with activists (some of whom identify themselves as "combatants") in the Black Liberation Army, American Indian Movement, and white anti-imperialist movements, Whitehorn maintains that the treatment of political captives in the United States has set the stage for the maltreatment of detainees today.

Countering the "ordinary" as excessive force directed against the racialized other, William F. Pinar argues that the abuse of Iraqi prisoners at Abu Ghraib becomes more fully intelligible when situated in cultural traditions of racialized torture and warfare in the United States. Pinar's "Cultures of Torture" situates the Abu Ghraib scandal in three "cultures" of torture in U.S. racial history: lynching; the nineteenth-century convict-lease system; and twentieth-century, racialized abuse by prison guards. Since "emancipation," Pinar argues, criminalization has been fashioned racially in the United States as "legalized lynchings" have slowly replaced extralegal executions. In the late nineteenth century, black men were imprisoned for social infractions that would have been non-criminal offenses for whites, and once imprisoned, they were exploited in a vicious convict-lease system, with exorbitant death rates and casualties that surpassed the cruelties of slavery. Currently, Pinar maintains, black and Latino men are still disproportionately imprisoned, at times for arbitrary reasons or as victims of a racially fashioned "war on drugs." Historical and contemporary "cultures of torture," argues Pinar, contradict President George W. Bush's 2004 assertion that the Abu Ghraib photographs "do not represent America."

Suffering and abandonment and the policing of black bodies and communities in post-Hurricane Katrina New Orleans are examined by Manning Marable in the closing chapter, "Katrina's Unnatural Disaster: A Tragedy of Black Suffering and White Denial," which originally appeared in *Souls: A Critical Journal of Black Politics, Culture, and Society*. The devastation in New Orleans, which was not necessarily a "natural disaster," brought global attention to punitive measures taken against black survivors and the existence of impoverished black communities as trauma sites. These spaces are distinct from the trauma sites of formal prisons, but inhabitants or residents in certain urban areas are still regulated by government control (or neglect) and policed in racially fashioned ways that contradict the stated ideals of American democracy yet, nevertheless, represent another aspect of dispossession rather than security in and belonging to the homeland.

9

Racial Profiling and the Societies of Control   Jared Sexton

Rather than a single *type* or a juxtaposition of particular *cases* to be classified in formal cate-gories, racism is itself a *singular history* . . . connecting together the conjunctures of modern humanity. —ETIENNE BALIBAR, "RACISM AND NATIONALISM" (1991), 40 (EMPHASIS ADDED)

Introduction

In *Resisting State Violence*, Joy James levies an important critique of the Fou-cauldian analytic of disciplinary power.[1] There she argues that the well-known late French philosopher failed to adequately comprehend the persistence of racist violence as a basic structural feature in the social formation of Western modernity. That is to say, discipline (as Foucault discusses it) simply does not supercede or even significantly displace punishment as the paradigmatic ex-ercise of state power against blacks. In this essay, I will build on, yet depart slightly from, this critical assessment. While I am in full agreement that blacks remain the preeminent objects of punishment in the United States (and be-yond), subject to the most vicious spectacles of state-sanctioned violence and precluded from the possibility of either granting consent (in the Gramscian sense) or achieving normalization (to stay with Foucault)—a historical status James refers to rightly as "unassimilable"—I would add to this position that, despite this fact, blacks are in fact nonetheless subjected to regimes of discipline and control as what we might understand as forms of supplemental violence.

I am not suggesting that blacks are therefore normalized, like the subjects of civil society, and then, in a gratuitous secondary moment, subjected to pun-ishment, as well. Black rights, in other words, are not revoked. Rather, I take punishment—or state-sanctioned direct relations of force—to be primary and foundational to black subjection, while the production of discipline provides a type of popular theater of cruelty that enters public debate under the terms of "emancipation," "enfranchisement," "integration," "multiculturalism," or other verities of a strained nationalist project. Punishment, on this account, represents neither a breakdown of the strategies of containment, assimilation, or social control nor an excess of entrenched power threatened by the prospect of change from below; it is not reactive or strategic. Organized, systemic racial violence against blacks, gratuitous violence that traverses the conceptual distinction between state and civil society is, on the contrary, the opening gesture of Western modernity as such, the demarcation of its most fundamental boundary. It is what allows for wars in the proper sense to be fought, even the most brutal one-sided massacres. It embodies the permanent state of exception par excellence.

Empire thus exceeds its political, economic, and military rationalities whenever blacks are concerned, and the multitude could stand to learn this lesson—the sooner, the better.[2] We must lend more attention to the pleasures of militarism itself, the pure enjoyment of collective destruction, the social fantasies of death and dismemberment, the delights of martial law.[3] To say this is no mere embellishment, however, no mere name calling. It is an analytical question begging for engagement. Too often commentators write off the obvious exhilaration displayed by those intent on "killing the black community" as a character flaw of a fanatical ruling-class faction,[4] its social-psychological Achilles' heel. But this attitude—sometimes smug, sometimes hopeful—conceals (at least) an ultimately unsustainable faith in a historical dialectic of oppression and resistance or the inexplicable inevitability of the masters' fatal error, a predictable product of hubris or the drunkenness of a seemingly absolute power. Prior to the events of September 11, 2001, the libidinal economy of antiblackness was brought into sharp relief by an international forum on the question of racial profiling in the United States, but most critical analyses to date have consistently retreated from its discussion in favor of what are by now hackneyed explanations or merely moral denunciations. Needless to say, the issue never fails to resurface, producing each time the most acute interference in the discourse and organization of radical politics.

A Genealogy of Policing

In the contemporary United States, the police operate as *the* unaccountable arbiters of lethal violence, the agents of a domestic militarism that underwrites all expansionism and interventionism. They are, as a rule, afforded impunity in their discretion to use what we continue to euphemize as "excessive force," which really means any manner of brutalization whatsoever, including so-called unjustified shootings. In each case, the police enjoy a virtual immunity from prosecution and rarely experience even interruptions in salary. This free rein is not only practical, however—the effect of negligent judicial oversight or disorganized civilian review boards—it is also codified as what the legal scholar Janet Koven Levit terms "constitutional carte blanche." There is simply no legal recourse against the violence and violation of the police; police departments are, according to a recent Human Rights Watch report, agencies "shielded from justice."[5] At this point of extremity, the power of life and death rests clearly in their hands, granted by official decree. Before the police, we do not live under constitutional (or other) protection of any sort. We are, in short, "naked before the state."[6]

Under such conditions, it should surprise no one that "racial profiling" as an institutionalized practice of the agencies of the police is not only possible or pervasive but entirely legal. There is nothing hyperbolic about my argument here. Reading the legal scholarship on racial profiling, one gets a distinct sense of vertigo. What one finds there is an infinite regress around the standards of "probable cause" set forth in the Fourth Amendment protection against "unreasonable searches and seizures." A number of scholars have amply demonstrated how, for instance, the recent cases of *Illinois v. Wardlow* (2000) and *United States v. Whren* (1996) effectively circumvented the standard of "reasonable suspicion" that previously governed the conditions under which the police might stop and frisk pedestrians or motorists during routine traffic stops.[7] That earlier standard of reasonable suspicion was established in *Terry v. Ohio* (1968), the case from which the well-known "Terry stop" takes its name. However, on even cursory examination, one sees that *Terry* itself instituted a loophole around the Fourth Amendment definition of probable cause, all of which enabled the police greatly during its war on drugs, as Reagan declared it in 1982.[8] We might lament this persistent whittling away of the standards of suspicion, yet if we look closely at the doctrinal history of Fourth Amendment protections, we find again that probable cause itself reduces down to an equally vague and problematic standard of protection. As H. Richard Uviller remarks in *Virtual Justice*:

> Probable cause is not a very apt term; it has little to do with probability and nothing whatever with causality. But it is the term chosen by the Framers to describe the degree of suspicion requisite for the government to move into

the citizen's private spaces. It means "damn good reason to believe," that's all. Not certainty beyond a reasonable doubt, not even more likely than not. But [just] more than a hunch or [mere] suspicion. That's the best we can do to define it.[9]

Of course, the Fourth Amendment was intended to preclude the use of the "general warrant" or "writ of assistance" carried by British colonial officers before the Revolution, which sanctioned the search and seizure of anything and everything in the home or on the person of a given "suspect." In other words, the parameters of search and seizure were at the discretion of the colonial police and not subject to any judicial review. It is safe to say that the police today have regained the general warrant, such that under present circumstances "we all become susceptible to the arbitrary whims and unsupported hunches of police officers."[10] The pretexts available to stop and frisk any pedestrian or motorist they so choose are as numerous as they are unavoidable. In a motor vehicle, any infraction of the traffic code, however minor, can lead to full-scale search and arrest. Given that "no one can drive for even a few blocks without committing a minor violation,"[11] one is imminently open to police encounter on the streets and highways. Simply walking away from the police is now grounds for a stop and frisk, despite the supposed constitutional right to do so. Standing still is also grounds for a stop, either in particular designated "high-crime areas" or in any setting in which the police judge your presence "incongruous."

In theory, everyone in the United States (and many outside its boundaries) is subject to these rules of engagement. Yet, as Ira Glasser, former director of the America Civil Liberties Union (ACLU), recently noted, while the police could, say, randomly raid apartment buildings on the Upper West Side of Manhattan and yield fruitful results, they clearly do not. As he puts it, "They don't do it because most of the folks who live in those apartment buildings are white. They don't do it because if they tried to do it, the outrage would become so big, so fast that it would become politically impossible to sustain."[12] We might wonder who would be outraged at such operations and whose outrage would make a difference? At any rate, the verdict of his analysis is clear:

> On our highways, on our streets, in our airports, and at our customs checkpoints, skin color once again, *irrespective* of class, and *without distinctions* based on education or economic status, skin color once again is being used as a cause for suspicion, and a sufficient reason to violate people's rights.[13]

For blacks in particular the situation is acute. The most recent attack on Fourth Amendment protections followed immediately the Warren Court's "due process revolution," as inaugurated by its decisions in the *Mapp* (1961) and *Miranda* (1966) cases. This shift in judicial opinion in favor of criminal suspects and defendants, disproportionately black and characteristically depicted as such, was supposed by some to be the criminal-law equivalent to or extension of then recent civil law reforms. The motion toward constitutional protections for blacks was, then, taken to be a byproduct of the limited success of the Civil Rights Movement, but its broader implications were rapidly conflated with the perceived threat of the radicalization of struggle dubbed "Black Power," which for the mainstream presented ominous criminal tendencies, among other things. The idea that blacks could or should have both civil and criminal rights thus entered the furor of an emergent "law and order" political culture whose executive, legislative, and judicial wings all feverishly and collaboratively retrenched. The legal history from Richard Nixon to Ronald Reagan to George W. Bush—from "war on crime" to "war on drugs" to "war on terror"—is alarmingly short. The liberal civil-rights legislation and judiciary review enjoyed a very brief and largely ineffective life. But the "revolution" in criminal rights never even got off the ground; it never actually happened except in the collective paranoid fantasy of "white America." There is, finally, no golden age for blacks before the criminal law. Therefore, in our discussions of a so-called creeping fascism or nascent authoritarianism or rise of the police state, particularly in the wake of the Homeland Security and PATRIOT acts, we might do better than trace its genealogy to the general warrant (or even the Executive Order), whose specter forever haunts the democratic experiment of postrevolutionary civil society. Instead, the proper object of investigation is the antebellum slave code and its antecedents in colonial statute, not because the trajectory of this legal history threatens to undo the rights of all, but precisely because the prevailing libertarian impulse in the United States has so resourcefully and recurrently *rendered the concrete situation of blacks in metaphoric terms.*

Under the force of this law, blacks, who were clearly in the polity but definitively not of it, were not only available to arbitrary search and seizure—the bane of the general warrant—but were, in the main, always already searched and seized. More to the point, they had, in the famous phrase, "no rights that a white man [was] bound to respect," including the right to life. The ethos of slavery—in other words, the lasting ideological and affective matrix of the white-supremacist project—admits no legitimate black self-defense, recognizes no legitimate assertions of black self-possession, privacy, or autonomy. A permanent state of theft, seizure, and abduction orders the affairs of the captive community and its progeny. Structural vulnerability to appropriation, perpetual and involuntary openness, including all the wanton uses of the body so finely detailed by scholars like Saidiya Hartman and Hortense Spillers, should be understood as the paradigmatic conditions of black existence in the Americas, the defining characteristics of New World antiblackness.[14] In short, the black, whether slave or "free," lives under the commandment of whites.[15] Policing blacks in the colonial and antebellum periods was, we recall, the prerogative of every white (they could assume the role or not) and was only later professionalized as the modern prison system emerged out of the ashes of Reconstruction.[16] Without glossing the interceding history, suffice it to say that such policing was organized across the twentieth century at higher orders of magnitude by the political, economic, and social shifts attending the transition from welfare to warfare state.[17]

"Racial profiling," then, is a young term, but the practice is centuries-old. In other words, the policing of blacks—whose repression has always been state-sanctioned, even as it was rendered a private affair of "property management"—remains a central issue today; it has not recently emerged. Amnesty International's public hearings on racial profiling, the stalled federal legislation termed "HR 1443," the ACLU's "Driving while Black" campaign, and the problematic reworking of the issue of racial profiling after September 11 all unfold against the backdrop of this long history of "policing black people." The effects of crude political pragmatism, legalistic single-mindedness, or historical myopia enable us to identify the unleashing of the police with the advent of the war on drugs or the xenophobic panic around the New Immigration or the emergence of Homeland Security against the threat of terrorism.[18]

The End of the Post–Civil Rights Era

On this score, Michael Moore's film *Fahrenheit 9/11* (2004) comes immediately to mind, an unmitigated failure as political cinema, regardless of having won the Palm d'Or at Cannes, having achieved unprecedented box-office success, and having enjoyed a warm reception in certain quarters of the liberal and progressive press.[19] This failure issues not so much from the many compelling reasons that various critics have already noted as from the film's desertion of the *only* line of investigation that might have yielded a meaningful critical analysis of the both the war on terror and its domestic corollary in Homeland Security.[20] I am referring, of course, to the opening scene in which is depicted the well-known controversy of the 2000 presidential election. The specific focus of this account is the blatant disenfranchisement of some tens of thousands of black voters in the State of Florida and the notorious connection suggested between the suspected oversight of that operation by Governor Jeb Bush, brother to the current heir, and the equally dubious appointment of George W. Bush by a conservative-majority Supreme Court that superseded the results of the popular and electoral vote (both of which apparently went in favor of his opponent, Vice President Al Gore). With all of Moore's characteristic sloppiness, it is implied (though never stated) that the road to the White House was paved over the eviscerated institution of black citizenship. In other words, despite the fact that judicial decree would ultimately render the electoral process moot, it seems as if there was something necessary about the systemic proscription of black civic participation to the full-scale inauguration of the New American Century.[21] This single insight—still suspended in the nonsense of debate around the film—is the sole contribution of Moore's latest work, and it is one that he makes despite his preoccupation with the waning integrity of relations between white Middle America and its government.

This observation is a curious thing, however, since, in the last instance, it cannot be argued, as most of the left continues to do, that the black vote—or lack thereof—in any way provided the crucial margin for the Bush campaign, either in Florida in particular or in the United States more generally. I am claiming, to the contrary, that the election did not come down to a dirty fight in this corner of the nation, to these several counties of predominantly black communities with strong sympathies for the Democratic Party. It is clear that the purging of voter rolls was a premeditated and well-coordinated endeavor and that its effects were intended to erode whatever advantage Gore might command in the state. It is also clear that this erosion was supposed to come at the expense of the disproportionately black segment of the electorate directly affected by the so-called ex-felon exclusion rule. However, the important point not to be missed is that there was no way that the Bush campaign could have known, in advance and with such precision, that the presidential race would have played out in the way that it did. There is simply no sampling instrument sophisticated enough to yield such predictive capacity. Even if this were the case, nothing mandated the voter gap be remedied by these particular methods. Nothing, that is, that rendered it strategically necessary to do so: Resources could have been differently allocated, the campaign could have targeted more intensely key swing-vote regions of Florida, the electoral votes potentially lost in Florida could have been made up in other states that were neglected or forfeited, etc.[22] And all of this could have been done without the risk of the political scandal that eventually broke across the bow of the Bush regime when its tactics came to light. Why pursue this agenda, then, when its potential costs are so high and its probability for success so low?

The answer to this question is to be found in a moment captured by Moore in a montage of found footage from C-SPAN. What it reveals is the collective response of the (currently all-white) U.S. Senate to the challenge of the Congressional Black Caucus (CBC) to the inauguration of George W. Bush, an impassioned petition of objection by House Democrats to the inclusion of Florida's disputed electoral votes: ridicule, disregard, and mockery. The point cannot be overstated. This was not a rearguard Republican filibuster resulting in a narrow partisan defeat. It was, rather, a unanimous refusal to co-sponsor the petition of their black colleagues on the matter (still, again) of black disenfranchisement. Not only were these black elected officials not able to block or even delay the ratification of the election; they were not even able to voice the basis of their objections (rules are rules, after all). In fact, their efforts were met with raucous shouts of impatience from those in attendance and—this might seem bizarre if it did not make sense—a series of flatly condescending remarks from the presiding official, the vanquished Al Gore himself.[23] The entire gesture of the CBC was, as a result, not recognized and therefore rendered nonexistent, off the record. Although control of the highest office in the land hung in the balance, and their party's loss of the forty-third presidency would consolidate Republican dominance in all three branches of the government for the foreseeable future, Democrats became accomplices—the real "coalition of the willing"—in the conspiracy of silence, tacitly agreeing to shuffle the national leadership. How could this jovial closing of ranks have followed on the heels of the most bitterly disputed election in more than a century—nearly six weeks of belligerent suspense, all the way to the Supreme Court—and why does the left remain so painfully inattentive to this profound peculiarity?[24] Well, prior to the congressional goose-stepping that rubber-stamped Bush's post-September 11 policy package (provoking such howls of false alarm and naive disappointment among the loyal opposition), there was this all too familiar embrace across the aisle on what has been, since before the Declaration of Independence, *the* issue of national division—blacks: subjects or objects, citizens or chattel?

This was the true political lesson of the year 2000: Gore's winning the race under the circumstances (that is, allegations of Republican fraud, an incipient recount, the pending litigation) would have required the official defense of black citizenship, a proposition that appears to have been entirely unacceptable to every member of the upper chamber of Congress—in the spirit of reconciliation, as it were. It seems that this gesture of advocacy—a nod, an admittance that there was, perhaps, something rotten in the Deep South—would have not only prolonged "what remains of partisan rancor" or besmirched any potential Gore administration (and who would care in any case?) but also thrown into question the functioning of the entire panoply of state apparatuses—"the honored institutions of our democracy."[25] Not, I suggest, because the black electorate posed a practical threat to a Republican agenda but, rather, because blacks pose—eternally—a symbolic threat to citizenship, the political equivalent to "there goes the neighborhood."[26]

In retrospect, it seems that this immanent crisis of legitimacy at the heart of "American civilization" threatened something more fundamental than the global instability brought about by the brazen flouting of all legal constraints—constitutional provisions, international law, United Nations conventions, etc.—that has characterized the Bush faction for the duration of its tenure. In fact, we have witnessed exactly the opposite. Bush has been taken more seriously since September 11 (as has the demonic Rudy Giuliani),[27] not just as a maniacal threat to the world, but as the legitimate leader of the United States. He is, to be sure, considered by most on the left to be dangerous, idiotic, and fanatical; however, he is not taken to be a usurper. For evidence of such, we need look no further than the fever-pitched center-left campaign to vote him out of office (from MoveOn.org to International ANSWER [Act Now to Stop War and End Racism]), as if he attained the position democratically, as if the position—President of the United States—can ever be attained democratically. Those who truly believe him, and the government over which he presides, to be a fraud must call for his immediate deposition, not demand his censure or impeachment, much less pray for his defeat at the polls. The latter posture simply yields to patriotism. "Regime change begins at home!" has been a frequent rallying cry at antiwar demonstrations across the United States. To those who sport such slogans, we can only say: Let it be changed then, as Bush and Company have changed so many others.

This position is largely unthinkable today, however, because, when taken to its logical conclusion, to radically oppose the Bush administration is, ipso facto, to foster the dissolution of the United States as we know it. This specter of "complete disorder" has always been essential to any prospect of black liberation in the United States.[28] (Recall, as I wrote above: "The road to the White House was paved over the eviscerated institution of black citizenship.") Needless to say, few on the left are willing to conscience as much. What prevails instead in the current conjuncture is a concrete preference for the national sacrifice of blacks as political entities (not only bearing rights, but also articulating legible demands in the public sphere) to pursue—under cover of an institutionalized disavowal—what amounts to an intensified partisan battle within the framework of an already anemic liberal democracy (anemic, that is, for those supposed to be its proper subjects; thus, the endless banter in the alternative press about "campaign finance reform," "media democracy," and so on). In my view, the determined inconsideration of the structural position of blacks in the social formation—that which makes the hoax of Election 2000 normal and not exceptional, a historical continuity—is absolutely vital to the range of progressive causes that have come of age in the wake of September 11: from the legal defense of those targeted by anti-terrorist profiling to debates about the standing and welfare of so-called enemy combatants to the efflorescence of the immigrant-rights movement. How else could the general public—now, since Clinton, expressly multiracial—acquiesce so readily in a bloodless coup d'état in the birthplace of the democratic experiment? Forget the snub of senatorial co-sponsorship for a wrist-slapping federal investigation (who looks to Congress for salvation?). The more important question is: Where were the broad-based, grassroots multiracial coalitions fighting on this front? And, as Election 2004 came and went, why were we not vociferously revisiting this political primal scene? In place of this absent solidarity with actually existing black communities (whose civic participation continues to be harassed, to put it mildly), we have instead a consistent analogizing to abstract black suffering that actually displaces black struggles even as it builds on their example: To wit, "Flying while Brown" is like "Driving while Black" (though police profiling, a practice legally rationalized as far back as the early 1960s, was off the radar of most Arab, Muslim, and South Asian community-based organizations up to September 10); the Immigrant Workers' Freedom Ride "builds on the history of the noble U.S. civil rights movement" (though immigrant rights groups are, as a rule, unconcerned with black workers or the exorbitant rates of black unemployment—black economic dislocation being one of the preconditions of immigrant labor);[29] the prisoner abuse at Abu Ghraib is reminiscent of the lynching of blacks (though most who publicly denounce such cruelty are relatively undisturbed about the similar treatment of a mostly black domestic prison population), and so on.[30]

Seen in this light, can we not detect in this pervasive indifference a historical revision of the election of 1876, in which the Republican Rutherford Hayes was appointed to the presidency by a special bipartisan commission despite having lost the popular vote to his Democratic challenger, Samuel Tilden? In other words, was not the month-long campaign that culminated in *Bush v. Gore*—and the marked silence that soon followed the high court's decision—an equivalent political event to that which formally ended the era of Reconstruction, the infamous Compromise of 1877? In the former instance, a program of unprecedented social spending, enforced by a massive domestic military presence, was terminated, and landmark civil-rights legislation, however watered down, was effectively abandoned, but only after each had already been rendered largely impotent by the often violent paramilitary and political maneuverings of a retrenched Confederacy against the first fateful hopes of a nominally emancipated slave population.[31] (The post-emancipation struggle for civil rights and racial justice would not reemerge with the force to wield significant national—and international—influence for nearly one hundred years.) The present moment, however, signals the true death-knell of the modern Civil Rights Movement, insofar as it pursued a second, more comprehensive Reconstruction, now in the twilight of the limited (though not insignificant) gains it momentarily secured under the headings of "antidiscrimination" and "affirmative action." Election 2000 designates the formal end of the post-civil-rights era, the genuine maturation of the new right, and the advent of a new redemption. The difference today is that the "racial reaction" is no longer a resurrection of new-fangled white supremacy, a project that has become untenable and perhaps even un-desirable.[32] It is, instead, an intensification of a capacious antiblackness that is entirely compatible with the emerging multiracial America.[33]

That is to say, quite insistently, that the most important shift produced by the ascension of the Bush junta regards the emergent consensus about the relative insignificance of what I can only inadequately term the rights of blacks in the United States. Even this is putting things too gently. For this stark rightward drift—which has affected the whole of the political spectrum—is not simply about the rollback of the liberal legislative gains of the 1960s or the deliber-ate dismantling of the most ameliorative aspects of the welfare state or even the endless narrowing of the scope of legal protections before the police (the latter tendency becoming especially prominent since the launch of Reagan's infamous war on drugs in the early 1980s). More profoundly, the "conservative restoration" names the retreat of the idea throughout the fabric of civil society that blackness and human being are not permanently and mutually exclusive.[34] The paradoxical notion of "black human being" has never enjoyed the reigning status of common sense, of course, but for a brief moment in recent history it seemed poised to enlarge its capacity to de-structure and redefine both terms of this strange compound. It was toward this potential threat, both material and symbolic, that the ill-named "white backlash" was finally aimed, and it has been so since before the first battle of the Civil War commenced. This "post-civil-rights" transformation of the national political culture, then, cannot be reduced to the assemblage of policy changes pursued since Nixon, because it constitutes a much more fundamental alteration of the background against which the po-litical operates altogether.

This alteration is, at once, a suturing of the wounded whiteness that survives the postwar mobilization of black political protest and an unparalleled enabling of race-based interest politics for non-black non-whites under the broad ban-ner, "people of color."[35] However, as mentioned earlier, the latter development issues forth not on a basis of solidarity with black struggle, as is supposed with-out warrant by the sentiment of coalition embedded in the notion, but, rather, in its wake, if not always at its expense. More precisely, it is a phenomenon made possible by the decline of the black movement and a development that flourishes in its stead. Over the past two decades, "people of color" politics has shifted from a path of capitalizing on historical opportunity (drawing from the

Civil Rights Movement and Black Power) to one of pursuing a defensive opportunism (demanding the transcendence of a supposedly outdated "black–white binary" model of racial politics). Thus, the populism of "angry white males" (reaching back at least to the 1964 Goldwater campaign) and the mass appeal of multiracial coalition politics (nurtured by demographic shifts brought about since the 1965 Immigration Act, a byproduct of the civil-rights era) represent two sides of the same coin. They are, in short, two aspects of the contemporary repression of postwar black radicalism. The former operates a frontal attack, twinning immense state-sponsored violence and overt propaganda against a civilian population (a terrorist scenario), while the latter displaces the insatiable demands and impossible questions posed by the specter of black liberation through absorption and redirection (a crowding-out scenario).[36]

It no doubt strikes one as counterintuitive to think about the proliferation of multiracial coalition politics—or, rather, the political mobilization of non-black people of color—as either an index of black powerlessness or, worse, a component of an active black disempowerment instituted via large-scale domestic structural adjustments. There is, after all, an almost universal acknowledgment among activists and organizers in Latino, Asian American, and, more recently, Arab and Muslim communities that the Civil Rights Movement and Black Power Movement were seminal to their current efforts (and occasional successes), both as practical training grounds for many a veteran political worker and as a continuing source of inspiration and instruction for younger generations now moving into the ranks of leadership. More important, consistent attempts are made to link, at least rhetorically, analogically, the struggle for immigrant rights (to use admittedly deficient shorthand) with the ongoing black struggle for racial justice.[37] This is usually done to promote a more effective and lasting spirit of collaboration among different communities of color; as an antidote for the destructive dynamics of "black–Asian conflict" or "blacks versus browns" and so on; and as a precondition for viable coalition, a search for common ground.[38]

However, on closer examination, one detects in the public commentary about both the histories of oppression and the contemporary forms of racial discrimination faced by non-black people of color not only a certain carelessness (a point I have already made), but also a strong undercurrent of open disdain toward the recent career of blacks in the United States, a subtext of antiblackness that appears to be both gratuitous (because it is not logically required by the arguments at hand, one can simply present the case as is, sans analogy) and utterly indispensable (because it is never not present in discernible form). We do not find, in other words, a coherent rationale for the animus that seems to lace the strategic calls for multiracial coalition or the conceptual deployment of metaphor between the station of blacks in U.S. society and culture and the evolving attacks on the welfare of non-black minorities. In each case, a claim is made that, say, the vicious assault on immigration reform (from bilingual education programs to health and human services for the undocumented to the militarization of the border), or the spectacular skepticism of government investigative agencies and the corporate media toward the loyalties of Asian Americans as such (from Japanese internment to the Democratic campaign-contribution fracas to the Wen Ho Lee affair[39]), or the implementation of aggressive policing against an "Arab–Muslim–Middle Eastern" terrorist profile, and so on, are offenses more egregious than those that have been happening to blacks in far greater proportion for nearly indefinite periods of time, in part because all of this is ostensibly unacknowledged as such, not by whites so much as by blacks.

Black suffering, in other words, is utilized as a convenient point of reference, the putative bottom line, in such a way that the specificity of antiblackness—which is to say, its inexorableness and fundamentality to racial formation in the United States—is almost entirely obscured. Meanwhile, blacks are faulted for failing to validate and embrace the political claims of non-black people of color. (We might be forgiven for wondering how it is that blacks are constituted here as a court of appeal or an audience in the first place, a question preliminary to any investigation of whether or to what extent blacks do or should or can recognize such claims.)

What the multiracial approach fails to appreciate—aside from the inherent injury and insult to the usual suspects of becoming concerned about a problem only when it happens immediately to you and yours—is the highly contingent nature of the injustices in question. This is, perhaps, the most tendentious point of the present argument: Whether one is talking about the attack on immigrants or the special registrations of Homeland Security, or even harking back to the internment of Japanese Americans during World War II, it is not unreasonable to conclude that these undeniably reprehensible and tragic events were nonetheless inessential—though clearly not unimportant—to the operations of the U.S. state and civil society (that is, it could have done otherwise without fear of crisis, catastrophe, or collapse). The mass imprisonment of citizens and non-citizens of Japanese descent, for instance, was dependent on both the hysteria of World War II and the foreign-policy objectives of the Roosevelt administration as a sufficient condition of possibility; the necessary condition was, to put it crudely, the history of anti-Asian racism in the United States.[40] The harassment, deportation, and demonizing effected by Homeland Security is fully entangled in the geopolitics of the United States' post–Cold War "Grand Strategy" and the unabated warfare required for capturing outstanding oil reserves, illicit drug markets, and natural resources that are becoming absolutely scarce.[41] The anti-immigration movement likewise must be understood as a key component of the regional integration of the Americas and Pacific Rim (to recite the acronyms: APEC, FTAA, IMF, NAFTA, WTO) and reflects not only political concessions to the obsessions of hard-line white supremacy but also—the dominant tendency—a disciplinary apparatus to regulate (not end or reverse) the migration of tractable labor pools, secure trade relations, and so on.[42]

We see this contingency at work again in the fact that racial profiling, to return to our central point, is operative for blacks anywhere and anytime, whereas for Latinos or certain Asian Americans it is more or less confined to poor or working-class neighborhoods.[43] Residential segregation, as well, is a class-bound issue for Latinos and Asian Americans; for blacks, it is a cross-class phenomenon, so much so that even the most segregated Asian Americans—including many Southeast Asian refugees—are more integrated than the most integrated middle-class blacks.[44] Poverty is principally transitional for immigrants but transgenerational and deeply entrenched for blacks ("underclass" signifying a segment of the black population permanently expelled from the political economy).[45] Nationally, Latinos are incarcerated at more than twice the rate of whites, but blacks are incarcerated at nearly three times the rate of Latinos.[46] This is all to say that, whereas the suffering of non-black people of color seems conditional to the historic instance (even if long-standing) and, even empirically, functions at a different scope and scale, the oppression of blacks seems to be invariant (which does not mean that it is simply unchanging; it mutates constantly). This sort of comparative analysis, which would unquestionably affect the formulation of political strategy and the demeanor of our political culture, is roundly discouraged, however, by the silencing mechanism of choice today in progressive political and intellectual circles: *Don't play Oppression Olympics!*[47] To tarry with such details, runs the dogma, is to play into the hands of divide-and-conquer tactics and, moreover, to engage a shameful, callous immorality.[48] One notes readily in this catch phrase the translation of a demand for or question of comparison (our conditions are alike or unlike) into an insidious posture of a priori competition (we will win so that you will lose). I suspect a deep relationship between this pervasive rhetorical strategy and the aggressive analogizing mentioned earlier, all of which boil down to assertions about being "like blacks" or, worse, "the new niggers."[49]

The good news, if it can be called that, is that this effort to repress a sustained examination of black positionality—"the position of the unthought"[50]—will only undermine multiracial coalition as politics of opposition. Every analysis that attempts to account for the vicissitudes of racial rule and the machinations of the racial state without centering black existence within its framework—which does not mean simply listing it among a chain of equivalents—is doomed to miss what is essential about the situation, because what happens to blacks indicates the truth (rather than the totality) of the system, its social symptom, and all other positions can (only) be understood from this angle of vision.[51] More important for present purposes, every attempt to defend the rights and liberties of the latest victims of racial profiling will inevitably fail to make substantial gains insofar as it forfeits or sidelines the fate of blacks, the prototypical targets of this nefarious police practice and the juridical infrastructure built up around it. Without blacks on board, the only viable option, the only effective defense against the crossfire will entail forging greater alliances with an antiblack civil society and capitulating further to the magnification of state power—a bid that carries its own indelible costs, its own pains *and* pleasures.

Notes

1. James, *Resisting State Violence*, 24–43.
2. I am referring, obviously, to Hardt and Negri, *Empire*; and idem, *Multitude*.
3. The classic texts on these questions are Freud, "Thoughts for the Times on War and Death"; idem, "Why War?" For a contemporary psychoanalytic account of similar themes, see Žižek, *For They Know Not What They Do*.
4. Scully, "Killing the Black Community." Scully is not among those who dismiss the

libidinal economy of antiblackness, even if it is not the primary object of her commentary.

5. Human Rights Watch, "Shielded from Justice: Police Brutality and Accountability in the United States" (1998), available online at http://www.hrw.org/reports98/police (accessed July 10, 2004).

6. Levit, "Pretextual Traffic Stops," 174.

7. See Calderón, "Race-Based Policing from Terry to Wardlow"; Harris, "Factors for Reasonable Suspicion"; Maclin, "*Terry v. Ohio*'s Fourth Amendment Legacy."

8. "Reasonable suspicion" is a standard determined solely within the purview of the police and not by judicial review (e.g., police manuals, police testimony, the naturalization of its norms of evaluative and investigatory procedures as "usual practices," all of which are developed with contempt for principles of individual rights and liberties, especially the Fourth Amendment). It was judicial review of police discretion to stop pedestrians and motorists that was forfeited in *Terry*, and now even the standards of conduct internal to the police (its "usual practices") are circumvented in favor of only the most cynical technical rationalization of arbitrary police powers of search and seizure (usual, reasonable, or otherwise). Find a justification, a pretext, for search and seizure after the idea occurs to make a stop: This is the essence of "aggressive patrol" as formulated in the early 1960s, and it took only a generation after the Civil Rights Movement to codify it entirely.

9. Uviller, *Virtual Justice*, 49.

10. Levit, "Pretextual Traffic Stops," 169.

11. Harris, "The Stories, the Statistics, and the Law," 311.

12. Glasser, "American Drug Laws," 712.

13. Ibid., 704. Emphasis added.

14. Hartman, *Scenes of Subjection*; Hortense Spillers, *Black, White, and in Color*. This point is valid not only in discussions of the slave societies of the Western Hemisphere. The global material and ideological transformations wrought by the centuries-long transatlantic political economy of slavery constructed the entire African diaspora as a slave population, real or imagined, actual or potential. This conflation in world history of "slaveness" and "blackness" is discussed brilliantly in Mbembe, *On the Postcolony*. This fact puts permanent stress on any notion of the postcolonial in Africa, the Caribbean, and Latin America and creates an incommensurable split between the position of the colonized subject and the position of the enslaved.

15. Mbembe, *On the Postcolony*, 24–65.

16. Walker, *The Police in America*.

17. Gilmore, "Globalisation and U.S. Prison Growth"; Parenti, *Lockdown America*.

18. That is to say, the construction of this vast legal architecture in defense of pretextual traffic stops or pedestrian stop and frisks indicates that a pervasive police practice

was already under way and in need of legal defense. Therefore, the danger it represents is not the return of some past tyranny (the general warrant) or some impending tumble down the path to totalitarianism (the jackboot imagery resurrected today in response to Homeland Security). Rather, it should be read as symptomatic of an extant structure of police power that cannot be announced otherwise but that can be read, in part, through the legal text. Such a reading lends coherence to the archive of testimonials regarding racial profiling, excessive use of force, and so on, and the conclusions that it suggests are important: not two forms of police power at the level of legal doctrine (Jim Crow *redux*) but, rather, a bifurcated juridical structure at the level of police practice, the moment of street-level discretion (which shifts debate from the beleaguered Fourth Amendment to nearly impossible Fourteenth Amendment considerations). For more on this point, see Martinot and Sexton, "The Avant-Garde of White Supremacy."

19. See, for instance, J. Hoberman, "Eviction Notice," *Village Voice*, June 21, 2004; Andrew O'Hehir, "Fahrenheit 9/11: Yea!" *Salon*, June 23, 2004, available online at salon.com/ent/movies/review/2004/06/23/fahrenheit_yay/index_np.html (last accessed August 23, 2006).

20. For instance, it is ambivalent to a fault about U.S. military intervention in Afghanistan; it is politically vague about Homeland Security; it mobilizes racist tropes of Arab/Muslim fanaticism and treachery with respect to Saudis even as it defends Iraqis as noble savages, and so on. See Robert Jensen, "Stupid White Movie," *Counterpunch*, July 5, 2004, available online at http://www.counterpunch.org/jensen07052004.html (accessed July 8, 2004); Terry Lawson, "Moore, Please," *Detroit Free Press*, June 24, 2004, available online at http://www.freep.com/entertainment/movies/far25_20040625.htm (last accessed August 23, 2006); Shlomo Svesnik, "Manufacturing Dissent," *World War 3 Report*, July 10, 2004, available online at http://www.worldwar3report.com/shlomo2.html (accessed July 12, 2004).

21. Arundhati Roy, "The New American Century," *The Nation*, January 22, 2004, available online at http://www.thenation.com/docprint.mhtml?i=20040209&s=roy (accessed January 25, 2004).

22. The notion that Florida was the final battleground of Election 2000 is pure illusion. One could just as easily claim that the presidential race came down to the battle over California, Colorado, Texas, or Virginia—all states reported to have suspected voter fraud or significant irregularities—or even to other states not steeped in controversy. The electoral vote, like the popular vote, is a national total, so the designation of one state or another as decisive is an arbitrary selection. To say that Bush could not have won without Florida or, conversely, that Gore would have won had he taken Florida is to imply "all other things remaining constant," precisely what we cannot maintain in such a dynamic situation.

23. Not surprisingly, Gore seemed most aggravated by the protest of Representative Maxine Waters (Democrat of California), reaffirming the racist/sexist notion that black women in elected office represent the sine qua non of political desecration. I thank Joy James for underscoring this point in her review of an earlier version of this article.

24. As described by the Associated Press, "Gore Presides in Bush Certification," January 7, 2001: "Gore pumped his right fist when California's 54 votes, the biggest electoral prize, were awarded to him. . . . At one point, Rep. Bill Thomas (R-CA), one of the four lawmakers who read the votes aloud, held Delaware's certificate up to the light and squinted. 'This one is different than all the others,' he said with a smile. His act, which provoked laughter, was a joking reference to the repeated televised recounts of Florida's votes." This report of bipartisan shuckin' and jivin' is available online at http://quest.cjonline.com/stories/010701/gor_0107017643.shtml.

25. Al Gore, "Transcript of Remarks," *Cable News Network*, December 13, 2000, available online at http://www.cnn.com/ELECTION/2000/transcripts/121300/t651213.html (accessed July 12, 2005).

26. This point should shed additional light on the fact that black people are again being rapidly disenfranchised in the present moment, most notably through the expansion of voter felony-exclusion laws. For a detailed discussion of this and other collateral consequences of mass imprisonment, see Garland, *Mass Imprisonment*; Mauer and Chesney-Lind, *Invisible Punishment*. In addition, electoral power at the state and national levels has been entirely undermined at this point, even for whites. See Martinot, "Deconstructing Electoral Politics for 2004." The idea that the black vote today poses a serious practical challenge to the operations of the two-party system, the state–corporate alliance, or even the populist agendas of the white middle and working classes (whether Republican, Democratic, Green, or Independent) is preposterous.

27. Thanks again to Joy James for the latter point.

28. Fanon, *The Wretched of the Earth*, 37.

29. I acknowledge the scholarship that demonstrates that blacks and immigrants are not generally in direct labor competition in the post-civil-rights-era United States, even if this is the case in some regions and industries. My point is to shift the debate. I am concerned not so much with the impact of immigration or immigrants on the quality of black life, including access to gainful employment—though this is an unavoidable question. More important, I am concerned with what dislocations and displacements had to be manufactured and institutionalized as components of a renewed mass immigration as a political economic prerequisite for the very struggles against the exploitation of immigrant labor that have since gathered steam. The razing of the black working class—the material base of the postwar black social

movement—by deindustrialization, downsizing, and outsourcing, and the dismantling of the welfare state and the erection of the prison-industrial complex remain
historically and ontologically prior to the plight of the post-1965 new immigrants.
See Peter Skerry, "The Black Alienation: African Americans versus Immigrants," *New
Republic*, January 30, 1995, available online at http://www.brook.edu/views/articles/
skerry/199550130.htm (accessed June 5, 2005).

30. See Richard Muhammad, "Voices from the Immigrant Workers Freedom Ride,"
AlterNet, September 25, 2003, available online at www.alternet.org/story/16835 (accessed August 23, 2006); Shora, "Guilty of Flying while Brown"; Susan Sontag, "Regarding the Torture of Others," *New York Times*, May 23, 2004, 25.

31. See DuBois, *Black Reconstruction in America*; Foner, *Reconstruction*.

32. Omi and Winant, *Racial Formation in the United States*.

33. Yancey, *Who Is White?*

34. Shor, *Culture Wars*.

35. Robinson, *Marked Men*; Gracia and De Greiff, *Hispanics/Latinos in the United States*;
Jaimes, *The State of Native America*; Robinson, *Marked Men*; Wu, *Yellow*.

36. See Wilderson, "Gramsci's Black Marx." To say that black liberation issues an insatiable demand and poses an impossible question is not hyperbole; it is this foreclo-
sure of redress that distinguishes black existence in the modern world from all else.
The contemporary reparations movement, for all of its humbleness to date, threatens
to throw the current domestic economy into recession if it is granted even half of
its demands. However, were it to assume the full ramifications of its cause—that is,
become a movement of justice rather than recompense—it could no longer shy away
from the utter devastation and ruin that it requires of the entire global system: its political economy, its civil society, its supranational institutions, its emergent common
culture. If the status quo is predicated on the historical terror of slavery, then to move
toward reparations in this light is to threaten not just an unprecedented challenge or
crisis but a catastrophe, total systemic collapse. What else could it mean to repair the
legacy of five centuries of slavery?

37. Julie Quiroz-Martínez, "Missing Link," *Colorlines* 4, no. 2 (2001), available online at
http://www.arc.org/C_Lines/CLArchive/story4_2_01.html (accessed June 5, 2005).

38. Conflicts arise between the native-born black population and black immigrant
groups, as well; however, black immigrants do not have available to them the racial
capital of non-black immigrants of color. They find themselves, in other words,
consistently folded back into the spaces of homegrown blackness, as it were, and
subjected to the same protocols of violence, especially in subsequent generations. It
gets worse, not better, as is the case with most immigrants. Moreover, a number of
the most sensational conflicts between "blacks and immigrants," as the dichotomy
is typically drawn, involve black immigrants against other, non-black immigrant

groups. Black immigrants do not, then, disrupt the paradigm so much as demonstrate why it is correct, at this level, to speak of an irresolvable discrepancy between blackness and immigrant status.

39. *Editor's note*: Wen Ho Lee, a Chinese nuclear scientist, was accused in 1999 by the CIA and FBI of passing nuclear secrets to Beijing while working at Los Alamos National Laboratory in New Mexico. The charges against Lee were based on anti-Chinese sentiment and irrational fear about domestic security rather than concrete evidence; the government dropped fifty-eight of fifty-nine counts, charging him with a single security violation. After spending 275 days in solitary confinement, Lee was released. See Lee and Zia, *My Country versus Me.*

40. Robinson, *By Order of the President.*

41. Deffeyes, *Hubbert's Peak*; Klare, *Resource Wars*; Scott, *Drugs, Oil, and War.*

42. Estevedeordal et al., *Integrating the Americas*; Hakim and Litan, *The Future of North American Integration*; Ravenhill, *Asian Pacific Economic Cooperation.*

43. Jeffrey Goldberg, "The Color of Suspicion," *New York Times Magazine*, July 20, 1999, available online at http://www.nytimes.com/library/magazine/home/19990620mag-race-cops.html (accessed June 5, 2005).

44. Massey, "The Residential Segregation of Blacks, Hispanics, and Asians, 1970–1990."

45. Wilson, *The Truly Disadvantaged.*

46. Human Rights Watch, "Race and Incarceration in the United States: Human Rights Watch Press Backgrounder" (February 27, 2002), available online at http://www.hrw.org/backgrounder/usa/race (accessed June 10, 2005). This fact is mediated by longstanding U.S. imperial interventions across Latin America for the purposes of regulating drug production, distribution, and consumption. See Marez, *Drug Wars*, for a detailed treatment of this history.

47. See, for instance, Martínez, *De Colores Means All of Us.*

48. Of course, this dogma is aided and abetted by certain black leaders, as well. Take, for instance, the chastising statement made recently by the longtime civil-rights activist, Reverend Richard Lowery, on the occasion of the Immigrant Workers Freedom Ride: "We may have come over on different ships but we're all in the same damn boat now" (as quoted in Chris McGann, "Busloads of Activists," *Seattle Post-Intelligencer*, July 8, 2003).

49. See, for instance, Hishaam Aidi, "Jihadis in the Hood: Race, Urban Islam and the War on Terror," in this volume.

50. Hartman, "The Position of the Unthought."

51. Something similar can be said about hip hop as a multiracial culture of resistance. The ubiquity of "nigga" as a term of address among non-blacks, including many whites, may provide a potent enjoyment of one's defiant sense of marginalization— degradation measured by one's proximity to blacks, literally or figuratively—but

it has only contributed to the loss of clarity, not a refinement, and the blunting of analysis, not an expansion. No doubt, hip hop brings people together, particularly young people—"one love"—but so do football games and Young Democrats meetings. If we are being honest, we must concede that, as a rule, hip hop promotes political obscurantism even when self-described as "conscious." Political radicalism in this realm is exceptional.

10

Jihadis in the Hood:
Race, Urban Islam, and the War on Terror   Hishaam Aidi

In his classic novel *Mumbo Jumbo*, Ishmael Reed satirizes white America's age-old anxiety about the "infectiousness" of black culture with "Jes Grew," an indefinable, irresistible carrier of "soul" and "blackness" that spreads like a virus contaminating everyone in its wake from New Orleans to New York.[1] Reed suggests that the source of the Jes Grew scourge is a sacred text, which is finally located and destroyed by Abdul Sufi Hamid, "the Brother on the Street." In a turn of events reminiscent of Reed's storyline, commentators are advancing theories warning of a dangerous epidemic spreading through our inner cities today, infecting misguided, disaffected minority youth and turning them into anti-American terrorists. This time, though, the pathogen is Islam—more specifically, an insidious mix of radical Islam and black militancy.

Since the capture of John Walker Lindh, the Marin County "black nationalist"-turned-Taliban,[2] and the arrest of the would-be terrorist José Padilla, a Brooklyn-born Puerto Rican ex-gang member who encountered Islam while in prison, terrorism experts and columnists have been warning of the "Islamic threat" in the American underclass and alerting the public that the ghetto and the prison system could very well supply a fifth column to Osama bin Laden and his ilk. Writing in New York City's *Daily News*, the black social critic Stanley Crouch reminded us that in 1986 the powerful Chicago street gang al-Rukn—known in the 1970s as the Blackstone Rangers—was arrested en masse for receiving $2.5 million from Libya's strongman, Muammar Qaddafi, to commit terrorist acts in the United States. "We have to realize there is another theater in this unprecedented war, one headquartered in our jails and prisons," Crouch cautioned.

Chuck Colson of the evangelical American Christian Mission, which ministers to inmates around the country, penned a widely circulated article for the *Wall Street Journal* charging that "al-Qaeda training manuals specifically identify America's prisoners as candidates for conversion because they may be 'disenchanted with their country's policies.' . . . As U.S. citizens, they will combine a desire for 'payback' with an ability to blend easily into American culture." Moreover, he wrote, "Saudi money has been funneled into the American Muslim Foundation, which supports prison programs," reiterating that America's "alienated, disenfranchised people are prime targets for radical Islamists who preach a religion of violence, of overcoming oppression by jihad."[3]

Since September 11, 2001, more than a few American-born black and Latino jihadis have indeed been discovered behind enemy lines. Before Padilla (Abdallah al-Muhajir), there was Aqil, the troubled Mexican American youth from San Diego found in an Afghan training camp fraternizing with one of the men accused of killing the journalist Daniel Pearl. Aqil, now in custody, is writing a memoir called *My Jihad*. In February, the *New York Times* ran a story about Hiram Torres, a Puerto Rican whose name was found in a bombed-out house in Kabul on a list of recruits to the Pakistani group Harkat al-Mujahedeen, which has ties to al-Qaeda. Torres, also known as Mohamed Salman, graduated first in his New Jersey high-school class and briefly attended Yale before dropping out and heading to Pakistan in 1998. He has not been heard from since. A June edition of *U.S. News and World Report* mentions a group of African Americans, their whereabouts currently unknown, who studied at a school closely linked to the Kashmiri militia Lashkar-e Taiba. L'Houssaine Kerchtou, an Algerian government witness, claims to have seen "some black Americans" training at al-Qaeda bases in Sudan and Pakistan.

Earlier this year, the movie *Kandahar* caused an uproar in the American intelligence community because the African American actor who played a doctor was the American fugitive David Belfield. Belfield, who converted to Islam at Howard University in 1970, is wanted for the 1980 murder of the Iranian dissident Ali Akbar Tabatabai in Washington. Belfield has lived in Tehran since 1980 and goes by the name Hassan Tantai.[4] The two most notorious accused terrorists now in U.S. custody are black Europeans, the French Moroccan Zacarias Moussaoui and the English Jamaican shoe bomber Richard Reid, who were radicalized in the same mosque in the London ghetto of Brixton. Moussaoui's ubiquitous mug shot in orange prison garb, looking like any American inner-city youth with his shaved head and goatee, has intrigued many and unnerved some. "My first thought when I saw his photograph was that I wished he looked more Arabic and less black," wrote Sheryl McCarthy in *Newsday*. "All African-

Americans need is for the first guy to be tried on terrorism charges stemming from this tragedy to look like one of our own."

But assessments of an "Islamic threat" in the American ghetto are sensational and ahistorical. As campaigns are introduced to stem the "Islamic tide," there has been little probing of why alienated black and Latino youth might gravitate toward Islamism. There has been no commentary comparable to what the British race theorist Paul Gilroy wrote about Richard Reid and the group of Britons held at Guantánamo Bay: "The story of black European involvement in these geopolitical currents is disturbingly connected to the deeper history of immigration and race politics." Reid, in particular, "manifest[s] the uncomfortable truth that British multiculturalism has failed."[5]

For over a century, African American thinkers—Muslim and non-Muslim— have attempted to harness the black struggle to global Islam, while leaders in the Islamic world have tried to yoke their political causes to African American liberation. Islamism, in the U.S. context, has come to refer to differing ideologies adopted by Muslim groups to galvanize social movements for "Islamic" political ends—the Nation of Islam's "buy black" campaigns and election boycotts or Harlem's Mosque of Islamic Brotherhood lobbying for benefits and cultural and political rights from the state. Much more rarely, it has included the jihadi strain of Islamism, embraced by foreign-based or foreign-funded Islamist groups (such as al-Rukn) attempting to gain American recruits for armed struggles against "infidel" governments at home and abroad. The rise of Islam and Islamism in American inner cities can be explained as a product of immigration and racial politics, deindustrialization and state withdrawal, and the interwoven cultural forces of black nationalism, Islamism, and hip hop that appeal strongly to disenfranchised black, Latino, Arab, and South Asian youth.

Islam in the Transatlantic

The West Indian–born Christian missionary Edward Blyden was the first African American scholar to advocate an alliance between global Islam and pan-Africanism, the system of thought that is considered his intellectual legacy. After studying Arabic in Syria and living in West Africa, Blyden became convinced that Islam was better suited for people of African descent than Christianity because of what he saw as the lack of racial prejudice, the doctrine of brotherhood, and the value placed on learning in Islam. His seminal tome, *Christianity,*

Islam and the Negro Race (1888), laid the groundwork for a pan-Africanism with a strong Islamic cultural and religious undergirding.

Blyden's counterpart in the Arab world was the Sudanese Egyptian intellectual Duse Muhammad Ali. In 1911, after the First Universal Races Congress held at the University of London, Duse Mohammed launched the *African Times and Orient Review*, a journal championing national liberal struggles and abolitionism "in the four quarters of the earth" and promoting solidarity among "nonwhites" around the world. Published in both English and Arabic, the journal was circulated across the Muslim world and African diaspora, running articles by intellectuals from the Middle East to the West Indies (including contributions from Booker T. Washington). Duse would later become mentor to the American black nationalist Marcus Garvey when he worked at the *Review* in London in 1913 and would leave his indelible stamp on Garvey's Universal Negro Improvement Association, whose mission "to reclaim the fallen of the race, to administer and assist the needy" would become the social-welfare principles animating myriad urban Islamic and African American movements.[6] In 1926, Duse created the Universal Islamic Society in Detroit, which would influence, if not inspire, Noble Drew Ali's Moorish Science Temple and Fard Muhammad's Temple of Islam, both seen as precursors of the modern-day Nation of Islam (NOI).

Blyden's and Duse's ideas, which underlined universal brotherhood, human rights, and "literacy" (i.e., the study of Arabic), had a profound impact on subsequent pan-Africanist and Islamic movements in the United States, influencing leaders such as Garvey, Elijah Muhammad, and Malcolm X. The latter two inherited an "Arabo-centric" understanding of Islam, viewing the Arabs as God's "chosen people" and Arabic as the language of intellectual jihad—ideas still central to the Nation of Islam today. The NOI's mysterious founder, Fard Muhammad, to whom Elijah Muhammad referred as "God himself," is widely believed to have been an Arab.[7] "Fard was an Arab who loved us so much so as to bring us al-Islam," Minister Louis Farrakhan has said repeatedly. For the past thirty-five years, Farrakhan's top adviser has been the Palestinian American Ali Baghdadi, though the two fell out earlier this year when Farrakhan condemned suicide bombings.[8] In the NOI "typologist" theology, Arabs are seen as a "Sign" of a future people, a people chosen by God to receive the Quran but who have strayed, and so God has chosen the American Negro, who like the Arab is "despised and rejected" with a "history of ignorance and savagery," to spread Islam in the West.[9]

Malcolm X was probably the most prominent African American Muslim leader to place the Civil Rights Movement not just in a pan-Islamic and pan-African context, but also within the global struggle for Third World independence. In addition to his historic visit to Mecca, where he would witness "Islamic universalism" and eventually renounce the NOI's race theology, Malcolm X would confer with Egyptian President Gamal Abdel Nasser and Algerian President Ahmed Ben Bella, leaders of the Arab League and Organization of African Unity, respectively, and consider taking African American problems to the floor of the United Nations General Assembly.

When Warith Deen Muhammad, who had been educated at al-Azhar University, took over the Nation of Islam after the death of his father, Elijah, in 1975, he renounced his father's race theology and changed his organization's name to the World Community of al-Islam in the West to emphasize the internationalist ties of Muslims over the nationalistic bonds of African Americans—leading to a split with Farrakhan, who then proceeded to rebuild the NOI in its old image. Arab and Islamic states would persistently woo Warith Deen Muhammad, apparently eager to gain influence over U.S. foreign policy. "But," lamented one scholar, "he has rejected any lobbying role for himself, along with an unprecedented opportunity to employ the international pressure of Arab states to improve the social conditions of black Americans."[10]

Targeting the Disaffected

Is there any truth to the claim that Muslim states or Islamist groups specifically targeted African Americans to lobby the U.S. government or to recruit them in wars overseas? *U.S. News and World Report* notes that, just in the 1990s, between 1,000 and 2,000 Americans—of whom "a fair number are African-Americans"—volunteered to fight with Muslim armies in Bosnia, Chechnya, Lebanon, and Afghanistan. Many were recruited by radical imams in the United States. According to several reports, in the late 1970s the Pakistani imam Sheikh Syed Gilani, now on the run for his alleged role in Daniel Pearl's murder, founded a movement called al-Fuqara (The Poor), with branches in Brooklyn and New Jersey, where he preached to a predominantly African American constituency. Using his *Soldiers of Allah* video, Gilani recruited fighters for the anti-

Soviet jihad in Afghanistan. Likewise, according to the FBI, working out of his "jihad office" in Brooklyn the blind cleric Sheikh Omar Abdel Rahman raised millions of dollars for the Afghan resistance and sent 200 volunteers to join the mujahedeen.

According to a recent study, Saudi Arabia has historically exerted the strongest influence over the American Muslim community, particularly since the rise of Organization of Petroleum Exporting Countries in 1973.[11] Through the Islamic Society of North America (ISNA), Muslim Student Associations, the Islamic Circle of North America, and the Saudi-sponsored World Muslim League, the Saudis have financed summer camps for children, institutes for training imams, speakers' series, the distribution of Islamic literature, mosque building, and proselytizing. In addition, the Saudi embassy, through its control of visas, decides who in the American Muslim community goes on the pilgrimage to Mecca. But there is absolutely no evidence suggesting a connection between this influence and terrorism against the United States, as has been alleged by several media outlets.[12]

In the early 1980s, Iran attempted to counter Saudi influence over the American Muslim community and to gain African American converts to Shiism. On November 17, 1979, Ayatollah Khomeini had ordered the release of thirteen African American hostages, stating that they were "oppressed brothers" who were also victims of American injustice. In 1982, a study commissioned by the Iranian government to appraise the potential for Shiite proselytizing in black America attacked the Nation of Islam and Sunni Muslims for their "insincerity" and argued that Saudi proselytizers were in cahoots with the CIA. The report stated: "Besides being dispirited, the African-American Muslims feel that nobody cares about them. [Everyone] only wants to use them for their own personal reasons as they languish. . . . The majority of African-Americans really want pure Islam. However, until and unless someone is willing, qualified and able to effectively oppose active Saudi oil money . . . the Islamic movement in America will plod on in a state of abject ineptitude and ineffectiveness."[13] But the Iranian revolution did not have much influence over African American Muslims, with the notable exception of the aforementioned Belfield.

The majority of African Americans, and increasingly Latinos, who embrace Islam do not end up wearing military fatigues in the mountains of Central Asia. For most, Islam provides order, meaning, and purpose to nihilistic and chaotic lives, but even if most do not gravitate toward radical Islamism, why the attraction to Islam in the first place?

Exiting the West

Many blacks and Latinos in American metropolises live in poverty and feel alienated from the country's liberal political and cultural traditions. Repelled by America's permissive consumerist culture, many search for a faith and culture that provides rules and guidelines for life. Often they are drawn to strands of Christianity that endorse patriarchy, "family values," and abstinence. But many young African Americans, and increasingly Latinos, reject Christianity, which they see as the faith of a guilty and indifferent establishment. Christian America has failed them and stripped them of their "ethnic honor." Estranged from the United States and, in the case of Latinos, from their parents' homelands, many minority youth search for a sense of community and identity in a quest that has increasingly led them to the other side of the Atlantic, to the Islamic world. Sunni Islam, the heterodox Nation of Islam, and quasi-Muslim movements such as the Five Percenters and Nuwaubians allow for a cultural and spiritual escape from the American social order that often entails a wholesale rejection of Western culture and civilization.

Family breakdown and family values come up often in conversations and sermons at inner-city mosques as explanations for the younger generation's disenchantment with American society and liberalism. The decline of the two-parent household, which preoccupies discussion of family values, has economic and political roots. In the 1970s and 1980s, the middle classes left for the suburbs, investors relocated, and joblessness in urban areas increased rapidly. As one analyst observed, "The labor market conditions which sustained the 'male breadwinner' family have all but vanished." Matrifocal homes arose in its place. The new urban political economy of the 1980s—state withdrawal and capital flight—led to "the creation of a new set of orientations that places less value on marriage and rejects the dominance of men as a standard for a successful husband–wife family."[14] But in the view of many inner-city Muslim leaders, family breakdown and economic dislocation result from racism, Western decadence, and immorality—they are the effect of straying from the way of God. Raheem Ocasio, imam of New York's Alianza Islamica, contends: "Latinos in the society at large, due to pressures of modern Western culture are fighting a losing battle to maintain their traditional family structure. . . . Interestingly, the effects of an Islamic lifestyle seem to mitigate the harmful effects of the Western lifestyle and have helped restore and reinforce traditional family values. Latino culture is at its root patriarchal, so Islam's clearly defined roles for men as responsible leaders and providers and women as equally essential and complementary were assimilated. As a result, divorce among Latino Muslim couples is relatively rare."[15]

By embracing Islam, previously invisible, inaudible, and disaffected individuals gain a sense of identity and belonging to what they perceive as an organized, militant, and glorious civilization that the West takes very seriously. One Chicano ex-convict tried to explain the allure of Islam for Latino inmates and why Mexican Americans sympathize with Palestinians: "The old Latin American revolutionaries converted to atheism, but the new faux revolutionary Latino American prisoner can just as easily convert to Islam. . . . There reside in the Latino consciousness at least three historical grudges, three conflicting selves: the Muslim Moor, the Catholic Spanish and the indigenous Indian. . . . [For the Mexican inmates] the Palestinians had their homeland stolen and were oppressed in much the same way as Mexicans."[16]

"Bringing Allah to Urban Renewal"

In the wretched social and economic conditions of the inner city, and in the face of government apathy, Muslim organizations operating in the ghetto and prisons deliver materially. As in much of the Islamic world, where the state fails to provide basic services and security, Muslim organizations appear, funding community centers, patrolling the streets, and organizing people.

As the state withdrew and capital fled from the city in the Reagan–Bush era, social institutions and welfare agencies disappeared, leaving an urban wasteland. Churches have long been the sole institutions in the ghetto, but Islamic institutions have been growing in African American neighborhoods for the past two decades. In Central Harlem, Brownsville, and East New York—areas deprived of job opportunities—dozens of mosques (Sunni, NOI, Five Percenter, and Nuwaubian) have arisen, standing cheek by jowl with dozens of churches that try to provide some order and guidance to these neighborhoods. In the ghettoes of Brooklyn, on Chicago's South Side, and in the barrios of East Harlem and East Los Angeles, where aside from a heavy police presence there is little evidence of government, Muslim groups provide basic services. The Alianza Islamica of New York, headquartered in the South Bronx, offers after-school tutorials, equivalency diploma instruction for high-school dropouts, marriage counseling, substance-abuse counseling, AIDS-awareness campaigns, and sensitivity talks on Islam for the New York Police Department. The Alianza has confronted gangs and drug posses, training young men in martial arts to help clean up the streets of the barrio with little reliance on trigger-happy policemen.

One quasi-Islamic group, the United Nation of Islam, which broke away from Farrakhan's NOI in 1993, has adopted the slogan "Bringing Allah to Urban Renewal" and is resurrecting blighted urban neighborhoods across the country, opening up health clinics, employment centers, restaurants, and grocery stores that do not sell red meat, cigarettes, or even soda because they are bad for customers' health.[17] The United Nation of Islam does not accept government funds, fearing that federal money would compromise its mission of "Civilization Development." Similarly, the NOI conducts "manhood training" and mentoring programs in inner cities across the country, earning the praise of numerous scholarly reports, which claim that young men who participate in these programs for an extended time show "positive self-conception," improved grades, and less involvement in drugs and petty crime.[18]

In addition to delivering basic services, the NOI today tries to provide jobs and housing. The NOI's Los Angeles branch is currently buying up homes for homeless young men (calling them "Houses of Knowledge and Discipline"), building AIDS treatment clinics, and starting up a bank specializing in small loans.[19] In 1997, Farrakhan announced a "three-year economic program" that aimed to eliminate "unemployment, poor housing and all the other detriments that plague our community."[20] Farrakhan seems to have reverted to the strategies of economic nationalism pursued by Elijah Muhammad. One scholar argues that under Elijah, the NOI was essentially a development organization emphasizing thrift and economic independence among poor black people, with such success that it turned many followers into affluent entrepreneurs. The organization itself evolved into a middle-class establishment, allowing Warith Deen Muhammad, after his father's death, to shed black-nationalist rhetoric and identify with a multiracial *umma* (community)—moves that resonated with his middle-class constituency.[21] In the 1970s, the NOI had owned thousands of acres of farmland, banks, housing complexes, retail and wholesale businesses, and a university and was described by C. Eric Lincoln as one of the "most potent economic forces" in black America, but Warith Deen Muhammad liquidated many of the NOI's assets. When Farrakhan resuscitated the NOI in the 1980s, he revived Elijah Muhammad's message of black economic empowerment (appealing to many poorer blacks) and began rebuilding the NOI's business empire. According to *Business Week*, in 1995 the NOI owned 2,000 acres of farmland in Georgia and Michigan, a produce-transport business, a series of restaurants, and a media-distribution company.

Islam behind Bars

Over the past thirty years, Islam has become a powerful force in the American prison system. Ever since the Attica prison riots in upstate New York in 1971, when Muslim inmates protected guards from being taken hostage, prison officials have allowed Muslim inmates to practice and proselytize relatively freely. Prior to the rise of Islam, the ideologies with the most currency among minorities in prison were strands of revolutionary Marxism—Maoism and Guevarism—and varieties of black nationalism. According to one report, nowadays one third of the million or more black men in prison are claiming affiliation with the Nation of Islam, Sunni Islam, or some quasi-Muslim group, such as the Moorish Science Temple.[22] Mike Tyson, during a stint in prison in the mid-1990s, seems to have combined all three currents, leaving prison as a Muslim convert, Malik Shabbaz, but with Mao and Ché Guevara tattoos. "I'm just a dark guy from the den of iniquity," the former heavyweight champion explained to journalists.

The presence of Muslim organizations in prisons has increased in the past decade as the state has cut back on prisoner services. In 1988, legislation made drug offenders ineligible for Pell grants; in 1992, this was broadened to include convicts sentenced to death or lifelong imprisonment without parole, and in 1994, the law was extended to all remaining state and federal prisoners. In 1994, Congress passed legislation barring inmates from higher education, stating that criminals could not benefit from federal funds, despite overwhelming evidence that prison educational programs not only help maintain order in prison but also prevent recidivism.[23] Legislation also denies welfare payments, veterans' benefits, and food stamps to anyone in detention for more than sixty days.

In 1996, the Clinton administration passed the Work Opportunity and Per-

sonal Responsibility Act, preventing most ex-convicts from receiving Medicaid, public housing, and Section Eight vouchers. Clinton forbade inmates in 1998 from receiving Social Security benefits, saying that prisoners "collecting Social Security checks" was "fraud and abuse" perpetrated against "working families" who "play by the rules."[24] All these cutbacks affected minorities disproportionately but African Americans in particular because of the disproportionately high incarceration rates of African American men. Disparate treatment by the criminal-justice system—which has a devastating effect on the black family, the inner-city economy, and black political power, since convicts and ex-convicts cannot vote in thirty-nine states—is another powerful factor fueling the resentment of minorities toward the establishment.

In this atmosphere, it is no surprise that Muslim organizations in prisons are gaining popularity. The Nation of Islam provides classes, mentorship programs, study groups, and "manhood training" that teaches inmates respect for women, responsible sexual behavior, drug prevention, and life-management skills. Mainstream American Muslim organizations also provide myriad services to prisoners. At ISNA's First Conference on Islam in American Prisons, Amir Ali of the Institute of Islamic Information and Education described the services and support system that his organization provides to Muslim inmates: regular visits to prisons by evangelists who deliver books and literature, classes in Arabic and Islamic history, correspondence courses in other subjects, twenty-four-hour toll-free phones and collect-calling services for inmates to call families, mentorship programs for new converts, and "halfway houses" to help reintegrate Muslim inmates into society after release.

Those who study Islam behind bars cast doubt on the assertions of Colson and Crouch. At ISNA's Third Annual Conference on Islam in American Prisons in July 2002, the keynote speaker, David Schwartz, who recently retired as religious services administrator for the Federal Bureau of Prisons, strongly rejected the notion that American prisons were a breeding ground for terrorists and stated that Islam was a positive force in the lives of inmates. Robert Dannin adds: "Why would a sophisticated international terrorist organization bother with inmates—who are fingerprinted and whose data is in the U.S. criminal justice system?"[25]

Islam and Hip Hop

The street life is the only life I know

I live by the code style it's made PLO

Iranian thoughts and cover like an Arabian

Grab a nigga on the spot and put a 9 to his cranium.

—METHOD MAN, "PLO STYLE" *TICAL*, DEF JAM, 1994

If Rastafarianism and Bob Marley's Third Worldist reggae anthems provided the music and culture of choice for marginalized minority youth two decades ago, in the 1990s "Islamic hip hop" emerged as the language of disaffected youth throughout the West.

Arabic, Islamic, or quasi-Islamic motifs increasingly thread the colorful fabric that is hip hop, such that for many inner-city and suburban youth, rap videos and lyrics provide a regular and intimate exposure to Islam. Many "Old School" fans will recall the video of Eric B and Rakim's "Know the Ledge," which featured images of Khomeini and Muslim congregational prayer, as Rakim flowed: "In control of many, like Ayatollah Khomeini. . . . I'm at war a lot, like Anwar Sadat."[26] Self-proclaimed Muslim rap artists proudly announce their faith and include "Islamic" messages of social justice in their lyrics. Followers of Sunni Islam ("al-Islam" in hip-hop parlance), Q-Tip (Fareed Kamal), and Mos Def are among the most highly acclaimed hip-hop artists, lauded as representatives of hip hop's school of "Afro-humanism" and positivity. Mos Def, in an interview with the Web site Beliefnet, described his mission as a Muslim artist: "It's about speaking out against oppression wherever you can. If that's gonna be in Bosnia or Kosovo or Chechnya or places where Muslims are being persecuted; or if it's gonna be in Sierra Leone or Colombia—you know, if people's basic human rights are being abused and violated, then Islam has an interest in speaking out against it, because we're charged to be the leaders of humanity."[27]

The fluidity and variegated nature of Islam in urban America is seen in the different "Islams" represented in hip hop, and most poignantly in the friction between Sunni Muslims and Five Percenters. Today, most "Islamic" references in hip hop are to the belief system of the Five Percent Nation, a splinter group of the NOI founded in 1964 by Clarence 13X. The Five Percent Nation (or the Nation of Gods and Earths) refashioned the teachings of the NOI, rejecting the notion that Fard was Allah and teaching instead that the black man was God and that his proper name is ALLAH (Arm Leg Leg Arm Head). They taught that 85 percent of the masses are ignorant and will never know the truth. Ten percent of the people know the truth but use it to exploit and manipulate the 85 percent; only 5 percent of humanity know the truth and understand the "true divine nature of the black man who is God or Allah."[28] In Five Percenter theology, Manhattan (particularly Harlem) is known as Mecca, Brooklyn is Medina, Queens is the desert, the Bronx is Pelan, and New Jersey is the New Jerusalem. Five Percenter beliefs have exerted a great influence on hip-hop argot and street slang. The expressions "word is bond," "break it down," "peace," "whassup G" (meaning God, not gangsta), and "represent" all come from Five Percenter ideology.

Orthodox Sunni Muslims see Five Percenters as blasphemous heretics who call themselves "Gods." They accuse Five Percenters of *shirk*, the Arabic word meaning polytheism—the diametrical opposite of the *tawhid* (unitary nature of God) that defined the Prophet Muhammad's revelation. Since Five Percenters often wear skullcaps and women cover their hair, Sunni Muslims will often greet them with *al-salam alaykum* (peace be upon you), to which the Five Percenters respond, "Peace, God." Five Percenters refer to Sunni Muslims as deluded and "soon to be Muslim." In the "10 percent," Five Percenters include the "white devil," as well as orthodox Muslims "who teach that Allah is a spook."

Busta Rhymes, Wu Tang Clan, and Mobb Deep are among the most visible Five Percenter rappers. Their lyrics—replete with numerology, cryptic "Islamic" allusions, and at times pejorative references to women and whites (as "white devils" or "cave dwellers")—have aroused great interest and controversy. The journalist and former rapper Adisa Banjoko strongly reprimands Five Percenter rappers for their materialism and ignorance: "In hip-hop a lot of us talk about knowledge and the importance of holding on to it, yet under the surface of hip-hop's 'success' runs the thread of ignorance [*jahiliyya*, the Arabic term referring to the pagan age in Arabia before Islam]."[29] Like "the original *jahiliyya* age," hip hop today is plagued by "*jahili* territorialism and clan affiliation," a "heavy disrespect of women" and a materialism that "borders on *jahili* idol worship."[30] The Five Percenter Ibn Dajjal responded angrily to Adisa's criticism:

No amount of *fatwas* or censorship will ever silence the sounds of the NOI and Five Percent *mushrik* (idolater) nations. The group will continue to rise in fame with customers coming from all walks of life: black, white and Bedouin. Far from a masterpiece of style, the book [the Quran] is literally rid-dled with errors and clumsy style which yield little more than a piece of sacred music. . . . Maybe there should be a new hip-hop album entitled *Al-Quran al-Karim Freestyle* by Method Man and Ghostface Killa![31]

Though it has nothing to do with the jihadi trend, the language of Islam in the culture of hip hop does often express anger at government indifference and U.S. foreign policy and challenge structures of domination. The outspoken rapper Paris, formerly of the NOI, who galled the establishment with his 1992 single "Bush Killer," has raised eyebrows again with the single "What Would You Do?" (included on his forthcoming LP, *Sonic Jihad*), which excoriates the "war on terror" and the USA PATRIOT Act and implies government involve-ment in the September 11 attacks. In early 2002, the Brooklyn-based Palestinian American Hammer Brothers, "originally from the Holy Land, living in the Belly of the Beast, trying to rise on feet of Yeast,"[32] released their pro-Intifada cut, "Free Palestine," now regularly blared at pro-Palestinian gatherings in New York. One particularly popular and articulate artist is the Palestinian American spoken-word poet Suheir Hammad, the author of *Born Black, Born Palestinian*, on growing up Arab in Sunset Park, Brooklyn. Hammad appeared on Home Box Office's "Def Poetry Jam" some weeks after September 11 and delivered a stirring rendition—to a standing ovation—of her poem "First Writing Since," on being an Arab New Yorker with a brother in the U.S. Navy.[33]

"No Real Stake"

Pan-Africanism and pan-Islam were fused together by African American and Muslim intellectuals over a century ago to fight colonialism, racism, and Western domination. Today, that resistance strategy has been adopted by tens of thou-sands of urban youth (judging by NOI rallies in the United States and Europe) in the heart of the West. The cultural forces of Islam, black nationalism, and hip hop have converged to create a brazenly political and oppositional countercul-ture that has a powerful allure. At root, the attraction for African American, La-tino, Arab, South Asian, and West Indian youth to Islam, and movements that espouse different brands of political Islam, is evidence of Western states' failure to integrate minority and immigrant communities and deliver basic life neces-sities and social-welfare benefits—policy failures of which Islamic groups (and right-wing Christian groups) are keenly aware.

Rather than prompt examination of why minority youth in the ghetto and its appendage institution, the prison, would be attracted to Islam—whether in its apolitical Sunni or Sufi, its Five Percenter, or its overtly political Nation of Islam or jihadi variety—the cases of Moussaoui, Reid, and Padilla have led to arguments about how certain cultures are "unassimilable," hysterical warnings of a "black (or Hispanic) fifth column," and aggressive campaigns to counter Islamic influence in the inner city. Evangelical groups are trying to exclude Islamic institutions from George W. Bush's faith-based development initiative. Jerry Falwell has stated that "it is totally inappropriate under any circumstances" to give federal aid to Muslim groups, because "the Muslim faith teaches hate. Islam should be out the door before they knock. They should not be allowed to dip into the pork barrel."[34] Another Christian effort, Project Joseph, conducts "Muslim awareness seminars" in inner cities across the country, warning that Muslim leaders are exploiting the weakness of black churches, informing African Americans that conversion to Islam does not imply "recovering their ethnic heritage," and publicly admonishing that "if the conversion rate continues unchanged, Islam could become the dominant religion in black urban areas by the year 2020."[35]

The aspirations of the very poor and disenfranchised in America will continue to overlap with the struggles and hopes of the impoverished masses of the Muslim Third World, who will in turn continue to look toward African Americans for inspiration and help. Minister Farrakhan's recent "solidarity tour" of Iraq and recent meetings between Al Sharpton and Jesse Jackson and Yasser Arafat show that Muslim causes continue to reverberate in the African American community. By and large, African Americans do not seem to share the hostility to Islam that has intensified since September 11. Akbar Muhammad, professor of history at the State University of New York, Binghamton, and son of Elijah Muhammad, wrote in 1985 that because African Americans have "no real political stake in America, political opposition to the Muslim world is unworthy of serious consideration."[36] These words still hold true for many minorities in post-September 11 America.

Notes

Originally published as "Jihadis in the Hood: Race, Urban Islam and the War on Terror," *Middle East Report* 224 (2002).

1. *Editor's note*: Ishmael Reed, *Mumbo Jumbo* (New York: Simon and Schuster, 1996).

2. Many say Lindh was corrupted by reading *The Autobiography of Malcolm X* and by his love of hip hop. See Shelby Steele, "Radical Sheik," *Wall Street Journal*, December 18, 2001. Lindh often posed as black online, going by the names "Doodoo" and "Prof J." He attacked Zionism, once writing: "Our blackness does not make white people hate us, it is THEIR racism that causes hate. . . . [The "N" word] has, for hundreds of years, been a label put on us by Caucasians . . . and because of the weight it carries with it, I never use it myself." See Clarence Page, "The 'White Negro' Taliban?" *Chicago Tribune*, December 14, 2001.

3. Chuck Colson, "Evangelizing for Evil in Our Prisons," *Wall Street Journal*, June 24, 2002. See also Mark Almond, "Why Terrorists Love Criminals (and Vice Versa): Many a Jihadi Began as a Hood," *Wall Street Journal*, June 19, 2002; Earl Ofari Hutchinson, "Hispanic or African-American Jihad?" *Black World Today*, June 12, 2002; *Christian Science Monitor*, June 14, 2002.

4. *Guardian*, January 10, 2002.

5. Paul Gilroy, "Dividing into the Tunnel: The Politics of Race between the Old and New Worlds," *Open Democracy*, January 31, 2002, available online at http://www.opendemocracy.net (accessed June 5, 2005).

6. Hill, *Marcus Garvey and the Universal Negro Improvement Association Papers*, 302.

7. Despite Farrakhan's claim to have renounced race theology, *The Final Call* still prints on its back page that "God appeared in the person of W. Fard Muhammad."

8. Ali Baghdadi, "Farrakhan Plans to Meet Sharon," *Media Monitors Network*, April 14, 2002, available online at http://www.mediamonitors.net (accessed April 20, 2002).

9. See Smith, *Conjuring Culture*.

10. Allen, "Minister Louis Farrakhan and the Continuing Evolution of the Nation of Islam," 73.

11. Dannin, *Black Pilgrimage to Islam*.

12. Gause, "Be Careful What You Wish For."

13. Muhammad Said, "Questions and Answers about Indigenous U.S. Muslims," unpublished ms., Tehran, 1982.

14. "In 1993, twenty-seven percent of all children under the age of eighteen were living with a single parent. This figure includes fifty-seven percent of all black children, thirty-two percent of all Hispanic children and twenty-one percent of all white children": Wilson, *When Work Disappears*, 85. Elsewhere, Wilson argues that the sharp increase in black male joblessness since 1970 accounts in large measure for the rise in the number of single-parent families. Since jobless rates are highest in the inner city, rates of single parenthood are also highest there.

15. Rahim Ocasio, "Latinos, the Invisible: Islam's Forgotten Multitude," *Message*, August 1997.

16. *Los Angeles Times*, June 23, 2002.

17. *Christian Science Monitor*, December 1, 1999.

18. Majors and Wiener, *Programs That Serve African-American Youth.*

19. *Los Angeles Times*, February 13, 2002.

20. *Final Call*, February 11, 1997.

21. Mamiya, "Minister Louis Farrakhan and the Final Call."

22. *Newsweek*, October 30, 1995.

23. Josh Page, "Eliminating the Enemy: A Cultural Analysis of the Exclusion of Prisoners from Higher Education" (M.A. thesis, University of California, Berkeley, 1997).

24. Bill Clinton, radio address, April 25, 1998, transcript available online at http://www .whitehouse.gov (accessed June 10, 2005).

25. Quoted in Hishaam Aidi, "Jihadis in the Cell Block," africana.com, July 22, 2002.

26. Eric B. and Rakim, "Juice (Know the Ledge)," *Juice*, MCA, 1992.

27. Hishaam Aidi, "Hip-Hop for the Gods," africana.com, April 31, 2001.

28. Nuruddin, "The Five Percenters."

29. Adissa Banjoko, "Hip-Hop and the New Age of Ignorance," *FNV Newsletter*, June 2001, available online at http://www.daveyd.com/ageofignorance.html (accessed August 22, 2006).

30. Ibid.

31. Ibid.

32. Hammer Brothers, "Free Palestine," *Free Palestine*, Wax Poetic Productions, 2002.

33. Suheir Hammad, "First Writing Since," appeared in *Middle East Report* 221 (Winter 2001), and is available online at http://www.teachingforchange.org/News%20Items/ first_writing_since.htm (accessed August 22, 2006).

34. *Washington Post*, March 8, 2001.

35. *USA Today*, July 19, 2000.

36. Muhammad, "Interaction between 'Indigenous' and 'Immigrant' Muslims in the United States."

MARILYN BUCK

Marilyn Buck was born in 1947 in Jasper, Texas. Her political involvement began when she was a student at the University of Texas. Buck was involved in anti-racist organizing, worked as the editor of the Students for a Democratic Society national newspaper, and protested U.S. military involvement in Vietnam. In 1968, she moved to California to work with San Francisco Newsreel, a radical filmmaking collective. Buck also worked in solidarity with indigenous groups and the black liberation movement, the Black Liberation Army, and international groups struggling in Vietnam, Palestine, and Iran.

In 1973, Buck became a target of the FBI's COINTELPRO and was captured in her apartment in San Francisco. She was subsequently imprisoned on charges of purchasing ammunition using a false identification. After going underground during a work furlough from the experimental behavior-modification program at the Federal Women's Prison in Alderson, West Virginia, Buck was accused in the 1979 liberation of Assata Shakur from prison and the 1981 "Brink's robbery" case. In 1985 Buck was captured and was tried in four cases, including the "Resistance Conspiracy" case (with Laura Whitehorn and Susan Rosenberg). In 1987, she went on trial for conspiracy under the Racketeer Influenced and Corrupt Organizations Act, used in counterinsurgency because it turned politically subversive movements into "criminal" organizations. Buck and Mutulu Shakur were convicted in 1987 of conspiracy to commit armed bank robbery in support of the New Afrikan Independence struggle. She was sentenced to fifty years in addition to twenty years for past convictions.

Since imprisonment, Buck has remained committed to antiracist, anti-imperialist political principles and has continued her involvement in movements for revolutionary social change. A poet and literary teacher, she works with women in prison on such issues as literacy and HIV/AIDS education. Studying for a master's degree in poetics, she continues to write and publish poetry and until recently wrote a column, "Notes from the Unrepenitentiary," for *Prison Legal News*. In 2001, she received a PEN Prison Writing Prize for her volume of poetry, *Rescue the Word*. Her poems also appear in *Concrete Garden*, *Sojourner*, BLU *Magazine*, and *Prosodia X*, and in the anthologies *Hauling up the Morning*, *Voices of Resistance*, *Doing Time: Twenty-Five Years of Prison Writing*, and *Women's Prison Writings, 200 A.D. to the Present*. Following the September 11, 2001, tragedy, under the orders of Attorney-General John Ashcroft, she was taken out of general population in her Dublin, California, prison and placed in isolation.[1]

The Effects of Repression on Women in Prison   Marilyn Buck

It is not necessary to be a political prisoner in order to be able to analyze our conditions as women prisoners. To go beyond reacting to this process, however, one must become conscious of oneself and one's keepers. A lack of developed consciousness is dominant. When one can curse out one's keepers and not be punished, one often thinks that she is impervious to the power exerted over her.

We delude ourselves a lot. We must do so in order to not go crazy. Knowing too much about what is happening to us creates a very uncomfortable state. But it is a state that is necessary not only to survive, but also to become active as an agent in history or society rather than an object to be acted on.

State Repression: The Prison

External repression acts to remove any power an individual (or group) may have that will aid her in becoming a subject in, rather than an object of, her own world. Psychologically, repression forces the individual to lose control of self and forces her, the group, or the class to submit. Submission and subjugation lead to both social and psychological alienation and division. Paulo Freire has stated: "Part of the oppressed I is located in the reality to which it adheres; part is located outside the self in the mysterious forces which are regarded as responsible for a reality about which nothing can be done."[2]

What does or does not constitute a crime depends on the historical time; who is charged with lawbreaking is politically—or socially—determined. As Joy James posits in *Resisting State Violence*, "Greater obedience is demanded from those whose physical difference marks them as aberrational, offensive, or threatening. . . . Frantz Fanon writes, in 'The Negro and Psychopathology' that 'the Negro symbolizes the biological danger.'"[3]

The Prison as Agent of Repression

Prisons function as small city-states or fiefdoms; the denizens—prisoners—are subject not only to society's laws, but also to the ever changing, arbitrary power of the overseers and keepers. Punishment is a province of the prison system, a policy of terror.

An argument can be made that since women as a class already endure both social and cultural oppression and repression from childhood on, institutional repression affects women in a qualitatively different way. As Karlene Faith sums up in her book *Unruly Women: The Politics of Confinement and Resistance*: "The history of unruly, defiant women is the history of men's efforts to control them and this translates into practical terms on the context of criminal justice."[4]

Punishment begins the moment one is incarcerated. One is stripped of possessions, clothing, family, and both civil and human rights. The legal sentence is not only a judgment of guilt but also an assessment of normality. The first step in this process is to criminalize the individual and strip her of her long-held social and personal identity. The individual enters the prison gates as an offender. The repressive apparatus seeks to forge a "delinquent—the object of the apparatus" out of the offender to expand capitalist industry (criminology, criminal-justice programs in academe, sociology, and so on). A few who enter may readily accept the concept that they are criminals, bad girls, or "outlaws." Most women, however, know they are not criminals and struggle against the dehumanization implicit in the process of criminalization. Nazim Hikmet, a Turkish poet and political prisoner, captures this struggle:

We are clutching the rags of time
and trying to come to terms with bits of selves
shelved on the day of arrest.[5]

What is normal and routine in this world would be a nightmare to one who has not had to experience such indignity: lack of control over one's own self, censorship, punishment, and even torture by the guards. The only comparable environments, besides mental institutions, are militarized, policed "ghettoes" or "barrios," state-of-siege arenas—situations that many white U.S.-born people have never experienced, unless one has been held hostage, as in abusive relationships.

Most new prisoners walk around in a state of shock, fear, and uncertainty. It is difficult for one to believe that she has so few rights, or that there is no due process when a guard tells her that she must either do as he or she says or suffer the consequences. Even being transferred to another prison causes a similar, though less intense response. One must learn to negotiate the unfamiliar mine-field—the personalities and boundaries of the prison guards as well as those of the prisoners, each of who is arduously negotiating each day.

Evelyn, a black woman now in her forties, has been in prison for more than fifteen years. She recalls her arrest: "I was so devastated that I believe I had a nervous breakdown. I felt my whole world was over. I felt I had done such a terrible thing and I needed punishing. What I didn't realize however, at the time, was the people who were in control of me and who I felt were in charge of dispensing 'justice' were much more corrupt than I." Another prisoner, Delia, a foreign national imprisoned almost five years, states emphatically that when she was arrested, she felt "violated [and] a loss of dignity." She felt she had been reduced to "hav[ing] no value" and that she had been "stripped of all personal prerogative."

Techniques of Control

Karlene Faith writes: "The claiming of the prisoner's body begins with admission and is unremitting for the duration of imprisonment."[6] Some women have been in various institutions and enter already acclimated. Some women may be more accustomed to the mortification, battering, and censorship that are the constant, inescapable circumstances of prison, because they have suffered physical and psychological oppression or exploitation before, including the sexual abuse common to so many of us. For a few, prison may even be an escape from the horrors of their daily, battered, and abused lives—at least, in the beginning—until the deadly, sustained monotony of constant hypervigilance, depersonalization, and infantilization set in. Other factors are also in play.

> *Infantilization*: This is a primary instrument of repression. It reinforces women's oppression and our roles in all social, political, and economic relations. Control over self is wrenched from us; we are reduced to the status of children—girls. Infantilization finds a correspondence in documented cases of abuse. Its goal is dependence and docility. It works.
>
> *Hypervigilance*: The conditions of prison order and regimentation demand constant attention to every thing around oneself. Every act or situation is a potential infraction of the rules. The first threat is the keepers—not only their rules, but also their individual attitudes and moods. The women also become vigilant of each other, constantly moving out of each other's way,

predicting the next move, somewhat like playing in a championship tennis tournament and trying to determine where the ball will land so one will not be caught "off guard" and lose. One's life depends on winning—that is, negotiating each situation successfully. This promotes aggression ("Better you than me") or despair and docility. At times, this programmed hypervigilance even leads a prisoner to enter into an alliance with an authority that will function as her protector or as an agent of vengeance and retaliation against real or perceived threats from other women prisoners.

Racism in the name of diversity: To avoid the punishment of white supremacy's degradations, women of color, particularly black and Latina women from inside the United States, are forced not to rebel or deviate from white dominant culture. They must become docile and submissive and either suppress their own culture or be subjected to the same kinds of physical and psychological harassment and assaults that occur daily in the world. Alternatively, the black or Latina prisoner must play the role of the rebel that is expected of her as the untrainable "other." This rebellion, however, is a false one and leaves her unprepared to function in the white-ruled world to which she must return.

Defilement. This is the state, so-called by Erving Goffman, in which prisoners are forced to witness degradation of others or to degrade themselves. In extreme cases, there may be extreme responses—suicide or suicide attempts. Defilement is the normal, expected state of prison life. In less extreme or more banal cases of defilement, prisoners tend to experience chronic anxiety and stress or even depression. They become inured to cruelty and degradation and begin to identify with the keepers. When a woman is charged with an infraction of the rules, she may be blamed by her peers, some of whom may become angry at the rule breaker because she "makes prisoners look bad." They accept the keeper's social construct that a prisoner deserves to be punished, even for things that are neither crimes nor social violations in the outside world. It takes a lot of conscious work not to succumb to a moral indifference and dehumanization.

Mortification: Although cloaked in the name of security procedures, mortification is used to objectify. Strip searches, and even pat searches, are sexual violations we are forced to endure. Cavity searches cause a humiliation that we never get used to. As Karlene Faith declares: "For the women who experience it, a forced vaginal exam is tantamount to state-authorized rape, and torturing and shaming women in this way seems clearly intended to reinforce their dehumanized prisoner status."[7] One prisoner confided that she has fears she never remembered having before because she has been the victim of sexual harassment more than once. She believes that had she not had a sense of her own competence from her previous life experience, she would have been unable or unwilling to challenge the harassment both during the course of it and after, when she protested and tried to expose it. She remembers: "I never had such fear of authority. . . . I never realized how corrupt they could be. They condone sexual harassment by intimidating women who refuse to be silent."

Effects

The changes in one's self as a result of incarceration are difficult to articulate. Several women prisoners have remarked that it is difficult to remember how they were before. "But I wasn't like this!" A few have discovered "internal freedom" and skills they did not know they had in earlier lives as wives or mothers.

In one group discussion, women prisoners agreed that they do not write letters about the world of prison because they do not want to burden families or friends with the pain and horror of the prison experience. Women tend to lock up, or repress, the full extent of their horrific experiences.

Audre Lorde, in "Uses of the Erotic," states:

> The fear of our desires keeps them suspect and indiscriminately powerful . . . for to suppress any truth is to give it strength beyond endurance. The fear that we cannot grow beyond whatever distortions we may find within ourselves keeps us docile and loyal and obedient, externally defined, and leads us to accept many facets of our oppression as women.[8]

Repression of self or self-censorship: The physical and social repression of incarceration results in deforming and shutting down a woman's sense of self. Self-repression is a response to the techniques of control as a form of avoidance or as a strategy of withdrawal or denial. A primary consequence is docility. One begins to accept at an even more intense level than women in society might the abnormal conditions of power and control over her body as something either deserved or that she has no power to refuse. This is not so different from the woman who is abused, controlled, and perhaps even imprisoned by her abuser.

Complex chronic Post-Traumatic Stress Disorder: Judith Herman, in *Trauma and Recovery*, discusses captivity as long-term traumatic stress disorder.[9] She compares women who are abused and controlled by men with political prisoners and concentration-camp survivors, both particular classes of prisoners. However, she does not investigate or acknowledge that women convicted of breaking the law are also abused, held captive, and controlled in a long-term systematic trauma-producing situation. The condition of social imprisonment is functionally no different from being locked up by a man or incarcerated as result of one's political or social standing. There may be differences in degree or harshness of treatment; nevertheless, the psychological and physical effects differ little, despite the underlying reasons for imprisonment.

Herman seems not to recognize that there may be differences in response to captivity based on one's status or situation.[10] She scarcely mentions even class background as a possible aggravating factor in effects of the abuse. Women who are abused and demonized because they are not white Euro-Americans are not considered at all. That she excludes these women reinforces a view that women prisoners are not to be considered victims of trauma, or to be free from dehumanization because they have transgressed the "law," or, increasingly for women of color, have been targeted and abducted by the law because of their race, nationality, or class. In the United States, such an invasion of women's lives is culturally and politically acceptable.

In *Unruly Women*, Karlene Faith lists some of the agonies of prison. I will not reiterate them all here, but her article is well worth reading. Evelyn and Delia are extremely competent people in their views of self and perceptions of their experiences as prisoners. Yet the racism and discrimination they experience daily wear both of them down. This is not so different from that which exists in "normal" society. In society, however, one can seek shelter from the constant pressure in the lap of one's family or community. Family and community are safety valves that are not available when most needed in the prison environment. One must wait for a visit or a phone call or a letter. Even then, the constant, pervasive surveillance of mail and phone calls necessitates a high level of self-censorship. The prisoner is mindful and on alert that she is being monitored.

A general response is one of emotional tiredness and failure of concentration, with undercurrents of despair and depression.

Delia notes: "Women are more afraid to demand proper treatment as human beings. We are not assertive enough. . . . The system is designed to undermine, diminish self worth. . . . It affects me in many ways—feeling powerless, not being able to do any thing about it productively."

Laura Whitehorn, a political prisoner incarcerated for nearly fifteen years, talks about particular situations where the guards denied her *basic* necessities like toilet paper to mortify her and to break her:

> The feelings were hard to suppress or repress, as I usually did. Once unleashed, my anger made me ashamed because I hated to "lose control." The image of me the government put forward was "someone out of control"—using armed struggle wasn't a strategic decision but rather an acting out of anger. This view . . . de-politicized me and the movement I'd been part of, and turned us into "terrorists." . . . So, anytime I felt I was acting in anything less than strategic fashion in fighting for my rights, I felt I was undermining my own argument that this was vicious government propaganda.[11]

Survival Responses

Some of the many survival responses utilized by women in prison are:

> *Activity,* from exercise to game playing. Activity is a fundamental act of survival. There are some prison programs that have existed in various institutions at various times, such as parenting and educational programs. Those who are most self-motivated remain most active.
>
> *Religion* becomes a major aspect of survival and redefinition of self for many women.
>
> *Reading* passes the time and enables the individual to step beyond the confines of prison walls.
>
> *Working* in programs and organizations strengthens one's resistance and sense of self-efficacy. Any such program, whether it be the Jaycees, Toastmasters, the National Association for the Advancement of Colored People, or cultural programs, often provides the only situation in which the individuals have any control to act as empowered adults.

At Bedford Hills, the New York State prison for women, AIDS Counseling and Education (ACE), the first prison-peer educator group in the United States, successfully empowered many women. These women wrote about their experiences: "We began to see ourselves as women in a new light. Many of us usually see things in individual and private terms. Now we were thinking in social and political terms. It made us angry and emboldened. We wanted to act."[12]

At the Federal Correctional Institution in Dublin, California, PLACE (Pleasanton AIDS Counseling and Education), another successful HIV/AIDS peer counseling and education groups, modeled after ACE, functioned for seven years. After a change of administration in the summer of 1997, the program was abolished. Some of the participants recalled: "We lost a driving sense of purpose. The frustration of being marginalized and banned, told we could not build consciousness through peer education was paralyzing for a while. We went into a kind of depression. We had no real way to fight this censorship and wave of repression."[13]

Several of the long-time activists in PLACE did find ways to reclaim the purpose and work. On an informal basis, some of the women maintained a support circle for at least one woman, a PWA (prisoner with AIDS). That smaller, "unregistered" group was an act of resistance and a continuation of purpose. Nevertheless, the mourning for that grievous loss of purpose and constructive, collective work has not ended.

Seeking resistance strategies, political prisoners—incarcerated for their actions in support of their political beliefs against state injustice and oppression—draw strength of purpose from their beliefs and goals.

Ida Luz Rodríguez, imprisoned for nearly twenty years, is one of more than a dozen Puerto Rican independence fighters—a prisoner of war. In an interview, she spoke about her imprisonment: "I find myself stronger now than before imprisonment and clandestinity. Not only that, one cannot lock one's self up in a narrow mentality because I feel the strength that is born from a desire to be free [as a people]."[14]

Conclusion

There is much more to be said about surviving prison on both the physical and the psychological level. Women's responses to the repressive prison environment, as well as the repressive defenses we employ in our own immediate survival, may lead to long-term harm to the self. Internalized repression impedes the struggle to achieve one's existential purpose as a human being—that is, to become more human, more productive, and therefore to develop oneself as a subject rather than object of history, subject to the power of others. Imprisonment promotes a variety of psychological disorders. It takes a particularly psychologically hardy individual—a woman who is clear on her efficacy as a human being and who finds the resources to resist the assault on her personality and self-identity through a variety of strategies—in order not to succumb. Even among the women who leave prison or continue to endure it seemingly intact, there is damage. Women who are the most conscious of self and their states of mental health, and of why this damage is occurring, are the most successful. Political prisoners and prisoners of conscience are among the most successful. Laura Whitehorn, recently released after nearly fourteen years of imprisonment, illustrates this point. She suffered exceedingly the effects of poor or barely existent medical attention. As a political prisoner, she endured isolation and deliberate psychological targeting and harassment. From all outward aspects, she is strong psychologically. Most observers see that she has handled well the nearly fifteen years of imprisonment; the system could not break her. In fact, she gives other women hope.

Nevertheless, Laura is very conscious that she has been damaged psychologically, both in ways she can identify and in ways she cannot yet grasp. That she is aware of the damage makes her mentally healthier than she would be absent such consciousness. If a woman does not have much critical consciousness, she cannot address the problems of her own destabilized condition in a healthy manner, whether she remains a prisoner or is released.

There is always hope that the human spirit can surmount the mortification of prison to use the experience to continue one's development as a human being. Freedom can be found in adversity. Ida Luz Rodríguez summed up her prison experience:

> I have always lived with hope. Prison has never made me feel desperate. Adversity does not depress me, nor crush me. It is a challenge that is important to me. Fortunately this is my way of living. . . . [But] I am ready to get out of here. What I can learn here I have already learned, and I'm ready to learn things in other places. I am tired and irritated. This routine sucks.[15]

Notes

1. Sources for Buck's biography include Baraldini, Buck, Rosenberg, and Whitehorn, "Women's Control Unit"; and Buck, "On Self-Censorship," and "Prisons, Social Control, and Political Prisoners."
2. Freire, *The Pedagogy of the Oppressed*.
3. James, *Resisting State Violence*, 26.
4. Faith, *Unruly Women*.
5. Hikmet, *Poems of Nazim Hikmet*.
6. Faith, *Unruly Women*.
7. Ibid.
8. Lorde, *Uses of the Erotic*, 53.
9. See Herman, *Trauma and Recovery*.
10. Laura Whitehorn interview with the author, FCI Dublin, 1997.
11. Herman, *Trauma and Recovery*, 74.
12. ACE Program of Bedford Hills Correctional Facility, *Breaking the Walls of Silence*, 86.
13. Anonymous prisoner in conversation with the author.
14. Mari Narváez, trans. Marilyn Buck, *Claridad* (San Juan, Puerto Rico), June 18–24, 1999, 14–15.
15. Ibid.

CAROL GILBERT, O.P.

Carol Gilbert was born in 1947 and entered the Grand Rapids, Michigan, Dominican Sisters on September 8, 1965. She has been a junior-high-school teacher and a peace activist for twenty-five years. Gilbert is currently involved in peace and justice organizing at Jonah House in Baltimore, Maryland, and is a member of the Atlantic Life Community.[1]

A participant in four Plowshares' actions, Carol Gilbert has twice been found guilty of "depredation of U.S. government property" for actions taken to oppose U.S. manufacturing of nuclear warheads. On May 17, 1998, Gilbert and four other Plowshares activists disarmed a B-52 Stratofortress nuclear bomber at Andrews Air Force Base in Maryland during an annual "Air Show." They used household hammers to beat holes in the doors of the world's largest nuclear bomber and poured their blood over the B-52, calling it "the bloodiest weapon of this the bloodiest century in human history."[2] Gilbert spent six months in prison for this action.

In July 2003, Gilbert, along with Sister Jackie Hudson and Sister Ardeth Platte, was sentenced to time in federal prison for nonviolent protest at the N-8 Minuteman III silo in Colorado. On the morning of October 6, 2002, the three nuns, dressed as a "Citizens Weapons Inspection Team," cut a chain around a farmer's gate to enter the active missile site. Carrying hammers and baby bottles filled with their own blood, they poured blood in the shape of six crosses, hammered on the railroad tracks used to transport the missile, and removed a portion of the chain-link fence surrounding the silo to expose one of the thousands of nuclear warheads housed on U.S. soil.

Gilbert, Hudson, and Platte, all members of the Sacred Earth and Space Plowshares, planned their nonviolent civil-resistance action for the first anniversary of the illegal bombing and invasion of Afghanistan by the United States and at a time when the United States was planning to invade Iraq for supposedly harboring weapons of mass destruction. Law-enforcement authorities responded to their actions with an extremely strong reprimand: Rather than being charged with a misdemeanor, they faced felony charges with sentences comparable to that of murder. The women were charged with obstruction and sabotage of national defense and depredation of government property—crimes that carry a maximum sentence of thirty years. Judge Robert Blackburn sentenced Carol Gilbert to thirty-three months in federal prison. (Platte received forty-one months and Hudson thirty months, based on prior convictions.) Blackburn waived their fines but ordered that the nuns reimburse the government $3,080.04—the reported cost of fixing the fence they damaged. Carol Gilbert was released from Alderson Federal Prison on May 23, 2005, and is currently on three years supervised probation.

Ponderings from the Eternal Now   Carol Gilbert, O.P.

Sentencing Statement, July 25, 2003

For many months I have pondered what to say, if anything at all. St. Francis once said, "Preach the Gospel at all times, if necessary use words." It seems that today a few words are necessary.

For the past ten months we have tried to cooperate with these courts. We have been asking since day one—what are the charges? What is Title 18, U.S. Code, Section 2155, if not sabotage?[3] We are not saboteurs. Today, we ask no more questions. We know something is very wrong with a system that can incarcerate us for years in prison for inspecting, exposing, and symbolically disarming America's weapons of mass destruction.

We know we should be acquitted for upholding the U.S. Constitution that declares all laws and treaties to be the supreme laws of the country. Article 6, Section 2 of the U.S. Constitution "declares this constitution and the laws of the United States which shall be made in pursuant thereof, and all Treaties made, or which shall be made under the Authority of the United States, shall be the supreme law of the land and the Judges in every State shall be bound thereby, anything in the Constitution of laws of any State to the Contrary notwithstanding."

We should be acquitted for upholding international laws that this court has deemed unnecessary but is bound to enforce under Article 6, Section 2 of the U.S. Constitution.[4] It hurts to hear the prosecutor continue to call Frances Boyle a "self-professed international law guru."

We should be acquitted for upholding the highest law—God's law.

Judge Robert Blackburn talked a lot about law.[5] He did not want this to be a political trial but a case about law. So did we. That was our deepest hope. But we were not the ones that turned this into a political trial, nor will we make of ourselves political prisoners—that will be the prosecutor and judge.

We have read in the press and in our pre-sentencing reports that the lengthy sentence is for deterrence—both for ourselves and for others. But what the government fails to recognize is that long prison sentences will only energize the movement. As a T-shirt in upstate New York reads, "You can jail the resister but not the resistance." We will not be silenced.

During our seven months in the Clear Creek County Jail we received thousands of letters from the United States and international community and over 1,000 signatures from people who stand in solidarity with us, and more than 1,000 letters were sent to the judge asking for compassion and justice. There have been four Plowshares actions since ours—one of them in the United States.[6] This Memorial Day [2003], four Plowshares activists enfleshed the Isaiah and Micah prophecies on the *U.S.S. Philippine Sea* in New York Harbor during Fleet Week, naming themselves Riverside Ploughshares. No charges were filed.

No, Judge Blackburn needs no more words from us. Judge Blackburn needs no character witnesses this morning. What Judge Blackburn needs is to listen to his God. He needs to heed these words from one of my church's social-justice documents, *Gadium et spes. no. 16*:

> Deep within their consciences men and women discover a law which they have not laid upon themselves and which they must obey. Its voice, ever calling them to love and to do what is good and to avoid evil, tells them inwardly at the right moment: do this, shun that. For they have in their hearts a law inscribed by God. Their dignity rests, in observing the law, and by it they will be judged. Their conscience is people's most secret core and their sanctuary. There they are alone with God whose voice echoes in their depths.

Tomorrow, nonviolent citizens in Colorado will inspect and expose America's weapons of mass destruction, the Minuteman 111, with others joining in solidarity in other states and others exposing other weapons systems at other sites.[7] Resistance will not be deterred. You cannot silence truth. Truth will be spoken. Law will be upheld.

Judge Blackburn and the prosecutor need to reflect on the story in the Acts of the Apostles of Gamaliel—Chapter 5, verses 17–42. Gamaliel was a Pharisee, a member of the council, and a teacher of the law. He was highly respected by all the people. As Peter and the other apostles were taken to the council and high priest, Gamaliel cautioned the council not to take any action against the men. He said, "If what they have planned and done is of human origin it will disappear, but if it comes from God, you cannot possibly defeat them."

Someday, history will prove what we did on the early morning of October 6, 2002—inspecting, exposing, and symbolically disarming a Minuteman 111, a weapon of mass destruction—was legal. Until that day, I will continue being led where I would rather not go. I will continue to resist with every fiber of my being so that not one child will ever ask, "Why were you complicit?" A story told of Daniel Berrigan, Jesuit priest, prophet, and friend, is that he was once asked to give the commencement address at a prestigious university.[8] He stood up, walked to the podium, and said, "Know where you stand and stand there," and then he sat down. My friends, "Know where you stand and stand there."

The following collection of letters, edited for this volume, was written between October 2003 and July 2004. The letters are posted on Jonah House Community's website under the title, "Ponderings from the Eternal Now."

October 2003

As I wait for my medical clearance and before I begin my "landscaping" job, I thought you might be interested in the costs of life here at Alderson.

1. Issued one pair of steel-toed shoes (men's);
   Shower thongs—$.90
   Tennis shoes—$50–$70
   Boots—$70 and up (special order)
2. No free typewriter or computer available
   Typewriter ribbon—$7.50
   Lift-off tape—$1.25
3. No lock is provided for our small lockers. Stealing is rampant.
   Cost of lock—$7
4. Thin cap and garden gloves provided—no scarf.
   Hat, gloves, scarf—$20
5. Issued one pair of men's long underwear
   Long tops—$8
   Long bottoms—$5 (both men's)
6. Headphones and radios control the TVs and videos in housing units and chapel
   Headphones—$30–$50

7. Twenty-four over-the-counter common medications are sold. This is where you are sent to treat yourself

   Yeast infection medication—$13

8. Grey sweatshirts and sweatpants are allowed after 4 P.M. and on weekends

   $14.20 each—more for larger sizes (men's)

9. Fruit and fruit juices are sold weekly for those who can afford and want fruit more than once a day or so

10. Wash is done in the main laundry, but only the clothes they issue are so washed. In the housing units:

    Wash—$.40; dry—$.40

    Laundry soap—$2–$6

11. Fans, alarm clocks, watches, sunglasses—all must be purchased.

12. Families need an extra stamp and envelope because money orders are no longer sent to the inmate with a letter. All money orders go to a National Lock Box in Marietta, Georgia.

And, of course, selling one's body for pay is the last resort for some of these women.

This gives you an idea of how the poor remain poor, since average jobs are $5.25–$18 a month, unless one works for the prison industry, UNICOR, for slave wages. If any fines or restitution are owed, money is taken monthly from these wages. Life can be unbearable for these poor women.

Well, this is prison! Read on. . . . The October 6 issue of the *Nation* has an article from Christian Parenti:

> This unit's rifles are retooled hand-me-downs from Vietnam. They have inadequate radio gear, so they buy their own unencrypted Motorola walkie-talkies. The same goes for flashlights, knives and some components for night-vision sights. The low-performance Iraqi air-conditioners and fans, as well as the one satellite phone and payment cards shared by the whole company for calling home, were also purchased out of pocked from civilian suppliers.[9]

Make one wonder what the difference is between the prison-industrial complex and the military-industrial complex? Who said we should follow the money trail?

I close with these words from George Orwell: "In times of universal deceit, telling the truth is a revolutionary act."

Deep peace, Carol

November 2003

Many of you have asked about my work scene at Alderson. As soon as a person receives medical clearance, a job is assigned. This is a designated work camp, and everyone, from the oldest to the youngest, the strongest to the weakest, works. Work can be as simple as polishing a water fountain.

My first weeks were spent searching for work so I would not be placed in CDR—Central Dining Room. I applied to laundry, commissary, outside chapel maintenance, cottage maintenance, and landscaping. Some jobs are more labor-intensive, like landscaping, and some can be completed in a few hours, with lots of idle time. Pay can range from the minimum $5.25 a month to $.12 an hour—about $18 a month. The exception is UNICOR, the prison industry. The weeks passed, and I waited for my name to appear on the daily call-out sheet. The end of October my name appeared—CDR. I groaned, and my friends groaned! My attitude was upbeat. This would be a learning experience.

My first and third day consisted of tables in sections seven and eight. Between five and eight of us are responsible for wiping off tables after all have eaten, sweeping the floor, and wet moping—this is not a large section. My second day was working in the dish room, with three to five of us separating silverware as it came from the machine and stocking it in appropriate containers. Because we are overrun with cockroaches, one was on the lookout as they fell from the ceiling and their babies ran around our work table! During our down time, we are allowed no books, magazines, cards, pens, yarn—nothing! We sit! This policy is for every job site but is ignored.

The women who leave for GED from 12–2 P.M. may bring homework or their books to work. If caught with any of the above items, a shot (disciplinary action) can be given. It was not possible for me to live this schedule and remain healthy. The boredom was too much. My work ethic was not appreciated by many of the women, as they feared extra work. My friends here were praying for a miracle, and one came! Ms. Flack, my new counselor, asked to see me and then couldn't remember why. I shared my pain. She moved me after three days of CDR to cottage maintenance bathrooms. So five days a week, four of us clean two large bathrooms for 100 to 125 women. The good news is that when the work is finished, we are free to fill in the hours. My time is spent in prayer, reading, writing letters, walking, listening, and knitting hats, mittens, and scarves for poor children.

In pondering these past two months on work, I keep wondering under what illusion this system operates. I keep telling myself that these people can't actually believe we are working these many hours with so many people . . . 7:45 A.M.– 3:45 P.M. for most jobs. Addicts are told not to live in denial. Isn't this one of the greatest denials of all?

P.S. Mr. Bowling, the head of CDR, tells us an outside firm is coming in next week to fog for cockroaches and then once a month. We shall see!

February 2004

Dear Friends,

I don't know about you, but many of us here are waiting for signs of spring and warmer temperatures. While the snow is magnificent to see, we are getting tired of standing in cold lines to eat, and folks are getting a bit stir crazy being confined to our warehouse/ barracks based on wind chills.

A few prison happenings:

—I had extra cleaning duty a few days into the new year because I thought the 4:15 P.M. stand-up count had cleared and sat on my bed. Two of us were screamed at first, as this is the method used here.

—Hundreds of women had to buy new umbrellas at $8 apiece because the old ones were artistically decorated to prevent stealing. Luckily, I never wrote on mine.

—I was one of 120 women from here randomly selected to be part of the "Survey of Inmates in State and Federal Correctional Facilities" from the Bureau of Justice Statistics. We were told that the information will be used by lawmakers and correctional staff to help them make informed decisions about policies and inmate needs. Most of us felt it was a complete and total waste of time. I told the woman I didn't see how any of this would help lawmakers. I said: You need to interview us?

Since trials have begun and more will follow, I share the following:

The Public Prosecutor was on record at the trial stating: "As men we can respect . . . [their] convictions, but what we cannot allow is that the State, through a false sentimentalism, tolerates such things. The State must take no account of personalities who, although they cannot be placed in the same category as criminals, nevertheless represent a continual danger to the very existence of the State."

No, this is not a transcript from the trial of Jackie Hudson, O.P., Ardeth Platte, O.P. and Carol Gilbert, O.P. in Colorado in 2003. It is a quote from the trial of Rupert Mayer, S.J., in Munich, Germany, in 1937. [Father] Mayer's crime was speaking out against Hitler and he paid for preaching his truth with time in prison and a concentration camp.

[Father] Mayer was beatified in 1987 and is called the Apostle of Munich. The city of Munich prays often at his shrine just off the bustling city center and takes seriously their responsibility to the world to speak the truth about injustice and the consequences of blindly obeying the State.[10]

The above comes to us from our Sister Diane Zerfas when she was in Munich to accept the Nuclear-Free Future Award in our names. Sounds familiar, doesn't it? Lastly, I share this Taoist meditation because it best describes what I've been feeling these cold winter days:

> Close your eyes and you will see clearly.
> Cease to listen and you will hear truth.
> Be silent and your heart will sing.
> Seek no contact and you will find union.
> Be still and you will move forward in the tide of the Spirit.
> Be gentle and you will not need strength.
> Be patient and you will achieve all things.
> Be humble and you remain entire.

My deepest gratitude and love, Carol

March 2004

One of the things I'm beginning to understand is the "mentality of a soup line." As we wait anywhere from ten to thirty minutes to eat, sometimes in bitter winds, and people cut lines, I find myself getting angry. My mantra is to see the face of God in these women! The hopeful sign is the birds are singing! On February 22, I saw my first robin of the season.

This past month I was given my first "breathalyzer." This is randomly given to whoever is in the right place at the wrong time. I wonder what this unnecessary cost is to taxpayers! While I'd like to think I'm kinder on the environment being in prison, this was not true this past month. The hot-water heater's temperature control broke, and we ate on Styrofoam with plastic silverware at the cost of $600 a day for four weeks. There was a somewhat unorganized boycott of the vending machines as prices increased dramatically. For example, candy bars went from $.55 to $.85. While this doesn't impact my life, it does impact the majority of women here.

We are so overcrowded that sixty women are being asked to transfer to the [Metropolitan Correctional Center] in downtown Philadelphia to finish out their sentences. They will be much closer to home.

Our job market (adult day-care center) is so overcrowded that a new "center" was created—the Captain's Crew. These women wear orange vests and do litter and yard maintenance, the same as landscaping. The Captain's Crew Day Care Center is so popular that two shifts had to be created to meet the demand!

During these Lenten days I'm taking a four-week Centering Prayer Course offered by Molly Bauer, S.S.J., and a six-hour video class on the Jewish Kabala. The most hopeful news I've received is the meeting at the United Nations from April 26–May 7, 2004. The governments of the world will gather to discuss the Nuclear Nonproliferation and Disarmament Treaties.[11] A demonstration is planned in New York City for May 1, 2004. For more information, go to http://w.1may04.org. Also Jonah House has a web site that is posting our letters and other good information. Check it out and pass the word: http://www.jonah house.org.

Lastly, the reflection I share is a poem from Tom Keene. It expresses my belief and gratitude for each of you!

Who Holds Us Together?
A sacred tradition has it
That at all times and all ages
There exists a minimum of ten souls,
Scattered and unknown
Even to one another,
Who with their hungers and thirsts,
Their prayers and deeds,
Hold the world together,

Ever gluing back our family shards,

Redoing our undoings, our killings,

Redeeming our failure

To stand under one another.

To know such a one is almost enough.[12]

Yashir koach (May you grow in strength), Carol

April 2004

Dearest Friends,

This month I've decided to share with you what I've come to call my gift of tears. As I write this, we are still in the season of Lent and await the seasons of spring, new life, and Resurrection. My story of the gift of tears began in the wee morning hours of September 5, 2003. Jackie and I left Ardeth behind a locked cell door in Oklahoma City, Oklahoma. We realized it was probably the last time we would all be together for a few years. What is this gift of tears? It is tears that come easily and unexpected. Tears at various times and places. Tears of joy, tears of sorrow, and tears of joy mingled with tears of sorrow. Tears have come when:

—A herd of deer feeds at our back window

—Listening to the desperate voices of women calling home

—The foothills of these mountains [are] immersed in fog, mist, and low clouds

—One wakes to a winter wonderland and snow sits heavy on the branches

—Mother and child are united in a visiting room

—Harsh words are exchanged between prisoners

—A pileated woodpecker is so close one can almost touch it, watching it peck a hole in a rotten tree and finding the grubs

—Listening in the early-morning dark to stories on BBC and NPR

—A crocus blooms

—Hearing stories of unjust sentences because of mandatory minimums

—Letters from around the world [come] filled with grace and wisdom

—Guards intimidate and demean

—A tufted titmouse pecks for food

—Letters arrive with news of friends with cancer or notices of death

—Full moons

—Listening to stories of incest, abuse, and addiction

—A song at church

—Walking these prison grounds and reflecting on the wisdom of the trees and the peacemakers who walked these same paths and left part of their spirits

I sometimes feel when I leave prison it is the only gift I'll have to bring you—this gift of tears. And, maybe that's OK. Maybe, that's the gift the world most needs. Speaking of tears, I want to share with you "National Wash the Flag Day," June 14. Wash the pain and the shame from our flag. Wash away the stains of racism, sexism, classism, violence, criminalization, environmental injustice, blind patriotism, imperialism, militarism, deception, oppression, corporate greed, and materialism. For more information, e-mail spirithouse@aol.com.

The good news is that I finished my first scarf on the loom for the nursing home and my first-ever knitted child's sweater for local social services.

The doctor has put me on a statin (ZOCOR) for my cholesterol, which has skyrocketed. I'm sure in part due to diet—prison food. My teeth were cleaned after eight months, which was a gift, as I suffer from gum problems. They are always cleaned every three to four months.

I'll close with this quote from Johann Wolfgang von Goethe: "What then is your duty? What the day demands."

My heart overflows with gratitude for each of you.

Deepest love, Carol

P.S. We welcome as gift to the world Amos Philip Mechtenberg-Berrigan, the first-born of Molly and Jerry and first grandchild of Liz McAlister and the late Philip Berrigan.[13]

May 2004

Dearest Friends,

This isn't the letter I was expecting to send you this month, but sometimes something so horrendous comes along it must take precedence. Such is the following story. In reading my May issue of *Harper's Magazine*, I came upon a small piece of interviews conducted by Human Rights Watch researchers in Pakistan and Vivian White, a reporter for the BBC, with recently released prisoners of Camp X-Ray, the U.S. detention center at Guantánamo Bay, Cuba.[14]

I was not shocked at the use of tape, cuffs, gas, chains, cages, bright lights, noise, beatings, sleep deprivation, and painful positions. What did horrify me were the "injections" and the "pills."

—"They injected me. I was unconscious." A. Khan

—"They gave us pills that made us feel numb or made us drunk." K. M.

—"The other method that the guards used to make us quiet was injections. Guards would enter the cell with sticks and masks, and two or three of them would hold a prisoner while one of them injected him in any part of his body. Immediately after the injection, the person would faint. Then he was put into isolation. Twice they injected me and took me to the isolation room, a dark room with cold air blowing." A. K.

—"Other countries torture prisoners with electric shocks, but they tortured me with injections. After I received an injection, my eyes would remain fixed upwards, and my muscles would get stiff. I would stay like that for a day and sometimes longer, until I was given another injection, which would relax me, and then I could move my eyes and muscles again. Sometimes they would give me pills after the first injection. I saw other prisoners receive injections as well." S. M. A.

According to the article, the United States is currently holding about 650 suspects at Guantánamo Bay. These interviews don't sound that different to me from the Nazi experiments. I reflect on the Chinese proverb: "To know what is going on takes sense; to know what to do about it takes wisdom. What do we do with this burden of knowing?"

Spring has arrived in all its glory at Alderson. We are in awe as we watch the birds build their nests and smell the lilacs and honeysuckles. The mountains are alive with various shades of green as the trees burst forth. As I write this, I've just seen two Baltimore orioles in one of the huge pines outside the recreation building.

Our population of 1,028 women saw 200 of us sign up for garden plots—two to a plot. We have ordered the seeds and await our planting date. Deep gratitude must go to our team of lawyers, who have worked tirelessly with no pay on an appeal these past months. It was submitted on April 30.

Again, my deepest gratitude to each of you. No one from the [School of the Americas] is coming here, and so I sit with the silence and the stillness of within.

I'll close with these words from the historian Howard Zinn, which express our Eternal Now:

> To be hopeful in bad times is not just foolishly romantic. It is based on the fact that human history is a history not only of cruelty, but also of compassion, sacrifice, courage, kindness. And if we do act, in however small a way, we don't have to wait for some grand, utopian future.
>
> The future is an infinite succession of presents, and to live now as we think human beings should live, in defiance of all that is bad around us, is itself a marvelous victory.[15]

With deep love, Carol

P.S. For those who ask about my work, I've been dubbed The "Bathroom Queen Cleaning Lady"!

June 2004

Dearest Friends,

This is one of those letters I've put off writing. It is an attempt to explain my participation in the Inmate Financial Responsibility Program (IFRP)—the payment of criminal debts.[16] It is one of the most difficult programs for women to participate in while in prison. I'm no exception. Our sentence included two debts:

1. Special Assessments: Anyone convicted of a crime is given a special assessment. The money is deposited in the Criminal Victims Fund. Our assessment was $200 for each of us.
2. Restitution: We were ordered to pay for the fence, but this was deferred by order of the judge until our release. We have agreed we will not pay the restitution.

The prison staff has honored this order from the judge, but that is not the case for all the women here. I am blessed! Failure to pay while in prison results in "refusal status." The harshest consequence is being subjected to a monthly commissary spending limit of $25, excluding stamps and telephone.

Two days after my arrival, I met with prison staff and was told I needed to pay $25 quarterly toward the special assessment or face consequence. One of those consequences was not being able to buy my tennis shoes and thus being stuck with steel-toed shoes. I signed! I rationalized that I needed shoes and other basic necessities while here. I felt terrible and weak.

I was told that the money didn't go to the courts but to a special fund for victims.[17] One example given to me by prison staff was that the fund helped pay for the psychologists after the tragedy at Columbine. I could live with that. After seven months and the payment of $50, I was told I must pay the $250 in one month or be placed on refusal status. (Payments are determined by taking all the money received in a six-month period and dividing it into a monthly amount. The women find this very unfair because initially folks need a few hundred dollars to get basics, and Christmas/birthday gifts are one-time surpluses.) One would think I would now refuse since I had purchased my "basic necessities." But this time, my job was at stake. Cleaning bathrooms allows me to do what I wish when not working. Also, picture the scene—a room full of five prison staff yelling at me to sign, allowing me no time to think or ask questions. Sign or else was the threat. I felt pressured. I signed! Then, I guess, more rationalizations.

I'm paid almost $20 a month to clean bathrooms three hours a day, five days a week. I'm using that money for the assessment. When I've been paid that amount, I will then spend $20 a month to help women who get no funds by buying some of their basic necessities. Of course, this is all a game, because the $250 has already been paid. It has taken me some time to feel good about my decision. I feel I can live with it and talk about it. I've come to realize that we are in the end very alone and we need to only answer to ourselves and our God.

On the lighter side, I want to share a story from prison this past month. I share it because so many of the women here asked me to write about it in my next letter. I was responsible for closing the entire prison compound on a Friday night about 7:30 P.M. I was to report to the warden's assistant, and the staff could not find me, even though I had signed out for my weaving class. No one bothered to check the sign-out book. So the whistle blew three times, signifying a possible escape. Everyone was to report to their housing unit for a census count. Not happy campers! I'm found, and because I had signed out, there were no repercussions. You can imagine the teasing I endured for a few days and the rumors that circulated among the 1,000-plus women. My favorite was "nun on the run!"

I close with a poem by Stephen Levine that expresses what I can do these days:

Just a cup of tea.
Noticing hot.
Noticing fragrance, texture.
The touch of warm tea
On the willing tongue.
The warmth that extends down
Into the stomach.
What a wonderful cup of tea.
The tea of peace,
Of satisfaction.
Drinking a cup of tea,
I stop the war.
If only it were that easy!

My deepest love, gratitude and prayer, Carol

July 2004

Dear Friends,

According to Ron Rolheiser, a modern-day spiritual writer, "To ponder is to take into oneself tensions, to hold it and to give it back transformed." These past months I've been pondering deeply what it means to "love your neighbor." I'm finding this more difficult than to "love your enemy." Every Saturday evening at our Episcopal mass, Chaplin Elizabeth Walker closes with this blessing:

May the Lord Jesus Christ who walks on wounded feet
Walk with you to the end of the road.
May the Lord Jesus Christ who loves with a wounded heart
Help you to love your neighbor and one another.
May the Lord Jesus Christ who serves with wounded hands
Help you to serve each other and your neighbors.
May you see the face of God on everyone you meet,
And may the blessing of God Almighty,
The Father, Son, and Holy Spirit
Be with you this day and remain with you always.
Amen.

The obscene language, loud talking, yelling, constant messy sinks and toilets, cutting in lines, unhealthy relationships, inconsiderate and immature women, etc., etc., begin to take their toll. My belief is that "class" determines how difficult or easy it is for me to "love my neighbor" these days rather than race or culture, unless the culture believes in quiet, order, and responsibility. If it's true that every thought, word, and deed ripples through our universe, then I must confess we are far from a nonviolent world if my life is typical. And so I pray many times a day to live more nonviolently, to see the face of God in everyone I meet, and to be transformed.

Lest you think your tax dollars are not wisely at work: I was awakened at 2:00 A.M. on a weekday to get dressed and go with the guard to the administration building for a drug/urine test and breathalyzer. As we rode the mile, I told her we had a problem, as I had just emptied my bladder at 1:30 A.M. and was back in a deep sleep. She informed me I had two hours to produce or be sent to Beckley County Jail. I sat on a wooden bench for forty-five minutes, when she took me to the bathroom and ran the faucets. Nothing! I returned to the bench, where she told me she had to leave and do 3:00 A.M. count. She gave me two six-ounce glasses of water and told me she would be back in an hour. The lieutenant was very kind and brought me a soft chair to sit in. At 4:00 A.M. the guard returned, and we tried again. A dribble! She said it must come up to the line. It comes. I sign the paperwork. The container is placed in a plastic bag and sent off for testing. I am back in my bed at 4:30 A.M. When I ask her why they wake us up in the middle of the night, she tells me that every shift has to do so many tests, and it is all random—the computer spews out the names. When I ask about wasted costs and if they ever find anything, she tells me that this is [Bureau of Prisons] policy.

If you get a chance, try to watch the film *The Big House—Alderson*. It was filmed in 1998 and produced for PBS, the History Channel.[18] It is well done and features our Nukewatch peacemaker Bonnie Urfer.

We survived a twenty-eight-hour water shutoff as the city of Alderson did some water-repair work—something to do with bacteria. We also survived a twenty-four-hour period with no guards. All the correctional officers went on a retreat, and we were left with the secretaries and medical staff counting us. Why don't they just send us all home?

Some nature observations have included:

- —Spider webs high in the branches of very old maple and oak tress with dew glistening in the sun
- —Cows from a nearby farm escaping to our property
- —Watching a rabbit eat our flower tops
- —A red-tailed deer eating apples almost out of our hands
- —A glimpse of a yellow warbler and an indigo bunting
- —Robins, starlings, sparrows, and finches teaching their babies to eat
- —Squirrels eating bananas, which are healthier than Jolly Ranchers (hard candy)

The irony is that while many people are afraid of us "convicts," the animals are not afraid. The birds and squirrels don't move as we pass. We don't disturb them in any way. It is really quite amazing.

The gardens are planted and growing. It is truly a miracle to see these plants coming through the clay, cracked ground. We are allowed to eat our veggies, but many get "stolen" by both humans and non-humans, so we shall see.

How many ways can I say thank you for your prayers, letters, articles, books, support, and love? My heart overflows with gratitude. I'll close with a quote from the priest, writer, and friend John Dear, S.J.:

The life of peace is both an inner journey
toward a disarmed heart and a public journey
toward a disarmed world.

These days, that inner journey is most difficult as I strive for a disarmed heart. Blessings on your inner and public journey!
Deep love, Carol.

Notes

The research and draft for the biography of Carol Gilbert were provided by Madeleine Dwertman. Sources included Colorado Communities for Peace and Justice. "Ardeth Platte, Carol Gilbert, and Jackie Hudson," available online at http://www.coloradopeace .org (accessed July 12, 2004); Laura Lewis, "A New Kind of Cell: Jonah House Says Farewell to Sisters Carol Gilbert and Ardeth Platte, who are Headed to Federal Prison," *Baltimore City Paper*, July 23, 2003, available online at http://www.citypaper.com/news/ story.asp?id=4671 (accessed on August 16, 2006); Howard Pankratz, "Nuns Who Raided Silo Stand Firm: Trio Contends International Law is on their Side, but Prosecutors Disagree," *Denver Post Legal*, February 3, 2003, available online at http://www.jonahhouse. org/stand_firm (accessed August 4, 2004); Hannah Shakespeare, dir., *Conviction: U.S. v. Gilbert, Hudson and Platte* (videocassette, Little Voice Productions, Denver, 2004); and William Wan, "Welcomed Back to the Fold: A Community Celebrates a Nun's Return after Her Protest Led to a Term in Federal Prison," *Baltimore Sun*, May 24, 2005, available online at http://www.jonahhouse.org/gilbert_may23.htm (accessed August 16, 2006).

1. "Shalom Salaam Shanti Peace Carol, Jackie, Anne, Ardeth," available online at http:// www.plowsharesactions.org/E&S%202%20Bios.htm (accessed July 11, 2004).

2. "Gods of Metal Plowshares Convicted, Jailed; Sentencing to be January 4," available online at http://www.plowsharesactions.org/GOM%20Convicted.htm (accessed July 11, 2004).

3. *Editor's note*: Title 18, U.S. Code, Section 2155, Destruction of National-Defense Materials, National-Defense Premises, or National-Defense Utilities, reads:

> (a) Whoever, with intent to injure, interfere with, or obstruct the national defense of the United States, willfully injures, destroys, contaminates or infects, or attempts to so injure, destroy, contaminate or infect any national-defense material, national-defense premises, or national-defense utilities, shall be fined under this title or imprisoned not more than 20 years, or both, and, if death results to any person, shall be imprisoned for any term of years or for life; (b) If two or more persons conspire to violate this section, and one or more of such persons do any act to affect the object of the conspiracy, each of the parties to such conspiracy shall be punished as provided in subsection (a) of this section.

See "Title 18, U.S. Code, Section 2155," available online at http://www.frwebgate .access.gpo.gov/cgibin/getdoc.cgi?dbname=browse_usc&docid=Cite: +18USC2155 (accessed August 16, 2004).

4. *Editor's note*: The International Court of Justice's 1996 Advisory Opinion on the Legality of the Threat or Use of Nuclear Weapons determined that the threat or use of nuclear weapons is generally illegal and the necessity to conclude negotiations on complete nuclear disarmament. Paragraph 105(2)(E) of the document states:

> The threat or use of nuclear weapons would generally be contrary to the rules of international law applicable in armed conflict, and in particular the principles and rules of humanitarian law. However, in view of the current state of international law, and of the elements of fact at its disposal, the Court cannot conclude definitely whether the threat or use of nuclear weapons would be lawful or unlawful in an extreme circumstance of self-defense, in which the very survival of a State would be at stake.

The court, however, did not accept the argument that threat or use in such an instance would be legitimate; in paragraph 22 of the document, it argued that a state cannot "exonerate itself from compliance with the '*intransgressible*' norms of international humanitarian law." For the complete text of the 1996 International Court of Justice Advisory Opinion on the Legality of the Threat or Use of Nuclear Weapons, see "International Court of Justice," available online at http://www.dfat.gov.au/intorgs/icj_nuc/unan5a_a.html (accessed July 11, 2004).

United Nations Resolution 54/54 (December 1, 1999) calls on states harboring nuclear weapons to make efforts to quickly and completely eliminate their nuclear arsenals. In addition, states are urged to accelerate the process of negotiations in order to achieve nuclear disarmament, to which they are committed under Article VI of the Nuclear Nonproliferation Treaty.

5. *Editor's note*: Prior to trial, Judge Robert Blackburn denied the defendants' pretrial motions, one of which requested a dismissal based on the legality of their actions under international law. Blackburn granted a motion by the prosecutor prohibiting the sisters from speaking about the moral and legal justification for their actions. Calling the nuns "grossly irresponsible," Blackburn said that their position in the community and service, combined with the minimal damage done, allowed him to give them less than the maximum sentences of eight years.

6. *Editor's note*: On January 29, 2003, Mary Kelly hammered on a U.S. Navy C-40 Clipper (the military version of the Boeing 737 aircraft often used to transport troops, weapons, and ammunition to the Middle East) at Shannon Airport in Ireland. She was arrested and charged with causing criminal damage "without lawful excuse" to the plane in the amount of approximately 1.5 million euros ($US 1.92 million). Her first trial in June 2003 resulted in a hung jury. Her second trial in June 2004 also collapsed, when her legal counsel resigned on the first day of hearings because he did not want to ask for discovery of the attorney general's advice to the government regarding the uncertain legality of the United States' military use of the civilian Shannon Airport. In October 2004, Kelly defended herself in her third trial. She was found guilty and issued a two-year suspended sentence. See "Mary Kelly Aims to Uphold Rule of Law, Justify Disarmament, Put Bush and Irish Government on Trial," Mary Kelly Web site, available online at http://www.freewebs.com/mary_kelly/tria12_ennisJune04.html (accessed August 14, 2006); "Third Time Lucky for Some?," Mary Kelly Web site, available online at http://www.freewebs.com/mary_kelly/tria13_ennisOctober04.html (accessed August 14, 2006); Margaretta D'Arcy, dir., *Big Plane Small Axe (The Mis-Trials of Mary Kelly)*, (videocassette, Ireland, 2005).

On February 3, 2003, five peace workers affiliated with the Catholic Worker in Dublin—Diedre Clancy, Karen Falton, Damien Moran, Nuin Dunlop, and Cairon O'Reily—cut through a fence at Shannon Airport, poured their blood on the runway, and hammered on the same plane Mary Kelly had damaged. The five—who came to be known as the Pit Stop Plowshares—were arrested and charged with two counts of criminal damage ($US 2.5 million). They spent four months in prison after refusing to cooperate with initial bail conditions before their release in July 2003.

When finally brought to trial in March 2005 in Dublin circuit criminal court,

Judge O'Donnell called a mistrial and dismissed the jury on the sixth day after admitting to his own "perception of bias." Again, in October 2005, their retrial collapsed on the tenth day after the Defense council called for Judge MacDonagh's removal from the case based on his personal relationship with President George W. Bush. In their third trial, which began on July 10, 2006 and lasted twelve days, a jury found the Pit Stop Plowshares unanimously not guilty of both charges, indicating that the five had acted with the intent to "protect life and property" in Iraq and Ireland. The transit of U.S. soldiers through Shannon Airport continues at a rate of more than 10,000 every month.

See Harry Browne, "The View from Dublin: A Funny Thing Happened on the Way to Iraq, *CounterPunch*, February 12, 2003, available online at http://www .counterpunch.org/browne02122003.html (accessed August 13, 2006); "CW5 Re-Trial Collapses: Probable Public Perception of Biased Judge, Again," *Indymedia Ireland*, November 8, 2005, available online at http://www.indymedia.ie/newswire .php?story_id=72875 (accessed August 12, 2006); "Not Guilty: The Pitstop Ploughshares All Acquitted on All Charges," *Indymedia Ireland*, July 25, 2006, available online at http://ireland.indymedia.org/article/77460 (accessed August 12, 2006); "They're On Trial for Us," Peace on Trial, website, available online at http://www .peaceontrial.com/ (accessed August 13, 2006).

On February 9, 2003, Barbara Smedema, a member of the Dutch Peace Action Camp, entered a NATO airbase in Vokel, the Netherlands, and hammered three satellite dishes to protest the war on Iraq. Arrested, detained by military police, and jailed, Smedema was charged with endangering flight traffic, belonging to a criminal organization, and damaging government property. Her first trial in March 2003 ended in a mistrial when a judge recused himself. As of October 2004, a new trial was pending. Information about the outcome of this specific trial could not be obtained. See Arthur Laffin, "The Plowshares Disarmament Chronology," available online at http:// plowshares.org/Chronology.html (accessed July 11, 2004).

Early on March 11, 2003, the Danish Plowshares activist Ulla Roder entered Royal Air Force Leuchars Air Base in County Fife, Scotland, and hammered on a British Tornado fighter jet preparing for deployment in Iraq. Arrested and charged with malicious damage, she was released from prison on August 9, 2003 due to a procedural error committed by the Procurator Fiscal. Roder has served several prison terms for Plowshares actions. See "Tornado Disarmament Action at Leuchars Airport," available online at http://www.tridentploughshares.org/article748 (accessed August 15, 2006).

On May 25, 2003, at 3:45 P.M., as part of Fleet Week in New York City, the Catholic Workers Sister Susan Clarkson, Mark Coleville, Brian Buckley, and Joan Gregory, along with numerous tourists, boarded the *U.S.S. Philippine Sea*, an Aegis Cruiser that fired missiles during U.S. wars in Kosovo, Afghanistan, and Iraq. They were arrested by Navy police but released by federal agents without charges. See Laffin, "The Plowshares Disarmament Chronology."

Between July 2003, when Gilbert made her sentencing statement, and August 2006, Plowshares activists carried out a number of additional actions in resistance to the military warfare against Iraq and other Middle Eastern countries. For additional information on Plowshares activists arrested and incarcerated during this time period, see Trident Ploughshares, website, available online at http://www.tridentploughshares.org/ (accessed August 15, 2006); Jonah House, website, available online at http://www.jonahhouse.org/actions.htm (accessed August 12, 2006).

7. *Editor's note*: The Rocky Mountain Peace and Justice Center, Code Pink Colorado, and other peace groups planned nonviolent protests at each of Colorado's forty-nine missile silos in support of Gilbert, Platte, and Hudson. The actions, informally called "adopt-a-silo," took place at 11 A.M. on July 26, 2003, a day after the three Dominican sisters were sentenced for sabotage and depravation of federal property. Over 100 religious and political activists prayed, sang, danced, and hung eviction notices at the missile sites. See Judith Kohler, "Hundreds Continue Work of Imprisoned Nuns," *Rocky Mountain News*, July 26, 2003, available online at http://www.ccmep.org/2003_articles/ Local/072603_hundreds_continue_work_of_impris.htm (accessed July 11, 2004); "Colorado Communities for Justice and Peace," available online at http:// www.coloradopeace.org/2003/Adopt-a-Silo/ (accessed July 11, 2004).

8. *Editor's note*: Daniel Berrigan, a Roman Catholic priest, writer, and long-time peace activist, served multiple prison sentences for his actions against the Vietnam War. He was first arrested in 1968 along with his brother Philip Berrigan for destroying Selective Service files in Catonsville, Maryland, and sentenced to six years in prison. In 1980, they and six others began the Plowshares Movement when they entered the General Nuclear Missile Re-entry Division in King of Prussia, Pennsylvania, and hammered on the nose cones of two warheads. Arrested and initially charged with more than ten different misdemeanor counts, they were finally resentenced in 1990, after ten years of trials and appeals, and paroled for up to twenty-three and a half months. See Berrigan, *Lights on the House of the Dead*, *To Dwell in Peace*, and *The Trial of the Catonsville Nine*; Polner and O'Grady, *Disarmed and Dangerous*.

9. *Editor's note*: See Christian Parenti, "Stretched Thin, Lied to and Mistreated: On the Ground with U.S. Troops in Iraq," *Nation*, October 6, 2003, available online at http:// www.thenation.com/docprem.mhtml?i=20031006&s=parenti (accessed on July 13, 2004).

10. *Editor's note*: Since 1998, the Nuclear-Free Future Award has honored individuals, groups, and communities working to end the "Atomic Age." Sisters Carol Gilbert, Ardethe Platte, and Jackie Hudson were awarded the 2003 "Resistance" Nuclear-Free

Future Award. See Diane Zerfas, "Nuclear-Free Future Award Given to Three Imprisoned Dominicans," *Nuclear-Free News*, available online at http://www.nuclear-free
.com/english/diane.htm (accessed August 16, 2004).

11. *Editor's note*: The Preparatory Committee for the 2005 Review Conference of the
Nonproliferation Treaty met in New York City from April 26 to May 7, 2004. At the
third and final meeting of the Preparatory Committee, the delegates were not even
able to agree on a provisional agenda and background documentation for the 2005
Review Conference. At the Review Conference, which took place on May 2–27, 2005,
in New York City, delegates did not reach any significant agreements. Background
information and official documents on the 2004 and 2005 United Nations gatherings can be viewed online at http://www.un.org/events/npt2005. See also Douglas
Roche, "Re-nuclearization or Disarmament—A Fateful Choice for Humanity: A Political Analysis of the Third Preparatory Meeting for the 2005 Review Conference of
the Non-Proliferation Treaty," *Middle Powers Initiative*, May 2004, available online at
http://www.gsinstitute.org/mpi/pubs/npt-analysis.pdf (accessed June 28, 2005).

12. *Editor's note*: Tom Keene, "Who Holds Us Together?" *National Catholic Reporter Online*,
available online at http://www.natcath.com/NCR_Online/archives/091401/091401g
.htm (accessed August 16, 2004).

13. *Editor's note*: Philip Berrigan, a Catholic priest, peace activist, and co-founder of the
Plowshares Movement and the Jonah House community of war resisters, spent more
than ten years in prison for over 100 acts of antinuclear resistance. He also wrote,
lectured, and taught extensively. Berrigan left the priesthood and eventually married
the peace activist Elizabeth McAllister. He died of cancer at Jonah House in Baltimore on December 6, 2002. See Berrigan and Wilcox, *Fighting the Lamb's War*; Philip
Berrigan with Amy Goodman and Jeremy Scahill, "It's Too Bad the Soil Couldn't Cry
Out from the Blood Shed upon It: An Interview with Philip Berrigan," in James, *The
New Abolitionists*.

14. *Editor's note*: For full text of the article, see "Out of Mind," *Harper's Magazine*, May
2004, 22–26.

15. *Editor's note*: Zinn, *You Can't Be Neutral on a Moving Train*, 208.

16. *Editor's note*: Initiated by the Federal Bureau of Prisons in 1985 and implemented
nationwide in 1987, the Inmate Financial Responsibility Program (Bureau of Prisons
Program Statement 5380.07) allows federal courts, when sentencing convicted federal offenders, to impose financial penalties such as assessments, fines, and restitution. Regardless of the extent of an inmate's resources, each inmate with a financial
obligation makes payments electronically through his or her trust-fund accounts,
which include earnings from prison work assignments. In 1999, the IFRP, which is
in all federal facilities within the Bureau of Prisons, generated 7.3 million dollars for
the Bureau of Prisons. See: "Inmate Financial Responsibility Program," available on-

line at http://www.bop.gov/cpdpg/cpdifrp.html (accessed August 16, 2004); Federal Bureau of Prisons, "Review of Inmate Financial Responsibility Program," available online at http://a257.g.akamaitech.net/7/257/2422/14mar20010800/edocket.access .gpo.gov/cfr_2002/julqtr/pdf/28cfr544.101.pdf (accessed August 16, 2004).

17. *Editor's note*: Each year, the U.S. Attorney's Office, U.S. Courts, and Bureau of Prisons collects millions of dollars from criminal fines, forfeited bail bonds, penalty fees, and special assessments and deposits it into the Crime Victims Fund, which was established by the Victims of Crime Act of 1984. According to the U.S. Department of Justice, the first 10 million dollars deposited into the fund is used to "improve the investigation and prosecution of child abuse cases"; remaining funds are given to unidentified state compensation and assistance programs that determine which organizations will receive funds (to pay medical costs, funeral costs, or lost wages, or to provide crisis intervention, counseling, emergency shelter, and other services). See U.S. Department of Justice, "Office of the Victims of Crimes Fact Sheet: Victims of Crime Act Crime Victims Fund," available online at http://www.ojp.usdoj.gov/ovc/publications/factshts/cvfvca.htm (accessed August 16, 2004); Office for Victims of Crimes, "Resource Center," available online at http://www.ncjrs.org (accessed August 16, 2004).

18. Scott Paddor, dir., *The Big House—Alderson* (videocassette, Arts and Entertainment Home Video, New York, 1999).

LAURA WHITEHORN

Laura Whitehorn was born in 1945, in Brooklyn, New York. She began organizing in the 1960s as a college student, participating in the Civil Rights Movement and the antiwar movement. She graduated from Radcliffe College (Harvard University) in 1966 and later received her master's degree from Brandeis University. Before her imprisonment in 1985, she worked to expose the FBI's COINTELPRO, organized in support of political prisoners and Puerto Rican prisoners of war and in support of prisoners' rights, and worked actively in support of the Black Panther Party and the Black Power Movement. In the Boston area, she collaborated with others to establish a women's school, helped lead a takeover of a Harvard building to protest the university's involvement in the war in Vietnam, and organized white leftists to defend the homes of black families who were the targets of racist attacks. In the late 1970s, she moved to New York City and joined the John Brown Anti-Klan Committee to fight white supremacy and Zionism and joined the Madame Binh Graphics Collective, an anti-imperialist women's art group.

In 1985, after having gone underground to work at building a clandestine revolutionary movement, she was arrested by the FBI in Baltimore and was eventually charged in the "Resistance Conspiracy" case for bombings of government buildings. Placed under "preventive detention," Whitehorn was denied bail on the grounds that she was deemed an escape risk and was held in preventative detention for five years, without sentence or bail, until her conviction in the "Resistance Conspiracy" case for which she was sentenced to twenty-three years. While imprisoned, Whitehorn worked on HIV/AIDS peer education. During her years in prison, she contributed artwork to publications and exhibitions and articles to journals and anthologies. In August 1999, Whitehorn was released from prison. She now works as an associate editor at *POZ*, a national magazine for those affected by HIV, and is planning a correspondence course on HIV.[1]

Resisting the Ordinary   Laura Whitehorn (with Susie Day)

I sit down to write this article not twenty-four hours after the death of the Attica veteran and hero Frank "Big Black" Smith. Black died at age seventy-one, after surviving torture and threats to his life by guards during New York State's retaking of Attica prison in September 1971.[2] In 1971, Black was in prison for robbery. When 1,300 prisoners seized control of Attica to protest its horrific conditions, Black was chosen chief of security, a position of trust that would require enormous courage and wisdom. But it was the photograph, taken after the National Guard repressed the rebellion, of him lying on his back, stripped naked, with a football under his chin that brought him to public attention. The guards dropped burning cigarettes on his naked body and told Black that if he allowed the football to slip, he would be killed—as were the vast majority of the thirty-three prisoners and nine of the ten guards killed the day before, in a massacre by State Troopers and National Guardsmen.

Over thirty years later, in 2004, photos of torture, atrocities, malign neglect of Iraqis held by the United States at the Abu Ghraib prison appear in our newspapers. What should be most surprising about the revelations out of Abu Ghraib is not that torture occurred, or its particularly abhorrent nature, or even the grinning faces of the fairly low-level U.S. military personnel who performed the acts. What is most surprising is that these images—of prisoners stripped naked and heaped atop one another in piles; of a prisoner hooded, standing on a box, with wires strapped to his body; of naked men being threatened by dogs and sexually tortured—were, for once, not hidden from sight. This might shock those who realize that such torture is not an unusual event but, rather, a constant, though usually concealed, effect of the policies that brought the U.S. military guards and their Iraqi prisoners to Abu Ghraib in the first place. And what should shock our consciences most, I believe, is that despite a torrent of words and analyses in U.S. media from liberal to radical left, there was no visible protest, no marching in the streets demanding an end to such abuse.

Problematic, too, was the plethora of analyses citing psychological factors underlying the actions of the military personnel. I don't think there is a psychological analysis to explain or rationalize this sort of act. I don't think the Abu Ghraib prisoners are tortured because the United States is obsessed with wiping out terrorism and has lost sight of its basic democratic values in the process. I don't think Iraqi and other Arabic prisoners are tortured solely because of racist attitudes, solely because they are *the other*, different from the torturers (and presumably from the citizens those torturers are supposed to represent). Racism does play a role but as a part of something larger, white supremacy—something more systemic than a motivator of individual behavior. I think these prisoners are tortured because torture is an integral element in a system it has become unfashionable to name: U.S. imperialism (with white supremacy as a fundamental element). By "torture" I mean the purposeful use of physical or psychological violence and pain to extract information, force a change of ideology—or to terrorize both an individual and a group or community. It is a weapon of domination.

Torture is far from an aberration in this system that continues to seek to rule and possess the wealth and lives of nations and peoples around the world. It goes on daily against oppressed communities inside the borders of the United States, as well. In periods of social upheaval it becomes endemic. For example, the dismemberment and burning of black men and women who were lynched has been designed to terrorize other black people and prevent them from asserting their humanity, their rights, and their desire for basic equality. Along the way, barbarism inflicts deep and lasting scars on the psyche of the target population, injuring entire communities. Thus is the social order—in this case, white supremacy—maintained. Such is the fabric of U.S. democracy. In fact, in prison black women refer to guards as "police," making little distinction between their functions in monitoring and controlling black bodies behind bars or in the general society.

Even when the domination occurs through forms more subtle than outright torture, state exercise of physical and psychological abuse is fundamental to the system. Such abuse is a reality in U.S. prisons, as well—and it will not stop completely until imperialism itself is stopped. If all of us could face these realities, perhaps the images of Abu Ghraib flooding the mass media would have provoked as many visible acts of protest as articles of analysis. Perhaps there would be a broader outcry over the very similar conditions and methods used in prisons inside this country, as well.

Another Day on the Plantation

When Big Black was at Attica, there were, according to the U.S. Justice Department, 198,061 prisoners in the United States; today there are about 2 million, and most of them live unseen in prison conditions comparable to those now decried by the media covering Iraq. While others may ignore these conditions in the midst of U.S. society, leftist political prisoners are articulate in describing them. In an essay written in August 2004 titled, "Some Thoughts on the Abu Ghraib Prison Revelations in Iraq," Herman Bell, a former Black Panther and a political prisoner since 1973, wrote: "Abu Ghraib is just another day on the plantation."

Silvia Baraldini, a political prisoner in the United States for sixteen years before being repatriated to her native Italy, where she now lives under house arrest, agrees.[3] "The reality that is inexorably emerging from Iraqi prisons should not surprise us," Baraldini wrote in her May 11, 2004, essay "Torture: The United States Underground," published by *Il Manifesto*. According to Baraldini, "For years, Amnesty International, Human Rights Watch, and the American Civil Liberties Union have all denounced the analogous conditions that exist in special ['control unit' or 'maxi-maxi'] prisons in the United States."[4]

Those who were taken by surprise by the ghastly revelations of Abu Ghraib have not been paying attention. Or worse: They have availed themselves of the right to know, and of the privilege to do nothing. "Prison is a very cruel reality," writes Leonard Peltier, a Native American political prisoner who has been in prison since 1977 for allegedly killing two FBI agents at the Lakota reservation in Pine Ridge, North Dakota, in 1975. (The killings occurred during a time when the reservation and the American Indian Movement were besieged and attacked by agents of the FBI and Bureau of Indian Affairs. The government has never claimed that Peltier himself fired the fatal shots. Amnesty International has recognized Peltier as a "political prisoner.") Peltier continues:

> But unusual? The Eighth Amendment should reflect the standards of a maturing society, and your correctional system shouldn't be just about depriving people of freedom, but about rehabilitation. But this is not how it works for me or many other prisoners. Protection against cruel and unusual punishment has faded away as have the rights of ordinary citizens under such things as the Patriot Act and Homeland Security. . . . The courts say prison

officials have to have acted with "deliberate indifference" to the safety, health and welfare of prisoners for punishment to be considered cruel and unusual. I don't know what this means because "deliberate indifference" is a way of life in prison.[5]

Prison Security: Business as Usual

I spent a little more than fourteen years, from 1985 to 1999, in U.S. federal prisons as a left-wing political prisoner, convicted of "conspiracy to protest, oppose and change policies and practices of the U.S. government in domestic and international matters by violent and illegal means." Those means included a series of bombings of the U.S. Capitol, U.S. War College, Israeli Aircraft Industries, the South African Consulate (during apartheid), the New York City Patrolmen's Benevolent Association and other government and military buildings (no one was ever injured in any of these actions). During my years in prison, I came to know what Peltier calls "deliberate indifference," daily and intimately.

Much of what I experienced and witnessed in my years in prison looked like what I would call "abuse": haphazard, unspectacular cruelties delivered daily to people who are viewed by administrators, staff, and guards as simply not worthy of decent treatment. This abuse, so much a part of life in prison, is not the stuff of newspaper headlines, yet psychologically, over even a short time, it serves the same purpose as torture and, indeed, I believe it is in essence the same thing. It can be as cruel, and it can result in convincing a prisoner, at a very deep level, that she or he is not quite alive, not quite human. Most of all, its goals are the same as those of outright torture.

When directed at left-wing political prisoners or any particularly rebellious prisoner, such abuse, like torture, can be a means to force a change of ideology or psychology, as well as to terrorize others (other prisoners; communities outside). While the prison guards who actually carry out the abuse may do so because they view prisoners as deserving of punishment, the essential nature of the abuse is exactly the same as that of the Abu Ghraib torture: The need of the system (that same imperialism, enacted inside the borders of the United States) to repress and ultimately destroy, psychologically if not physically, black people and other oppressed people who seek human rights and self-determination, women who seek equality and personhood, and those, like left-wing political prisoners, who refuse to stop resisting and challenging the government.

What makes abuse like this palatable, often in the eyes of both the abuser and the abused, is its very ordinariness, the fact that it is a routine part of the regimen of prison "life," of prison security. For example, prisoners are regularly tested for drugs, so humiliating urine tests under the direct observation of guards are mandated.

While I was held in the federal women's prison in Dublin, California, in 1987, I learned that women were being forced to strip naked in front of (female) corrections officers and urinate into a cup while standing on one foot with the one leg raised, like a dog. I learned of this when my cellmate and dear friend, a politically conscious African American woman, was made to undergo the procedure and, enraged, came back to tell me of it. This practice had gone on for quite some time, partly because officials explained it was necessary to make sure the women weren't substituting someone else's urine, but largely because the women themselves were too humiliated to object. As my cellie and I asked a few other women if they had experienced this, we found that it had been common.

When procedures are this egregious, you can sometimes succeed in stopping them—as we did in that instance (and as, one expects, the more visibly disgusting forms of torture at Abu Ghraib have been stopped—temporarily). We immediately confronted the unit manager of our cellblock and asked for a grievance form—and won right away. Forcing women to stand naked with one leg raised, like dogs, shocked even some prison administrators. Before the grievance form was even filed, the procedure was stopped, though not, of course, the urine tests. More often, though, less dramatically objectionable and degrading procedures are maintained as "necessary to security," "standard operating procedures," and you don't win.

A most common example: In federal prisons, strip searches are a regular practice. In some prisons, we were required to be strip searched in groups, standing naked in front of one another. Then the guards would ask us to lift our breasts, bend over, cough, expose our genitals. "Let me see the pink!" the (female) guards would yell. "Let me see the pink!" That was standard operating procedure. Federal regulations permit male guards to strip search female prisoners only in vaguely defined emergency situations; ordinarily, strip searches in federal women's prisons are carried out by female guards. But it was standard for us to be pat searched by male officers.

The practice of having male guards pat search female prisoners is particularly reprehensible given that, as any woman who has spent time in prison or who has talked to women prisoners knows, many women prisoners have been abused, often sexually, by men in their lives. In that context, being pat searched by men can cause severe emotional distress. But I think there is an even more basic reason why pat searches of both women and men prisoners qualify as a human-rights abuse: Over time, they have the effect of erasing your humanity. When you are reminded, in a starkly physical way, that you do not retain the right to protect your own body from unwanted touching, you begin to feel you do not, should not exist, that you are an object or an animal, less than human.

What begins as humiliation, repeated daily, ends up eroding your sense of self and ultimately your energy to resist. It is a form of sexual violence similar to the use of rape as a tool of warfare. Even five years later, this paper is almost impossible for me to write. As I describe these procedures, I find that the terror inflicted daily on my body and my heart by living under these conditions still reverberates. Nightmares sometimes return me to feelings of powerlessness I could barely afford to acknowledge while I was locked up and subjected daily to these procedures.

My continuing attempts to resist (most often in concert with other prisoners, but sometimes alone) during the years in prison helped mitigate these effects and served to protect me to some degree from the damage they caused. But even the means by which you are permitted to fight back are closely controlled. It is illegal, for instance, to circulate any kind of petition, to file a grievance signed by more than one person, or to gather to meet to discuss any problems in a group. And often you can receive additional years on your sentence if you attempt to fight back—a fact in prisons that is itself elemental to abuse.

When I was in the federal women's prison in Lexington, Kentucky, from 1990 to 1991, there was a particularly vicious male officer who, during pat searches, liked to grab and squeeze my breasts and the breasts of the other women he knew to be lesbians. We filed a grievance, asking that the officer be prohibited from performing pat searches. While he was (quietly) admonished to stop grabbing our breasts, he was allowed to continue doing pat searches. And on paper, our grievance was rejected. We were informed that the officer was performing his job in a "professional and routine manner." Our grievance was interpreted as a challenge to the basic policy of men pat searching women and as an attempt by prisoners to assert control over the conditions of our incarceration.

Years before, when I had been an activist on the street, I had studied karate so that when a man on the street grabbed me like that, I could fight him off. If I had done that in prison, I would have been charged with assault on an officer and given extra time (the standard was three to five years for attacking a guard) in prison, as well as time in the hole. That was my reality. Now, multiply it by 2 million.

A Nation Apart

There is a crucial political meaning to all this. Prison abuse is a means for imperialism to undermine and weaken antigovernment movements. Whether or not people sit around in board rooms and think these policies up, I believe that a major purpose of incarcerating huge numbers of poor and working-class women and men—predominantly people of color, the majority black—is to disable communities from participating in rebellions such as those that shook this country in the 1960s and 1970s (or such as the exercise of black political power during Black Reconstruction after the Civil War). It also helps to explain the enormous surge in the number of incarcerated people since the 1970s, disproportionate to any rise in crime. Treating prisoners as subhuman helps ensure that, if and when they get out, they will not think or feel for themselves as political agents for change. These women and men, and their communities, are as much targets of U.S. warfare as any overseas nation invaded and disrupted by the U.S. military. The incorporation of torture or abuse into the daily fabric of prison life is ultimately a tool of counterinsurgency applied to all the oppressed and exploited classes of human beings represented in the prison population.

Even so, sad to say, pat searches and urine tests are only two, rather small components of prison reality. Herman Bell was convicted with Jalil Muntaqim and Albert Nuh Washington, also black liberationists, of shooting two police officers after what, to many observers, should have been a mistrial.[6] In "Some Thoughts," he writes of his three decades of incarceration:

In 1975, as a newly admitted federal prisoner at USP [United States Penitentiary] Marion [Illinois], I was locked in its infamous "control unit" for better than two years. I had violated no prison rules. Before building the control unit at this new prison, prison bureaucrats consulted with the renowned behavioral scientist B. F. Skinner on its design. Its primary function was designed to induce sensory deprivation on those confined who were individuals associated with high profile cases and political prisoners. I counted six political prisoners held there, three of whom were former Black Panthers. The principal effects of sensory deprivation are associated with isolation and loneliness that engender hallucinations, disorientation, and schizophrenia. The aim is to break one's will. After prolonged indoor isolation, the brushing of open air against the skin-hair causes extreme discomfort. Two prisoners died in the unit while I was there. Some prisoners in the unit, but not all of us, were medicated with drugs. I recall only the names of Thorazine and Prolixine. Marion was a nightmare. We were never told when we would be released from the unit. I hear that the new [maximum-security control unit] prison, USP Florence, which is patterned after Marion, is even worse.

All the prisons I was held in were not hell-holes on a par with Marion, Florence, pre-1971 Attica, or even with New York State's Clinton [prison] of the '60s and '70s, wherein upon entering grown men were frequently forced to kneel on all fours and bark like a dog; where, as a form of punishment, men were placed in restraints, wrapped in a blanket and thrown bodily down tall iron stairs. But I can say with certainty that America's prison system is unjust. It is unjust in the manner in which people are imprisoned and in the way prisons are administered.[7]

So many people experiencing this suffering for so many years. You would think somebody from the mainstream news media would sense a story here. But prisoners are a nation apart in this country, and the media seldom think to go there for more than one dateline. When the voice is that of a political prisoner, the media are even more hesitant to listen: Isn't this one of the domestic terrorists against whom Attorney General Ashcroft has warned them?

Even with the justified furor made in the media about Abu Ghraib, there is almost nothing heard from any prisoner who was held there—and when, after a long silence, some voices are heard, they are only briefly allowed space to speak through any mass media. It is important that we, who are now out, recall the others. Silvia Baraldini, with whom I spent three years in the maximum-security federal women's prison in Mariana, Florida, remembers, in "Torture," other political prisoners held in U.S. prisons, who have often endured mistreatment, specifically because of their politics:

If a journalist had tracked down Rafael Cancel Miranda, he would be able to testify that in the not-so-distant years of the 1970s, in the undergrounds of

Marion, prisoners were handcuffed to walls and left for hours. Samuel Brown would be able to tell us about his severe neck injury that was purposely left untreated as a strategy for softening him before he was interrogated by the FBI. And Sekou Odinga could tell us how, after he was arrested, his chest was used as an ashtray by members of the task force that interrogated him. Alejandrina Torres would be able to tell us about herself—a Puerto Rican political prisoner later pardoned by President Clinton, who was violated in federal prison in Phoenix, Arizona, not with a broomstick but with the gloved fists of a so-called nurse. Or Susan Rosenberg, who [along with Baraldini herself and Alejandrina Torres] spent two months in the winter of 1988 without sleep in a cell of the special unit of Lexington Prison where the lights were turned on every twenty minutes, where the curtainless shower was observed by one of the twenty-one surveillance cameras of that unit, who experienced the humiliation of having to ask a male prison guard for a tampon every time she needed one. The women prisoners in Georgia state prison and in Dublin federal prison would be able to testify how in prison one can be sexually abused by the same individuals who are supposed to protect you. In [California's maximum-security control unit] Pelican Bay and Florence, journalists would find the prisons upon which Guantánamo was modeled.[8]

Mumia Abu-Jamal, the African American radical and journalist on Pennsylvania's death row since 1985, has already told us of his own brutal treatment at the hands of Charles Graner, a corrections officer at SCI [State Correctional Institution] Greene, Pennsylvania. Graner is now one of the GIs accused of carrying out the torture of prisoners at Abu Ghraib.

Medical Abuse

I don't live under a prison regime anymore. I work as an editor at a magazine for people who are HIV-positive. But many of the magazine's readers are prisoners who have HIV. Virtually none of these people with HIV—or hepatitis C or any other disease—receives competent health care, much less the sympathy we on the outside require of our doctors. Hepatitis C is approximately ten times more common among the prison population than it is in the population at large, yet few prisoners are able to receive care and treatment for the virus. New Jersey, Pennsylvania, and Oregon are only three of the states in which prisoners have had to file class-action lawsuits to try to get such treatment. Often, prisoners were tested for hepatitis C and not even informed that they had the disease until they were released from prison years later. HIV care in this country has advanced significantly over the past ten years, yet prisoners regularly receive inadequate care for the condition—and are then blamed in inflammatory media stories for the spread of HIV in the communities to which they return on release. Like "Army Intelligence," "Prison Health Care" is another governmental oxymoron, because prisoners, no matter how ill, are still "dangerous," and any decision about a prisoner's health begins and ends with "security."

In this environment, survival is left to the prisoner alone. "Imagine suffering a stroke, as I did," writes Leonard Peltier in "Cruel and Unusual Punishment," "and slowly losing part of your sight in an environment where all of your senses are required for survival; or suffering extreme jaw pain for years, until the United Nations forced your government to stop the torture and provide the necessary health care."[9]

The political prisoner Robert Seth Hayes, an ex-Panther incarcerated in New York prisons since 1973, has, over the years, developed both hepatitis C and diabetes. Like hundreds of thousands of people with diabetes, Hayes requires daily blood-sugar-level testing and insulin-dose calibration—which are suspended at New York state's Clinton Correctional Facility, his current prison, simply because the health regulations there don't require them. Hayes—and scores of other prisoners at Clinton—risks insulin shock every day. So far, the prison remains indifferent to repeated outside campaigns to secure adequate medical treatment for Hayes and other diabetic prisoners.

Sometimes prisoners don't survive. In 2000, Albert Nuh Washington, one of Herman Bell's co-defendants, was allowed to die slowly of liver cancer in an upstate New York prison because the administration refused—for security reasons—to release him to an outside hospice so he could die among his family and friends.

It's hard to know whether to call "health-care" practices like this "abuse" or "neglect," but they happen, at some point, to almost all prisoners—and, as in U.S. prisons in Iraq, Afghanistan, and Guantánamo, the doctors themselves are often complicit.[10] As we return from the media stories of Abu Ghraib to business as usual, we should know that it is that very "business as usual" that causes Abu Ghraibs in the first place.

Back in Connecticut in the early 1990s, a woman in FCI Danbury became so ill that she was transferred to a women's prison hospital unit in Texas, where she died. Women at the prison later told me that her family told them the following story: The Texas prison shipped her body home to her family for burial. When the people at the funeral home opened the woman's casket to prepare her for burial, they discovered that her dead body had been—according to prison regulation—shackled and handcuffed for shipping. I do not find this essentially different from the mutilation of enemy soldiers' corpses during a war—another method of displaying the spectacle of torture to terrorize, to deliver the message: You are at our mercy.

My longtime comrade, the anti-imperialist political prisoner Tom Manning, in federal prison since 1985, sent me the following letter on prison and Abu Ghraib, which I share in its entirety here.[11] Tom has no release date.

IN MY TIME
Political Prisoner, U.S.A., May 10, 2004
I became aware through newspaper photographs that the prison cells built by KBR/Halliburton at Guantánamo Bay (Gitmo) do not have plumbing. That surprised me, considering the price that KBR/Halliburton charged the U.S. taxpayers for those cells.

In the early [1960s] I was a Seabee in the U.S. Navy, stationed at Quonset Point/Davisville, Rhode Island, with Mobile Construction Battalion One (MCB #1).

We were deployed for sea duty, to Gitmo, to build emergency housing for ten thousand Cuban refugees that America anticipated would flee Cuba for the confines of Gitmo in 1958, when Fidel liberated this island nation. It took nine months to complete and was named "Tin City."

We dredged hundreds of tons of living coral from the ocean in proximity to the base and deposited it in a lagoon that was enlarged to accommodate the project. The coral was crushed and leveled to form a floor surrounded by cliff-like excavated walls on three sides, with one side remaining open toward the sea.

Then the housing was built, of Quonset huts, which are corrugated tin barrel-like dwellings in groups, or pods, of nine huts; eight sleeping huts with no plumbing surrounding a ninth hut that was supplied with fresh water and sewage. I worked on the plumbing, from digging the supply and waste ditches, then leveling them, to laying in the supply and waste pipes and septic tanks and leach fields. I was on the crews that installed twelve toilets, twelve wash basins, and twelve head shower rooms in each central (ninth) hut.

During our time in Cuba, we had to adapt to the blistering heat by working tropical hours; working from five in the morning, until two in the afternoon, with a half hour lunch and two fifteen-minute breaks. We further voluntarily opted to forgo the lunch and two breaks so that we could get off the job site by 1 P.M., due to the midday heat.

Given this personal knowledge of the area, and recognizing the surrounding terrain in the current news photos as the old Seabee/Kittery Beach area, my initial thought was that it would be terrible to be confined in a metal cage there, without adequate water.

Add to that being at the mercy of young, poorly trained military personnel for what water you do get, and what toilet access you get.

I have been held in cells during my time in U.S. prisons (twenty-four years, six months, at this writing) without water or toilet a number of times. I have been subjected to the whims of whatever guards happened to be working the block on any given shift. I know that having a guard that consistently acts in a proper manner is the exception, not the rule.

While thinking about how to write about these thoughts and observations concerning water, the pictures from Abu Ghraib prison in Iraq have come out. And the information and pictures continue to come.

Automatically my mind goes into replay mode.

During my time in U.S. prisons my right knee has been permanently damaged by being stomped on during a cell beating by five guards (Walpole State Prison, Ten Block DSU [Drug Strategy Unit], 1969). The leg was up on a bunk while I was on my back on the floor with several guards "monkey piling" me, another guard stomped the knee, hyper-extending it, causing me to pass out from the pain. After that, I only had 15 percent flex of the knee, until I had it surgically corrected, when I got out of prison in 1971.

Shortly after being captured in 1985, I was body slammed onto a concrete floor while cuffed to a waist-chain, with black-boxed handcuffs and leg irons. That resulted in a fractured hip that wasn't repaired until 1999 with a total artificial left hip replacement. The Motrin I took for pain in the intervening years gave me ulcers and damaged my kidneys, which now function at less than 50 percent efficiency. I've often had to take iron pills to overcome anemia, caused by internal bleeding, and am currently on calcium pills to make up for the calcium my kidneys are spilling.

My shoulders have both been severely damaged during beatings, while I was cuffed behind my back, during forced blood takings. This resulted in surgery on both shoulders. These joint surgeries on the knee, hip, and shoulders is evidenced by twenty-one collective inches of surgical scars, not counting three arthroscopic surgeries.

I have been stun-gunned twelve times in one night, resulting in temporary paralysis of my left side, like a stroke. And then, on two other occasions, I was also stun-gunned, once each time.

I have been photographed naked numerous times in federal prison and also by [New Jersey] State Police and the FBI; gratuitously strip-searched uncountable times.

Dragged and slung around by leg irons, into walls and up and down stairs.

Strapped to a gurney with my head overhanging the front, and then run through the prison; rammed into every doorframe or door and corners.

Tear gassed in my cell at least six times.

Forced to exit my cell naked, with my fingers laced on top of my head, and told by a squad of six ninja-turtle-suited guards that if I lowered my arms it would be considered an act of aggression and treated accordingly, while a German shepherd dog was barking so close to my genitals that I could feel his breath and spittle striking me. Then forced to run down six flights of stairs, like that, with a dog and handler at every landing, shepherding us along.

The group that I was in was then herded into a large visiting room where all twenty-four of us stayed, naked, from 2 A.M. until 8 A.M., while our cells were wrecked; our personal property destroyed.

I've lost count of the number of times I've been left in cells for hours while black-box handcuffed and leg ironed; spending as much as seventeen and twenty hours in such restraints during transport and waiting delays, with no water and no toilet access. I have numb areas on my hands, wrists, and ankles from this treatment and from being kept in control-unit prisons for years, locked down for twenty-three hours or more a day; never less than this (six years in [New Jersey]; three years at Marion; three years at ADX, Florence [Colorado]; and two years in Walpole [Massachusetts] in the 1960s) for a total of fourteen years of lock down.

So pardon my being unpleasantly bemused at the "shocked and amazed" reaction of the U.S. public to this most recent "scandal." I'll be interested to see how long "the public's" attention can be focused on this one. And I invite every prisoner, and ex-prisoner, who reads this to sit down and write out and send out her/his own experiences of imprisonment and abuse. Or tell of the most memorable abuse you witnessed.

Example: When I was newly arrived at Trenton, New Jersey's, control unit, I heard laughter and whimpering. I looked out of my cell to see a very fat, young white prisoner stretched out on the floor, his arms extended beyond his head, hands cuffed and legs shackled. His shirt was pulled up, off his body, over his head and onto his arms; his pants were down around his ankles, leaving him naked from calves to forearms. Guards were standing on his restraints on both ends, and a baton was protruding from his rectum. Nobody else in the control unit cells was responding. I went nuts, screaming and kicking my cell door. I believe that over my years in MCU, I helped to heighten the resistance to such treatment. Of course, the treatment was worsened, accordingly.

But then, I would rather die on my feet than linger on my knees.

The Struggle Continues!

Tom Manning, Leavenworth Penitentiary, Kansas, U.S.A.[12]

Conclusion

All prisoners, at some point, have looked into the eyes of the guards, the police, the bureaucrats who commit abuse and torture. We have heard these people complain of low pay and long work hours—and then go on to carry out the orders of their bosses. Every one of us has heard them tell us that they are just doing their jobs. And they are. Their job is to be foot soldiers of a system. Years ago, those of us in the radical white left followed a strategy to try to challenge—and ultimately, we hoped, to destroy—that system. Today, I find it much harder to discern a path for anti-imperialism. And yet, protest against torture, protest against imperialist war on the people of Iraq and the Middle East, protest against the prison system must continue as the heart of any struggle for human rights. If we can face the significance of such things, we can travel beyond shock to action.

To listen, to be moved, is the first step. It is my fervent wish that we refuse to go back to business as usual. I said earlier, that this paper has been painful to write. Another reason why that is so is that I am all too aware that, on the day I walked through the gates at FCI Dublin, the women I left behind the walls remained to suffer daily humiliation, daily torture. It is as deeply infuriating to be unable to defend their humanity as it was to be unable to defend my own. I can only hope that progressive people, even in the absence of a clear revolutionary strategy, will do what we all can to stop this insensate destruction of human psyches. The longer it takes to do that, the deeper and more irreparable the damage is to the moral fabric of society as a whole—a prospect at least as frightening as the images from Abu Ghraib.

Notes

1. Sources of biographical material include Silvia Baraldini, Marilyn Buck, Susan Rosenberg, and Laura Whitehorn, "Women's Control Unit," in *Criminal Injustice: Confronting the Prison Crisis*, edited by Elihu Rosenblatt (Boston: South End Press, 1996), and "Preventive Detention: A Prevention of Human Rights?" in *Cages of Steel: The Politics of Imprisonment in the United States*, edited by Ward Churchill and Jim Vander Wall (Washington, D.C.: Maisonneuve Press, 1992); "Resistance at Lexington," 108–10 in Rosenblatt, ed., *Criminal Injustice*; Sonja De Vries and Rhonda Collins. *Out: The Making of a Revolutionary* (New York, Third World Newsreel, 2000, Videocassette); and *Resistance Conspiracy, San Francisco*, distributed by Bay Area Committee to Support the Resistance Conspiracy Defendants (Oakland, Peralta Colleges Television Production Company, 1990, Videocassette).

2. *Editor's note*: In the aftermath of the Attica rebellion, Frank "Big Black" Smith, designated chief of security by fellow inmates, was struck in the testicles by officers and burned with cigarettes and hot shell casings on his chest. Mistakenly regarded as a leader of the uprising, Smith was indicted on thirty-four counts of kidnapping, two counts of coercion, and two counts of unlawful imprisonment. All charges were eventually dropped. After his release, Smith moved to New York City, became a paralegal, and worked on a 2.8 billion dollar civil liability suit filed in 1974, which alleged that over 1,200 prisoners had been tortured or denied medical care. Smith was awarded 4 million dollars in 1997 by a federal jury in Buffalo, New York, but the award was overturned in 1999 by the U.S. Court of Appeals for Manhattan on the basis that his case could not be separated from the larger group. A general settlement

of 8 million dollars was awarded to survivors in 2002. Frank Smith died two years later. See Douglas Martin, "Frank Smith, 71, Is Dead: Sought Justice after Attica," *New York Times*, August 3, 2004.

3. *Editor's note*: Silvia Baraldini, an Italian citizen, was arrested in 1982 on RICO charges for allegedly aiding in the escape of Assata Shakur of the Black Panther Party and Black Liberation Army. She received a forty-year sentence and an additional three years for refusing to testify before a grand jury investigating the Puerto Rican Independence Movement. In 1989, Italy petitioned for Baraldini's return. She was returned to Italy in 1999 and remains under house arrest.

4. Sylvia Baraldini, "Torture: The United States Underground," *Il Manifesto* (May 11, 2004), available online at http://www.ilmanifesto.it/Quotidiano-archivio/11-Maggio-2004/art87.html (accessed August 15, 2006).

5. Leonard Peltier, "Cruel and Unusual Punishment: In the Eye of the Beholder," July 27, 2004, *Socialist Viewpoint* (September 2004), available online at http://www.socialist viewpoint.org/sept_04/sept_04_13.html (accessed August 14, 2006).

Editor's note: Leonard Peltier, a leader of the American Indian Movement (AIM), was given two life sentences for the killing of a police officer during the 1975 FBI shootout at Pine Ridge, at which AIM protected citizens of the reservation from unlawful police attacks. Although he has been imprisoned for almost three decades, the evidence of his guilt remains questionable. See Leonard Peltier, *Prison Writings: My Life is My Sun Dance* (New York: St. Martin's press, 1999).

6. *Editor's note*: On August 28, 1971, Jalil Muntaqim and Albert Nuh Washington were arrested in California for allegedly attempting to kill a San Francisco police sergeant. New York police proceeded to charge Muntaqim and Washington, along with Herman Bell, another member of the Black Panther Party and Black Liberation Army who was arrested two years later, with the killings of two Harlem police officers, Waverly Jones and Joseph Piagentini. Police entered the gun Muntaqim possessed in San Francisco as evidence in the New York City trial. In 1992, Muntaqim, Washington, and Bell proved the government's illegal conduct and suppression of evidence in their original trial, but federal and state courts denied their appeals. In April 2000, Washington died of liver cancer at the Coxsackie Correctional Facility in New York. Both Muntaqim and Bell were denied parole in 2004 and remain incarcerated in New York.

7. Herman Bell, "Some Thoughts on the Abu Ghraib Prison Revelations in Iraq," letter to author for inclusion in chapter, August 2004.

8. Baraldini, "Torture."

9. Peltier, "Cruel and Unusual Punishment."

10. See Lifton, "Doctors and Torture."

11. *Editor's note*: Tom Manning, a Vietnam veteran and former member of the white

anti-imperialist organizations Sam Melville/Jonathan Jackson Unit and United Freedom Front, was sentenced to fifty-eight years for a series of bombings carried out in resistance to U.S. imperialism in Latin America, Puerto Rican colonialism, and apartheid in South Africa. Manning was sentenced to eighty years in New Jersey for the killing of a State Trooper, which he maintains was an act of self-defense. Having spent over twelve years in solitary confinement, Manning is currently incarcerated at the U.S penitentiary at Leavenworth, Kansas.

12. Tom Manning, "In My Time," is available online at http://www.jerichony.org/manning.html (accessed August 17, 2006).

Cultures of Torture

William F. Pinar

While most immediately attributable to the "culture" of the Bush administration, the abuse of Iraqi prisoners in Abu Ghraib becomes more fully intelligible when situated in cultural traditions of racialized torture in the United States, among them lynching, the convict-lease system, and abuse by prison guards. Since "Emancipation," criminalization has been profoundly racialized in the United States, as "legalized lynchings" slowly replaced the extralegal kind.[1] In the late nineteenth century, black men were imprisoned for nearly any reason and, once imprisoned, exploited in a vicious convict-lease system that made slavery almost look attractive.[2] A century later, black men are still imprisoned for almost any reason, victims of a racialized "war on drugs"—in effect, a war on young black and Latino men.[3]

   In this chapter I situate the Abu Ghraib incident in three "cultures" of torture in U.S. history: nineteenth-century and twentieth-century lynching, the nineteenth-century convict-lease system, and twentieth-century abuse by prison guards. These "cultures of torture" contradict President Bush's assertion that what is shown the Abu Ghraib photographs "do[es] not represent America."[4] Given the sexualized cultures of racial torture in the United States, these photographs would seem to represent "America" rather exactly.

"America's National Crime"

Black men did not provoke lynching by raping white women. —JACQUELYN DOWD HALL, *REVOLT AGAINST CHIVALRY* (1979), 163

Of all the emotional determinants of lynching none is more potent in blocking the approach to a solution than sex, and of all the factors, emotional or otherwise, none is less openly and honestly discussed. —WALTER WHITE, *ROPE AND FAGGOT* (1929), 54

The black phallus, of course, was the focus—indeed, very often, the site of—much of lynching's ritualistic concern and energy. —MICHAEL AWKWARD, *NEGOTIATING DIFFERENCE* (1995), 191

In the early hours of October 27, 1934, in the deep woods of northwestern Florida, near Marianna, white men lynched a black laborer named Claude Neal.[5] The National Association for the Advancement of Colored People (NAACP) investigator, a white North Carolinian named Howard Kester, learned the details of the torture ten days after it occurred. For one hour and forty minutes he interviewed a member of the mob. Confessing that he was "quite nauseated by the things which apparently gave this man the greatest delight to relate," Kester reported the man's story, "corroborated by others."

> "After taking the nigger to the woods about four miles from Greenwood, they cut off his penis. He was made to eat it. Then they cut off his testicles and made him eat them and say he liked it." (I gathered that this barbarous act consumed considerable time and that other means of torture were used from time to time on Neal.) "Then they sliced his sides and stomach with knives and every now and then somebody would cut off a finger or toe. Red hot irons were used on the nigger to burn him from top to bottom. From time to time during the torture a rope would be tied around Neal's neck and he was pulled up over a limb and held there until he almost choked to death when he would be let down and the torture began all over again."[6]

"It was terrible," one white woman remarked about the mob, "but nothing which could have been done to the Negro would have been too much."[7]

Claude Neal was hardly the first black man to be lynched in the United States. Nor would he be the last. While reliable data exist only after 1882, it is estimated that between 2,400 and 10,000 Americans—overwhelmingly young black men—were lynched in the United States.[8] Between one-half and two-thirds of threatened lynchings failed, so the actual number of lynching incidents is much higher.[9] The lynching of Claude Neal occurred during the denouement of lynching. Its apex was 1892, a period when Southern (and many Northern) whites believed that black men were raping white women on a mass scale. It was a belief contradicted by the facts.[10] Despite continuing white fantasies of black male attacks on white women, rape in America has been an overwhelmingly intraracial event, with the conspicuous exception of white slave owners' repeated rape of black slave women and, in all likelihood, of men.[11] The late-nineteenth-century rape fantasy was a collective hallucination.

Statistically, as Fitzhugh Brundage has shown, allegations of murder, not rape, provoked most lynchings.[12] No matter, white Southerners still insisted that rape was the key to lynching. It was, I argue, if in a different sense: Lynching was mangled homosexual rape.[13] Several scholars—among them Trudier Harris, Winthrop Jordan, Joel Williamson, and Cornel West—have suggested that it was white sexual envy and fear of black men that accounted for this extreme and savage ritual of racial hatred. When it is without basis in reality, fear can be inverted desire.[14]

In many lynchings—such as Claude Neal's—the black man was castrated. In the act of castration, did white men imagine that black men's sexual power was transferred to them? Why would white men destroy what they wanted? Why would lynchers divide pieces—souvenirs—of the murdered man's body among themselves? Such murder was not only racial torture and sexual mutilation; it was not only the "retrieval" of qualities projected onto an abstract disembodied "other." Lynching was an explicit sexual act, however conflated with other issues and forces. As Robyn Wiegman has observed: "Castration is also an inverted sexual encounter between black men and white men."[15] Literal and symbolic, castration defines a racial politics of emasculation in the United States.

The Convict-Lease System

During the slave regime, the southern white man owned the Negro body and soul. It was to his interest to dwarf the soul and preserve the body. . . . But Emancipation came and the vested interests of the white man in the Negro's body were lost. —IDA B. WELLS, *A RED RECORD* (1892)

The image of black convicts in striped uniforms laboring under the gaze of armed white guards has endured as one of the most telling symbols of the American South.
—EDWARD L. AYERS, *VENGEANCE AND JUSTICE* (1984), 222

Racisms are never pure and unencumbered. —ANN LAURA STOLER, *RACE AND THE EDU-CATION OF DESIRE* (1995), 204

Prisons do not exist in a vacuum, of course; they are integral elements of the American political, social, economic, and racial order. In the late-nineteenth-century South, thousands of mostly young black men spent their short lives imprisoned in the convict-lease system, working underground in mines or nearly underwater in swamps during the day, collapsed in filthy shacks or cages during the night. Women made up 7 percent of the South's postwar imprisoned population; nearly all were black. About half of those in the lease system had been sentenced for theft or burglary, often involving petty amounts. White men with capital, from the North as well as the South, bought the labor of these imprisoned, re-enslaved black people. The largest mining and railroad companies in the region, as well as small businesses, fought each other to win leases. Deteriorating antebellum penitentiaries were few and relatively unpopulated. Only a few white men convicted of murder, a few black men too sick to work, and a few women (white and black) remained in the dilapidated penitentiaries. Wardens had little to do, for the state had become almost irrelevant in the punishment of criminals.[16]

On the surface, the convict-lease system was a source of political patronage for local and state politicians, providing jobs for their unemployed party workers. The system was thoroughly corrupt. Kickbacks and bribes to public officials usually accompanied the awarding of convict leases to private industry.[17] But those details of convict-campus life that survive suggest that more than political patronage was at work. They compel us to accept that "Emancipation" was, fundamentally, an illusory event. As Dylan Rodríguez points out, slavery was never materially abolished in the United States; it was simply transposed.[18] And as in lynching, the black male body remained the site of white desire, disavowal, and fetishization.

In many camps, guards aroused the sleeping prisoners at 4:30 in the morning and had them at work within half an hour. Prisoners received forty minutes for dinner and "then worked until after sundown, and as long as it is light enough for a guard to see how to shoot. They are worked every day, rain or shine, cold or wet."[19] "Obviously," observes Edward Ayers, "the roots of such forced labor reached into slavery."[20] Like those of the slaves, the conditions under which convicts lived and worked were, at best, brutal.[21] As the sentences from Ida B. Wells that opened this section and those from James Weldon Johnson Jr. quoted later suggest, the conditions in which young black male convicts labored were often worse than those their fathers and mothers had suffered in slavery:

> Our Civil War freed the slaves in name only. It left them illiterate, homeless, and penniless, and at the economic mercy of their former masters. Masses

of them entered a new slavery in which there was neither legal nor moral obligation on the masters; there was not even so much as a financial interest in the "new slaves."[22]

The convict-lease system discloses the intersections between race and sexuality in postbellum Southern society. There is no hint of rehabilitation in these examples of "Southern living." In rolling iron cages, "prisoners slept side by side, shackled together, on narrow wooden slabs. They relieved themselves in a single bucket and bathed in the same filthy tub of water. With no screens on the cages, insects swarmed everywhere. It was like a small piece of hell, an observer noted—the stench, the chains, the sickness, and the heat."[23] The young black men were supervised by armed white guards "notorious for shooting with little provocation."[24]

Many mining companies exploited convicts via the "task system," in which a group of three inmates had to mine a certain amount of coal each day or the entire group would receive floggings. In Alabama, prisoners leased to mining companies were subjected to torture, including being "hung from makeshift crucifixes, stretched on wooden racks, and placed in coffin-sized sweatboxes for hours at a time."[25] In many mining camps, convicts were forced to work throughout the winter without shoes; they stood in cold, putrid water much of the time. In turpentine camps, convicts, chained together, were forced to work at a trot for the entire workday.[26] Indeed, black convicts had no value and were easily replaced. Under convict leasing, replacement of injured or dead convicts involved little if any extra expense for the lessee, who could count on a constant supply of able-bodied convicts from the criminal-justice system.[27] Leased convicts suffered continual illness, brutal punishments, starvation, and, for most, early death.[28]

Prison officials tried to hide the reality of the system. Their reports were exemplary instances of obfuscation and officialese. Reports in Alabama, for instance, praised the "good order" of the convict camps, yet even a glance at the statistical tables accompanying these reports indicated that during some years almost half of the prisoners died—and not from old age. Two-thirds to three-fourths of the convicts working and dying in the convict-lease system were in their twenties or younger. In Mississippi, for example, black children and adolescents made up one-fourth of all convicts leased to private entrepreneurs.[29]

Sexual assaults in convict-lease camps were common. One investigating committee reported that Tennessee's branch prisons were "hell holes of rage, cruelty, despair, and vice." Homosexual rape of young men occurred daily, and "gal boys" were in constant demand.[30] Women were only occasionally separated from men. Men and women were chained together sometimes, pressed together on the same bunks, reminiscent of the Middle Passage. Like young men, women prisoners were regularly raped.[31]

Accompanying the convict-lease system was the largest number of lynchings in American history. Lynching and convict leasing were two sides of the same white coin: white male mutilation of black (mostly) male bodies. Not until the first two decades of the twentieth century did the South finally discontinue the practice of leasing convicts.[32] On May 3, 1995, more than forty years after it had abolished the practice, Alabama reintroduced the chain gang, a contemporary version of nineteenth-century convict leasing.[33]

Abuse by Prison Guards

The nation's prisons are reservations and shelters for black men. —ESSEX HEMPHILL, *BROTHER TO BROTHER* (1991), xx

Is it surprising that prisons resemble factories, schools, barracks, hospitals, which all resemble prisons? —MICHEL FOUCAULT, *DISCIPLINE AND PUNISH* (1979), 228

The law is clearly a system of desire. —GUY HOCQUENGHEM, *HOMOSEXUAL DESIRE* (1978), 52

For accuracy's sake, the "war on drugs" ought to be renamed the "war on young black and Latino men." While failing to curb drug use in the United States, the war on drugs has intensified urban violence. Despite these two facts, the war goes on, and a disproportionate number of African American and Latino men are sent to prison. Jerome Miller argues: "The prosecution of the war on drugs has done more to shatter the inner cities of America than decades of neglect and ineffective social programs."[34] Especially for young black men, the experience of arrest and imprisonment has become "something of a puberty rite, a transition to manhood." The experience "comes with deep, historical racially anchored roots" and often involves a subjective struggle over whether to meekly assume or to aggressively reject the bifurcated identity the ritual demands. It is, Miller continues, an ambiguous puberty rite of disrespect and symbolic castration—from "assuming the position": being handcuffed; placed in a police van; moved from place to place; shackled to a line of peers and older African-American males; posed for a mug shot; tagged with an I.D. bracelet attached to a wrist or ankle; confined in crowded "tanks" or holding cells (a common toilet or open hole in the middle)—to appearing before a robed judge; being assigned a lawyer who controls one's destiny but whom one seldom meets; having a price set on one's head as bail; and, finally, joining one's peers or anxious relatives outside.[35]

Imprisonment today is too often a form of "legal lynching," except now the torture occurs very slowly, over the duration of a long prison sentence, punctuated by the sadism of prison guards.[36]

While, as Miller describes, the contemporary arrest ritual echoes historically, its sadism is experienced in the racialized present, and it is specifically sexualized. In Abu Ghraib, the sadism of U.S. prison guards as they fetishized male bodies of "color" recalls the sexualized torture of lynching and convict leasing. While the historical and geographical circumstances differ significantly, the American culture of sexualized and racialized torture remains recognizable. In the United States, the contemporary black male experience of arrest and imprisonment, Miller asserts, is a mark of continuing subjugation. It becomes an occasion of solidarity, as well, but I will focus here on the latter.[37]

Because many U.S. prisons are located in remote rural areas, guards tend to be drawn from the ranks of the unemployed (or the marginally employed) in small towns and farm areas. They tend to white and undereducated. A consistent demand of prison reformers, national commissions, and rioting prisoners has been the recruitment of minority personnel to replace veteran rural white prison guards, who have been regularly charged with being, at best, unsympathetic, and at worst, brutal, sadistic, and racist. But the recruitment of minority prison guards has not proved simple or always helpful in reducing abuse by prison guards.[38]

The racialized sadism of Southern prisons was legendary. For example, not until August 1974 was the Mississippi Department of Corrections forced to abolish its so-called prisoner trust system. Under this scheme of state-sponsored racial violence, some 300 designated white convicts were given state-owned guns and whips (known as the "Black Annie") and ordered to maintain prison law and order.[39] This system of discipline was found "deplorable and subhuman" by the Federal District Court in Gainesville, Mississippi.[40] Documented incidents include one prisoner who reported being scalded with hot water by a guard; a paraplegic prisoner who testified to being beaten unconscious by guards; two male prisoners who reported homosexual rapes by guards; and one prisoner who witnessed another prisoner hang himself to death while guards stood by laughing. Slightly more than one half of the informants reported that black men were singled out for severe discipline.[41]

Brutality was also widespread in the Texas system throughout the post–World War II years. Physical punishment in Texas prisons included beatings with clubs and fists, as well as the use of blackjacks, riot batons, and aluminum-cased flashlights. Then there was the practice of "tap dancing." Was "tap dancing" a form of relaxation? Not exactly: "On one such occasion, the inmate was thrown to the floor by several officers. One literally stood on the inmate's head (called the tap dance) while another 'spanked' him on the buttocks and thighs with a riot baton." White men's rape of women is well known and ongoing. As we saw in lynching, white men also use power to sexually assault other men.[42]

Not all prison-guard brutality is restricted to the South, of course. One Washington State prisoner reported to Inez Cardozo-Freeman that a guard had sodomized another prisoner with a police baton.[43] That use of the baton was not unprecedented in the prison Cardozo-Freeman studied. On another occasion, several inmates watched as guards took another inmate into the strip cell upside down. The prisoner was handcuffed while another guard repeatedly thrust a baton into his rectum. Substituting a baton for one's penis is an idea still in circulation. From Abu Ghraib, an as yet anonymous prisoner testified:

> And one of the police he put a part of his stick that he always carries inside my ass and I felt it going inside me about two centimeters, approximately, And I started screaming, and he pulled it out and he washed it with water inside the room. And then two American girls that were there when they were beating me, they were hitting me with a ball made of sponge on my dick. And when I was tied up in my room, one of the girls, with blonde hair, she is white, she was playing with my dick. . . . And they were taking pictures of me during all these instances.[44]

Such "economies of visibility" structure racial representation in the public sphere in contemporary America. The body remains the cultural screen of sexualized racial specularity.[45]

In August 1997, four New York City police officers were formally accused of acting on racist motivations in the case of a Haitian immigrant named Abner Louima, thirty-one, and another Haitian immigrant, Patrick Antoine. Hospitalized with a perforated colon, Louima alleged he had been beaten and sodomized by police. Both black men had been arrested outside a nightclub on assault charges that were later dropped. Officers Justin Volpe, Charles Schwarz, Thomas Wiese, and Thomas Bruder were charged with assaulting Louima in a patrol car. Volpe and Schwarz were accused of attacking Louima in the bathroom at a precinct stationhouse, kicking him, and shoving a stick into his rectum and mouth while his hands were cuffed behind his back.[46]

The racial politics of these sexualized assaults is unmistakable. As recently as thirty years ago, Ku Klux Klan members were employed as prison guards, a situation one cannot assume is not true today. In the Pendleton Reformatory in Indiana during the winter of 1972, a group of black prisoners refused to return to their cells. One black inmate raised his hand in the Black Power salute. One white guard was overheard saying, "That one is mine!" The young man was shot five times; he died immediately. Testimony before the U.S. Senate later revealed that nearly 50 percent of the correctional officers involved in the incident were members of the Ku Klux Klan. Dylan Rodríguez points out that several racist/ hate groups now claim representation among U.S. prison guards.[47]

The events in 1971 at Attica prison in upstate New York are infamous. In the four days beginning with the recapture of Attica, New York State Troopers and correctional personnel struck, prodded, and assaulted injured prisoners, many of whom were semiconscious and lying on stretchers. Other prisoners were stripped naked, then beaten, sometimes in the genital area. These "disciplinary" actions are well documented.[48] Relying on Tom Wicker's *A Time to Die*, Paul Hoch points out that guards had been under the impression—due to a rumor that spread rapidly among them (and that was "corroborated" by state correctional administrators) that rebellious inmates were castrating those guards held hostage.[49] This fantasy—the rumor was completely false—was attributed to a particularly muscular inmate with the nickname "Big Black" (Frank Smith) who was later captured and tortured by white guards who casually applied burning cigarettes to his genitals. In ordering that injunctive relief be granted against further brutality, the Second Circuit Court stated:

> Detailed evidence was furnished by plaintiff to the effect that beginning immediately after the State's recapture of Attica on the morning of September 13 and continuing at least until September 16, guards, State Troopers, and correctional personnel had engaged in cruel and inhuman abuse of numerous inmates. Injured prisoners, some on stretchers, were struck, prodded, or beaten with sticks, belts, bats, or other weapons. Others were forced to strip and run naked through gauntlets of guards armed with clubs, which they used to strike the bodies of the inmates as they passed. Some were dragged on the ground, some marked with an "X" on their backs, some spat upon or burned with matches, others were poked in the genitals or arms with sticks. According to the testimony of inmates, bloody or wounded inmates were apparently not spared in this orgy of brutality.[50]

Additional testimony indicated that accompanying the physical violence inflicted on inmates were threats of death or brutality. White correctional officers called inmates "niggers" or "coons" and threatened to "get rid of" them.[51]

The sexualized character of abuse by prison guards is well known to researchers.[52] In one documented incident, a prisoner screamed for over an hour while he was gang raped in his cell within earshot of a correctional officer. Not only did the guard ignore the screams, but he laughed as the young man, shaken, stumbled from his cell afterward.[53] In other cases, correctional-staff members forced prisoners to have sex with one another while the guards watched. In another documented incident, an inmate reported that a friend had been coerced by a guard to have sexual intercourse with a known homosexual prisoner. When the friend refused to do so, he was taken to a private room and beaten. After he was made submissive, the counselors brought in the homosexual prisoner; the two prisoners had sex while the guards watched.[54]

In one Southern institution, a prisoner could purchase a young man from correctional officers, including from deputy wardens. Young men were used as "gifts" from prison officials to inmate leaders who helped them keep the institution quiet. One ex-prisoner claims to have been presented to

> . . . an entire wing of the prison, as a bonus to the convicts for their good behavior. In this wing, any prisoner who wanted his services, at any time and

for any purpose, was given it; the guards opened doors, passed him from one cell to another, provided lubricants, permitted an orgy of simultaneous oral and anal entry, and even arranged privacy.[55]

On occasion staff members become sexually involved with inmates. In one incident, several young men accused several officials of forcing them to participate in homosexual relations. The purely exploitative aspects of these incidents are difficult to verify, for after these young men alleged that they had been forced into performing sexual acts, they changed their stories. In the new versions, they admitted they were willing partners.[56] One young man described his "affair" with a youth leader: "He had some intercourse with me about every two weeks. I did not want to do it, but he talked about getting me out of [here] faster and I wanted to get out because I have been here a long time."[57]

Abuse by prison guards continues today, and not only in Abu Ghraib. In November 1999, for instance, four guards at Corcoran in California—allegedly the nation's most dangerous prison—were acquitted of setting up the rape of a prisoner named Eddie Dillard in March 1993 by leaving him in the cell of a well-known sexual predator, Wayne Robertson. Robertson testified that he had in fact raped Dillard, repeatedly. He said that the guards knew his reputation and employed him regularly to "punish" disobedient inmates. After several failed efforts at bringing charges in the case, a special grand jury had indicted the four prison guards when a former guard, Roscoe Poindexter, broke ranks and testified in support of Dillard.[58]

Robertson was a muscular six foot three and weighed 230 pounds, a convicted murderer and serial inmate rapist who was known in the house as the Booty Bandit. The guards knew Robertson would teach "punks" like Dillard "how to do time."[59] Depending on his mood, Robertson would either beat Dillard or rape him. Dillard fought back, but Robertson overpowered him. While being beaten or raped, Dillard screamed, but for hours no guard responded. When Officer Joe Sanchez did appear and Dillard told him he was being raped, Sanchez laughed at him. During the next two days, Robertson raped Dillard regularly. The pattern is a familiar one: "If you surrender, you're a bitch, a punk. Bitches are cut loose, cast out of the group to become prey for other gangs."[60] In Abu Ghraib, those "other" gangs were the prison guards themselves.

Lynching, convict leasing, and contemporary abuse by prison guards capture the conflations of "race" and "sex" in American cultures of torture. As

Katherine M. Blee perceptively observes, the gender of racial violence in America is masculine.[61] Despite the radical discontinuities between these historical periods and geographical locations—from the post-Reconstruction American South to twentieth-century and present-day U.S. prisons and U.S.-administered Iraqi prisons—certain cultural continuities and historical through lines are discernible. The photographs from Abu Ghraib portray a white-supremacist sadistic culture structured by sexualized compulsions to torture. In its institutionalizations of power, such as prison, the sexualized and racialized character of these cultures of torture is clearly visible.

Conclusion

The specific apparatuses and instruments of punishment—the technologies of penal power—correspond with larger relations of political power. —MARK COLVIN, *PENITENTIARIES, RE-FORMATORIES, AND CHAIN GANGS* (1997), 19

In the United States, the distinction between "culture" and "prison" blurs. What has been learned about the organizational life of prisons is not peculiar to that institution. Rather, it reproduces various aspects of the racialized and gendered culture outside the institution. What has happened and happens still in prisons is not segregated from the sadistic structure of culture outside, as students of the institution have acknowledged: "Living and working conditions, the legitimacy or illegitimacy of various disciplinary mechanisms, and the structure of punishments and rewards all depend upon how the prison articulates with the political, economic, and legal system of the whole society."[62] America has been and is now a culture of discipline and punishment structured by racialized criminalization, imprisonment, and sexualized torture.

The sexualized and racialized culture of torture that Americans created in Abu Ghraib prison becomes intelligible as an extension of U.S. history and culture. So situated, the Army's "few bad apples" defense becomes ludicrous.[63] From the sexualized torture of lynching and the convict-lease system to late-twentieth-century abuse by prison guards, the refrain is constant: sexualized racial assault. One prisoner at Abu Ghraib, Salem Uraiby, an Iraqi who had worked for Reuters for twelve years as a cameraman, testified that guards whispered that they wanted to have sex with him: "Come on, just for two minutes."[64] Another Reuters employee, Ahmad, reported that he was forced to insert a finger into his anus and lick it.[65] In Abu Ghraib, Danner reports, there was a constant "parade" of naked bodies punctuated by "forced masturbation."[66] The photographs "do not represent America," George W. Bush insisted.[67] It would seem they do.

Notes

1. Wright, *Racial Violence in Kentucky, 1865–1940.*
2. Ayers, *Vengeance and Justice.*
3. Miller, *Search and Destroy.*
4. Quoted in Danner, "The Logic of Torture," 74.
5. For this section's title, see Jane Addams, "Respect for Law," in Addams and Wells, *Lynching and Rape*, 28–34; Ida B. Wells-Barnett, "Lynching and the Excuse for It" (1901), ibid.
6. McGovern, *Anatomy of a Lynching*, 80.
7. Ames, *The Changing Character of Lynching*, 58.
8. Raper, *The Tragedy of Lynching*; Tolnay and Beck, *A Festival of Violence*; Wright, *Racial Violence in Kentucky, 1865–1940.*
9. Griffin et al., "Narrative and Event."
10. Tolnay and Beck, *A Festival of Violence.*
11. Looby, "Innocent Homosexuality." To have sex while disavowing it, late-nineteenth-century Southern white men imaginatively "relocated" that desire onto (imaginary) white women's bodies, bodies with whom they were already unconsciously identified. After inhabiting the bodies of their imaginary white ladies, they then positioned them in the originary fantasy—the interracial rape scenario—enabling them to get laid without anyone the wiser. See Chodorow, *The Reproduction of Mothering*, n. 17; Silverman, *Male Subjectivity at the Margins.* As Dylan Rodríguez (personal communication) points out, the collective "hallucination" achieved social materiality, a vicious and tragic materiality.
12. Brundage, *Lynching in the New South.*
13. Pinar, *The Gender of Racial Politics and Violence in America.*
14. Harris, *Exorcising Blackness*; Jordan, *White over Black*; West, *Race Matters*; Williamson, *The Crucible of Race.* While no longer taken seriously by most practicing psychoanalysts, Freud's theorization of paranoia as an effect of repressed homosexual desire may not always be mistaken. See Freud, "Psychoanalytic Notes upon an Autobiographical Account of a Case of Paranoia."
15. Wiegman, "The Anatomy of Lynching." See also idem, *American Anatomies.* As Dylan Rodríguez points out, "genital mutilation" is the more precise and descriptive term. I employ "castration" because the term has symbolic as well as literal meaning in U.S. racial politics and in part because scholars whose work I admire—such as Robyn Wiegman—use the term.

16. Ayers, *Vengeance and Justice.*
17. Ayers, *The Promise of the New South.* See also *Vengeance and Justice.*
18. Rodríguez, personal communication. Others—such as Saidiya Hartman—also emphasize the illusory character of "Emancipation." For the pedagogical reinscription of slavery in the postbellum period, see Hartman, *Scenes of Subjection*, chaps. 4–5.
19. Ayers, *Vengeance and Justice*, 193.
20. Ibid., 191.
21. Woodward, *The Origins of the New South, 1877–1913.*
22. Johnson, *Along This Way*, 346. Appointed executive secretary of the NAACP in December 1920, James Weldon Johnson, along with Walter White, W. E. B. Du Bois, and other early-twentieth-century NAACP leaders, fought unsuccessfully for federal anti-lynching legislation. See Pinar, *The Gender of Racial Violence and Politics in America*, chap. 11. Hazel Carby has observed: "Johnson situates the black male body at the center of what he perceives as a national crisis, a crisis conceived in the dual terms of black body and white soul." See Carby, *Race Men*, 47.
23. Oshinsky, *Worse than Slavery*, 59.
24. Ayers, *The Promise of the New South*, 126. Dylan Rodríguez suggests that the Marxist critique of racial violence falls apart in the face of such torture and assault.
25. Oshinksy, *Worse than Slavery*, 79. See Mancini, *One Dies, Get Another*, 76, 115, 123, for additional reports of torture in convict-leasing camps.
26. Colvin, *Penitentiaries, Reformatories, and Chain Gangs.*
27. See Mancini, *One Dies, Get Another.*
28. See Colvin, *Penitentiaries, Reformatories, and Chain Gangs.*
29. Ayers, *Vengeance and Justice.*
30. Ibid., 200.
31. See Ayers, *Vengeance and Justice*; Colvin, *Penitentiaries, Reformatories, and Chain Gangs*; Mancini, *One Dies, Get Another*; Oshinsky, *Worse than Slavery*; Woodward, *The Origins of the New South, 1877–1913.*
32. Ayers, *Vengeance and Justice.*
33. "The Return of the Chain Gang," *Washington Post*, May 4, 1995, A1.
34. Miller, *Search and Destroy*, 120.
35. Ibid., 99.
36. Wright, *Racial Violence in Kentucky, 1865–1940.*
37. It is also in the American prisons where subjugated black men sometimes achieve political solidarity and enact what I have called Claude Neal's revenge. See Pinar, *The Gender of Racial Violence and Violence in America*. It is a particular revenge: interracial prison rape.
38. Jacobs, *New Perspectives on Prisons and Imprisonment*. As we saw in Abu Ghraib, black guards can become assimilated to those cultures of torture that historically surfaced around black enslavement.

39. McWhorter, *Inmate Society*.

40. Hamm et al., "The Myth of Humane Imprisonment," 175.

41. Ibid.

42. Crouch and Marquart, *An Appeal to Justice*, 79–80. Regarding the "gender of violence," see Pinar, *The Gender of Racial Politics and Violence in America*, chaps. 13–15.

43. Dannes, "The Logic of Torture," 73.

44. Cardozo-Freeman, *The Joint*.

45. Danner, "The Logic of Torture," 71. Also see Wiegman, *American Anatomies*, 3.

46. Associated Press, "Officers Indicted in Torture Case," *Star Phoenix*, August 23, 1997, B16.

47. Bowker, *Prison Victimization*. Rodríguez (personal communication) recommends the following website for additional information: www.splcenter.org/intel/hatewatch.

48. Ibid.

49. Wicker, *A Time to Die*; Hoch, *White Hero, Black Beast*.

50. Deutsch et al., "Twenty Years Later."

51. Ibid.

52. See Pinar, *The Gender of Racial Politics and Violence in America*, chaps. 16–17.

53. Bowker, *Prison Victimization*.

54. Ibid.

55. Ibid., 110.

56. Bartollas et al., *Juvenile Victimization*.

57. Ibid., 214.

58. Richard Stratton, "The Making of a Bonecrusher," *Esquire*, September 1999, 214.

59. Ibid., 191.

60. Ibid., 208.

61. Blee, *Women of the Klan*.

62. Jacobs, *New Perspectives on Prisons and Imprisonment*, 17–18.

63. Danner, "The Logic of Torture," 71.

64. Ibid.

65. Ibid.

66. Ibid., 72.

67. Ibid., 74.

Katrina's Unnatural Disaster: A Tragedy of Black Suffering and White Denial

Manning Marable

Unquestionably, the September 2005 Hurricane Katrina was the largest natural disaster in U.S. history. Yet contrary to the assertions of President George W. Bush that no one could have "anticipated the breach of [New Orleans's] levees" and the massive flooding and destruction of one of America's historic cities in the wake of a major hurricane, the catastrophe we have witnessed was widely predicted for decades.[1] A 2002 special report of the New Orleans *Times-Picayune*, for example, warned, "It's only a matter of time before South Louisiana takes a direct hit from a major hurricane. . . . Levees, our best protection from flooding, may turn against us." The *Times-Picayune* predicted that such a disaster might "decimate the region" from flooding, and that in New Orleans, "100,000 will be left to face the fury."[2] That same year, in a *New York Times* editorial opinion, Adam Cohen predicted coldly, "If the Big One hits, New Orleans could disappear." A direct major hurricane strike, Cohen estimated, would certainly force Lake Pontchartrain's waters "over levees and into the city. . . . There could be 100,000 deaths." Thousands "could be stranded on roofs, surrounded by a witches' brew of contaminated water."[3]

A natural disaster for New Orleans was statistically inevitable. But what made the New Orleans tragedy an "unnatural disaster" was the federal government's gross incompetence and indifference in preparing the necessary measures to preserve the lives and property of hundreds of thousands of its citizens. The Federal Emergency Management Agency (FEMA), established in 1979, has been plagued for years with financial mismanagement, administrative incompetence, and cronyism.

The litany of FEMA's bureaucratic blunders has been amply documented: its insistence that vital supplies of food, water, and medical aid were impossible to deliver to thousands of people stranded at New Orleans's downtown Morial Convention Center, though entertainers and reporters easily reached the site; its inability to rescue thousands of residents marooned on the roofs and in flooded houses for days; the failure to seek deployment of active-duty troops in large numbers until three days after Hurricane Katrina struck the Gulf Coast region. But the incompetence goes deeper than that. FEMA's Director Michael Brown actually instructed fire departments in Louisiana, Mississippi, and Alabama not to send emergency vehicles or personnel into devastated areas unless local or state officials communicated specific requests for them—at a time when most towns and cities lacked working telephones, fax machines, and Internet access. Florida's proposal to send 500 airboats to assist rescue efforts was blocked by FEMA. Thousands of urgently needed generators, communications equipment, and trailers and freight cars of food went undelivered for weeks. Meanwhile, hundreds of dead bodies floated in New Orleans's streets and rotted in desolated houses. Millions of desperate Americans who attempted to phone FEMA's toll-free telephone number for assistance heard recorded messages that all lines were busy or were disconnected.[4]

Even before Katrina struck, it was obvious that the overwhelming majority of New Orleans residents who would be trapped inside the city to face the deluge would be poor and working-class African Americans, who made up nearly 70 percent of the city's population. As the levees collapsed and the city's Ninth Ward flooded, tens of thousands of evacuees were herded into the Superdome and Convention Center, where they were forced to endure days without toilets and running water, food, electricity, and medical help. Hundreds of black evacuees seeking escape on a bridge across the Mississippi River were confronted and forcibly pushed back into the city. One paramedic who witnessed the incident stated: "I believe it was racism. It was callousness, it was cruelty."[5]

As the media began to document this unprecedented tragedy, the vast majority of New Orleans's victims were "the faces at the bottom of America's well—the poor, black and disabled," as Monica Haynes and Erv Dyer, reporters for the Pittsburgh *Post-Gazette*, observed. "The indelible television images of mostly black people living in subhuman conditions for nearly a week have prompted some to ask whether race played a role in how quickly or how not-so-quickly federal and state agencies responded in [Katrina's] aftermath."[6]

However, much of the media coverage cruelly manipulated racist stereotypes in its coverage. In one well-publicized example, the Associated Press released two photographs of New Orleans residents wading through chest-deep water, carrying food obtained from a grocery store. The whites were described as carrying "bread and soda from a local grocery store" that they found; the black man pictured was characterized as having "loot[ed] a grocery store."[7] A London *Financial Times* reporter, on September 5, 2005, declared New Orleans had become "a city of rape" and "a war zone," with thousands subjected to "looting" and "arson."[8] Administrators in Homeland Security and FEMA justified their lack of emergency aid by claiming that they had not anticipated that "people would loot gun stores . . . and shoot at police, rescue officials and helicopters." The flood of racialized images of a terrorized, crime-engulfed city prompted hundreds of white ambulance drivers and emergency personnel to refuse to enter the New Orleans disaster zone. Television reports locally and nationally quickly proliferated false exposés about "babies in the Convention Center who got their throats cut" and "armed hordes" hijacking ambulances and trucks. Baton Rouge's Mayor Kip Holden imposed a strict curfew on its facility that held evacuees, warning of possible violence by "New Orleans thugs."[9] That none of these sensationalized stories was true hardly mattered: As Matt Welch of the online edition of *Reason* magazine noted, the "deadly bigotry" of the media probably helped to "kill Katrina victims."[10]

The terrible destruction of thousands of homes and businesses, and the relocation of over 1 million New Orleans and Gulf area residents, was perceived as a golden opportunity by corporate and conservative political elites who had long desired to "remake" the historic city. Even before the corpses of black victims had been cleared from New Orleans's flooded streets, corporations closely associated with George W. Bush's administration secured noncompetitive, multibillion-dollar reconstruction contracts. Brown and Root, a subsidiary of Halliburton, for example, was awarded the contract to reconstruct Louisiana and Mississippi naval bases. Bechtel was authorized to provide short-term housing for several hundred thousand displaced evacuees. Shaw, the Louisiana engineering corporation, received lucrative contracts for rebuilding throughout the area. Bush waived provisions of the Davis-Bacon Act, allowing corporations to hire workers below the minimum wage. After Congress authorized over 100 billion dollars for the region's reconstruction, Halliburton's stock price surged on Wall Street.[11] Local corporate subcontractors and developers who directly profited from federal subsidies set into motion plans for what local African Americans feared could quickly become a gentrification removal of thousands of black households from devastated urban neighborhoods.

Behind the plans to "rebuild" New Orleans may be racially inspired objectives by Republicans to reduce the size of the city's all-black voting precincts.

About 60 percent of New Orleans's electorate is African American, which normally turns out at 50 percent in local elections. All-white affluent neighborhoods have turnout rates exceeding 70 percent. In the 1994 mayoral race, only 6 percent of the city's white voters supported the successful black candidate Marc Morial.[12]

The African American political analyst Earl Ofari Hutchinson speculated that "the loss of thousands of black votes" could easily "crack the thirty years of black, and Democratic dominance of City Hall in New Orleans." The seat of the black Democrat William Jefferson, who represents the city in Congress, could be in jeopardy. Even more seriously, Hutchinson observed, the massive African American vote in New Orleans in 2000 and 2004 "enabled Democrats to bag many top state and local offices, but just narrowly. A shift of a few thousand votes could tip those offices back to Republicans."[13]

Nationally, most African American leaders, public officials, and intellectuals were overwhelmed and outraged by the flood of racist stereotypes in the media and their government's appalling inaction to rescue thousands of black and poor people. They observed that the most devastated sections of the city were nearly all black and mostly poor. Local blacks had been largely ignored in preparations for evacuating the city.[14] Beverly Wright, the director of Xavier University's Deep South Center for Environmental Justice, expressed the general sentiment of most African Americans by declaring: "I am very angry, and I really, really believe that [the crisis] is driven by race. . . . When you look at who is left behind, it is very disturbing to me."[15] Wright's viewpoint was echoed by many black intellectuals. For example, Harvard's Professor Lani Guinier observed that, in American society, "poor black people are the throw-away people. And we pathologize them in order to justify our disregard."[16] Some reporters assigned to the Katrina crisis soon began to reflect these mounting criticisms. Desiree Cooper, a columnist for the *Detroit Free Press*, drew parallels between the economic devastation of New Orleans and Detroit, noting that "the poverty rate in both cities rivals that of Third World nations. So as I watched the hurricane coverage, with racism and poverty creating the perfect storm, I couldn't help but think: If Detroit were underwater, no one would bother to rescue us either."[17]

By mid-September, 2005, 60 percent of African Americans surveyed in a national poll believed that "the federal government's delay in helping the victims in New Orleans was because the victims were black." By contrast, only 12 percent of white Americans agreed.[18] In response, the Bush administration unleashed its black apologists to deny any racial intent of its policies and actions. Secretary of State Condoleezza Rice insisted, "Nobody, especially the President, would have left people unattended."[19] The black conservative ideologue John McWhorter, a senior fellow at the Manhattan Institute, ridiculed the accusations of racism as "nasty, circular, [and] unprovable. . . . It's not a matter of somebody in Washington deciding we don't need to rush [to New Orleans] because they're all poor jungle bunnies anyway."[20]

African Americans were stunned and perplexed by white America's general apathy and denial about the racial implications of the Katrina catastrophe. On a nationally televised fundraiser for the hurricane's victims, the rap artist Kanye West sparked controversy by denouncing "the way America is set up to help the poor, the black people, the less well off as slow as possible."[21] Blacks were especially infuriated with the descriptions of poor black evacuees as "refugees" by officials and the media. Black Congresswoman Diane Watson protested vigorously, " 'Refugee' calls up to mind people that come here from different lands and have to be taken care of. . . . These are American citizens."[22] But the racial stigmatization of New Orleans's outcasts forced many African Americans to ponder whether their government and white institutions had become incapable of expressing true compassion for the suffering of their people. The prominent Princeton University professor Cornel West, at a Columbia University forum sponsored by the Institute for Research in African-American Studies, pondered whether "*black suffering* is required for the preservation of white America."[23]

West's provocative query ought to be explored seriously. The U.S. government and America's entire political economy were constructed on a racial foundation. Blacks were excluded by race from civic participation and voting for several hundred years; they were segregated into residential ghettoes, denied credit and capital by banks, and relegated to the worst jobs for generations. Over time, popular cultural and social attitudes about black subordination and white superiority were aggressively reinforced by the weight of discriminatory law and public policy. Psychologically, is the specter of black suffering and death in some manner reaffirming the traditional racial hierarchy, the practices of black exclusion and marginalization?

Even before Katrina's racial debate had receded from the media, the question of racial insensitivity was posed again by William Bennett, secretary of education under Ronald Reagan. In early October 2005, Bennett announced to his national radio audience: "I do know that it's true that if you wanted to reduce crime, you could—if that were your sole purpose—you could abort every black baby in this country, and your crime rate would go down." Perhaps covering his racial gaffe, Bennett immediately added, "That would be an impossible, ridiculous and morally reprehensible thing to do, but your crime rate would go down."[24] The *New York Times* columnist Bob Herbert interpreted Bennett's remarks as the central aspect of the Republican Party's "bigotry, racially divisive tactics and outright anti-black policies. That someone who's been a stalwart of that outfit might muse publicly about the potential benefits of exterminating blacks is not surprising to me at all. . . . Bill Bennett's twisted fantasies are a malignant outgrowth of our polarized past."[25] Bennett's repugnant statements, combined with most white Americans' blind refusal to recognize a racial tragedy in New Orleans, illustrate how deeply rooted racial injustice remains in America.

Has the public spectacle of black suffering and anguish evolved into what might be defined as a "civic ritual," reconfirming the racial hierarchy, with blackness permanently relegated to a subordinate status? In the summer of 2005, the U.S. Senate seemed to confirm Cornel West's hypothesis, as it was forced to confront the civic ritual of lynching. Between 1882 and 1927, over 3,500 blacks were lynched in the United States, about 95 percent in the South. An unknown number of additional African Americans were killed, especially in rural and remote areas where we have few means to reconstruct these crimes.

In Marion, Indiana, on August 7, 1930, a massive white mob stormed the jail in the local county courthouse, seizing two incarcerated African American teenagers, Thomas Shipp and Abram Smith, who had been accused of raping a white woman. Within less than an hour, a festive gathering of several thousand white women and men armed with baseball bats, crowbars, and guns beat and then lynched the two black boys. A photograph of the Marian lynching that was reproduced in my book *Freedom*, co-written with Leith Mullings, depicts smiling young adults, a pregnant woman, teenage girls, and a middle-aged man pointing proudly to one of the dangling corpses.[26]

A third young African American, a sixteen-year-old shoeshine boy named James Cameron, was also seized and beaten by the mob that night. Several men lifted Cameron up, and a noose was slipped around his neck. Just at that moment, a local white man in the crowd pushed forward and declared that young Cameron was innocent. Years later, on June 13, 2005, speaking at a U.S. Senate new conference, ninety-one-year-old James Cameron recalled: "They took the rope off my neck, those hands that had been so rough and ready to kill or had already killed, they took the rope off my neck and they allowed me to start walking and stagger back to jail, which was just a half-block away."[27] Cameron, the only known survivor of an attempted lynching, had come to the Capitol as part of an effort to obtain a formal apology from the Senate for its historic refusal to pass federal legislation outlawing lynching. For decades, Southern senators had filibustered legislative attempts to ratify anti-lynching legislation, denouncing such bills as an unnecessary interference with states' rights. Prompted by the emotional testimony of Cameron and the family members and descendants of lynching victims, the Senate finally issued an apology for lynching—the first time in U.S. history that Congress has acknowledged and expressed regret for historical crimes against African Americans—in a formal resolution. What was most significant, perhaps, was that only eighty-five of the one hundred U.S. senators had co-sponsored the resolution when it came up for a voice vote. The fifteen senators who did not initially co-sponsor the bill were Republicans. Belatedly, seven senators subsequently signed an oversize copy of the Senate's anti-lynching resolution, which was to be publicly displayed. The eight senators who still refused to concede an apology are Lamar Alexander (Republican of Tennessee), Thad Cochran (Republican of Mississippi), John Cornyn (Republican of Texas), Michael Enzi (Republican of Wyoming), Judd Gregg (Republican of New Hampshire), Trent Lott (Republican of Mississippi), John Sununu (Republican of New Hampshire), and Craig Thomas (Republican of Wyoming).[28]

Why the steadfast refusal to acknowledge the forensic evidence and the obvious human pain and suffering inflicted on not only the victims of racist violence but on their descendants? Because in a racist society—by this I mean a society deeply stratified, with "whiteness" defined at the top and "blackness" occupying the bottom rungs—the obliteration of the black past is absolutely essential to the preservation of white hegemony, or domination. Since "race" itself is a fraudulent concept, devoid of scientific reality, "racism" can only be rationalized and justified through the suppression of black accounts or evidence that challenges society's understanding about itself and its own past. Racism is perpetuated and reinforced by the "historical logic of whiteness," which repeatedly presents whites as the primary (and frequently sole) actors in the important decisions that have influenced the course of human events. This kind of history deliberately excludes blacks and other racialized groups from having the capacity to become actors in shaping major social outcomes.

In this process of falsification, two elements are crucial: the suppression of evidence of black resistance, and the obscuring of any records of white crimes and exploitation committed against blacks as an oppressed group. In this manner, white Americans can more easily absolve themselves of the historical responsibility for the actions of their great-grandparents, grandparents, parents—and of themselves. Thus, the destructive consequences of modern structural racism that can be easily measured by social scientists within contemporary U.S. society today, as well as the human suffering we have witnessed in New Orleans, can be said to have absolutely nothing to do with "racism." Denial of responsibility for racism permits the racial chasm in America to grow wider with each passing year.

When the "unnatural disaster" of the New Orleans tragedy of race and class is examined in the context of American structural racism, the denial by many whites of the reality of black suffering becomes clear. It parallels the denial of the Turkish government of the massive genocide of the Armenian population committed by the Ottoman Empire in 1915–16. It mirrors the repulsive anti-Semitism of those who to this day deny the horrific reality of the Holocaust during World War II. Until the denial of suffering ceases, there is no possibility of constructing meaningful, corrective measures in addressing the racial chasm that continues to fracture the foundations of democratic life and a truly civil society in America.

Notes

Originally published in *Souls: A Critical Journal of Black Politics, Culture, and Society* 8, no. 1 (winter 2006): 1–8

1. Ted Steinberg, "A Natural Disaster, and a Human Tragedy," *Chronicle of Higher Education*, vol. 52, no. 5, September 23, 2005, 811–12.
2. "Washing Away," *Times-Picayune* (New Orleans), June 23–27, 2002.
3. Adam Cohen, "If the Big One Hits, New Orleans Could Disappear," *New York Times*, August 11, 2002. See also Jon Nordheimer, "Nothing's Easy for New Orleans Flood Control," *New York Times*, April 30, 2002.
4. "Truly Clueless at FEMA," editorial, *Boston Herald*, September 8, 2005; "Political Ap-

pointments, Loss of Focus, Crippled Disaster Relief Agency," editorial, *U.S.A. Today*, September 8, 2005; Tina Susman, "FEMA: Effort Mired in Bureaucratic Hash," *Newsday*, September 11, 2005; Jonathan S. Landay, Alison Young, and Shannon McCaffrey, "Was FEMA's Brown the Fall Guy?" *Seattle Times*, September 14, 2005; Angie C. Marek, Edward T. Pound, Danielle Knight, Julian E. Barnes, Judd Slivka, and Kevin Whitelaw, "A Crisis Agency in Crisis," *U.S. News and World Report*, September 19, 2005; and "FEMA: Just a Money Pit?" editorial, *Hartford Courant*, September 23, 2005.

5. Andrew Buncombe, "'Racist' Police Blocked Bridge and Forced Evacuees Back at Gunpoint," *Independent* (London), September 11, 2005.

6. Monica Haynes and Erv Dyer, "Black Faces Are Indelible Image of Katrina," *Independent* (London), September 4, 2005.

7. Aaron Kinney, "'Looting' or 'Finding'?" available online at http://www.salon.com/new/features/2005/09/01/photo_controversy/print.html (accessed December 13, 2005).

8. Guy Dinmore, "City of Rape, Rumour and Recrimination," *Financial Times* (London), September 5, 2005.

9. David Caruso, "Disaster Official at New York Symposium: Planners Didn't Anticipate Gun Problem after Katrina," *Newsday*, September 12, 2005.

10. Matt Welch, "The Deadly Bigotry of Low Expectations? Did the Rumor Mill Help Kill Katrina Victims?" available online at http://www.reason.com/links/links090605.shtml (accessed December 13, 2005).

11. Katherine Griffiths, "Firms Linked with Bush Get Katrina Clean-Up Work," *Independent* (London), September 17, 2005; Scott Van Voorhis, "Katrina Boon to Builders," *Boston Herald*, September 6, 2005.

12. Coleman Warner, "Primary Turnout Makes Black Vote Crucial in Runoff," *Times-Picayune* (New Orleans), February 7, 1994.

13. Earl Ofari Hutchinson, "Katrina Wallops Black Voters," September 16, 2005, available online at www.blackvoicenews.com/content/view/38603/16/ (accessed February 15, 2007).

14. Jonathan Curiel, "Disaster Aid Raises Race Issue: Critics Say Poor Blacks Not Considered in Planning for Emergencies, Evacuations," *San Francisco Chronicle*, September 3, 2005.

15. Alex Tzon, "Katrina's Aftermath: Images of the Victims Spark a Racial Debate," *Los Angeles Times*, September 3, 2005.

16. Lynne Duke and Teresa Wiltz, "A Nation's Castaways: Katrina Blew In, and Tossed up Reminders of a Tattered Racial Legacy," *Washington Post*, September 4, 2005.

17. Desiree Cooper, "Outrage, Carrying Mix in Katrina Response," *Detroit Free Press*, September 15, 2005.

18. CNN, *U.S.A. Today*, and Gallup poll, released September 13, 2005, cited ibid. Other

opinion polls confirmed that most black Americans believed that racism was behind the federal government's inaction to aid Katrina's victims. A Pew Institute poll, for example, indicated that 66 percent of blacks surveyed "felt the government would have reacted faster if the stranded victims had been mainly white than black." See Alex Massie, "Racial Tensions Simmer as Blacks Bear Brunt of Slow Official Response," available online at http://news.scotsman.com/opinion.cfm?id=1920892005 (accessed December 13, 2005).

19. Elisabeth Bumiller, "Gulf Coast Isn't the Only Thing Left in Tatters: Bush's Status with Blacks Takes a Hit," *New York Times*, September 12, 2005.
20. Duke and Wiltz, "A Nation's Castaways."
21. Kanye West, quoted on *The O'Reilly Factor*, Fox News Network, September 8, 2005.
22. Robert E. Pierre and Paul Farhi, " 'Refugee': A Word of Trouble," *Washington Post*, September 7, 2005.
23. Cornel West, "When Affirmative Action Was White," remarks at symposium, Institute for Research in African-American Studies, Columbia University, New York, October 1, 2005.
24. Bob Herbert, "Impossible, Ridiculous, Repugnant," *New York Times*, October 6, 2005.
25. Ibid.
26. See Marable and Mullings, *Freedom*, 132.
27. Sheryl Gay Stolberg, "Senate Issues Apology over Failure on Anti-Lynching Law," *New York Times*, June 14, 2005.
28. "Eight U.S. Senators Decline to Co-Sponsor Resolution Apologizing for Failure to Enact Anti-Lynching Legislation," *Journal of Blacks in Higher Education Weekly Bulletin*, June 30, 2005; Avis Thomas-Lester, "Repairing Senate's Record on Lynching," *Washington Post*, June 11, 2005.

Bibliography

Abu-Jamal, Mumia. *Live from Death Row.* New York: Avon Books, 1996.

———. *We Want Freedom: A Life in the Black Panther Party.* Cambridge, Mass.: South End Press, 2004.

ACE Program of Bedford Hills Correctional Facility. *Breaking the Walls of Silence: AIDS and Women in a New York State Maximum Security Prison.* Woodstock, N.Y.: Overlook Press, 1998.

Addams, Jane, and Ida B. Wells. *Lynching and Rape: An Exchange of Views,* ed. Bettina Aptheker. New York: American Institute for Marxist Studies, 1977.

Allen Jr., Ernest. "Minister Louis Farrakhan and the Continuing Evolution of the Nation of Islam." In *The Farrakhan Factor,* ed. Amy Alexander. New York: Grove Press, 1998.

Ames, Jessie Daniel. *The Changing Character of Lynching,* reprint ed. Atlanta: Commission on Interracial Cooperation, 1942; New York: AMS Press, 1972.

Amin, Samir. "Confronting the Empire." *Monthly Review* 55, no. 3 (July–August 2003).

———. *Empire of Chaos,* trans. W. H. Locke Anderson. New York: Monthly Review Press, 1992.

Amnesty International, London. *United States of America: The Death Penalty and Juvenile Offenders,* October 1991.

Amnesty International U.S.A. *Allegations of Mistreatment in Marion Prison, Illinois, U.S.A.* Doc. no. AMR 51/26/87, May 1987.

Andrews, William L., and Henry Louis Gates Jr. *Slave Narratives.* New York: Library of America, 2000.

Aptheker, Bettina. *Morning Breaks: The Trial of Angela Davis,* reprint ed. New York: International Publishers, 1975; Ithaca, N.Y.: Cornell University Press, 1999.

Arendt, Hannah. *The Human Condition.* Garden City, N.Y.: Doubleday, 1959.

Artières, Philippe, Laurent Quéro, and Michelle Zancarini-Fournel, eds. *Le Groupe d'information sur les prisons: Archives d'une lutte, 1970–1972.* Paris: Editions de l'Institut Mémoires de l'édition contemporaine, 2003.

Awkward, Michael. *Negotiating Difference: Race, Gender, and the Politics of Positionality.* Chicago: University of Chicago Press, 1995.

Ayers, Edward L. *The Promise of the New South: Life after Reconstruction.* New York: Oxford University Press, 1993.

———. *Vengeance and Justice: Crime and Punishment in the Nineteenth Century American South.* New York: Oxford University Press, 1984.

Balibar, Etienne. "Racism and Nationalism." In *Race, Nation, Class: Ambiguous Identities*, ed. Etienne Balibar and Immanuel Wallerstein. New York: Verso, 1991.

Bamford, James. *Body of Secrets: Anatomy of the Ultra-Secret National Security Agency from the Cold War through the Dawn of a New Century*. New York: Doubleday, 2001.

Bandele, Asha. *The Prisoner's Wife*. New York: Scribner, 1999.

Baraldini, Silvia, Marilyn Buck, Susan Rosenberg, and Laura Whitehorn. "Women's Control Unit." In *Criminal Injustice: Confronting the Prison Crisis*, ed. Elihu Rosenblatt. Boston: South End Press, 1996.

Barreto, Amilcar Antonio. *Vieques, the Navy and Puerto Rican Politics*. Gainesville: University Press of Florida, 2002.

Bartollas, Clemens, Stuart J. Miller, and Simon Dinitz. *Juvenile Victimization: The Institutional Paradox*. New York: John Wiley/Sage Publications, 1976.

Bartov, Omer. *Murder in Our Midst: The Holocaust, Industrial Killing and Representation*. New York: Oxford University Press, 1996.

Baum, Dan. *Smoke and Mirrors: The War on Drugs and the Politics of Failure*. New York: Little, Brown, 1996.

Behrendt, Stephen D. "Crew Mortality in the Transatlantic Slave Trade in the Eighteenth Century." In *Routes to Slavery*, ed. David Eltis and David Richardson. London: Frank Cass, 1997.

Bennett, James R. *Political Prisoners and Trials: A Worldwide Annotated Bibliography, 1900 through 1993*. Jefferson, N.C.: McFarland and Company, 1995.

Bennett Jr., Lerone. *Before the Mayflower: A History of Black America*, 5th ed. New York: Penguin Books, 1984.

Berrigan, Daniel. *Lights on the House of the Dead: A Prison Diary*. New York: Doubleday, 1974.

———. *To Dwell in Peace: An Autobiography*. San Francisco: Harper and Row, 1987.

———. *The Trial of the Catonsville Nine*. Boston: Beacon Press, 1970.

Berrigan, Philip, and Fred A. Wilcox. *Fighting the Lamb's War: Skirmishes with the American Empire, the Autobiography of Philip Berrigan*. Monroe, Maine: Common Courage Press, 1996.

Berry, Mary Frances. *Black Resistance/White Law: A History of Constitutional Racism in America*. New York: Appleton-Century-Crofts, 1971.

Bowker, Lee H. *Prison Victimization*. New York: Elsevier, 1980.

Black Liberation Army. "On the Black Liberation Army." Pamphlet. September 18, 1979.

Black Prison Movements U.S.A.: NOBO Journal of African Dialogue. Trenton, N.J.: Africa World Press, 1995.

Blackston, Nelson. COINTELPRO: *The FBI's Secret War on Political Freedom*. New York: Vintage Books, 1976.

Blassingame, John W. *The Slave Community: Plantation Life in the Antebellum South*. New York: Oxford University Press, 1972.

Blee, Katherine M. *Women of the Klan: Racism and Gender in the 1920s.* Berkeley: University of California Press, 1991.

Blum, William. *Killing Hope: U.S. Military and CIA Interventions since the Cold War.* Monroe, Maine.: Common Courage Press, 1995.

Boyle, Robert. "Tribunal Urges Freedom for U.S. Political Prisoners," *Guild Notes* (Winter 1991).

Breitman, George. *The Last Year of Malcolm X: The Evolution of a Revolutionary.* New York: Schocken, 1967.

Brown, David J., and Robert Merrill, eds. *Violent Persuasions: The Politics and Imagery of Terrorism.* Seattle: Bay Press, 1993.

Brundage, W. Fitzhugh. *Lynching in the New South: Georgia and Virginia, 1880–1930.* Urbana: University of Illinois Press, 1993.

Buck, Marilyn. *On Self-Censorship.* Berkeley, Calif.: Parentheses Writing Series, Small Press Distribution, 1995.

———. "Prisons, Social Control, and Political Prisoners." *Social Justice* 27, no. 3 (2000): 25–28.

———. *Rescue the Word: Poems.* San Francisco: Friends of Marilyn Buck, 2001.

Buck, Marilyn, and Laura Whitehorn. "Legal Issues for Women in Federal Prisons: FCI Dublin California." *Legal Journal* 10, no. 11 (Winter 1996).

Burns, Haywood. "Racism and American Law." In *Law against People*, ed. Robert Lefcourt. New York: Bintae Books, 1971.

Burton-Rose, Daniel, Dan Pens, and Paul Wright, eds. *The Celling of America: An Inside Look at the U.S. Prison Industry.* Monroe, Maine: Common Courage Press, 1998.

Calderón, Tovah Renee. "Race-Based Policing from Terry to Wardlow: Steps down the Totalitarian Path." *Howard Law Journal* 44, no. 73 (2000).

Call Me Nuh and Last Statement, 2000. Videocassette, Real Dragon Productions, San Francisco, 2000.

Committee to End the Marion Lockdown. *Can't Jail the Spirit,* 5th ed. Chicago: Committee to End the Marion Lockdown, 2002.

Carby, Hazel V. *Race Men.* Cambridge, Mass.: Harvard University Press, 1998.

Cardozo-Freeman, Inez. *The Joint: Language and Culture in a Maximum Security Prison.* Springfield, Ill.: Charles C. Thomas, 1984.

Carey, Henry C. *The Slave Trade: Domestic and Foreign* (1853), reprint ed. New York: Augustus M. Kelley Publishers, 1967.

Carson, Clayborne. *In Struggle: SNCC and the Black Awakening of the 1960s.* Cambridge, Mass.: Harvard University Press, 1981.

Chinosole. *Schooling the Generations in the Politics of Prison.* Berkeley, Calif.: New Earth Publications, 1995.

Chodorow, Nancy J. *The Reproduction of Mothering.* Berkeley: University of California Press, 1978.

Chomsky, Noam. *The Culture of Terrorism*. Boston: South End Press, 1988.

Churchill, Ward, and Jim Vander Wall. *Agents of Repression: The FBI's Secret Wars against the Black Panther Party and the American Indian Movement*. Boston: South End Press, 2002.

———. *The COINTELPRO Papers: Documents from the FBI's Secret Wars against Domestic Dissent*. Boston: South End Press, 2002.

Churchill, Ward, and Jim Vander Wall, eds. *Cages of Steel*. Washington, D.C.: Maisonneuve Press, 1992.

Clausewitz, Carl von. *On War*, ed. and trans. Michael Howard and Peter Paret. Princeton: Princeton University Press, 1976.

Cleaver, Eldridge. *Soul on Ice*. New York: McGraw-Hill, 1968.

Cleaver, Kathleen, and George Katsiaficas, eds. *Liberation, Imagination, and the Black Panther Party*. New York: Routledge, 2001.

Coetzee, J. M. *White Writing: On the Culture of Letters in South Africa*. New Haven: Yale University Press, 1988.

Colvin, Mark. *Penitentiaries, Reformatories, and Chain Gangs*. New York: St. Martin's Press, 1997.

Conway, Marshall Eddie. "Imprisoned Black Panther Party Members: Criminals or Political Prisoners?" M.A. thesis, California State University, Dominguez Hills, 2004.

Copley, Esther. *A History of Slavery and Its Abolition*. London: Houlstom and Stoneman, 1839.

Coutin, Susan Bibler. *The Culture of Protest: Religious Activism and the U.S. Sanctuary Movement*. Boulder: Westview Press, 1993.

Crouch, B. M., and J. W. Marquart. *An Appeal to Justice: Litigated Reform of Texas Prisons*. Austin: University of Texas Press, 1989.

Curtin, Philip. *The Atlantic Slave Trade: A Census*. Madison: University of Wisconsin Press, 1969.

Dannin, Robert. *Black Pilgrimage to Islam*. New York: Oxford University Press, 2002.

Davis, Angela Y. *Angela Davis: An Autobiography*. New York: Random House, 1974.

———. *The Angela Y. Davis Reader*, ed. Joy James. Malden, Mass.: Blackwell, 1998.

———. *Are Prisons Obsolete?* New York: Seven Stories Press, 2003.

———. "From the Prison of Slavery to the Slavery of Prison." In *The Angela Y. Davis Reader*, ed. Joy James. Malden, Mass.: Blackwell, 1998.

Davis, Angela Y., and Bettina Aptheker, eds. *If They Come In the Morning; Voices of Resistance*. New York: Third Press, 1971.

Day, Susie, and Laura Whitehorn. "Human Rights in the United States: The Unfinished Story of Political Prisoners and COINTELPRO." *New Political Science* 23, no. 2 (June 2001): 285–97.

Deffeyes, Kenneth. *Hubbert's Peak: The Impeding World Oil Shortage*. Princeton: Princeton University Press, 2003.

DeSantis, John. *For the Color of His Skin: Yusuf Hawkins and the Trial of Bensonhurst.* New York: Pharos Books, 1991.

Deutsch, Michael E. "The Improper Use of the Federal Grand Jury: An Instrument for the Internment of Political Activists." *Northwestern School of Law Journal of Criminal Law and Criminology* 75 (Winter 1984): 1–45.

Deutsch, Michael E., and Jan Susler. "Political Prisoners in the United States: The Hidden Reality." *Social Justice* 18, no. 3 (2000).

Deutsch, Michael E., Dennis Cunningham, and Elizabeth Fink. "Twenty Years Later: Attica Civil Rights Cases Finally Cleared for Trial." In *Prison Crisis: Critical Readings,* ed. Edward P. Sbarbaro and Robert L. Keller. New York: Harrow and Heston, 1995.

Diaz-Cotto, Juanita. *Gender, Ethnicity and the State: Latina and Latino Prison Politics.* Albany: State University of New York Press, 1996.

Diedrich, Maria, Henry Louis Gates Jr., and Carl Pederson, eds. *Black Imagination and the Middle Passage.* New York: Oxford University Press, 1999.

Dieter, Richard C. *The Death Penalty in Black and White: Who Lives, Who Dies, Who Decides.* Washington, D.C.: Death Penalty Information Center, 1998.

DuBois, W. E. B. *Black Reconstruction in America,* reprint ed. New York: Free Press, 1998.

Durden-Smith, Jo. *Who Killed George Jackson?* New York: Knopf, 1976.

Dyer, Joel. *The Perpetual Prisoner Machine: How America Profits from Crime.* Boulder: Westview Press, 2000.

Eltis, David. "The Volume and Structure of the Transatlantic Slave Trade: A Reassessment." *William and Mary Quarterly* 58, no. 1 (January 2001): 17–31.

Eltis, David, and James Walvin, eds. *The Abolition of the Atlantic Slave Trade: Origins and Effects in Europe, Africa, and the Americas.* Madison: University of Wisconsin Press, 1981.

Eltis, David, David Richardson, and Stephen D. Behrendt. "Patterns in the Transatlantic Slave Trade, 1662–1867." In *Black Imagination and the Middle Passage,* ed. Maria Diedrich, Henry Louis Gates Jr., and Carl Pederson. New York: Oxford University Press, 1999.

Equiano, Olaudah. *Equiano's Travels: The Interesting Narrative of the Life of Olaudah Equiano, or Gustavus Vassa the African* (1789), ed. Paul Edwards. Repr. ed. New York: Praeger, 1966.

Eribon, Didier. *Michel Foucault,* trans. Betsy Wing. Cambridge, Mass.: Harvard University Press, 1991.

Escobar, Edward J. "The Dialectics of Repression: The Los Angeles Police Department and the Chicano Movement, 1968–1971." *Journal of American History* (March 1993): 1483–514.

Estevedeordal, Antoni, Dani Rodrik, Alan M. Taylor, and Andres Velasco, eds. *Integrating the Americas: FTAA and Beyond.* Cambridge, Mass: Harvard University Press, 2004.

Evans, Linda, and Eve Goldberg. *The Prison Industrial Complex and the Global Economy.* San Francisco: AK Press Distribution, 1998.

Eyerman, Ron, and Andrew Jamison. *Social Movements: A Cognitive Approach.* University Park: Pennsylvania State University Press, 1991.

Faith, Karlene. *Unruly Women: The Politics of Confinement and Resistance.* Vancouver: Press Gang Publishers, 1993.

Falcón, Luis Nieves. *Violations of Human Rights in Puerto Rico by the U.S.* San Juan: Ediciones Puerto, 2002.

Fanon, Frantz, *Black Skin, White Masks,* trans. Charles Markmann. New York: Grove Press, 1967.

———. *The Wretched of the Earth,* trans. Constance Farrington. New York: Grove Press, 1963.

Feldman, Allen. *Formations of Violence.* Chicago: University of Chicago Press, 1991.

Fernández, Ronald. *Prisoners of Colonialism: The Struggle for Justice in Puerto Rico.* Monroe, Maine: Common Courage Press, 1994.

Fletcher, B. R., L. D. Shaver, and D. B. Moon, eds. *Women Prisoners: A Forgotten Population.* Westport, Conn.: Praeger, 1993.

Fletcher, Jim, Tanaquil Jones, and Sylvère Lotringer, eds. *Still Black, Still Strong: Survivors of the U.S. War against Black Revolutionaries.* New York: Semiotext(e), 1993.

Foner, Eric. *Reconstruction: America's Unfinished Revolution, 1865–1877.* New York: HarperCollins, 1988.

Foner, Philip S., ed. *Jack London, American Rebel.* New York: Citadel Press, 1947.

———. *The Black Panthers Speak.* Philadelphia: Lippincott, 1970.

Forgacs, David, ed. *The Antonio Gramsci Reader: Selected Writings, 1916–1935.* New York: New York University Press, 2000.

Foucault, Michel. *Discipline and Punish: The Birth of the Prison,* trans. Alan Sheridan. New York: Vintage Books, Random House, 1979.

———. *Power/Knowledge: Selected Interviews and Other Writings, 1972–1977,* ed. Colin Gordon. New York: Pantheon, 1980.

———. "14 January 1976." In *"Society Must Be Defended": Lectures at the Collége de France, 1975–1976,* ed. Mauro Bertani and Alessandro Fontana, trans. Graham Burchell. New York: Picador, 2003.

Franklin, H. Bruce. *Prison Literature in America: The Victim as Criminal and Artist.* New York: Oxford University Press, 1989.

Freed, Donald. *Agony in New Haven: The Trial of Bobby Seale, Ericka Higgins, and the Black Panther Party.* New York: Simon and Schuster, 1973.

Freire, Paulo. *The Pedagogy of the Oppressed,* trans. Myra Bergman Ramos. New York: Continuum, 1981.

Freud, Sigmund. "Psychoanalytic Notes upon an Autobiographical Account of a Case of Paranoia" (1911), reprinted as "Dementia Paranoides." In *Three Case Histories*, ed. Philip Rieff. New York: Collier, 1963.

———. "Thoughts for the Times on War and Death" (1915). In *The Standard Edition*, vol. 14. London: Vintage, 2001.

———. "Why War?" (1933). In *The Standard Edition*, vol. 22. London: Vintage, 2001.

Friedman, Lawrence. *Crime and Punishment in American History*. New York: Basic Books, 1993.

Garland, David. *Mass Imprisonment: Its Causes and Consequences*. London: Sage, 2001.

———. "The Rationalization of Punishment." In *Punishment and Modern Society: A Study in Social Theory*. Chicago: University of Chicago Press, 1990.

Gates Jr., Henry Louis, ed. *Frederick Douglass*. New York: Library of America, 1994.

———. *Six Women's Slave Narratives*. New York: Oxford University Press, 1988.

Gates Jr., Henry Louis, and William L. Andrews, eds. *Pioneers of the Black Atlantic: Five Slave Narratives from the Enlightenment, 1772–1815*. Washington, D.C.: Counterpoint, 1998.

Gause, Gregory. "Be Careful What You Wish For: The Future of U.S.-Saudi Relations." *World Policy Journal* 19, no. 1 (Spring 2002).

Gerassi, John. *The Coming of the New International*. New York: World Publishing, 1970.

Gilmore, Ruth. "Globalisation and U.S. Prison Growth: From Military Keynesianism to Post-Keynesian Militarism." *Race and Class* 40, nos. 2–3 (1998).

Glasser, Ira. "American Drug Laws: The New Jim Crow." *Albany Law Review* 63, no. 703 (2000).

Griffin, Larry J., Paula Clark, and Joanne C. Sandberg. "Narrative and Event: Lynching and Historical Sociology." In *Under Sentence of Death: Lynching in the South*, ed. W. Fitzhugh Brundage. Chapel Hill: University of North Carolina Press, 1997.

Goldberg, David Theo. *Racial Subjects: Writing on Race in America*. New York: Routledge, 1997.

Goldstein, Robert Justin. "An American Gulag? Summary Arrest and Emergency Detention of Political Dissidents in the United States." *Columbia Human Rights Law Review* 10 (1978).

Goodell, Charles. *Political Prisoners in America*. New York: Random House, 1973.

Gracia, Jorge, and Pablo De Greiff, eds. *Hispanics/Latinos in the United States: Ethnicity, Race, and Rights*. New York: Routledge, 2000.

Gramsci, Antonio. *The Prison Notebooks*. New York: Columbia University Press, 1991.

———. *Selections from the Prison Notebooks*, ed. and trans. Quintan Hoare and Geoffrey Nowell Smith. New York: International Publishers, 1971.

Green, Sam, and Bill Seigel (interviewers). *David Gilbert: A Lifetime of Struggle*, ed. Claude Marks and Lisa Rudman. Videocassette, Freedom Archives, San Francisco, 2004.

Greenberg, Karen J., and Joshua L. Dratel, eds. *The Torture Papers: The Road to Abu Ghraib*. New York: Cambridge University Press, 2005.

Grobsmith, E. *Indians in Prison: Incarcerated Native Americans in Nebraska*. Lincoln: University of Nebraska Press, 1994.

Gross, Samuel R., and Robert Mauro. *Death and Discrimination: Racial Disparities in Capital Sentencing*. Boston: Northeastern University Press, 1989.

Groupe d'information sur les prisons (GIP). *Intolerable 1: Enquête dans 20 prisons*. Paris: Editions Champ Libre, 1971.

———. *Intolerable 2: Enquête dans une prison-modèle: Fleury-Mérogis*. Paris: Editions Champ Libre, 1971.

———. *Intolerable 3: L'Assassinat de George Jackson*. Paris: Gallimard, 1971.

———. *Intolerable 4: Suicides de prison*. Paris: Gallimard, 1973.

Hakim, Peter, and Robert Litan, eds. *The Future of North American Integration: Beyond NAFTA*. Washington, D.C.: Brookings Institution, 2000.

Hall, Jacquelyn Dowd. *Revolt against Chivalry: Jesse Daniel Ames and the Women's Campaign against Lynching*. New York: Columbia University Press, 1993.

Halperin, Morton H., Jerry Berman, Robert Borosage, and Christine Marwick. *The Lawless State: The Crimes of the U.S. Intelligence Agencies*. New York: Penguin, 1976.

Hamm, Mark S., Therese Coupez, Francis E. Hoze, and Corey Weinstein. "The Myth of Humane Imprisonment: A Critical Analysis of Severe Discipline in U.S. Maximum Security Prisons, 1945–1990." In *Prison Violence in America*, ed. Michael Braswell, Steven Dillingham, and Reid Montgomery Jr. Cincinnati: Anderson Publishing, 1994.

Haney, Craig. "Infamous Punishment: The Psychological Consequences of Isolation." *National Prison Project Journal* (Spring 1993).

Harding, Vincent. *There Is a River: The Black Struggle for Freedom in America*. New York: Vintage Books, 1981.

Hardt, Michael, and Antonio Negri. *Empire*. Cambridge, Mass.: Harvard University Press, 2000.

———. *Multitude: War and Democracy in the Age of Empire*. New York: Penguin, 2004.

Harlow, Barbara. *Barred: Women, Writing and Political Detention*. Hanover, N.H.: Wesleyan University Press, 1992.

Harris, Cheryl. "Whiteness as Property." *Harvard Law Review* 106, no. 1707 (1993).

Harris, David A. "Factors for Reasonable Suspicion: When Black and Poor Means Stopped and Frisked." *Indiana Law Journal* 69, no. 659 (1994).

———. "The Stories, the Statistics, and the Law: Why 'Driving while Black' Matters." *Minnesota Law Review* 84, no. 265 (1999).

Harris, Trudier. *Exorcising Blackness: Historical and Literary Lynching and Burning Rituals*. Bloomington: Indiana University Press, 1984.

Hartman, Saidiya. "The Position of the Unthought: An Interview with Frank Wilderson." *Qui Parle* 13, no. 2 (2003).

———. *Scenes of Subjection: Terror, Slavery, and Self-making in Nineteenth Century America.* New York: Oxford University Press, 1997.

Hemphill, Essex. *Brother to Brother: New Writings by Black Gay Men.* Boston: Alyson Publications, 1991.

Herman, Judith Lewis. *Trauma and Recovery.* New York: Basic Books, 1992.

Hikmet, Nazim. *Poems of Nazim Hikmet,* trans. Mutlu Konuk Blassing, rev. ed. New York: Persea Books, 2002.

Hill, Robert A., ed. *Marcus Garvey and the Universal Negro Improvement Association Papers,* Vol. 3. Berkeley: University of California Press, 1989.

Hoch, Paul. *White Hero, Black Beast: Racism, Sexism and the Mask of Masculinity.* London: Pluto Press, 1979.

Hocquenghem, Guy. *Homosexual Desire,* trans. Daniella Dangoor. Durham: Duke University Press, 1993.

Holland, Sharon Patricia. *Raising the Dead: Readings of Death and Black Subjectivity.* Durham: Duke University Press, 2000.

Human Rights Watch. *Cold Storage: Super-Maximum Security Confinement in Indiana.* New York: Human Rights Watch, October 1997.

———. "Darfur Destroyed: Ethnic Cleansing by Government and Militia Forces in Western Sudan." *Human Rights Watch Report* 16, no. 6A (May 2004).

———. *No Escape: Male Rape in U.S. Prisons.* New York: Human Rights Watch, 2001.

Hynes, Charles J., and Bob Drury. *Incident at Howard Beach: The Case for Murder.* New York: Putnam, 1990.

In Defense of Self-Defense and Self-Determination: A Conversation with Mabel Williams and Kathleen Cleaver. Videocassette, Freedom Archives and Crash Collision Video Productions, San Francisco, 2004.

Inikori, Joseph, and Stanley Engerman, eds. *The Atlantic Slave Trade.* Durham: Duke University Press, 1992.

International Indian Treaty Council. "Violations of American Human Rights by the United States: Wounded Knee, 1973." In *Illusions of Justice: Human Rights Violations in the United States,* by Lennox S. Hinds. Iowa City: University of Iowa, 1979.

Irwin, John, and James Austin. *It's about Time: America's Imprisonment Binge.* Belmont, Calif.: Wadsworth Publishing, 1997.

Jackson, George. *Blood in My Eye,* New York: Random House, 1972; repr. ed., Baltimore: Black Classic Press, 1990.

———. *Soledad Brother: The Prison Letters of George Jackson.* New York: Bantam, 1970; repr. ed., Chicago: Lawrence Hill Books, 1994.

———. "Toward the United Front." In *If They Come in the Morning: Voices of Resistance,* ed. Angela Y. Davis and Bettina Aptheker. San Francisco: National United Committee to Free Angela Davis, 1971.

Jacobs, James B. *New Perspectives on Prisons and Imprisonment*. Ithaca, N.Y.: Cornell University Press, 1983.

Jaimes, M. Annette, ed. *The State of Native America: Genocide, Colonization, and Resistance*. Boston: South End Press, 1991.

James, Joy. *Resisting State Violence: Radicalism, Gender and Race in U.S. Culture*. Minneapolis: University of Minnesota Press, 1996.

James, Joy, ed. *Imprisoned Intellectuals: America's Political Prisoners Write on Life, Liberation, and Rebellion*. Lanham, Md.: Rowman and Littlefield, 2003.

———. *The New Abolitionists: (Neo)Slave Narratives and Contemporary Prison Writings*. Albany: State University of New York Press, 2005.

———. *States of Confinement: Policing, Detention and Prisons*. New York: St. Martin's Press, 2002, rev. paperback edition.

Johnson, Anita, and Claude Marks, prods. *Prisons on Fire: George Jackson, Attica and Black Liberation*. Audio CD, AK Press, Oakland, Calif., 2002.

Johnson Jr., James Weldon. *Along This Way*. New York: Viking, 1933.

Johnson, Troy, Joan Nagel, and Duane Champagne, eds. *American Indian Activism: Alcatraz to the Longest Walk*. Urbana: University of Illinois Press, 1997.

Jones, Charles E., ed. *The Black Panther Party (Reconsidered)*. Baltimore: Black Classic Press, 1998.

Jordan, Winthrop D. *White over Black*. Chapel Hill: University of North Carolina Press, 1968.

Kay, George F. *The Shameful Trade*. London: Frederick Muller, 1967.

Kohn, Stephen M. *American Political Prisoners: Prosecutions under the Espionage and Sedition Acts*. Westport, Conn.: Praeger, 1994.

Klare, Michael. *Resource Wars: The New Landscape of Global Conflict*. New York: Owl Books, 2002.

Klein, Herbert S. *The Middle Passage: Comparative Studies in the Atlantic Slave Trade*. Princeton: Princeton University Press, 1978.

Laffin, Arthur J. *Swords into Plowshares: A Chronology of Plowshares Actions, 1980–2003*. Chicago: Rose Hill Books, 2004.

Larana, Enrique, Hank Johnston, and Joseph Gusfield, eds. *New Social Movements: From Ideology to Identity*. Philadelphia: Temple University Press, 1994.

Lew-Lee, Lee. *All Power to the People! The Black Panther Party and Beyond*. Videocassette, Filmmakers Library, New York, 1996.

Lee, Wen Ho, and Helen Zia. *My Country versus Me: The First Hand Account by the Los Alamos Scientist Who Was Falsely Accused*. New York: Hyperion, 2002.

Levit, Janet Koven. "Pretextual Traffic Stops: *United States v. Whren* and the Death of *Terry v. Ohio*." *Loyola University of Chicago Law Journal* 28, no. 145 (1996).

Levy, Howard, et al. *Going to Jail: The Political Prisoner.* New York: Grove Press, 1971.

Liberatore, Paul. *The Road to Hell: The True Story of George Jackson, Stephen Bingham, and the San Quentin Massacre* New York: Atlantic Monthly Press, 1996.

Lichtenstein, Alex. *Twice the Work of Free Labor: The Political Economy of Convict Labor in the New South.* New York: Verso, 1995.

Lifton, Robert J. "Doctors and Torture." *New England Journal of Medicine* 351, no. 5 (July 29, 2004).

London, Jack. *The Call of the Wild.* New York: Daily Worker, 1915.

———. "The Pen: Long Days in a County Penitentiary." In *Prison Writing in 20th-Century America*, ed. H. Bruce Franklin. New York: Penguin, 1998.

———. "'Pinched': A Prison Experience." In *Prison Writing in 20th-Century America*, ed. H. Bruce Franklin. New York: Penguin, 1998.

Looby, Christopher. "'Innocent Homosexuality': The Fielder Thesis in Retrospect." In *Mark Twain, Adventures of Huckleberry Finn: A Case Study in Critical Controversy*, ed. Gerald Graff and James Phelan. New York: St. Martin's Press, 1995.

López, Alfredo. *Doña Licha's Island—Modern Colonialism in Puerto Rico.* Boston: South End Press, 1987.

Lorde, Audre. *Uses of the Erotic: The Erotic as Power.* Brooklyn, N.Y.: Out and Out Books, 1978.

Lott, Tommy L., ed. *Subjugation and Bondage: Critical Essays on Slavery and Social Philosophy.* New York: Rowman and Littlefield, 1998.

Lovejoy, Paul E. "The Volume of the Atlantic Slave Trade: A Synthesis." *Journal of African History* 23, no. 4. (1982).

Maclin, Tracey. "*Terry v. Ohio*'s Fourth Amendment Legacy: Black Men and Police Discretion." *Saint John's Law Review* 72, no. 1271 (1998).

Majors, Richard, and Susan Wiener. *Programs That Serve African-American Youth.* Washington, D.C.: Urban Institute, 1995.

Mamiya, Lawrence H. "Minister Louis Farrakhan and the Final Call: Schism in the Muslim Movement." In *The Muslim Community in North America*, ed. Earl H. Waugh, Baha Abu-Laban, and Regula B. Qureshi. Edmonton: University of Alberta Press, 1983.

Mancini, Matthew. *One Dies, Get Another: Convict Leasing in the American South, 1866–1928.* Columbia: University of South Carolina Press, 1996.

Mann, Eric. *Comrade George: An Investigation into the Life, Political Thought, and Assassination of George Jackson.* New York: Harper and Row, 1974.

Manning, Patrick, ed. *Slave Trades, 1500–1800: Globalization of Forced Labor.* London: Ashgate Publishing, 1996.

Marable, Manning. *How Capitalism Underdeveloped Black America.* Boston: South End Press, 1983.

Marable, Manning, and Leith Mullings. *Freedom: A Photographic History of the African American Struggle*. London: Phaidon, 2002.

Marable, Manning, and Leith Mullings, eds. *Let Nobody Turn Us Around: Voices of Resistance, Reform, and Renewal*. Lanham, Md.: Rowman and Littlefield Press, 2000.

Marez, Curtis. *Drug Wars: The Political Economy of Narcotics*. Minneapolis: University of Minnesota Press, 2004.

Marín, Heriberto. *Eran Ellos*. Río Piedras: Ediciones Ciba, 1979.

Marquart, James W., Sheldon Edland-Olson, and Jonathan R. Sorenson. *The Rope, the Chair, and the Needle: Capital Punishment in Texas, 1923–1990*. Austin: University of Texas Press, 1994.

Martínez, Elizabeth. *De Colores Means All of Us: Latina Views for a Multi-Colored Century*. Boston: South End Press, 1998.

Martinot, Steve. "Deconstructing Electoral Politics for 2004." *Synthesis/Regeneration* 33 (2004).

Martinot, Steve, and Jared Sexton. "The Avant-Garde of White Supremacy." *Social Identities* 9, no. 2 (2003).

Massey, Douglas. "The Residential Segregation of Blacks, Hispanics, and Asians, 1970–1990." In *Immigration and Race: New Challenges for American Democracy*, ed. Gerald Jaynes. New Haven: Yale University Press, 2000.

Massey, Douglas, and Hajnal Zoltan. "The Changing Geographic Structure of Black-White Segregation in the United States." *Social Science Quarterly* 76, no. 3 (September 1995): 533–34.

Masters, Jarvis Jay. *Finding Freedom: Writings from Death Row*. Junction City, Calif.: Padma Publishing, 1997.

Mauer, Marc. *Race to Incarcerate*. New York, New Press: 2001.

Mauer, Marc, and Meda Chesney-Lind, eds. *Invisible Punishment: The Collateral Consequences of Mass Imprisonment*. New York: New Press, 2002.

May, John P., and Khalid R. Pitts, eds. *Building Violence: How America's Rush to Incarcerate Creates More Violence*. Thousand Oaks, Calif.: Sage Publications, 2000.

Mbembe, Achille. *On the Postcolony*. Berkeley: University of California Press, 2001.

McGovern, James R. *Anatomy of a Lynching: The Killing of Claude Neal*. Baton Rouge: Louisiana State University Press, 1982.

McWhorter, W. L. *Inmate Society: Legs, Half-Pants and Gunmen: A Study of Inmate Guards*. Saratoga, Calif.: Century Twenty One, 1981.

Meyer, Matt. "Freedom Now." *Nonviolent Activist* (November–December 1993).

Miller, James. *The Passion of Michel Foucault*. Cambridge, Mass.: Harvard University Press, 1993.

Miller, Jerome G. *Search and Destroy: African-American Males in the Criminal Justice System*. Cambridge: Cambridge University Press, 1996.

Minor, W. William, "Political Crime, Political Justice, and Political Prisoners." *Criminology* 12 (February 1975): 385–98.

Morris, Norval, and David J.Rothman, eds. *The Oxford History of the Prison: The Practice of Punishment in Western Society*. New York: Oxford University Press, 1995.

Morrison, Toni. "Home." In *The House That Race Built: Black Americans, U.S. Terrain*, ed. Wahneema H. Lubiano. New York: Pantheon, 1997.

———. "Rootedness: The Ancestor as Foundation." In *Black Women Writers*, ed. Mari Evans. New York: Doubleday, 1984.

Muhammad, Akbar. "Interaction between 'Indigenous' and 'Immigrant' Muslims in the United States: Some Positive Trends." *Hijrah* (March–April 1985).

Nathanson, Nathaniel L. "Freedom of Association and the Quest for Internal Security: Conspiracy from Dennis to Dr. Spock," *Northwestern University Law Review* 65, no. 2 (May–June 2003).

Newton, Huey P. *War against the Panthers: A Study of Repression in America*. New York: Harlem River Press, 1996.

Nkrumah, Kwame. *Handbook of Revolutionary Warfare: A Guide to the Armed Phase of the African Revolution*. New York: International Publishing, 1968.

Northrup, David, ed., *The Atlantic Slave Trade*. Lexington, Mass.: D. C. Heath and Company, 1994.

Nuruddin, Yusuf. "The Five Percenters: A Teenage Nation of Gods and Earths." In *Muslim Communities in North America*, ed. Yvonne Haddad and Jane Idleman Smith. Albany: State University of New York Press, 1994.

Obadele, Imari A. *Revolution and Nation-Building: Strategy for Building the Black Nation in America*. Detroit: House of Songhay, 1970.

———. "A People's Revolt for Power and an Up-Turn in the Black Condition: An Appeal and a Challenge." In *The New Abolitionists: (Neo)Slave Narratives and Contemporary Prison Writings*, ed. Joy James. Albany: State University of New York Press, 2005.

O'Hare, Kate Richards. *In Prison*. Seattle: University of Washington Press, 1976.

Oliverio, Annamarie. *The State of Terror*. Albany: State University of New York Press, 1998.

Omi, Michael, and Howard Winant. *Racial Formation in the United States: From the 1960s to the 1990s*. New York: Routledge, 1994.

Oppenheimer, Martin. *The Urban Guerrilla*. Chicago: Quadrangle Books, 1969.

O'Reilly, John, dir. *Jalil Muntaqim: Voice of Liberation*, ed. and prod. Eve Goldberg and Claude Marks. Videocassette, Freedom Archives, San Francisco, 2004.

O'Reilly, Kenneth. "The FBI and the Politics of the Riots, 1964–1968." *Journal of American History* 75, no. 1 (June 1988): 91–114.

Oshinsky, David. *Worse than Slavery: Parchman Farm and the Jim Crow Justice System*. New York: Free Press, 1996.

Owen, Barbara. *"In the Mix": Struggle and Survival in a Women's Prison*. Albany: State University of New York Press, 1998.

Paralatici, Jose Ché. *Sentencia Impuesta: 100 Años de Encarcelamientos per la Independencia de Puerto Rico*. San Juan: Ediciones Puerto, 2004.

Parenti, Christian. "Assata Shakur Speaks from Exile: Postmodern Maroon in the Ultimate Palenque." z *Magazine* (March 1998): 27–32.

———. *Lockdown America: Police and Prisons in the Age of Crisis*. New York: Verso, 1999.

Patterson, Orlando. *Slavery and Social Death: A Comparative Study*. Cambridge, Mass.: Harvard University Press, 1982.

Peltier, Leonard. *Prison Writings: My Life Is My Sun Dance*. New York: St. Martin's Press, 1999.

Perkinson, Robert. "Shackled Justice: Florence Federal Penitentiary and the New Politics of Punishment." *Social Justice* 21, no. 3 (Fall 1994): 117–32.

Pinar, William F. *The Gender of Racial Politics and Violence in America: Lynching, Prison Rape, and the Crisis of Masculinity*. New York: Peter Lang, 2001.

Pisciotta, Alexander W. *Benevolent Repression: Social Control and the American Reformatory-Prison Movement*. New York: New York University Press, 1994.

Political Prisoners in the United States. Washington, D.C.: Center for Constitutional Rights, September 1988.

Polner, Murray, and Jim O'Grady. *Disarmed and Dangerous: The Radical Life and Times of Daniel and Phillip Berrigan*. Boulder: Westview Press, 1998.

Postma, Johannes. *The Atlantic Slave Trade*. Westport, Conn.: Greenwood Press, 2003.

Prashad, Vijay. *Keeping Up with the Dow Joneses: Debt, Prison, Workfare*. Boston: South End Press, 2003.

Pratt, John. *Punishment and Civilization*. London: Sage Publications, 2002.

Raper, Arthur F. *The Tragedy of Lynching*, repr. ed. Chapel Hill: University of North Carolina Press, 1933; Montclair, N.J.: Patterson Smith, 1969.

Ravenhill, John. *Asian Pacific Economic Cooperation: The Construction of Pacific Rim Regionalism*. New York: Cambridge University Press, 2001.

Reagon, Bernice Johnson. "Coalition Politics: Turning the Century." In *Home Girls: A Black Feminist Anthology*, ed. Barbara Smith. Albany: Kitchen Table/Women of Color Press, 1983.

Roberts, Les, Riyadh Lafta, Richard Garfield, Jamal Khudhairi, and Gilbert Burnham. "Mortality before and after the 2003 Invasion of Iraq: Cluster Sample Survey." *Lancet* 364, no. 9448 (November 20, 2004): 1857–64.

———. "Mortality after the 2003 Invasion of Iraq: A Cross-sectional Cluster Sample Survey." *Lancet* 368, no. 95 45 (October 2006): 1421–28.

Robinson, Greg. *By Order of the President: FDR and the Internment of Japanese Americans*. Cambridge, Mass.: Harvard University Press, 2003.

Robinson, Sally. *Marked Men: White Masculinity in Crisis*. New York: Columbia University Press, 2000.

Rodríguez, Dylan. *Forced Passages: Imprisoned Radical Intellectuals and the Formation of the United States Prison Regime*. Minneapolis: University of Minnesota Press, 2005.

Ross, Luana. *Inventing the Savage: The Social Construction of Native American Criminality*. Austin: University of Texas Press, 1998.

Rotman, Edgardo. "The Failure of Reform: United States, 1865–1965." In *The Oxford History of the Prison: The Practice of Punishment in Western Society*, ed. Norval Morris and David J. Rothman. New York: Oxford University Press, 1998.

Sabatini, Rafael. *The Writings of Rafael Sabatini*. Boston: Houghton Mifflin, 1924.

Sabo, Donn, Terry A. Kupers, and Willie London, eds. *Prison Masculinities*. Philadelphia: Temple University Press, 2001.

Scott, Peter Dale. *Drugs, Oil, and War: The United States in Afghanistan, Columbia, and Indochina*. New York: Rowman and Littlefield, 2003.

Scully, Judith. "Killing the Black Community: A Commentary on the United States War on Drugs." In *Policing the National Body: Race, Gender, and Criminalization*, ed. Jael Silliman and Anannya Bhattacharjee. Boston: South End Press, 2002.

Shakur, Assata. *Assata: An Autobiography*. Chicago: Lawrence Hill Books, 1987.

Shakur, Sanyika. "Flowing in File: The George Jackson Phenomenon." *Wazo Weusi (Think Black): A Journal of Black Thought* 2, no. 2 (1995).

Shor, Ira. *Culture Wars: School and Society in the Conservative Restoration*. Chicago: University of Chicago Press, 1992.

Shora, Kareem. "Guilty of Flying while Brown." *Air and Space Lawyer* 1, no. 17 (2002).

Silverman, Kaja. *Male Subjectivity at the Margins*. New York: Routledge, 1992.

Simon, John K. "Michel Foucault on Attica: An Interview." *Telos*, no. 19 (1974): 154–61.

Sklar, Morton, ed. *Racial and Ethnic Discrimination in the United States: The Status of Compliance by the U.S. Government with the International Convention on the Elimination of Racial Discrimination*. Washington, D.C.: Coalition against Torture and Racial Discrimination, 1998.

———. *Torture in the United States: The Status of Compliance by the U.S. Government with the International Convention against Torture and Other Cruel, Inhuman or Degrading Treatment or Punishment*. Washington, D.C.: World Coalition against Torture, 1998.

Smith, Jennifer. *An International History of the Black Panther Party*. New York: Garland Publishing, 1999.

Smith, Theophus Harold. *Conjuring Culture: Biblical Formations in Black America*. New York: Oxford University Press, 1994.

Solzhenitsyn, Aleksandr. *The Gulag Archipelago, 1918–1956*, trans. Thomas P. Whitney. New York: Harper and Row, 1973.

Spillers, Hortense. *Black, White, and in Color: Essays on American Literature and Culture.* Chicago: University of Chicago Press, 2003.

Staples, William G. *The Culture of Surveillance: Discipline and Social Control in the United States.* New York: St. Martin's Press, 1997.

Stoler, Ann Laura. *Carnal Knowledge and Imperial Power: Race and the Intimate in Colonial Rule.* Berkeley: University of California Press, 2002.

————. "Toward a Genealogy of Racisms: The 1976 Lectures at the Collége de France." In Stoler, *Race and the Education of Desire: Foucault's* History of Sexuality *and the Colonial Order of Things.* Durham: Duke University Press, 1995.

————. *Race and the Education of Desire: Foucault's* History of Sexuality *and the Colonial Order of Things.* Durham: Duke University Press, 1995.

Street, Paul. "Race, Prison, and Poverty: The Race to Incarcerate in the Age of Correctional Keynesianism." *Z Magazine* (May 2001): 26.

Susler, Jan. "Puerto Rican Political Prisoners." *Radical Philosophy Review* 3, no. 1 (January 2000).

————. "Unreconstructed Revolutionaries: Today's Puerto Rican Political Prisoners of War." In *The Puerto Rican Movement,* ed. Andres Torres and Jose E. Valazquez. Philadelphia: Temple University Press, 1998.

Tate, Greg. *Everything but the Burden: What White People Are Taking from Black Culture.* New York: Harlem Moon, 2003.

Theoharis, Athan. *The FBI: An Annotated Bibliography and Research Guide.* New York: Garland Publishing, 1994.

Tolnay, Stewart E., and E. M. Beck. *A Festival of Violence: An Analysis of Southern Lynchings, 1882–1930.* Urbana: University of Illinois Press, 1995.

Tomsho, Robert. *The American Sanctuary Movement.* Austin: Texas Monthly Press, 1987.

Tonry, Michael. *Malign Neglect—Race, Crime and Punishment in America.* New York: Oxford University Press, 1995.

Torres, Andrés, and José E. Velázquez. *The Puerto Rican Movement: Voices from the Diaspora.* Philadelphia: Temple University Press, 1998.

United Nations. *Standard Minimum Rules for the Treatment of Prisoners.* New York, 1984.

U.S. Commission on Civil Rights. *The Navajo Nation: An American Colony.* Washington, D.C.: U.S. Government Printing Office, September 1975.

U.S. Senate. *Final Report of the Select Committee to Study Government Operations with Respect to Intelligence Activities.* Washington, D.C.: U.S. Government Printing Office, 1976.

Uviller, H. Richard. *Virtual Justice: The Flawed Prosecution of Crime in America.* New Haven: Yale University Press, 1996.

Wagner, Peter. *The Prison Index: Taking the Pulse of the Crime Control Industry.* Northampton, Mass.: Western Prison Project and Prison Policy Initiative, 2003.

Wagner-Pacifici, Robin. *Theorizing the Standoff: Contingency in Action*. New York: Cambridge University Press, 2000.

Walker, Samuel. *The Police in America: An Introduction*. New York: McGraw-Hill, 1999.

Wall Tappings: An International Anthology of Women's Prison Writings, 200 A.D. to the Present. New York: Feminist Press, 2002.

Watterson, Kathryn. *Women in Prison*. Boston: Northeastern University Press, 1996.

Wells, Ida B. *A Red Record* (1892). Repr. in *Southern Horrors and Other Writings: The Anti-Lynching Campaign of Ida B. Wells, 1892–1900*, ed. Jacqueline Jones Royster. Boston: Bedford Books, 1997.

West, Cornel. "Black Strivings in a Twilight Civilization." In *The Future of the Race*, ed. Henry Louis Gates Jr. and Cornel West. New York: Alfred A Knopf, 1996.

———. *Race Matters*. Boston: Beacon Press, 1993.

White, Walter. *Rope and Faggot: A Biography of Judge Lynch*. New York: Alfred A. Knopf, 1929.

Whitehorn, Laura. "Preventive Detention: A Prevention of Human Rights?" In *Cages of Steel: The Politics of Imprisonment in the United States*, ed. Ward Churchill and Jim Vander Wall. Washington, D.C.: Maisonneuve Press, 1992.

Wicker, Tom. *A Time to Die*. New York: Quandrangle/New York Times Books, 1975.

Wiegman, Robyn. *American Anatomies: Theorizing Race and Gender*. Durham: Duke University Press, 1995.

———. "The Anatomy of Lynching." *Journal of the History of Sexuality* 3, no. 3 (January 1993): 445–67.

Wilderson III, Frank. "Gramsci's Black Marx: Whither the Slave in Civil Society." *Social Identities* 9, no. 2 (2003).

———. "The Prison Slave as Hegemony's (Silent) Scandal." *Social Justice* 30, no. 2 (2003): 18–27.

Williams, Eric. *Capitalism and Slavery*, reprint ed. Chapel Hill: University of North Carolina Press, 1994.

Williams, William Appleman. *Empire as a Way of Life*. New York: Oxford University Press, 1980.

Williamson, Joel. *The Crucible of Race: Black–White Relations in the American South since Emancipation*. New York: Oxford University Press, 1984.

Wilson, William Julius. *The Truly Disadvantaged: The Inner City, the Underclass, and Public Policy*. Chicago: University of Chicago Press, 1987.

———. *When Work Disappears: The World of the New Urban Poor*. New York: Alfred A. Knopf, 1996.

Woodward, C. Vann. *The Origins of the New South, 1877–1913*, reprint ed. Baton Rouge: Louisiana State University Press, 1971.

Wright, George C. *Racial Violence in Kentucky, 1865–1940: Lynchings, Mob Rule, and "Legal Lynchings."* Baton Rouge: Louisiana State University Press, 1990.

Wu, Frank. *Yellow: Race in America beyond Black and White*. New York: Basic Books, 2001.

Yancey, George. *Who Is White? Latinos, Asians, and the New Black/Nonblack Divide*. Boulder: Lynne Rienner, 2003.

Yee, Min S. *The Melancholy History of Soledad Prison*. New York: Harper's Magazine Press, 1973.

Zinn, Howard. *A People's History of the United States*. New York: Harper and Row, 1980.

———. *You Can't Be Neutral on a Moving Train*. Boston: Beacon Press, 1994.

Žižek, Slavoj. *For They Know Not What They Do: Enjoyment as a Political Factor*. New York: Verso, 1991.

Zulaika, Josebam and William A. Douglass. *Terror and Taboo: The Follies, Fables, and Faces of Terrorism*. New York: Routledge, 1996.

Contributors

Hishaam Aidi, a research fellow at Columbia University's Middle East Institute, works on the university's Islam in New York Project, sponsored by the Ford Foundation. His work is published in *Middle East Report*, and a longer version of the essay printed in this volume appears in his anthology *Islam and Urban Youth Culture*, co-edited with Yusuf Nuruddin.

Dhoruba Bin Wahad (Richard Moore), a leader of the New York chapter of the Black Panther Party, is a former political prisoner. Falsely incarcerated for over nineteen years as a result of COINTELPRO operations, Bin Wahad was released from prison in 1990; the District Attorney's Office of New York dismissed his case in 1995. Since his release, he has founded the Campaign to Free Black and New Afrikan Political Prisoners and established the Institute for the Development of Pan-African policy in Accra, Ghana. His writing appears in *Still Black, Still Strong, Criminal Injustice: Confronting the Prison Crisis*, and *Imprisoned Intellectuals*.

Marilyn Buck is a white antiracist political prisoner serving a virtual life sentence for her work with the Black Liberation Army. Her writing appears in the *Social Justice*; *Enemies of the State*; *Criminal Injustice: Confronting the Prison Crisis*; and *Imprisoned Intellectuals*. She is currently incarcerated in a California prison: 00482–285, 5701 8th Street, Camp Parks B, Federal Corrections Institute, Dublin, Calif. 94568.

Catherine von Bülow was a member of the *Groupe de Informacion sur les Prisons* (Prison Information Group, or GIP), a collective of French writers, including Michel Foucault, interested in penal reform.

Marshall Eddie Conway, a former Black Panther Party member incarcerated for over three decades as a result of COINTELPRO, is a political prisoner serving a sentence of life plus thirty years. Despite a lack of evidence against Conway, the government has refused to release him or grant him a new trial. He has founded numerous prison-based educational programs and has led legislative battles to improve basic living conditions in Maryland state correctional institutions. Conway is completing his master's degree and actively working to reopen public hearings on the legacies of the U.S. government's counterintelligence program. Marshall Eddie Conway is held in a Maryland prison: #116469, P.O. Box 534, Jessup, Md., 20794.

Susie Day, a freelance writer, lives in New York City and contributes to feminist and lesbian/gay publications, including *Sojourner, Advocate, Z Magazine, LGNY,* and *Outlines.*

Daniel Defert, a noted French sociologist and longtime partner of Michel Foucault, taught at the University of Paris VIII. In 1984, he founded AIDES, the first French association to fight against AIDS, and served as president of the organization until 1992. A member of Le Haute Comité de la Santé Publique (High Committee of Public Health) in France until 1998, he continues to speak publicly about health, AIDS, and the political economy of disease.

Madeleine Dwertman graduated from Brown University with a bachelor of arts in Africana studies and American civilization. She is active with a number of organizations working on issues of policing and incarceration.

Michel Foucault (1926–84), a prominent French philosopher, is the author of numerous books. His publications include *Madness and Civilization, The Order of Things, Discipline and Punish, The History of Sexuality* (3 vols.), *"Society Must Be Defended": Lectures at the Collége de France 1975–1976,* and *Abnormal: Lectures at the Collége de France 1974–1975.*

Carol Gilbert, O.P., a Dominican nun and a peace activist for over twenty-five years, is a member of the Sacred Earth and Space Plowshares. She organizes at Jonah House in Baltimore. Sister Gilbert was charged with obstruction of national defense and was sentenced to a thirty-three month prison sentence for her participation in an anti-nuclear warfare protest in October 2002.

Sirène Harb, assistant professor of English at the American University of Beirut, specializes in postcolonial studies, literary theory, women's studies, and American literature. Harb has translated three novels: *Le mystère des six compagnons* (French to Arabic, as *Sirr al-asdiqua al-sitta,* 1993), *No Promise of Love* (English to Arabic, as *La wou'oud bil houbb,* 1994), and *Les six compagnons et le poste èmetteur* (French to Arabic as *Al-asdiqua al-sitta wa al-moughamarat fi al-bahr,* 1993). Her writing also appears in *Discursive Geographies* and *Romance Languages Annual.*

Rose Heyer is the Geographic Information Systems (GIS) analyst for Prison Policy Initiative in Massachusetts and consults with other organizations on the use of GIS for criminal-justice-reform advocacy.

George Jackson (1941–71), former field marshal of the Black Panther Party and a founder of the Soledad Brothers, was killed by San Quentin prison guards on August 12, 1971. His books include *Soledad Brother: The Prison Letters of George Jackson* and *Blood in My Eye.* He completed the latter a week before his death.

Joy James is John B. and John T. McCoy presidential professor and chair of Africana studies and college professor in political science at Williams College in Williamstown, Massachusetts. She is the author of *Shadowboxing: Representations of Black Feminist Politics*; *Transcending the Talented Tenth: Black Leaders and American Intellectuals*; and *Resisting State Violence*. Her edited collections include *The New Abolitionists: (Neo)Slave Narratives and Contemporary Prison Writings*; *Imprisoned Intellectuals*; *States of Confinement*; and *The Angela Y. Davis Reader*. James is currently writing a book on the Central Park case.

Oscar López Rivera was actively involved in the Puerto Rican Independence Movement of the 1960s, '70s, and '80s. In 1981, he was convicted of seditious conspiracy ("to overthrow the government of the United States in Puerto Rico by force") and armed robbery. Sentenced to fifty-years in prison, with an additional fifteen years for conspiracy to escape in 1988, he declined the Clinton administration's 1999 offer of a ten-year sentence reduction in exchange for his renunciation of armed struggle. During his incarceration, López Rivera has written many short stories and articles for *Libértad* and *Patria Libre*. He is currently serving his seventy-year sentence at the U.S. Penitentiary at Terre Haute: #87651–024, P.O. Box 33, Terre Haute, Ind. 47808.

Manning Marable is professor of public affairs, political science, and African-American studies at Columbia University. He was the founding director of the Center for Contemporary Black History, established in 2002, and the Institute for Research in African-American Studies, where he served from 1993 to 2003. A prolific author, Marable's publications include: *Beyond Black and White: Transforming African-American Politics*; *The Crisis of Color and Democracy*; *The Great Wells of Democracy: The Meaning of Race in American Life*; and *Living Black History: How Reimagining the African-American Past can Remake America's Racial Future*. Among his works-in-progress is a comprehensive biography of Malcolm X, entitled *Malcolm X: A Life of Reinvention*.

William F. Pinar teaches curriculum theory at the University of British Columbia, where he holds a Canada Research Chair and directs the Centre for the Study of the Internationalization of Curriculum Studies. In 2000, Pinar received an AERA (American Educational Research Association) Lifetime Achievement Award; in 2004, he received an American Educational Association Outstanding Book Award for *What Is Curriculum Theory?* He is the author of *Autobiography, Politics, and Sexuality*, *The Gender of Racial Politics and Violence in America*, and the forthcoming *The Body of the Father and the Race of the Son: Noah, Schreber, and the Curse of the Covenant*.

Dylan Rodríguez, an associate professor in the Department of Ethnic Studies at the University of California, Riverside, is the author of *Forced Passages: Imprisoned Radical Intellectuals and the U.S. Prison Regime*. A founding member of the Critical Resistance organizing collective, Rodríguez is active in a variety of struggles for social change.

Jared Sexton is assistant professor of Africana studies at the University of California, Irvine. His dissertation, "The Politics of Interracial Sexuality in the Post-Civil Rights Era U.S.," lays the groundwork for his forthcoming book, tentatively titled *Amalgamation Schemes: Interracial Sexual Politics and Anti-Blackness in the Americas*," a critical mediation on the "Latin Americanization of U.S. race relations."

Laura Whitehorn is a former political prisoner, having spent over fourteen years in federal prison for "conspiracy to oppose, protest and change policies and practices of the U.S. government in domestic and international matters by violent and illegal means." The "illegal means" included bombings of government and military targets, in which no one was injured. Both before and after her incarceration, she has worked in campaigns to release leftist political prisoners and to challenge criminal-justice policies against all U.S. prisoners. She is currently an editor at *POZ*, a magazine for people with HIV. She lives in New York City with her partner Susie Day. Her writing appears in *States of Confinement* and *Imprisoned Intellectuals*.

Frank B. Wilderson III, assistant professor in African American studies and drama at the University of California, Irvine, is a documentary filmmaker. A longtime human-rights activist and organizer against racism and the prison-industrial complex, he spent five and a half years in South Africa in underground structures and as an elected official in the African National Congress. Wilderson's memoir, *Incognegro*, and a film studies book, *Red, White, and Black: Cinema and the Structure of U.S. Antagonisms* (Duke University Press) are forthcoming.

Permissions

Contributors to this volume, as well as *Social Justice, Middle East Report*, and Black Classic Press, granted free access to reprint their respective essays. Lawrence Hill Books and MIT Press provided essays for a reduced fee.

Illustration: "U.S. Prison Proliferation: 1900–2004," by Rose Heyer, appears by permission of the author/artist.

Chapter 1: "The Prison Slave as Hegemony's (Silent) Scandal," by Frank B. Wilderson III, is reprinted by permission of the author and of *Social Justice: A Journal of Crime, Conflict and World Order*.

Chapter 2: "Forced Passages," by Dylan Rodríguez, appears by permission of the author.

Chapter 3: "Sorrow: The Good Soldier and the Good Woman," by Joy James, appears by permission of the author.

Chapter 4: "War Within: A Prison Interview with Dhoruba Bin Wahad" is reprinted by permission of MIT Press.

Chapter 5: "Domestic Warfare: A Dialogue with Marshall Eddie Conway" appears by permission of Marshall Eddie Conway.

Chapter 6: Excerpts from *Soledad Brother: The Prison Letters of George Jackson* and *Blood in My Eye*, by George Jackson, are reprinted by permission of Lawrence Hill Books and Black Classic Press, respectively.

Chapter 7: *The Assassination of George Jackson*, by Michel Foucault, Catherine von Bülow, and Daniel Defert, was originally published in 1971 by Gallimard, but the press has no copyright records for the pamphlet. The English translation of "The Masked Assassination" and the introduction appear by permission of the translator, Sirène Harb.

Chapter 8: "A Century of Colonialism: One Hundred Years of Puerto Rican Resistance," by Oscar López Rivera, appears by permission of the author.

Chapter 9: "Racial Profiling and the Societies of Control," by Jared Sexton, appears by permission of the author.

Chapter 10: "Jihadis in the Hood: Race, Urban Islam, and the War on Terror," by Hishaam Aidi, is reprinted by permission of the author and *Middle East Report*.

Chapter 11: "The Effects of Repression on Women in Prison," by Marilyn Buck, appears by permission of the author.

Chapter 12: "Ponderings from the Eternal Now," by Carol Gilbert, O.P., appears by permission of the author.

Chapter 13: "Resisting the Ordinary," by Laura Whitehorn (with Susie Day), appears by permission of Laura Whitehorn.

Chapter 14: "Cultures of Torture," by William F. Pinar, appears by permission of the author.

Chapter 15: "Katrina's Unnatural Disaster: A Tragedy of Black Suffering and White Denial," by Manning Marable, appears by permission of the author and the journal *Souls: A Critical Journal of Black Politics, Culture and Society.*

Index

Abu Ghraib: doctors and, 66; legacy of lynching and, 64, 195, 207, 296; sexualization of torture and, 62, 297–98, 300–302; torture in U.S. prisons and, 274–77, 279–87. *See also* Iraq war

Abu-Jamal, Mumia, 281

ACLU (American Civil Liberties Union), 200, 202, 275

Acquired Immune Deficiency Syndrome (AIDS), 61, 236, 272

ADX Control Prison (Colo.), 48–49, 159, 280, 286

Afghanistan, xv, 68, 72, 282

Africa, 63, 67–68, 71, 98. *See also* Middle Passage; slave trade

African Americans: Hurricane Katrina and, 306–9, 312, 314 n. 18; incarceration of, xv, 7, 22, 195, 229; Islam and, 220–26, 230–33; as perceived terrorists, 220–21. *See also* blacks, blackness

AFSC (American Friends Service Committee), 113

Aidi, Hishaam, 193, 219–35

AIDS (Acquired Immune Deficiency Syndrome), 61, 236, 272

AIDS Counseling and Education Project (ACE), 246; in prisons, 281–82

AIM (American Indian Movement), 98, 105, 168, 275, 288 n. 5

Alabama, 294–95, 306

Albizu Campos, Don Pedro, 160, 163–67, 185 n. 19

Alderson Penitentiary (W.Va.), 176, 236, 249, 252–65

Alexander, Lamar, 311

Ali, Duse Muhammad, 222

Ali, Noble Drew, 222

Alianza Islamica of New York, 225–27

Alien and Sedition Acts (1798), 187 n. 25

All-Afrikan Peoples' Revolutionary Party (A-ARPR), 100, 117 n. 4

alliances, 3, 14 n. 4, 23–33, 116, 206, 208–12

al-Qaeda, 52, 219

al-Rukn, 219

Amazon (Brazil), 65

American Civil Liberties Union (ACLU), 200, 202, 275

American Friends Service Committee (AFSC), 113

American Indian Movement (AIM), 98, 105, 168, 275, 288 n. 5

American Indians, xv, 22, 30–31, 34 n. 11, 81

Amnesty International, 202, 275

antiterrorism. *See* terrorism; "war on terror"

antiwar movement, 107, 205–6, 248, 272. *See also* Plowshares; Vieques

Arab League, 223

Arabs, Arab Americans: community organizing and, 209; internment of, 22; profiling of, 207, 210

Arendt, Hannah, 11–12 n. 1

Armed Forces of National Liberation (FALN), 90, 94 n. 11, 172, 183 n. 5, 188 n. 29. *See also* Puerto Rican Independence Movement

Armed Revolutionary Forces of the People (FARB), 173. *See also* Puerto Rican Independence Movement arms trafficking, 67

Arriví, Carlos Soto, 173, 185–86 n. 21

Ashcroft, John, 61–62, 236, 280

Ashkelon Prison (Israel), 157, 158 n. 16

Asians, Asian Americans, xv, 207, 209–11, 221

Assassination of George Jackson, The, 5, 21, 138–39, 140–57

Atlanta, 185 n. 19; Buttermilk Bottom, 88, 94 n. 9

Attica Prison (N.Y.), 7–9, 14 n. 9, 157, 228, 274–75, 280, 287 n. 2, 298–99

"Avant-garde of White Supremacy" (Martinot), 25

Ayers, Edward L., 292–93

Baltimore, 96, 248

Bandele, Asha, 6–7

Banjoko, Adissa, 231

Baraldini, Silvia, 275, 280–81, 288 n. 3

Barceló, Carlos Romero, 178, 185–86 n. 21

Beauchamp, Hiram, 160, 163

Behrendt, Stephen, 45

Belfield, David (Hasan Tantai), 220

Bell, Herman, 275, 279–80, 288 n. 6

Beltràn, Haydee, 174–75, 188–89 n. 32

Bennett, William, 310

Bensonhurst, 85, 93 n. 6

ben-Yahweh, Shemuel (Imari A. Obadele), 11, 117 n. 7

Berrigan, Daniel, 118 n. 8, 252, 269 n. 8

Berrigan, Philip, 118 n. 8, 269 n. 8, 270 n. 13

Berríos, Luz, 176

Berríos, Rubén, 171, 185–86 n. 21

"Big Pun" (Christopher Rios), 71

Billingslea, Fred, 123

Binetti, Nicholas, 74

Bingham, Steven, 143–45

bin Laden, Osama, 193, 219

Bin Wahad, Dhoruba (Richard Moore), 19, 74–95

Blackburn, Robert, 249–51, 267 n. 5

Black Guerrilla Family, 120

Blackhawk Rangers, 93 n. 3

black liberation, 32, 206, 216 n. 36

Black Liberation Army (BLA), 20, 60–61, 78, 83, 105, 194–95, 236

Black Liberation Movement, 112, 120, 160

Black Panther Party (BPP): Baltimore Chapter of, 96–97, 99–100; Chicago Chapter of, 93 n. 3, 137 n. 12; founding of, 136 n. 9; government repression of, 83–84, 89–91, 92 n. 1, 99–104, 112, 116 n. 3, 117 n. 6; New Haven Chapter of, 100, 117 n. 5; New York Chapter of, 74–79, 87, 101, 117 n. 5; Oakland Chapter of, 77, 99, 117 n. 4; political education programs of, 81; self-defense viewed by, 84–86; Southern California Chapter of, 135 n. 6; survival programs of, 86, 98–99, 102, 110–11, 154; Ten-Point Platform of, 81. *See also* COINTELPRO

Black Power Movement, 112, 120, 160

blacks, blackness: criminalization of, xii, 81–82, 87, 195, 290, 310; disenfranchisement of, 203–4, 215 n. 26; gender and, 58–73; genealogy of prison regime and, 39–54; identity theft of, 5–9; positionality of, 19, 23–33, 197–202, 206–12, 215–16 n. 29; revolutionary potential of, 131–33. *See also* African Americans; Black Panther Party; prisoners; racism

Blackstone Rangers, 219

Blood in My Eye (Jackson), xvi, 21, 58, 121, 131–35

Blyden, Edward, 221–22

Bosch, Orlando, 180

Bosnia and Herzegovina, 73

Bottom, Anthony (Jalil Muntaqim), 279, 288 n. 6

Bronx, 74, 227

Brooklyn, 226, 272

Brown, Michael, 306
Brown, Samuel, 281
Bruder, Thomas, 298
Buck, Marilyn, 89, 194, 236–47
Bukhari-Alston, Safiya, 58, 60–61
Bureau of Indian Affairs, 275
Bush, George H. W., 180
Bush, George W.: on Abu Ghraib, 290, 302;
    environmental policy of, 72; faith-based
    initiatives of, 233; Hurricane Katrina
    and, 305–8; in 2000 election, 203–8, 214
    n. 22; Vieques naval base closed by, 181;
    "war on terror" and, xvii n. 4, 195, 201
Bush, Jeb, 203–4
Busta Rhymes, 231

California, 101, 122–23, 152. *See also* Los
    Angeles
California Correctional Peace Officers As-
    sociation (CCPOA), 49–50
California Youth Authority, 120
Calipatria State Prison, 49
Camacho Negrón, Antonio, 188 n. 32
Cambodia, 98, 108
Cameron, James, 310–11
Campos, Don Pedro Albizu, 160, 163–67,
    185 n. 19
capitalism, 27–29, 46, 98, 106, 111, 131, 134
Cardozo-Freeman, Inez, 297
Carmichael, Stokely (Kwame Toure), 100,
    117 n. 4
Carr, James, 120, 144
Carriles, Luis Posada, 181
Cartenga Flores, Miguel, 187 n. 21
Carter, "Bunchy" Alprentice, 122, 130, 135
    n. 6
Carter, Jimmy, 172, 186 n. 21
castration, 291, 302 n. 15. *See also* lynching
Castro, Fidel, 180–81, 184 n. 16
CCPOA (California Correctional Peace
    Officers Association), 49–50

Central Intelligence Agency (CIA), 108,
    118–19 n. 12; "Operation Chaos" of, 83; in
    Vietnam, 80, 82, 93 n. 7; in Wen Ho Lee
    Affair, 217 n. 39
Cerro Maravilla Massacre, 172–73, 178,
    185–87 n. 21
Chicago, 64, 79, 89, 120, 159, 175, 177, 180,
    187 n. 22, 219
Chicanos, 81, 127, 129, 226
Chihuahua, 64
China, 71, 91, 105
Christianity, 221, 225, 233, 250–51, 263–64
Christmas, William, 121, 157 n. 4
Church Committee, 78, 80, 93 n. 4. *See also*
    COINTELPRO
CIA (Central Intelligence Agency), 108,
    118–19 n. 12; "Operation Chaos of," 83; in
    Vietnam, 80, 82, 93 n. 7; in Wen Ho Lee
    Affair, 217 n. 39
Ciudad Juárez, 64
Civiletti, Benjamin R., 185–86 n. 21
civil rights movement, 201, 272
civil society, 23–33, 54, 197–98, 210–12
Civil War, 208, 293
Clarence 13X, 230–31
Claridad, 169, 184 n. 17
Clark, Mark, 137 n. 12
Cleaver, Eldridge, 122, 129–30, 135 n. 6, 136
    n. 9, 154
Clinton, Bill, 206; Puerto Rican prisoners
    granted clemency by, 159, 175, 180, 188 n.
    32, 281; Work Opportunity and Personal
    Responsibility Act signed by, 228–29
Clinton Correctional Facility (N.Y.), 280,
    282
Cluchette, John, 21, 121, 130, 137 n. 13, 141,
    150, 156
coalitions, 3, 14 n. 4, 23–33, 116, 206, 208–12
Coetzee, J. M., 29–30
COINTELPRO (FBI Counterintelligence
    Program): agent-provocateurs used by,

Falcón, Luis Nieves, 161–62, 182 n. 1

family, 58–59, 64, 66–72, 225–26, 229, 243

Fanon, Frantz, 24–25, 31, 32, 111–12, 238

Fahrenheit 9/11 (documentary), 62, 202–3

FARB (Armed Revolutionary Forces of the People), 173. *See also* Puerto Rican Independence Movement

Farrakhan, Louis, 222–23, 227–28, 233

FBI (Federal Bureau of Investigation), 20; domestic repression and, 119 n. 16, 275, 281, 285; Prison Activist Program of, 90; in Puerto Rico, 187 n. 21, 188 n. 27; in Wen Ho Lee Affair, 217 n. 39. *See also* COINTELPRO

FEMA (Federal Emergency Management Agency), 305–7. *See also* Hurricane Katrina

Fernández, Ronald, 177

Figueroa Cordero, Andrés, 167, 172, 187 n. 23

Five Percent Nation (Nation of Gods and Earths), 225–26, 230–31

Flores Rodríguez, Irvin, 167, 173

Florida: Hurricane Katrina and, 306; in 2000 election, 203–4, 214 n. 22, 215 n. 24

Ford, Gerald, 72

Fort Leavenworth Prison (Kan.), 159, 286, 289 n. 11

foster care, 70

Foucault, Michel, xv–xvi, 4–5, 21, 37–38, 140–57, 157 n. 2, 197; *Discipline and Punish*, 295; "Michel Foucault on Attica," 7–9, 15 n. 10

Fourteenth Amendment, 59

Fourth Amendment; due process and, 201; probable cause and, 199–200, 213 n. 8, 213–14 n. 18

Freire, Paulo, 238

Fuerzas Armadas de Liberación (FALN), 90, 94 n. 11, 172, 183 n. 5, 188 n. 29

Gallardo Santiago, Juan, 160, 164

gangs, 74, 91, 93 n. 3, 219

Garvey, Marcus, 222

Gates, Henry Louis, Jr., 47–48

gender. *See* women

Genet, Jean, 138

Geneva Convention, 68

genocide, 59, 64, 134, 312

Gerassi, John, 134

Gerena, Victor, 177, 188 n. 27

Ghana, 75, 117 n. 4, 136 n. 10

Giap, Vo Nguyen, 129, 136 n. 10

Gilani, Sheikh Syed, 223–24

Gilbert, Carol, 194, 248–65, 267–69 n. 6

Gilroy, Paul, 221

GIP (Groupe d'information sur les prisons), 21, 138, 157 nn. 1–2

Glasnost, 92, 94 n. 12

Glasser, Ira, 200

Gonzales, Alberto, 60

González Malavé, Alejandro, 172, 185–86 n. 21

Goode, Wilson, 5

Gore, Al, 203–5, 214 n. 22, 215 nn. 23–24

Gramsci, Antonio, 26–29

Graner, Charles, 281

Grangers, 107, 118 n. 10

Grito de Jayuya, 185 n. 19

Grito de Lares, 183 n. 5

Guantánamo Bay (Cuba), xv, 52, 194, 221, 259–60, 281–84. *See also* torture

Guillermo Morales, William, 187 n. 22

Guinier, Lani, 308

gulag, xiii

Gulag Archipelago, The (Solzhenitsyn), xiii, 13 n. 2

Guzmán Rodríguez, Manuel, 162

Haley, Harold, 121, 157 n. 4

Halliburton, 283, 307

Puerto Rico: Armed Revolutionary Independence Movement and, 183 n. 5; Cerro Maravilla Massacre in, 172–73, 178, 185–87 n. 21; Charter of Autonomy of, 160–62, 174, 182 n. 1, 183 n. 4; citizenship status and, 160, 162–63, 182 n. 2; colonialism in, 160–67, 171, 174, 182, 182–83 n. 2, 185 n. 21; Committee on Government Reform in, 180; Free Associated State vs. Commonwealth status, 166; Grito de Jayuya in, 185 n. 19; Grito de Lares in, 183 n. 5; Truth and Justice Committee of, 183 n. 5, United Nations status of, 166–67. *See also* Puerto Rican Independence Movement

Qaddafi, Muammar, 219

racial profiling, 25–26, 193–95, 198–202, 211–12, 213–14 n. 18
racism, 81, 87–88, 92, 96, 113–16, 133, 154, 197, 306–12; in prison: 121–31, 147, 241, 243. *See also* blacks, blackness; racial profiling; white supremacy
Racketeer Influenced and Corrupt Organizations (RICO) Act, 109, 119 n. 14, 236
Rackley, Alex, 117 n. 5
Rahman, Sheikh Omar Abdel, 224
Rakim, 230
rape: homosexuality and, 290–302, 302 n. 11; incidence of, 67; marital, 65–66; of prisoners, 11, 62, 66, 72, 286; racial stereotypes and, 32, 290–302; slavery and, 84; war and, 10, 15 n. 12, 59, 62, 64, 69–71, 73, 278
Reagan, Ronald, xiii, 119 n. 16, 123, 128–29, 199, 201, 208, 310
Reagon, Bernice Johnson, 14 n. 4
Reconstruction, 39, 202, 207, 279
Reed, Ishmael, 219

reform, 26, 115, 131
Reid, Richard, 220–21
religion, 193, 245. *See also* Christianity; Islam
Republic of New Afrika (RNA), 105, 117–18 n. 7
Reserve Officer Training Corps (ROTC), 169–71
resistance, 9, 11, 22, 83, 110–11, 129, 278; nonviolent, 248–51
Resistance Conspiracy Case, 236, 272
revolution, xvi, 129, 131–34, 140, 147, 149, 154
Revolutionary Boricua Volunteers (OVRB), 173. *See also* Puerto Rican Independence Movement
Reynolds, Charles, 97
Rice, Condoleezza, 309
Riggs, Francis E., 160, 163
Rios, Christopher "Big Pun," 71
Rios, Lisa, 71
Rivera, Oscar López, 22, 159–82
Roberts, Gene, 100–101
Robertson, Wayne, 300
Rockefeller, Nelson A., 9
Roder, Ulla, 267–69 n. 6
Rodríguez, Alberto, 175, 187 n. 22, 188 n. 32
Rodríguez, Alicia, 174, 178, 188 n. 32
Rodríguez, Dylan, 19, 35–57, 99, 106–7, 112, 293, 298
Rodríguez Cristóbal, Angel, 173
Rodríguez García, Erich, 179–80
Rolheiser, Ron, 263
Roosevelt, Franklin Delano, 118–19 n. 12, 164, 211
Rosa, Luis, 174, 188 n. 32
Rosado, Elias, 160, 163
Rosado Ortiz, Pablo, 160, 164
Rosenberg, Susan, 51, 54, 236, 281
Rumsfeld, Donald, 72
Rwanda, 59, 64

Weigman, Robin, 292
Wells Fargo, 177, 188 n. 27
West, Cornel, 309–10
West, Kanye, 309
White, Walter, 290, 303 n. 22
Whitehorn, Laura, 194–95, 236, 272–89
white left, 88–90, 113, 133, 204–6, 286
white supremacy, 6, 25–27, 30, 80–81, 106, 114–16, 201–2, 208, 211, 241, 274. *See also* racial profiling; racism
White Writing (Coetzee), 29–30
Wiese, Justin, 298
Wilderson, Frank B., III, 19, 23–33
Wilson, Woodrow, 182 n. 2
Winshop, Blanton, 163, 165
women: as prisoners, 175–76, 193–94, 238–47, 253–65, 277–78, 281; race and, 65–68, 153, 241; as soldiers, 58–73; warfare and, 144–45. *See also* rape

Work Opportunity and Personal Responsibility Act (1996), 228–29
World Community of al-Islam in the West, 223
World War I, 107, 118 n. 11; draft during, 160, 162–63
World War II, 22, 107–8, 118 n. 12, 165, 210–11, 302
Wretched of the Earth, The (Fanon), 24–25, 31
Wright, Beverly, 308

Young Lords, 74, 93 n. 3
Young Patriots, 74, 93 n. 3

Zedong, Mao, 120, 129
Zerfas, Diane, 256
Zinn, Howard, 261

Joy James is John B. and John T. McCoy Presidential Professor of Africana Studies and College Professor in Political Science at Williams College. She is the author of *Shadowboxing: Representations of Black Feminist Politics* (1999), *Transcending the Talented Tenth: Black Leaders and American Intellectuals* (1997), and *Resisting State Violence: Radicalism, Gender, and Race in U.S. Culture* (1996). She is the editor of *The New Abolitionists: (Neo)Slave Narratives and Contemporary Prison Writings* (2005); *Imprisoned Intellectuals: America's Political Prisoners Write on Life, Liberation, and Rebellion* (2003); *States of Confinement: Policing, Detention and Prisons* (2000; rev. ed. 2002); and *The Angela Y. Davis Reader* (1998), and the coeditor (with Steve Martinot) of *The Problems of Resistance: Studies in Alternate Political Cultures* (2001). James is completing a book on the Central Park case.

Library of Congress Cataloging-in-Publication Data
Warfare in the American homeland : policing and prison in a penal democracy /
edited by Joy James.
p. cm.
Includes bibliographical references and index.
ISBN 978-0-8223-3909-0 (cloth : alk. paper)
ISBN 978-0-8223-3923-6 (pbk. : alk. paper)
1. Prisons—United States. 2. Prisoners—United States. 3. Imprisonment—United States. 4. Discrimination in criminal justice administration—United States. 5. Discrimination in law enforcement—United States. 6. Minorities—United States. 7. Social control—United States. I. James, Joy.
HV9471.W363 2007
364.3'400973—dc22   2006101925